Studies in the Social and
Cultural Foundations of Language No. 12

Language diversity and thought

Studies in the Social and Cultural Foundations of Language

The aim of this series is to develop theoretical perspectives on the essential social and cultural character of language by methodological and empirical emphasis on the occurrence of language in its communicative and interactional settings, on the socioculturally grounded "meanings" and "functions" of linguistic forms, and on the social scientific study of language use across cultures. It will thus explicate the essentially ethnographic nature of linguistic data, whether spontaneously occurring or experimentally induced, whether normative or variational, whether synchronic or diachronic. Works appearing in the series will make substantive and theoretical contributions to the debate over the sociocultural-function and structural-formal nature of language, and will represent the concerns of scholars in the sociology and anthropology of language, anthropological linguistics, sociolinguistics, and socioculturally informed psycholinguistics.

Language diversity and thought examines the Sapir–Whorf linguistic relativity hypothesis: the proposal that the grammar of the particular language we speak affects the way we think about reality. Adopting an historical approach, the book reviews the various lines of empirical inquiry which arose in America in response to the ideas of anthropologists Edward Sapir and Benjamin L. Whorf. John Lucy asks why there has been so little fruitful empirical research on this problem and what lessons can be learned from past work. He then proposes a new, more adequate approach to future empirical research. A companion volume, *Grammatical categories and cognition*, illustrates the proposed approach with an original case study. The study compares the grammar of American English with that of Yucatec Maya, an indigenous language spoken in southeastern Mexico, and then identifies distinctive patterns of thinking related to the differences between the two languages.

Language diversity and thought

A reformulation of the linguistic relativity hypothesis

JOHN A. LUCY

University of Pennsylvania

CAMBRIDGE
UNIVERSITY PRESS

Published by the Press Syndicate of the University of Cambridge
The Pitt Building, Trumpington Street, Cambridge CB2 1RP
40 West 20th Street, New York, NY 10011-4211, USA
10 Stamford Road, Oakleigh, Melbourne 3166, Australia

First published 1992
Reprinted 1993, 1996

A catalogue record for this book is available from the British Library

Library of Congress cataloguing in publication data

Lucy, John Arthur, 1949–
Language diversity and thought: a reformulation of the linguistic relativity
hypothesis / John A. Lucy. (Studies in the Social and Cultural Foundations
of Language)
     p.   cm.
Includes bibliographical references and index.
ISBN 0 521 38418 4. – ISBN 0 521 38797 3 (pbk.)
1. Sapir–Whorf hypothesis.   2. Language and languages – Variation.
3. Thought and thinking.   I. Title.
P35.L84   1992
401'.9 – dc20   91–27644   CIP

ISBN 0 521 38418 4 hardback
ISBN 0 521 38797 3 paperback

Transferred to digital printing 1999

CE

Contents

Figures

Acknowledgments

I must first thank my teachers who stimulated, guided, and supported this work. Ruth and Robert Munroe, with whom I worked as an undergraduate, introduced me to the problems of culture and cognition. At the University of Chicago, where the present project was begun, my interdisciplinary orientation was consistently supported both within the Committee on Human Development and by the University as a whole. Robert LeVine long provided intellectual support, and to him I owe the insights that scholarly differences stem as much from disciplinary history and habitual methods as from principled theory and that true interdisciplinary work must therefore deal with these existing traditions and their diverse methods. Richard Shweder has been a patient and enthusiastic supporter of the project and has provided a critical perspective on social science methodology that has strongly affected the present work. David McNeill first introduced me to the history and problems of research on the relation of thought and language. Finally, Michael Silverstein, in addition to teaching me most of what I know about language, provided me with a model of how to balance critical analysis with constructive theory and method. I am also in his debt for the actual substance of his research, which informs the discussion at several levels, and for his steady support of this work over many years.

During the writing of this book I had the good fortune to have the intellectual and financial support of the Center for Psychosocial Studies in Chicago. I thank Bernard Weissbourd, Chairman of the Board of Directors of the Center, for making my period of residence possible and for his and the Center's continuing commitment to integrative social science research. My involvement at the Center has been marked by continuing contact with a stimulating group of colleagues who have made this book better: Benjamin Lee, Elizabeth Mertz, Richard Parmentier, Moishe Postone, Lee Schlesinger, Greg Urban, and James Wertsch. Of these I must single out Ben Lee for special thanks as having given this project his personal and intellectual support during some difficult times.

Finally, I thank my immediate family – my wife Suzanne Gaskins and my sons Robert and Steven – for their personal support during the writing of this work. There are no words that can adequately express the extent of Suzanne's contribution to this book. She made it possible.

Permission to quote copyrighted work has been granted by the following: American Council of Learned Societies; American Psychological Association; Australian Journal of Linguistics; Keith Basso; Alfred Bloom; Chicago Linguistic Society; Harcourt, Brace, & Co.; Holt, Rinehart, and Winston, Inc.; Dell Hymes; Indiana University; Lawrence Erlbaum Associates, Inc., Publishers; Dorothy Lee; Edith Lenneberg; Linguistic Society of America (from "Cognition in ethnolinguistics" by E. Lenneberg, *Language 29*, 463–71, © 1953); Macmillan Publishing Company (from "Language" by Edward Sapir in *Encyclopaedia of the social sciences*, Edwin R. A. Seligman, Editor in Chief, Vol. IX, pp. 155–69, Copyright © 1933 by Macmillan Publishing Company, and renewed © 1961; from *The mind of primitive man*, by Franz Boas, Copyright © 1938 by Macmillan Publishing Company, renewed © 1966 by Mrs. Franziska Boas Nichelson; from *Race, language, and culture*, by Franz Boas, Copyright © 1940 by Franz Boas, renewed © 1967 by Mrs. Franziska Boas Nichelson; from *Words and things: an introduction to language*, by Roger Brown, Copyright © 1958 by The Free Press, a Division of Macmillan, Inc.); MIT Press (from *Language, thought, and reality: selected writings of Benjamin Lee Whorf*, edited by J. Carroll, Copyright © 1956 by The Massachusetts Institute of Technology); Mouton de Gruyter; Peter de Ridder Press; Prentice Hall, Inc.; Michael Silverstein; Simon & Schuster, Inc.; Society for Research in Child Development; Southwestern Educational Laboratory; University Microfilms International; University of California Press (from *Basic color terms: their universality and evolution*, by Brent Berlin and Paul Kay, Copyright © 1969 The Regents of the University of California; from *Selected writings of Edward Sapir*, edited by D. Mandelbaum, Copyright © 1949); University of Chicago Library Microfilm Collection; University of Chicago Press (from *Anthropology today*, edited by A. Kroeber, Copyright © 1953; from *Language in culture*, edited by H. Hoijer, Copyright © 1954); University of Nebraska Press (from *Introduction to handbook of American Indian languages*, by Franz Boas, Copyright © 1966 by the University of Nebraska Press); Department of Anthropology, University of New Mexico; John Wiley & Sons (from *Biological foundations of language*, by E. Lenneberg, Copyright © 1967); Williams and Wilkins Company (D. Lee, Conceptual implications of an Indian language, *Philosophy of Science 5*, 89–102, Copyright © 1938 by Williams & Wilkins).

Introduction

General orientation

This study examines the linguistic relativity hypothesis, that is, the proposal that diverse languages influence the thought of those who speak them. This has been an important issue in our intellectual tradition for several hundred years. How far back the concern can be traced is largely a function of how one understands the terms language and thought and how explicit an hypothesis one requires. Relatively contemporary formulations begin to appear in eighteenth-century Germany with the work of Machaelis, Hamann, and Herder (R. L. Brown, 1967; Koerner, 1977; Penn, 1972; Stam, 1980; cf. Aarsleff, 1982; Friedrich, 1986). Interest continues in the nineteenth century, again particularly in Germany, and begins to separate from speculative philosophy, especially in the work of Wm. von Humboldt. In the twentieth century the main line of empirical research moves to America with the development of Boasian anthropology. There are undoubtedly important connections between this new work in America and the earlier nineteenth-century German work of Humboldt, Müller, and Steinthal (Haugen, 1977; Hymes, 1963; Stam, 1980), but there was fresh impetus too deriving from firsthand contact with the incredible diversity of native American linguistic forms and from the emergence in contemporary anthropology of an anti-evolutionary project with an emphasis on the functionally and temporally equivalent value of these diverse languages (Stocking, 1974).

The general roots of our interest in the problem of linguistic relativity have never been extensively examined, although this is an important problem (Lucy, 1985a; cf. Friedrich, 1986). Such an analysis is beyond the scope of this book, which focuses almost entirely on an internal analysis of twentieth-century empirical research in America. However, an attempt is made within this framework to place the research in historical sequence so as to indicate more accurately the course of the evolving debate. This is important for two reasons. On the one hand,

1

most of the historical studies of the development of the hypothesis are seriously deficient in their characterizations of twentieth-century approaches. Most often this is because they do not understand the evolving tradition but rather focus on a given text in isolation. On the other hand, there is a consistent tendency by those conducting contemporary empirical research to read the works from earlier in this century without reference to or sympathy for their historical context and genuine achievements but only with reference to contemporary concerns. A balanced and detailed contextual understanding of this earlier work is a prerequisite to building upon it.

Contemporary interest in the relation of linguistic diversity to thought springs from three central concerns. First, there has been growing recognition in recent decades of the central importance of semiotic phenomena in general and of language in particular in the social and behavioral sciences. The emphases can vary quite widely from assigning language a theoretical significance in the constitution of human thought and culture to simply noting its methodological importance as the primary source of data used in evaluating various theories in the human sciences. Many of these theories work with "language in general," disregarding the diversity among languages. An hypothesis of linguistic relativity assigns special importance to language variation and raises problems for theories which have ignored this diversity.

Second, individual thought occupies a central position in most modern theories of human behavior as the immediate cause of or guide for overt behavior. This leads naturally to a concern with the nature and origins of thought itself. The claim that thought is "relative" in some way immediately creates serious problems for a wide assortment of theories which presuppose a commonality of thought everywhere. An hypothesis that thought is influenced by the varying particulars of language raises just this issue.

The final problematic governing research in this century concerns the reflexive implications of the notion of relativity. If there is a linguistic relativity, then it may create real dilemmas for the conduct of research, because researchers themselves are not exempt from these linguistic influences. Not only might there be difficulties in understanding or characterizing the forms of thought of those speaking other languages, but the very generality and validity of our own linguistically formulated theories are brought into question. A linguistic relativity, if there is such, will not only lie *out there* in the object of investigation but will also penetrate right *into* the research process itself. This "reflexivity" is a general problem in the social sciences (Lucy, 1988; 1992).

In this respect the problem intersects with the more general issue of the development of a methodology (in the broad sense of methodology as a mode of inquiry) adequate to the goals of social science investigation. Thus, the hypothesis of linguistic relativity challenges assumptions which lie at the heart of much modern social and behavioral research – namely its claim to be discovering general laws and to be truly scientific. This is also the reason that the topic generates controversy and even hostility among so many social and behavioral scientists.

In contrast to the widespread importance of and interest in the topic, there is a virtual absence of empirical research on the problem. The reasons for the absence of research are diverse, but three principal ones can be identified. First, there is a common tendency to reduce or caricature the problem into a simplified form which can then be regarded as obviously true or obviously false. One construal of a relativity hypothesis is the claim that the specific structure of a language *determines* thought, in the sense that a self-conscious speaker can never be free from constraints imposed by it; this is a view that nearly everyone agrees is untenable. An alternative argument is the claim that variable structures of specific languages *influence* thought, in the sense that there may be some identifiable cognitive correlates (outside of the specifically linguistic realm) associated with using a particular language; this is a view that nearly everyone can agree with. Thus, under either conceptualization there is really no reason to conduct research, because the hypothesis is either obviously true or obviously false. These reductions (or simplifications) sidestep the crucial issues: what are the influences, how important are they, when and how do or can they operate, etc.

A second obstacle to research in this area is its inherently interdisciplinary nature. One must first have a grasp of how languages work. Usually this would involve an understanding of linguistics and of some auxiliary field encompassing some of the uses of language such as anthropology, folklore studies, or comparative literature. Secondly, one must have substantial knowledge of the domain of thought under consideration. For some this has meant the *contents* of thought, that is, a speaker's conceptualizations of the world as part of a cultural system studied, for example, by cultural anthropologists or historians; for others this has meant the *processes* of thinking, that is, the activities of attending, remembering, reasoning, etc. as studied, for example, by cognitive psychologists. Either way, some knowledge other than the strictly linguistic is necessarily entailed. There may be further requirements depending on the approach taken. For example there are certain methodological skills required in linguistic analysis, for anthropological fieldwork, for experimental psychology, and so forth. Whichever of these are involved must also be mastered. This very real interdisciplinary nature of the hypothesis represents a significant obstacle given the present state of research training, which sharply limits the acceptable topics and methods in most social science fields.

This leads directly to the third obstacle to research of this type, namely that it is intrinsically contrary to some of the central assumptions of the relevant disciplines. For example, the hypothesis, if correct, would jeopardize the assumption tacitly accepted by most psychologists that each individual can be conceptualized from a scientific standpoint as a psychological entity autonomous in both development and mature functioning. The notion that what is distinctive about human activity in contrast with other species lies precisely in its embeddedness in an historically transmitted social, linguistic, and cultural ecosystem is simply alien to most psychologists – widespread lip service to the importance of culture notwithstanding.

This psychological assumption endures for a variety of reasons, the most important perhaps being that the view of the individual as an autonomous entity is in harmony with our own cultural premises. It is difficult to recognize the relativity of one's own psychological functioning and scientific theories. This would involve not only entertaining the possibility that the notion of the autonomous individual stems in large part from our own cultural norms and assumptions but also recognizing that there may be limits to the degree of human self-understanding achievable within the methodologically strict positive scientific paradigm.

Further, a reconceptualization of the individual as being to some degree intrinsically social would raise a number of difficult methodological and conceptual problems which are more easily not faced. Recognition that the central objects of study in an individual psychology depend on radically different, socially constituted contextual systems would pose the need to formulate a general method (in the sense of global procedure) for conducting grounded comparison across such contexts where the presence of an a priori "objective" external framework is ruled out and where no specific individual case can rightly serve as a privileged standard for comparison. (This is a social [or cultural] version of the central problem in any psychology: how can any two individuals justifiably be compared in a valid way?) Such a psychology would need to integrate into the investigation a broad range of methods (in the sense of specific techniques), drawing on related, yet often unfamiliar, social science disciplines so as to address the full complexity of the issues adequately. Even the preliminaries for a comparative psychology of this sort remain undeveloped. This problem has its complement in the more "social" sciences, such as anthropology and sociology, which try to account for distinctively human social organization either without reference to a comprehensive theory of individual functioning or by gratuitous assumptions about the nature of such functioning. Most cultural accounts depend heavily on such assumptions.

These issues all come to a head in certain problems which by their very nature simply cannot be addressed in the traditional ways: the problem of linguistic relativity is one such problem. Incorporated within the very hypothesis itself is a question about the validity of generalizing to others on the basis of our own experience. What is required, as the empirical companion to this study will make clear, is that the problem must be formulated comparatively from the beginning. One does not formulate an approach without reference to other groups and then seek to "generalize" it or "test" it. Such an approach will guarantee misleading results because it must ultimately regiment and interpret the other groups in terms of our categories, categories that are demonstrably appropriate only for the first term of comparison.

The decision to focus on the relation between language and thought in this study stems directly from these various concerns. The study is conceived of as a contribution to the more general enterprise of developing the theoretical and methodological approaches necessary to address properly the intrinsically social and cultural nature of individual human psychological functioning. The linguistic relativity hypothesis offers several advantages in this regard. Languages are clearly different from one another, and the possible significance of such differences is a recognized problem within psychology. The reflexive (or self-critical) implications of linguistic influences on thought for the research enterprise itself are especially clear in this area, since language is the central intellectual tool in the social sciences. Further, the outline of a general comparative method for the investigation of language forms which is sensitive to both universal and variable factors is emerging within linguistics and can be instructive in guiding attempts to construct comparative methods in other domains. Finally, the emergence in recent years of a recognition of the relevance of linguistic phenomena to inquiries within a wide variety of social science disciplines offers an especially good opportunity for building interdisciplinary dialogue. Thus the relation of language and thought represents an ideal area in which to examine more general problems of the relation of individual and society. These broader issues ultimately motivate and structure the particular research reported here.

Focus of the present research

The present study focuses on the influence of linguistic diversity, cross-language variation in formal structure, on speakers' habitual cognitive responses to the world. There are, of course, a number of related problems which fall under the general heading of the inter-relationship of language and thought, and which, in fact, bear on the discussion in important ways although they are not the focus here. Perhaps the best way to make clear the bounds of this work and to give preliminary content to the just-mentioned statement of focus is to contrast briefly the problem to be examined in this book with these related problem areas.

First, this study focuses on *the influence of language on thought* and not, for the most part, on the influence of thought on language. The latter concern is an important one and underlies many studies of language universals, language acquisition, and language as an index of cultural experience. Further, there are a great many studies of par-ticular languages (e.g., English) which purport to demonstrate the role of thought in determining language structure, but these are, on the whole, methodologically misguided since both cognitive performance and linguistic structure are assessed only in a single language group. In establishing a cross-linguistic comparative frame for the empirical portion of the present research, a procedure for isolating underlying cognitive influences on language structure will emerge, although it will not be fully developed.

Second, this study focuses on *the cognitive significance of the diversity of linguistic structures* across languages. It is not concerned with the importance of what might be termed *Language*, the general properties of the vocal-communicational behavioral skill and cognitive "faculty" pos-sessed by virtually all members of the human species, for *Thought*, the generalized cognitive capacity we associate with adult members of the species. This latter issue has been of interest to physical anthropologists, biologists, and most psychologists, but it is not of immediate concern here except insofar as linguistic variability is itself a characteristic of human Language which warrants theoretical attention. The cognitive significance ascribed to the universal presence of Language in members of the species has been considerable, leading many to identify Language as *the* definitive element in a distinctively human cognition. This book will of necessity deal with the problem of the general role of Language in Thought in developing a hypothesis about the possible cognitive import-ance of linguistic variation; but the focus will be on the question of whether the particular formal organization of meaning characteristic of the speech of a group of persons influences the thought of the group in a discernible way. This particular question has been of most interest from a research standpoint to sociocultural anthropologists, to those interested in the comparative study of languages, and to a small subset of those who study psycholinguistics. There is at present little agreement about the influence of linguistic variety on thought or on the proper approach to studying the issue.

Third, this study focuses on the *formal structuring of meaning in language*. Thus, we will not be concerned at all with the phonological level, and only indirectly with the social uses of language. Differences among languages at the level of grammatical processes (i.e., techniques of formal marking such as inflection) will be discussed in passing, but will not be the focus of the empirical research. The focus rather will be on differences in the grammatical structuring of meaning, that is, the ways syntactic and lexical categories interact to signal meaning in language-specific ways.

Fourth, this study focuses on *habitual thought*, by which is meant everyday, routine ways of attending to objects and events, categorizing them, remembering them, and perhaps even reflecting upon them. The focus on habitual thought is meant to contrast with two more extreme alternatives. First, it contrasts with a focus on specialized thought, that is, cognitive routines or structures restricted to particular subgroups within a culture (e.g., ritual or technical specialists) or restricted to particular domains in a culture (e.g., kinship or illness). Thus, for example, if certain specialists memorize vast amounts of information about a particular topic or have a highly differentiated classification scheme for a certain domain, it will be of secondary interest from the point of view of this work. These specialized practices will be overlooked here in order to facilitate cultural comparison – not because language effects are any less likely in these areas. Second, the focus on habitual thought contrasts with a concern for "potential" thought, that is, with what a given speaker or group of speakers could conceivably think like or think about in some circumstances. The notion of an abstract underlying thought potential will be avoided, as it is theoretically problematic and bears a very uncertain relationship to any actual behavior. In a sense, such potential thought is thought conceived of without any reference to actual contextual bounds. As such it lies at the opposite pole from specialized thought, which is contextually specific. Habitual thought, in the sense intended here, is intermediate in nature, being actually general across behavioral contexts within a culture.

Whether or not patterns of habitual thought can or should be summed up into an overall notion of worldview is a difficult problem which will be addressed only briefly in this study. For the purpose of this project, the critical question is whether there is or can be solid empirical evidence *linking* distinctive language patterns to distinctive habitual behavior or belief at the level of the aggregable individual social actors. In subsequent work it may be possible to tackle more effectively the problems of specialized modes of speech and thought within a given culture and of the role of language in promoting a degree of generality and integration in habitual everyday thought.

Overview of the research

The study consists of two parts, this book and a companion volume, *Grammatical categories and cognition*, that together present an historical, theoretical, and empirical re-examination of the linguistic relativity hypothesis, that is, the hypothesis that differences among languages in the grammatical structuring of meaning influence habitual thought.

This book presents an analytic review of the historical development of the hypothesis and previous attempts to provide empirical evidence directly relevant to it. The review is concerned with methodology in the broad sense, that is, with identifying the general requirements of adequate empirical work on this problem. The review analyzes in detail the flaws and the achievements of existing studies with the aim of formulating an improved approach to research. The companion volume *Grammatical categories and cognition* provides a concrete case study which utilizes this improved approach.

Chapter 1 details the historical context within which current formulations developed. The focus is on the work of American anthropologists Franz Boas and Edward Sapir. Other research traditions, particularly those of nineteenth- and twentieth-century philosophy are not described, but the distinguishing characteristics of the American tradition are explained.

Chapter 2 examines in considerable detail the work of Benjamin Lee Whorf. In one way or another Whorf's work is the starting point for all contemporary research. Despite the significance of his work, it has often been greatly misunderstood. The goal in this chapter is to work through exactly what Whorf did say and, implicitly, to correct many of the prevalent misunderstandings.

Chapters 3, 4, 5, and 6 summarize subsequent empirical research by anthropological linguists and psycholinguists on the ideas of Sapir and Whorf. En route most of the important objections to Whorf's approach are described. Two other themes are stressed. First, empirical research in these two traditions strongly reflects both longstanding disciplinary perspectives and methods and the shifting tides of research concern over the years. Second, many of the concepts and methods that have been developed complement each other in important ways and suggest the lines of a more adequate and comprehensive approach. The chapters come in pairs. Chapter 3 describes the traditional approach within anthropological linguistics, indicating its strengths and weaknesses; and chapter 4 outlines more recent developments in this discipline which can solve some of the traditional problems. Chapter 5 discusses the dominant approach within psycholinguistics and its strengths and weaknesses; chapter 6 discusses a variety of minority approaches within this discipline, some of which point the way towards remedying the weaknesses of the dominant tradition.

Chapter 7 distills this historical material and presents a theoretical reformulation which characterizes the issues in contemporary terminology, identifies those elements or aspects which deserve prior attention, and indicates which existing research techniques can be effectively applied to the problem.

The companion volume *Grammatical categories and cognition* presents a new empirical investigation based on the theoretical reformulation developed in chapter 7. The aim is to illustrate by means of a specific study the general approach being advocated and the sorts of results which can be expected. There is an emphasis throughout the second work on how the approach might be generalized. The substantive focus is on the influence of different nominal number marking patterns on attending, classifying, and remembering. The specific linguistic focus is developed by comparing American English with Yucatec Maya and looking for points of difference. Once a suitable linguistic contrast is found, specific cognitive hypotheses based on this linguistic focus are developed and then tested.

The introduction to *Grammatical categories and cognition* recapitulates the main goals laid out in this book and outlines the structure of the case study presented there.

Chapter 1 describes in general terms the background of the comparative research in Yucatán, Mexico, outlining pertinent aspects of the culture and language as well as the general conduct of the field research.

Chapter 2 describes the linguistic differences between American English and Yucatec Maya in grammatical number marking. Each language is first described independently. The two descriptions are followed by a detailed contrast of the two languages framed within a broader comparative perspective. Formal syntactic number marking is shown to be more frequent and structurally significant in English than in Yucatec, and this difference is shown to relate intimately to the structure of lexical reference in the two languages.

Chapter 3 describes the cognitive assessment. On the basis of the linguistic analysis, general hypotheses are developed regarding probable cognitive consequences. Then specific hypotheses are explored in tasks involving attention, memory, and classification to verify more precisely the linguistic patterns and to assess how they correlate with behaviors that do not overtly involve linguistic production. The tasks utilize a variety of different stimulus materials and procedures.

Chapter 4 summarizes the empirical findings and shows their relevance to the historical and theoretical concerns reviewed in *Language diversity and thought*. The chapter contrasts this study with earlier approaches and closes with specific recommendations for further work.

Various appendices provide more detailed information on the linguistic and cognitive materials, information which may be of use to those who wish to reinterpret, replicate, or extend the specific empirical research.

1. Development of the linguistic relativity hypothesis in America: Boas and Sapir

Although many scholars have concerned themselves with the questions of whether and how diverse languages influence thought, contemporary social science research centers on the claims of Benjamin Lee Whorf, a student of native American Indian languages. Whorf drew extensively upon the prior work of anthropologists Franz Boas and Edward Sapir in his formulation of the problem, so it will be useful to examine their contributions first.[1] The discussion will be relatively detailed, since an understanding of Whorf's position and an evaluation of his contribution depend on a comparison with these two predecessors.

Language as the reflection of culture: Boas

Franz Boas (1858–1942)[2] was born and educated in Germany. He later emigrated to the United States, where he was the person primarily responsible for building anthropology into a professional discipline. He made contributions to most of the subfields of anthropology, including physical anthropology, social and cultural anthropology, and linguistic anthropology. His primary concerns were to break away from racial and evolutionary conceptions of culture by arguing on the one hand for the psychic unity of mankind and on the other hand for a notion of distinct cultures and culture areas, each to be studied on its own terms. In this chapter only his work on language will be discussed, although his broader agenda shapes his argument at several points.

The linguistic analysis of experience

Boas made three arguments about the nature of language that are important for the eventual development of the view that language plays a role in shaping thought. First, he argued that languages classify experience:

Since the total range of personal experience which language serves to express is infinitely varied, and its whole scope must be expressed by a limited number of phonetic groups, it is obvious that an extended classification of experiences must underlie all articulate speech.   (Boas, 1966a [1911], p. 20)

Thus, each language of necessity contains intrinsic classifications which group elements of experience as "alike" for the purposes of speech.[3] In this passage Boas is referring primarily to lexical items,[4] but it seems clear from the overall discussion (1966a [1911], pp. 24–43) that he also considered other sorts of grammatical categories to be classificatory of experience and, in some ways, more important.[5]

Second, different languages classify experience differently. Boas emphasized that

the groups of ideas expressed by specific phonetic groups show very material differences in different languages, and do not conform by any means to the same principles of classification.   (Boas, 1966a [1911], p. 21, and 1916 [1911], p. 145)

In various cultures these classifications may be founded on fundamentally distinct principles.   (Boas, 1965 [1938], p. 190)

the principles of classification which are found in different languages do not by any means agree.   (Boas, 1916 [1911], p. 198)

Thus it happens that each language, from the point of view of another language, may be arbitrary in its classifications; that what appears as a single simple idea in one language may be characterized by a series of distinct phonetic groups in another.   (Boas, 1966a [1911], p. 22, and 1916 [1911], pp. 146–47)

Boas gave many examples (1966a [1911], sect. 2) to show the great variety among different languages. The majority of these examples consist of showing how a given experience would be differently rendered in various languages or how a set of experiences would be differently · grouped by different languages. His most famous example concerns the various words in Eskimo relating to snow:

Another example of the same kind, the words for SNOW in Eskimo, may be given. Here we find one word, *aput*, expressing SNOW ON THE GROUND; another one, *qana*, FALLING SNOW; a third one, *piqsirpoq*, DRIFTING SNOW; and a fourth one, *qimuqsuq*, A SNOWDRIFT.   (1966a [1911], pp. 21–22)

Less familiar examples show the inverse relation with English having multiple words for what is a single modified form in another language:

As an example of the manner in which terms that we express by independent words are grouped under one concept, the Dakota language may be selected. The terms *naxta'ka* TO KICK, *paxta'ka* TO BIND IN BUNDLES, *yaxta'ka* TO BITE, *ic'a'xtaka* TO BE NEAR TO, *boxta'ka* TO POUND, are all derived from the common element *xtaka* TO GRIP, which holds them together, while we use distinct words for expressing the various ideas.   (1966a [1911], p. 22)

In his concluding discussion of grammatical categories he made much the same point:

> many of the categories which we are inclined to consider as essential may be absent in foreign languages, and ... other categories may occur as substitutes.
>
> (Boas, 1966a [1911], p. 38)

> When we consider for a moment what this implies, it will be recognized that in each language only a part of the complete concept that we have in mind is expressed, and that each language has a peculiar tendency to select this or that aspect of the mental image which is conveyed by the expression of the thought.
>
> (Boas, 1966a [1911], p. 39)

The additional examples that follow this passage make these differences clear by putting into overt surface forms some of the distinctions implicit in the grammatical categories of different languages.[6] In general, in considering grammatical categories, Boas was concerned with obligatory categories (1966a [1911], pp. 38–39; 1965 [1938], pp. 193–94; 1966b [1917], p. 207; see also Jakobson, 1959), but he also mentioned that optional categories may be another source of cross-language variation (1966a [1911], p. 39).

Third, linguistic phenomena are unconscious in character, apparently because of their highly automatic production.[7] Boas observed:

> It would seem that the essential difference between linguistic phenomena and other ethnological phenomena is, that the linguistic classifications never rise into consciousness, while in other ethnological phenomena, although the same unconscious origin prevails, these often rise into consciousness, and thus give rise to secondary reasoning and to re-interpretations. (Boas, 1966a [1911], p. 63)[8]

> the infinitely large number of ideas have been reduced by classification to a lesser number, which by constant use have established firm associations, and which can be used automatically. (Boas, 1916 [1911], p. 145)

> the use of language is so automatic that the opportunity never arises for the fundamental notions to emerge into consciousness. (Boas, 1966a [1911], p. 64)

Thus, while an extensive classification of experience is implicit in language, speakers individually and collectively typically remain unaware of it because of its highly automatic nature.[9]

The relation of languages to thought and culture

Boas's essential view was that linguistic classifications reflect but do not dictate thought, that is, the conceptual ideas and forms of thinking characteristic of a culture. Boas was rarely systematic or explicit in presenting his ideas on the relation of language and thought, but his most general attitude seems to have been that language categories directly reflect (or express) ideas and hence linguistic data can be used to study those ideas.[10] So, on the one hand, variations among languages reflect the divergent historical experience of the group and, on the other hand, universals across languages reflect the psychic unity of man:

> it seems well worth while . . . to seek in the peculiarities of the groupings of ideas in different languages an important characteristic in the history of the mental development of the various branches of mankind. From this point of view, the occurrence of the most fundamental grammatical concepts in all languages must be considered as proof of the unity of fundamental psychological processes.
>
> (Boas, 1966a [1911], p. 67)

This view flows quite naturally from Boas's general argument that individual performance and ability are much the same in every culture, but that individuals are enmeshed in different traditions; apparent differences in thought arise from the amalgamation of new perceptions and ideas to different traditional bodies of knowledge (1916 [1911], pp. 197–243, especially p. 203; see also Stocking's, 1974, discussion of this point).

Occasionally, Boas spoke more directly to the interrelation of language and thought, but within the context of a general debate about higher levels of thought as distinctive of civilized man. He felt that the presence of some linguistic devices in a society such as a lexical item corresponding to an abstract concept might facilitate abstract thought, but he felt this was a relatively minor matter with respect to cross-language comparison, and he concluded:

> It seems very questionable in how far the restriction of the use of certain grammatical forms can really be conceived as a hindrance in the formulation of generalized ideas. It seems much more likely that the lack of these forms is due to the lack of their need.
>
> (Boas, 1966a [1911], p. 60)

> Thus it would seem that the obstacles to generalized thought inherent in the form of a language are of minor importance only, and that presumably the language alone would not prevent a people from advancing to more generalized forms of thinking if the general state of their culture should require expression of such thought.
>
> (Boas, 1966a [1911], p. 63; also 1965 [1938], pp. 195–98)[11]

On the other hand, he argued that language form can also be a source of error in thought, but again this was not unique to any particular language:

> When we try to think at all clearly, we think, on the whole, in words; and it is well known that, even in the advancement of science, inaccuracy of vocabulary has often been a stumbling-block which has made it difficult to reach accurate conclusions. The same words may be used with different significance, and by assuming the word to have the same significance always, erroneous conclusions

may be reached. It may also be that the word expresses only part of an idea, so that owing to its use the full range of the subject-matter discussed may not be recognized. In the same manner the words may be too wide in their significance, including a number of distinct ideas the differences of which in the course of the development of the language were not recognized.

(Boas, 1966a [1911], pp. 67–68)

But

All these traits of human thought, which are known to influence the history of science and which play a more or less important role in the general history of civilization, occur with equal frequency in the thoughts of primitive man.

(Boas, 1966a [1911], p. 68)

In short, language categories may facilitate or confuse thought in various ways, but there is no basis for ascribing intrinsic privilege to any one language (or group of speakers) over another in this regard.

While Boas did not put these arguments together to make an argument regarding language-specific influences on thought, such a view does emerge in his later writings in at least one passage:

The general concepts underlying language are entirely unknown to most people. They do not rise into consciousness until the scientific study of grammar begins. Nevertheless, the categories of language compel us to see the world arranged in certain definite conceptual groups which, on account of our lack of knowledge of linguistic processes, are taken as objective categories and which, therefore, impose themselves upon the form of our thoughts. (Boas, 1966c [1920], p. 289)

Everything is present for an argument of linguistic relativity based on taking our linguistic categories as objective reality except for an emphasis on the diversity of these conceptual groups. It is not until the end of his life, perhaps under the influence of Sapir and Whorf, that the possible influence of linguistic diversity was integrated with these views, and Boas remained highly cautious in his formulation:

It is another question in how far the categories of grammar and the general classification of experience may control thought . . . The obligatory categories of language differ fundamentally . . . It is obvious that the mental picture aroused by a spoken sentence will be fundamentally different according to these categories . . . The form of our grammar compels us to select a few traits of thought we wish to express and suppresses many other aspects which the speaker has in mind and which the hearer supplies according to his fancy . . .

There is little doubt that thought is thus directed in various channels. . . . Such a tendency pervading the language may well lead to a different reaction to the incidents of everyday life and it is conceivable that in this sense the mental activities of a people may be in part directed by language. I should not be inclined to overestimate this influence because devices for expressing . . . [various ideas] are ever-present, and may rise into idiomatic use. In this sense, we may say that language exerts a limited influence on culture.   (Boas, 1942, pp. 181–83)

In the end, it seems that Boas's two desires, to assert the psychic unity of man and to avoid premature generalization at the theoretical level, kept him from going further along this line of thought to the claim of significant differences in thought among different linguistic-cultural groups. Nonetheless, most of the elements necessary for such an argument are already present in his work.

Concerning the broader related topic of the connection of language and culture, Boas felt that language and culture could covary freely (see, e.g., his discussion of the independence of race, language, and culture in Boas, 1966a [1911], pp. 1–10). However, if there were influences, they were those of culture on language, and not vice versa:

> It does not seem likely, therefore, that there is any direct relation between the culture of a tribe and the language they speak, except in so far as the form of the language will be moulded by the state of culture, but not in so far as a certain state of culture is conditioned by morphological traits of the language.
>
> (Boas, 1966a [1911], p. 63)

(See also 1942, pp. 178–83.) However, in his examples of how elements of language can affect our thinking, he repeatedly showed how linguistic patterns may influence custom. So various extensions of kinship terms lead to historical changes in actual kin categories; a failure to distinguish a name from the personality named is connected to naming children after ancestors; and metaphoric descriptions of social events and personae are interpreted literally in the historical development of ritual and myth (Boas, 1966a [1911], pp. 68–69). Thus, as indicated in the passages quoted earlier, language can influence culture via its influence on thought. In each of these cases, however, it is the lexical level of language which is implicated, and we can conclude conservatively that Boas was open to the mutual interaction of vocabulary with culture in general, though for various reasons he did not develop a detailed argument.[12]

Summary

So Boas emphasized that every language represents a classification of experience, these classifications vary dramatically from language to language, and they are so automatic that they typically lie outside the sphere of conscious awareness. Boas tended to see language reflecting elementary psychological functioning (hence its universal character) and specific historical experience (hence its variable character). He tended to reject the claims for a general effect of language on culture, seeing them as in free variation, but he did note that language can be an aid in abstraction and a source of error. Quite late in his life he voiced, somewhat tentatively, the possibility of a shaping role for language in thought and culture.

Language and the relativity of the form of thought: Sapir

Edward Sapir (1884–1939) was Boas's premier student in the area of linguistic studies. He is known for both the quality and the quantity of his empirical research on specific languages and also for the breadth and clarity of his theoretical vision. He also played an important role in developing the subfield of culture and personality, which is concerned with the interaction between psychological functioning and cultural patterns. His concern for the relationship between language and thought stands at the intersection of these two areas of interest.

The linguistic analysis of experience

Sapir elaborated on Boas's arguments in a number of ways, the most important of which was his emphasis on the formal completeness of each language as a symbolic *system*:

> The outstanding fact about any language is its formal completeness ... To put this ... in somewhat different words, we may say that a language is so constructed that no matter what any speaker of it may desire to communicate ... the language is prepared to do his work ... The world of linguistic forms, held within the framework of a given language, is a complete system of reference ...
>
> (Sapir, 1949c [1924], p. 153)

(See also Sapir, 1949e [1921], p. 98; 1949j [1927], pp. 550–53; and 1964 [1931], p. 128.) Because each language constitutes a complete system of reference, any specific formal or substantive element of language must be seen as a component of such a system.[13]

Sapir echoed Boas's ideas about implicit classification of experience in language in much the same terms, but he also emphasized the social function of these shared formal classifications:

> the single experience lodges in an individual consciousness and is, strictly speaking, incommunicable. To be communicated it needs to be referred to a class which is tacitly accepted by the community as an identity.
>
> (1949e [1921], pp. 12–13)

And since language categories are interrelated in a coherent system of forms, so too, by extension, are the various individual experiences they represent. These language forms serve to establish a definite relational feeling or attitude towards all possible contents of expression and, through them, towards all possible contents of experience, in so far, of course, as experience is capable of expression in linguistic terms.

(Sapir, 1949c [1924], p. 153)

(See also Sapir 1949h [1929], p. 166.) Under this interpretation, experience is considerably more ordered by language than it would be with a simple unorganized assortment of classifications.[14] This emphasis on the formal, systematic aspect of language represents a crucial development in Sapir's argument.

Second, like Boas, Sapir emphasized the formal diversity of languages (see especially 1949e [1921], chs. 4 and 5), but again he went further, noting that the systemic nature of language was itself one source of this diversity:

Inasmuch as languages differ very widely in their systematization of fundamental concepts, they tend to be only loosely equivalent to each other as symbolic devices and are, as a matter of fact, incommensurable in the sense in which two systems of points in a plane are, on the whole, incommensurable to each other if they are plotted out with reference to differing systems of coordinates.

(Sapir, 1964 [1931], p. 128)

So he added to Boas's views regarding the differences among the categories of various languages the notion that these categories are *arranged* into formally complete yet incommensurate systems.

Sapir's evidence for variety among languages, like that of Boas, consists essentially of detailed comparisons of the different ways in which the same experience would be differentially encoded by an expression in each of two languages. The most extended and useful examples are given as part of his discussion of grammatical concepts in his book *Language* (1949e [1921], ch. 5),[15] where he also develops a preliminary classification of the basic kinds of concepts expressed in languages. His central example examines the English sentence *the farmer kills the duckling*. He shows that this simple five-word sentence entails thirteen distinct concepts. He then contrasts this English sentence with others from German, Yana, Chinese, Kwakiutl, and so forth, showing that many of these concepts need not be expressed, but that others must be expressed in their stead.

Third, in addition to repeating Boas's arguments regarding the unconscious, automatic nature of language (Sapir, 1949f [1912], pp. 100–1; 1949c [1924], pp. 155–56; 1949j [1927], pp. 548–49), Sapir noted that the systematic formal aspect of language is another factor which helps account for the unconscious nature of linguistic phenomena. On the one hand

the reasoning intelligence seeks to attach itself rather to the functions than to the forms of conduct.

(Sapir, 1949j [1927], p. 547)

Hence the formal aspect of cultural and linguistic patterns tends to be overlooked easily. On the other hand, the complexity of formal relations and the unified nature of the whole add to the impenetrability of linguistic forms – especially when each is examined in isolation. Sapir first made this point in a general way about all cultural patterns:

Why are the forms of social behavior not adequately known by the normal individual? . . . I believe that the answer to this question rests in the fact that the relations between elements of experience which serve to give them their form and significance are more powerfully "felt" or "intuited"[16] than consciously perceived. It is a matter of common knowledge that it is relatively easy to fix the attention on some arbitrarily selected element of experience, such as a sensation or an emotion, but that it is far from easy to become conscious of the exact place which such an element holds in the total constellations of behavior.

(1949j [1927], p. 548)[17]

This is followed by extensive exemplification from linguistics, with the conclusion that

In the simple facts of language we have an excellent example of an important network of patterns of behavior, each of them with exceedingly complex and, to a large extent, only vaguely definable functions, which is preserved and transmitted with minimum consciousness.   (1949j [1927], p. 555)

Thus, the systematic formal nature of linguistic (and other cultural) phenomena makes them particularly resistant to folk analysis. Although both of these arguments – natural focus on function over form and difficulty in comprehending the role of a particular form in a complex network of forms – probably play a role in the unconscious nature of linguistic phenomena, they are not distinctive, in Sapir's view, of linguistic as opposed to other aspects of culture. In this sense his observations did not advance the argument for the special nature of language even as far as the position advocated by Boas, although he did identify additional factors accounting for the lack of awareness of all cultural forms.

The relation of languages to thought and culture

Sapir, led in part by these observations, essentially reversed Boas's claim that linguistic classifications reflect thought and argued rather that organized linguistic classifications channel thought. His argument had two parts.

First, he saw thought as arising from an interpretation of, or reading into, language classifications of their full conceptual potential:

From the point of view of language, thought may be defined as the highest latent or potential content of speech, the content that is obtained by interpreting each of the elements in the flow of language as possessed of its very fullest conceptual value

... It is, indeed, in the highest degree likely that language is an instrument originally put to uses lower than the conceptual plane and that thought arises as a refined interpretation of its content.   (1949e [1921], pp. 14–15)[18]

Note here that Sapir holds this to be true quite aside from arguments about linguistic variation.

Sapir did not thereby equate language and thought – in fact he explicitly claimed the opposite (1949e [1921], p. 15) – but argued rather that whether or not thought is a natural domain apart from speech, it is nonetheless only through language (i.e., *some particular*, socially conventional symbolism) that we are led to fully conceptual thought. He dismissed the intuition we have of being able to think without language as due either to a confusion of imagery with thought or to the confusion of the auditory aspect of language with its formal structure (1949e [1921], pp. 15–16). Finally he acknowledged that the development of speech itself was probably dependent in a high degree on the development of thought:

The instrument makes possible the product, the product refines the instrument.
                                                        (Sapir, 1949e [1921], p. 17)

Secondly, this process of reading into linguistic categories interacts with the formally complete nature of language to yield, in fact, a systematic (re)constitution of reality:

Language is ... a self-contained, creative symbolic organization, which not only refers to experience largely acquired without its help but actually defines experience for us by reason of its formal completeness and because of our unconscious projection of its implicit expectations into the field of experience ... [Language] categories ... are, of course, derivative of experience at last analysis, but, once abstracted from experience, they are systematically elaborated in language and are not so much discovered in experience as imposed upon it because of the tyrannical hold that linguistic form has upon our orientation in the world.   (Sapir, 1964 [1931], p. 128)

(See also Sapir 1949d [1933], p. 10.) In short, Sapir claims we anticipate (or read) experience in terms of language categories which, by virtue of their abstraction and elaboration in the linguistic process, no longer correspond to experience in a direct way.

It only remained to add to this the argument that these categories are only loosely equivalent to derive the conclusion that particular languages channel thought (i.e., conceptual interpretations of reality) in diverse ways:

It would be possible to go on indefinitely with such examples of incommensurable analyses of experience in different languages. The upshot of it all would be to make very real to us a kind of relativity that is generally hidden from us by our naive acceptance of fixed habits of speech as guides to an objective understanding of the nature of experience. This is the relativity of concepts or, as it might be called, the relativity of the form of thought.   (1949c [1924], p. 159)

(See also Sapir, 1949c [1924], p. 153; Sapir and Swadesh, 1964 [1929–46], p. 103.)

It is worth highlighting that this "relativity of thought" is of "concepts" or of "the form of thought." Thus there are diverse *conceptual* interpretations[19] of experience based upon a *naive reliance* upon our linguistic classifications as a *guide* to objective reality when in fact many possible linguistic classifications, and hence conceptualizations, are possible. Sapir intends here to encompass more than ordinary everyday thought. He remarks, "no matter how sophisticated our modes of interpretation become, we never really get beyond the projection and continuous transfer of relations suggested by the forms of our speech" (1949d [1933], p. 11). Thus conceived, the relativity of thought does not jeopardize the Boasian principles of the psychic unity of man, because it operates at the level of conceptual interpretations of reality and not at the level of basic psychological processes or functions. However, this view requires that we look "through" the peculiarities of linguistic forms, and the rationalizations and extensions built upon them, to discover the nature of this underlying psychological unity:

All forms of linguistic expression are reducible to a common psychological ground, but this ground cannot be properly understood without the perspective gained from a sympathetic study of the forms themselves.

(Sapir and Swadesh, 1964 [1929–46], p. 101)

In other words the common psychological ground of language can only be gotten at by working *through* the diversity of manifest forms of languages.[20]

Regarding the connection between language and culture more generally, Sapir shared Boas's views that culture influenced language (and not vice versa) and that this influence was chiefly evident in the vocabulary and not in the morphological,[21] or formal, part of language, which Sapir regarded as especially self-contained (for example, Sapir, 1949f [1912], pp. 90–100; 1949i [1916], p. 432; 1949e [1921], pp. 218–19; 1949h [1929], pp. 164–65; 1949d [1933], pp. 26–27; 1947, p. 3; etc.).

In his early writings on this topic, Sapir argued that a connection between language and culture might be deducible through the intervening variable of thought modes, but he concluded that the evidence was essentially negative:

Linguistic morphology, on the other hand, as giving evidence of certain definite modes of thought prevalent among the speakers of the language, may be thought to stand in some sort of relation to the stock of concepts forming the mental stock in trade, as it were, of the group. As this stock of concepts, however, is necessarily determined by the physical and social environment, it follows that some sort of correlation between these environments and grammatical structure might be looked for. And yet the negative evidence is as strong in this case as in the parallel [phonetic[22]] one just disposed of.   (Sapir, 1949f [1912], p. 97)

This contradiction between analysis and evidence may be the basis for a discussion some years later in which Sapir divided thought into a content (or cultural) aspect and a formal/processual (or linguistic) aspect which, he argued, need not be causally linked:

Nor can I believe that culture and language are in any true sense causally related. Culture may be defined as *what* a society does and thinks. Language is a particular *how* of thought. It is difficult to see what particular causal relations may be expected to subsist between a selected inventory of experience (culture, a significant selection made by society) and the particular manner in which the society expresses all experience.   (Sapir, 1949e [1921], p. 218)

Thus, by splitting thought into two natures (a "what" and a "how") Sapir could retain the relation of thought to both culture and language without the difficulty (or contradiction) implied by a lack of connection in turn between language and culture. Sapir did mention that if it could be shown that "culture has an innate form," then it might once more become interesting to contrast language with culture.[23]

Exceptions to the generalization that Sapir did not argue for a reverse influence, that is, for language having an influence on culture, include the following oft-quoted lines:

Language is a guide to 'social reality' ... Human beings do not live in the objective world alone, nor alone in the world of social activity as ordinarily understood, but are very much at the mercy of the particular language which has become the medium of expression for their society ... the 'real world' is to a large extent unconsciously built up on the language habits of the group. No two languages are ever sufficiently similar to be considered as representing the same social reality. The worlds in which different societies live are distinct worlds, not merely the same world with different labels attached.
     ... We see and hear and otherwise experience very largely as we do because the language habits of our community predispose certain choices of interpretation ... From this standpoint we may think of language as the *symbolic guide to culture*.   (Sapir, 1949h [1929], p. 162)[24]

These comments follow by only two years Sapir's paper "The unconscious patterning of behavior in society" (1949j [1927]), in which he draws stronger conclusions than earlier about the organization or formal patterning of cultural phenomena and of the general similarity of such phenomena to linguistic patterning. These remarks may reflect a change in belief by Sapir, namely that the notion of "form" in culture was now a viable concept.[25]

Indeed, two years later Sapir reaches much the same conclusion and appears to be moving toward a conception of culture based more on shared symbolic understandings:

> it is obvious that language has the power to analyze experience into theoretically dissociable elements and to create that world of the potential intergrading with the actual which enables human beings to transcend the immediately given in their individual experiences and to join in a larger common understanding. This common understanding constitutes culture, which cannot be adequately defined by a description of those more colorful patterns of behavior in society which lie open to observation.   (Sapir, 1949d [1933], p. 10)

However, another clear comment on this topic published posthumously (Sapir, 1947) seems to indicate a consistency with earlier views, in that there is hesitancy once more regarding the relation of the formal aspects of language to culture:

> If ... there are fundamental relations between cultural and formal linguistic phenomena, they cannot be of the type which so many linguistic philosophers and social scientists are in the habit of discovering.   (Sapir, 1947, p. 3)

We may interpret this as a disavowal of evolutionary or specific culture trait connections of the type rejected by Boas before (and Whorf after), but not of any connections whatsoever, if properly conceptualized.

Summary

Sapir worked out the implications of the fact that the implicit classifications of experience in language (described by Boas) cohere into *formally complete systems*. Thus, the differences among languages lie not merely in the content of the individual classifications themselves, but, among other things, in their systematic formal arrangement. The formal, systemic nature of these classifications is one factor contributing to their remaining out-of-awareness. Whereas Boas saw language as primarily reflecting thought and culture and only on occasion having a direct influence back on them, Sapir began to see in language a powerful shaping factor because of the impact of using this creative symbolic tool in the interpretation of experience. He argued that the use of this tool transforms and, in part, constitutes conceptual thought; the naive acceptance of language-specific properties as guides to reality channels and shapes the speakers' view of physical and social reality. While Sapir recognized the logical plausibility of the influence of language on culture via its influence on thought, he felt the evidence on this issue was negative. However, in his later writings certain reconceptualizations of thought and culture emerged which pointed toward a notion of culture involving shared symbolic understandings, which of necessity depend largely on a linguistic base.

Conclusion

Boas and Sapir lay the groundwork for a notion of linguistic relativity by showing that each language represents a classification of experience which can vary considerably. However, they differ in their sense as to the importance of this variation for thought and culture. Boas believed that the influences on thought and culture were minimal and, if anything, that stronger influences ran in the other direction. Sapir felt (particularly in the later period) that there was an influence on thought, although he did not investigate this in detail, but he felt that the linkage to culture was questionable given the available evidence.

2. Development of the linguistic relativity hypothesis in America: Whorf

Introduction

Benjamin Lee Whorf (1897–1941) was trained as a chemical engineer at the Massachusetts Institute of Technology and worked as a fire-prevention engineer for the Hartford Insurance Company for his entire professional career. Avocationally, however, he pursued a wide variety of interests, centering for the most part on a deep concern for the apparent conflict between science and religion. This general interest eventually became focused on linguistic problems, and it is in the area of language-related studies that he made his most important scholarly contributions. (Biographical accounts of Whorf's life and his interests can be found in Carroll, 1956, and Rollins, 1972 and 1980. Whorf, 1956a,[1] also contains a bibliography of most of Whorf's published and unpublished works.)

Whorf was initially self-taught in linguistics, but later (after 1931) benefited significantly from interaction with Sapir and his circle of students at nearby Yale. His interest in and formulation of the specifically linguistic relativity principle probably stemmed in large part from this contact with Sapir. It is important to realize that despite his "amateur" status, Whorf's work in linguistics was and still is recognized as being of superb professional quality by linguists. He produced general descriptive works on the modern Nahuatl (Aztec) and Hopi languages, partial descriptive studies of a variety of other languages contemporary and ancient, historical reconstructions of the Uto-Aztecan and adjacent language families, epigraphic studies of Mayan and central Mexican hieroglyphic writings, and a number of theoretical articles. Most of these works are still of contemporary relevance.

The linguistic analysis of experience

Language classifies experience

Whorf shared with Boas and Sapir the view that language was classificatory, isolating and organizing elements of experience (Whorf, 1956a, pp. 55, 102, 162, 210–13, 240). And, like Sapir, he emphasized the productive formal completeness of the linguistic system of classifications and the dependency of meaning on the patterns of relations among classifications (1956a, pp. 58–59, 67, 102, 156). Further, he agreed with Sapir that the analysis of experience implicit in a language might only be in accord with objective experience up to a point; thereafter, the role of the socially conventional linguistic scheme itself becomes important in further defining the nature of what is classified and in what way (1956a, pp. 92, 102, 212–13). However, Whorf went much further than Sapir by examining less obvious morphological categories to reveal the full classificatory nature of language and hence the true extent of the possible interactions of language classifications with thought.[2]

Whorf went beyond Boas and Sapir to distinguish two types of classification implicit in language: *overt categories* and *covert categories*.[3] Overt and covert categories differ from each other in their degree of systematic formal marking:

An overt category is a category having a formal mark which is present (with only infrequent exceptions) in every sentence containing a member of the category. The mark need not be part of the same word to which the category may be said to be attached in a paradigmatic sense; i.e. it need not be a suffix, prefix, vowel change, or other "inflection," but may be a detached word or a certain patterning of the whole sentence. Thus in English the plural of nouns is an overt category, marked usually in the paradigm word (the noun in question) by the suffix '-s' or a vowel change, but in the case of words like 'fish, sheep,' and certain gentilic plurals, it is marked by the form of the verb, the manner of use of the articles, etc....

A covert category is marked, whether morphemically or by sentence-pattern, only in certain types of sentence and not in every sentence in which a word or element belonging to the category occurs. The class-membership of the word is not apparent until there is a question of using it or referring to it in one of these special types of sentence, and then we find that this word belongs to a class requiring some sort of distinctive treatment, which may even be the negative treatment of excluding that type of sentence. This distinctive treatment we may call the REACTANCE of the category. In English, intransitive verbs form a covert category marked by lack of the passive participle and the passive and causative voices; we cannot substitute a verb of this class (e.g. 'go, lie, sit, rise, gleam, sleep, arrive, appear, rejoice') into such sentences as 'It was cooked, It was being cooked, I had it cooked to order.'   (1956a, pp. 88–89)[4]

It should be stressed that covert categories *are* marked in the language, but their marking emerges only in certain contexts of use.[5] Whorf noted:

> Grammatical classes are not to be set up on the absence of any markers at all; from a *grammatical* configurative standpoint an entirely unmarked class would be a fiction . . . Covert marking is very definitely marking. (1956b [1938], p. 5)

Whorf pointed out that such marking (whether covert or overt) sometimes might not occur in the immediate sentence but rather in a "small group of sentences (immediate field of discourse)" (1956b [1938], p. 5).

Whorf occasionally applied an alternative set of labels to covert and overt categories, namely *cryptotype* and *phenotype*, respectively. He used the term cryptotype initially (in 1936 and 1937) to highlight those covert categories that have subtle meaning and no overt marks other than their impact on the structural possibilities of various overtly marked forms:

> A covert linguistic class . . . may have a very subtle meaning, and it may have no overt mark other than certain distinctive "reactances" with certain overtly marked forms. It is then what I call a CRYPTOTYPE. (1956a, p. 70)

He later shifted to using the less stringent criterion of relatively infrequent reactances while retaining essentially the same definition:

> A covert category may also be termed a CRYPTOTYPE, a name which calls attention to the rather hidden, cryptic nature of such word-groups, especially when they are not strongly contrasted in idea, nor marked by frequently occurring reactances such as pronouns. (1956a, p. 92)

(See also Whorf, 1956a, pp. 80–83, 105.) The term cryptotype, then, had two senses, one referring to a relative lack of marking and the other referring to relative obscurity of meaning. The discussion of phenotypes follows the same pattern, beginning with the use of the term to emphasize the conjunction of clear meaning and very regular marking:

> I give the name PHENOTYPE to the linguistic category with a clearly apparent class meaning and a formal mark or morpheme which accompanies it; i.e., the phenotype is the "classical" morphological category. (1956a, p. 72)

This later shifted slightly, as with the case above, to a greater focus on the degree of formal marking, essentially permitting the use of the term for the mark:

> The contrasting term PHENOTYPE may be applied to the overt category and, when no ambiguity results, to the mark which accompanies the overt category in the sentence. (1956a, p. 93)

Whorf then used these terms rather freely as alternates to the terms covert and overt.

Whorf's use of these alternate terms can be confusing. He sometimes spoke as if they were fully equivalent with the terms overt and covert, yet in other places they are clearly used to refer to subsets of the broader terms. (Contrast, for example, the pairs of citations in the previous paragraph.) Further, by referring sometimes to the relative clarity of meaning and sometimes to the relative ubiquity of marking with the same term, he invited further confusion. In a later writing on the subject of overt and covert categories (in 1938), Whorf moved toward using phenotype and cryptotype more exclusively for meaning as opposed to marking, but in a way that was inconsistent with his earlier uses:

> Grammatical classes which appear ordinarily "without" markers do have markers appearing with them under certain particular circumstances – such a class is "covert", and its marker a "reactance". Its grammatical meaning, if distinguishable, is a "cryptotype" ... *Overt* categories are accompanied by markers in all or nearly all sentences ... Their grammatical meanings are "phenotypes".   (1956b [1938], p. 5)

Thus, phenotype and cryptotype refer to the *grammatical meanings*[6] of overt and covert categories respectively. This usage has the advantage of permitting unambiguous reference to the meaning of a category independently of its marking. (There are some earlier hints of movement in this direction, e.g., in Whorf, 1956a, pp. 105 and 109, but nothing this definite.) In the following discussion, Whorf's last usage will be followed.[7]

It should be emphasized that only the degree of formal marking makes a category overt or covert. The substantive content of the category is generally not at issue. Whorf pointed out that a given classification may be overt in one language and covert in another; he gave examples which include the gender classes of various European languages and the shape classes of various American Indian languages (1956a, pp. 90–91; see also pp. 69–70). Although Whorf occasionally used the term cryptotype to imply that the meaning of a covert category is subtle or elusive, this was not the basis of its classification as a covert category.

However, by contrast, the relative covertness of a category does appear to affect its meaning, or content. For example, as we have seen, Whorf implied by his use of the term cryptotype that many covert categories do have subtle, elusive meanings that are not readily brought into consciousness at least in part because of their covert status (1956a, pp. 70–71, 83, 92, 104–5, 132). Further, he argued that such categories were more likely to be "rational," by which he meant in accordance with his view of nonlinguistic fact and not merely a cultural or linguistic convention. This happens because the category, in the absence of many formal marks, is free to crystallize around an idea:

> Indeed, covert categories are quite apt to be more rational than overt ones. English unmarked [i.e., covert] gender is more rational, closer to natural fact,

than the marked [i.e., overt] genders of Latin or German. As outward marks become few, the class tends to crystallize around an idea – to become more dependent on whatever synthetizing principle there may be in the meanings of its members.   (1956a, p. 80)

Overt categories, then, are more likely to be at variance with classifications that might be made on purely rational grounds (in Whorf's sense of the term). (This is more often implied than directly stated by Whorf, 1956a, pp. 69, 80–81, 91, 109, 261–62.) To say that covert categories are more rational, however, does not mean that they are completely so:

Likewise with various covert categories of exotic languages: where they have been thought to be recognitions of objective differences, it may rather be that they are grammatical categories that merely accord up to a certain point with objective experience. They may represent experience, it is true, but experience seen in terms of a definite linguistic scheme.   (1956a, p. 92)

Thus, for example, even though he has suggested that English gender is more rational than Latin or German gender (1956a, p. 80), he explains in considerable detail how a good part of the English gender system is not deducible from "a knowledge of actual sex and of scientific biological and physical classification of objects" (1956a, p. 90), but rather depends to a considerable extent on linguistic and cultural conventions, some of which he describes (1956a, pp. 90–92).

   Overt and covert categories do not operate independently of one another. Both need analysis to provide a full understanding of the category meanings of a language:

The meaning of a PHENOTYPE, though ostensibly plain, can really not be understood in all its subtlety until the cryptotypes that go with it have been dredged up from their submerged state and their effective meanings to some extent brought into consciousness. Thereupon the different effects produced by the same phenotype with different cryptotypes, and vice versa, result in a more pronounced consciousness and clearer understanding of the phenotype itself.

                              (1956a, p. 109; see also pp. 105 and 110)

One aspect of this interdependence that particularly interested Whorf was the possibility that languages might use covert categories to different degrees – and, in particular, that a language that was overtly very simple might in fact be more complex in its covert categories:

It may turn out that the simpler a language becomes overtly, the more it becomes dependent upon cryptotypes and other covert formations, the more it conceals unconscious presuppositions, and the more its lexations become variable and indefinable.   (1956a, p. 83)

Whorf pointed out that Hopi and English were particularly rich in covert categories and that this might not be true of all languages (1956a, pp. 82,

110), but he appeared to believe in the general utility of the overt–covert distinction since he included it in his general theoretical discussions without such warning (1956a, pp. 88–93, 129, 132). Certainly, throughout his work he stressed the importance of hierarchical levels of patterning as contributing to meaning and the inadequacy of analyzing a linguistic element (e.g., a lexeme) in isolation from its associated patterns. (See, for example, the early remarks in 1936 [1956a, pp. 67–69] and the later remarks in 1941 [1956a, pp. 246–70].[8])

Much as Sapir's insight that the classifications in language form a self-contained, formally complete symbolic universe led to his more sophisticated understanding of the mechanism and potential significance of language influences on thought, so too did Whorf's conceptualization of covert categories lead to a still more sophisticated theory on these issues. Where Sapir had to make generalized, somewhat vague references to form-feeling, intuition, or relational feeling arising from the overall patterns of relations in a language, Whorf was able to discuss specific, empirically investigable covert linkages among the forms in a language:

A covert concept like a covert gender is as definable and in its way as definite as a verbal concept like 'female' or feminine, but is of a very different kind; it is not the analogue of a word but of a rapport-system, and awareness of it has an intuitive quality; we say that it is sensed rather than comprehended.

(1956a, pp. 69–70)

The concepts involved might be intuitive for the speakers of a language, but they could become explicit and well defined for the analyst, as Whorf demonstrated repeatedly through his illustrative analyses (see, for example, 1956a, pp. 68–70, 90–91, 102–11). It is crucial to Whorf's subsequent arguments that the cognitive influences he traces to grammatical regularities need not derive solely from the most obvious and systematic overt categories in a language, but may involve large numbers of underlying covert linkages which work together as a unified psychic complex:

There is no evident reason why such a [psychic] complex [of covert linkages] should not enter into various functional relations with other material of thought without necessarily requiring the activation of any of the individual words or class marks with which it is connected.   (1956a, p. 69)

The covert classes may have a far-reaching connection with the type of thinking, the "philosophy" or "implicit metaphysics" of a [language] . . . The manifestations of these class-distinctions in thinking and the character of the sometimes rather deeply-hidden and seldom-appearing reactances suggest the phenomena associated with the unconscious, subconscious, or foreconscious in psychology, though on a more socialized and less purely personal plane, and may connect in a significant manner therewith.   (1956b [1938], p. 5)

(See also Whorf, 1956a, p. 81.) Thus the influence of language on thought need not arise only through the influence of the more straight-forward, easily described morphological categories, but may also arise from covert categories in the language. Further, because cryptotypes can play such an important role in defining phenotypes, a simple, naive analysis of overt morphology is not a sure guide either to the meanings of those elements or to their significance in cognition. Thus, in Whorf's view, overt morphology is doubly unreliable: it neither accurately reflects the "objective" *nonlinguistic* reality (in line with the arguments of Sapir) nor adequately represents the full *linguistic* reality. Although Whorf did not cast his later, popularized discussions of the relations between language and thought in terms of the overt–covert distinction,[9] his insights in this area clearly provide the groundwork for his com-parison of English and Hopi and for a much more sophisticated theory of language and thought interaction.

Language classifications vary across languages

Although Whorf followed Boas and Sapir in indicating that the classifi-cations implicit in linguistic forms varied considerably across languages, he was able to add new depth and scope to the traditional arguments. By emphasizing detailed case studies (1956a, pp. 134–59, 207–19, 233–45), rather than the citation of isolated examples typical of his predecessors, he was able to show how specific, often minor, differences in such classifications could cumulatively signal quite general, often major, underlying differences in fundamental approach to the linguistic repre-sentation of reality – what he came to call different "fashions of speaking." In his case studies, Whorf worked to show that differences in the classifications of various languages are *semantically integrated* and *structurally pervasive*. They are semantically integrated in that each conceptual distinction works with many others to form a coordinated, coherent set within each language – hence many differences between languages are better characterized in terms of patterns of differences that operate across entire systems. For example, a pattern of treating imaginary entities as if they were concrete objects ("objectification," in Whorf's terminology) can be identified in rules of English pluralization, quantification, time expressions, etc., while the Hopi language differs in each case so as to deny, or ignore, such a pattern of treatment (1956a, pp. 134–59). A series of minor differences cumulate to indicate a significant underlying pattern. The classifications are structurally per-vasive in that they operate, or are carried, in multiple kinds of formal apparatus. Thus, to continue the previous example, morphological, syntactic, and lexical devices all contribute to the English pattern of classification. Whorf summarized these points by noting that such conceptual differences between languages

do not depend so much upon ANY ONE SYSTEM (e.g., tense, or nouns) within the grammar as upon the ways of analyzing and reporting experience which have become fixed in the language as integrated "fashions of speaking" and which cut across the typical grammatical classifications, so that such a "fashion" may include lexical, morphological, syntactic, and otherwise systemically diverse means coordinated in a certain frame of consistency.   (1956a, p. 158)

Essentially, Whorf drew out in detail the implications of Sapir's arguments about the systemic, interlocking nature of the linguistic analysis of experience for the project of linguistic comparison. His studies reveal that differences in linguistic classifications may range across the whole of the morpholexical and syntactic structures of the languages.[10]

Whorf realized that the very variety of languages posed a problem for comparison of linguistic categories. Contrary to the popular image of Whorf as a dogmatic relativist, he firmly believed in the possibility of meaningful comparison and generalization.[11] The key concern in his approach, however, was to find a frame of reference for comparison that would be independent of the particularities of any given language:

To compare ways in which different languages differently "segment" the same situation or experience, it is desirable to be able to analyze or "segment" the experience first in a way independent of any one language or linguistic stock, a way which will be the same for all observers.   (1956a, p. 162)

Whorf proposed both nonlinguistic and linguistic solutions to this problem of "calibration," as he termed it (1956a, p. 214) – solutions which are also important for the insight they give regarding his general views on the nature of linguistic variation and universals.

Whorf occasionally raised the possibility that frames of comparison based on nonlinguistic grounds could be found:

In describing differences between [languages] ... we must have a way of describing phenomena by non-linguistic standards, and by terms that refer to experience as it must be to all human beings, irrespective of their languages or philosophies.   (1956b [1938], p. 6)

The principal such standard directly suggested by Whorf lay in the laws of visual perception discovered by Gestalt psychology:

A discovery made by modern configurative or Gestalt psychology gives us a canon of reference for all observers, irrespective of their languages or scientific jargons, by which to break down and describe all visually observable situations, and many other situations, also. This is the discovery that visual perception is basically the same for all normal persons past infancy and conforms to definite laws, a large number of which are fairly well known.   (1956a, p. 163)

Whorf gives examples of the application of this technique in a description of Shawnee stem composition (1956a, pp. 160–72) and in the relative modes of expressing figure and ground relations in English and Hopi (1956b [1938], pp. 7–9). The latter example, which is the only one that tries to use Gestalt ideas for language comparison, is, unfortunately, only slightly developed and was never published by Whorf. It should perhaps be clarified that the principal role played by Gestalt psychology in Whorf's thinking was the much more general one of reinforcing his belief (and that of Sapir's circle) in the importance of pattern and configuration in all human activity (e.g., 1956a, pp. 41–42, 158, 248) – and that these specific applications were secondary. Nonetheless, they clearly point to a concern on Whorf's part to give language comparison an unbiased foundation.[12]

At times, Whorf also seemed to embrace the view that modern physical science or logic could serve as bases for nonlinguistic evaluation, and hence calibration, of language categories. This view emerges in his early writings when he discusses the superior fit of implicit Hopi metaphysics with modern physics, in contrast to the implicit metaphysics of the Indo-European languages (1956a, pp. 55–56, 85). These arguments reflect his concern, in line with the Boasian tradition, with defending Indian and other exotic languages against those who would label them "primitive" in some respect. A similar view emerges when he makes reference to a language category being "more rational, closer to natural fact" (1956a, p. 80), in his attempt to establish the reality and significance of covert categories.

Most of Whorf's writings, however, reflect a more balanced view of the referential equivalence of various languages and a more skeptical view of the utility of modern physical science as a basis for comparison. He usually argued that the alternative views of the world encapsulated in language categories are functionally equivalent or equal in value. Writing on the Hopi language, he remarked:

the Hopi language is capable of accounting for and describing correctly, in a pragmatic or operational sense, all observable phenomena of the universe ... Just as it is possible to have any number of geometries other than the Euclidean which give an equally perfect account of space configurations, so it is possible to have descriptions of the universe, all equally valid, that do not contain our familiar contrasts of time and space.   (1956a, p. 58)

The differences among languages are those of "emphasis" (1956a, pp. 147–48) or of relative ease in making some distinction which might be of use in certain circumstances (1956a, pp. 217, 265) – not of fundamental referential potential or subtlety (1956a, pp. 84–85, 263; 1941, pp. 13–14).[13] Further, in his later writings directed toward an audience of natural scientists, he became especially critical of modern physical science and Western logic as sure guides to reality. He referred to the underlying vagueness of their concepts (1956a, p. 260), to their dependence on naive concepts in the Indo-European type of language (1956a, pp. 214–19, 221–22, 263, 266, 269), and to the tendency of scientific sublanguages to build in points of view that impede the acceptance of alternative views (1956a, pp. 246–47). Thus, on the whole, Whorf was skeptical of using contemporary physical science and logic as a basic frame for the comparison of the categories of diverse languages.

Most often, Whorf advocated building a vocabulary or frame of comparison directly from the study of languages. Unfortunately, the grammatical terms developed in the study of European languages are inadequate because of the close historical relationship among these languages, which limits the range of observed variation. The close historical relationship operates on several levels:

Among these [European] tongues there is a unanimity of major pattern which . . . exists only because these tongues are all Indo-European dialects cut to the same basic plan, being historically transmitted from what was long ago one speech community; because the modern dialects have long shared in building up a common culture; and because much of this culture, on the more intellectual side, is derived from the linguistic backgrounds of Latin and Greek. (1956a, p. 214)

The commonalities are so great that, in contrast with other languages in the world such as Hopi, Whorf felt comfortable in grouping them together as a single language which he called Standard Average European (SAE) (1956a, p. 138). To remedy the problems stemming from concepts developed on so narrow a basis, Whorf advocated a widescale survey of languages to provide the basis for an adequate understanding of the true range of variation among languages (1956a, pp. 76–78, 84, 87, 239, 244–45). What is needed is a true "contrastive" linguistics to plot "the outstanding differences among tongues – in grammar, logic, and general analysis of experience" (1956a, p. 240). From such a linguistics will come a more correct image of the nature both of language in general and of particular languages.

Whorf realized that such a contrastive survey would of necessity involve the use of traditional, inadequate terms, but he felt that with an awareness of the problem, new conceptual frames could eventually be developed:

The very natural tendency to use terms derived from traditional grammar, like verb, noun, adjective, passive voice, in describing languages outside of Indo-European is fraught with grave possibilities of misunderstanding. At the same time it is desirable to define these terms in such a way that we can avail ourselves of their great convenience and, where possible, apply them to exotic languages in a scientific and consistent way. To do this, we must re-examine the types of grammatical category that are found in languages, using a worldwide view of linguistic phenomena, frame concepts more or less new, and make needed additions to terminology. (1956a, p. 87)

Cautious use of such terms may be helpful, perhaps unavoidable, but it must be remembered that in their ranges of meaning they are but the creatures of modern Indo-European languages and their subsidiary jargons, and reflect the typical modes of segmenting experience in these tongues. (1956a, p. 162)

(See also Whorf, 1956a, pp. 59, 242.) Whorf went beyond exhortation on this issue. He developed new conceptualizations of grammatical categories (some of which have been discussed above) more suitable for the general comparison of languages (1956a, pp. 87–101) and indicated the proper approach to the development of generic taxonomic categories for grammatical comparisons (1956a, p. 101). He also provided the detailed beginnings of a format for the systematic survey of languages, one founded on both his own theoretical insights and the experience of the Boas–Sapir and Bloomfield schools of linguistic study (1956a, pp. 125–33). He felt that by a process of iterative reformulation, a vocabulary adequate to the task of linguistic description could be built.

In suggesting the development of a specifically linguistic frame of comparison built on the contrastive study of languages, Whorf implied that he believed there is a specifically linguistic level of generality for the description of both language variation and commonality. Occasionally he was explicit on this point:

Just as cultural facts are only culturally determined, not biologically determined, so linguistic facts, which are likewise cultural, and include the linguistic element of thought, are only linguistically determined. They are determined not merely by language, but by languaɢes. (1956a, p. 67 [n5])[14]

But there are some passages that suggest that if commonalities among languages exist, they may not in fact reflect specifically linguistic regularities:

The different tongues are the real phenomena and may generalize down not to any such universal as "Language," but to something better – called "sublinguistic" or "superlinguistic" – and NOT ALTOGETHER unlike, even if much unlike, what we now call mental. (1956a, p. 239)

(See also Whorf, 1956a, p. 36.) Although this remark seems to contradict the ones cited just above, in fact it does not. It merely asserts that it may be the case that a nonlinguistic level exerts its influence not on some general capacity "Language" but rather on individual "languages." And the postulation of a general "Language" faculty that lies behind the cross-linguistic pattern may add nothing of descriptive or theoretical interest.

Although Whorf's first concerns were to stress the importance of linguistic variation and the need for a frame of comparison independent of any single language or language group, these discussions also show his positive attitude toward the search for commonalities, or universals, across languages and his openness to considering both specifically linguistic and extralinguistic factors as the basis for such commonality. Specifically, his search for an unbiased frame of comparison, his desire for a broad survey of the world's languages, and his interest in the general categories of description for language all reflect this positive attitude. Too often Whorf's concern with pressing the significance of linguistic variation – both for linguistics and for the other sciences – has led to the neglect by others of this aspect of his work. Whorf explored the variation and hence the "relativity" of linguistic categories in the service of overcoming their influence, and not as an end in itself. As he remarked on one occasion: "science CAN have a rational or logical basis even though it be a relativistic one" (1956a, p. 239), once we control for the biases of our language through contrastive linguistics.

Language classifications are out-of-awareness

Turning next to the out-of-awareness, or unconscious, nature of linguistic categories, Whorf agreed for the most part with Boas and Sapir, but he elaborated their arguments in some crucial ways. Whorf did not explicitly mention Boas's early arguments about automaticity. Instead, he emphasized a related argument that languages are background phenomena for speakers and are not easily brought to conscious attention because of the lack of contrasting examples:

if a rule has absolutely no exceptions, it is not recognized as a rule or as anything else; it is then part of the background of experience of which we tend to remain unconscious. Never having experienced anything in contrast to it, we cannot isolate it and formulate it as a rule until we so enlarge our experience and expand our base of reference that we encounter an interruption of its regularity.

(1956a, p. 209)

(See also Whorf, 1956a, pp. 138 and 211.) In this, language is not distinctive from other parts of culture. In fact, the background nature of language is guaranteed precisely by the social (or interpersonal) nature of language, which compels agreement to effect communication:

We cut nature up, organize it into concepts, and ascribe significances as we do, largely because we are parties to an agreement to organize it in this way – an agreement that holds throughout our speech community and is codified in the patterns of our language. The agreement is, of course, an implicit and unstated one, BUT ITS TERMS ARE ABSOLUTELY OBLIGATORY; we cannot talk at all except by subscribing to the organization and classification of data which the agreement decrees. (1956a, pp. 213–14)[15]

Thus, this background quality is not an accidental and easily modified characteristic of language, but rather is an intrinsic part of the social process of language usage.

Speakers are so powerfully bound by this background agreement that even when they are exposed to a very different language, they will tend to analyze it in terms of their own language categories. In spite of this, Whorf consistently advocated the study of the novel modes of expression in exotic languages[16] as the surest and perhaps the only route to bringing many linguistic categories into consciousness:

the best approach is through an exotic language, for in its study we are at long last pushed willy-nilly out of our ruts. Then we find that the exotic language is a mirror held up to our own. (1956a, p. 138)

(See also Whorf, 1956a, p. 112.) In a sense, we de-automatize our own language categories by contrasting them with those of other languages. This view led quite naturally to Whorf's concern with a world-wide comparison of languages with the goal of identifying general grammatical types that could be used to give an "objective" characterization of each language, that is, one free of the particular background assumptions of the investigator's native tongue.

Whorf also discussed Sapir's argument that people attend more to function than form, but he directed his remarks somewhat more specifically to language. He pointed out that people see language as a vehicle for expressing thought, that is, they see language as functional, and regard its form as irrelevant (1956a, p. 207). Further, they equate agreement about subject matter with knowledge of language processes (1956a, p. 211). Sapir also discussed the difficulty of segmenting out one element in a cultural pattern and understanding its relation to the whole. Whorf made similar remarks, stressing the tremendous complexity of linguistic patterns (e.g., 1956a, pp. 211 and 256), and the difficulty, even for the specialist, of analyzing these forms. This all formed part of Whorf's general argument that pattern in language is more important than lexation (1956a, pp. 246–70).

But Whorf went somewhat further than Sapir in making reference to speakers' explicit beliefs (or ideologies) about language itself. He emphasized that speakers have the view that language reflects an independently organized reality and thought rather than shapes or affects them in a significant way (1956a, pp. 207, 221, 238, 251, 257). He also referred on occasion to native "theories" about the structure and meaning of linguistic categories (e.g., 1956a, pp. 258–63). Whorf's principal claim was that speakers can readily reflect on lexical meanings but tend to be completely oblivious to the patterned grammatical meanings which ultimately govern a lexical item. And overt categories were more susceptible to the critical consciousness of speakers than covert categories with their cryptotypes. In short, some aspects of language are more susceptible to *conscious awareness* than are others. These remarks suggest that under certain circumstances speakers can and do reflect upon some aspects of their linguistic categories and that these reflections will be skewed by differential awareness of those categories.

Further, at another level, Whorf's argument for analogical influences of language on thought (discussed below) depends on there being a specific directionality of influence among connected categories because of their formal properties or substantive content. This implies a differential *salience* for thought of some aspects of linguistic form and meaning relative to other aspects. This might be characterized as a differential *intuitive awareness*. Whether we speak of intuitive or conscious awareness, however, the implication remains the same: speakers do not respond to all aspects of their language in an unbiased way. They bring to both use and reflection a differential awareness of some forms and meanings relative to others. This emphasis on differential sensitivity to or awareness of language structure represents a crucial and novel element in Whorf's subsequent arguments about the influence of language on thought and culture.

The relation of languages to thought and culture

Language classifications influence thought

Whorf, like Sapir before him, felt that language classifications influenced thought and, therefore, that the diversity of those classifications insured a certain diversity of thought among the speakers of different languages. Whorf referred to this as the linguistic relativity principle:

These automatic, involuntary patterns of language are not the same for all men but are specific for each language and constitute the formalized side of the language, or its "grammar" . . .

From this fact proceeds what I have called the "linguistic relativity principle," which means, in informal terms, that users of markedly different grammars are pointed by the grammars toward different types of observations and different evaluations of externally similar acts of observation, and hence are not equivalent as observers but must arrive at somewhat different views of the world.

(1956a, p. 221)

(See also Whorf, 1956a, p. 214.) Unlike Sapir, however, Whorf took up in considerable detail just how speakers are "pointed by their grammars." His central treatment of the problem is given in his article "The relation of habitual thought and behavior to language" (1956a, pp. 124–59), which serves as the principal basis for the discussion in this section, although his other writings will be used to supplement the analysis.[17] In this article he specified the focus of research, laid out a theoretical mechanism to account for the influence of language on thought, and provided empirical evidence in support of his claims.

Focus of research

Whorf was very explicit about the focus of his research, summarizing his concerns as follows:

> That portion of the whole investigation here to be reported may be summed up in two questions: (1) Are our own concepts of 'time,' 'space,' and 'matter' given in substantially the same form by experience to all men, or are they in part conditioned by the structure of particular languages? (2) Are there traceable affinities between (a) cultural and behavioral norms and (b) large-scale linguistic patterns? (1956a, p. 138)

Embedded within these two questions are clear indications of the aspects of language and of thought that were of concern to Whorf in his study. On the linguistic side he was interested in the pervasive structural (or grammatical) patterns which are characteristic of particular languages. On the cognitive side he was interested in the fundamental conceptual ideas habitually used by speakers of those languages. The importance of language for culture more broadly will emerge in the discussion of Whorf's evidence for his ideas and will also be treated explicitly below in a separate section, following Whorf's own division of the research problem into two distinct, though admittedly related, questions.

Whorf's concern with "the structure of particular languages" and with "large-scale linguistic patterns" was consistent with his emphasis elsewhere on complex grammatical categories and on the importance of overall patternment in language, issues that have been discussed in detail above. Whorf did describe how the "names" of situations influence behavior in the prelude to the above quotation, but only because these lexations and other simple overt patterns provide especially clear examples of the point he wished to make.[18] His basic concern with more complicated and pervasive patternment is made quite explicit in his transition from these introductory examples to the two central questions quoted above:

The linguistic material in the above examples is limited to single words, phrases, and patterns of limited range. One cannot study the behavioral compulsiveness of such material without suspecting a much more far-reaching compulsion from large-scale patterning of grammatical categories, such as plurality, gender and similar classifications (animate, inanimate, etc.), tenses, voices, and other verb forms, classifications of the type of "parts of speech," and the matter of whether a given experience is denoted by a unit morpheme, an inflected word, or a syntactical combination.   (1956a, p. 137)

In short, although Whorf did not deny that more limited, or isolated, aspects of a language might have effects on thinking, he felt that broad patterns of signification and formal structure in language are a more potent source of effects. His subsequent analyses and examples constituted an attempt to identify differences in the broad patterns of the two particular languages with which he was concerned – Hopi and English.[19] The patterns that he finds "do not depend . . . upon ANY ONE SYSTEM . . . within the grammar" but rather "cut across the typical grammatical classifications" (1956a, p. 158). It is more this complex patterning, or "fashion of speaking," that Whorf sought to connect with thought rather than, as some have supposed, particular isolated differences between languages.

On the cognitive side, Whorf said that his interest was in our own "concepts" such as "'time,' 'space,' and 'matter.'" This indicates that his focus was on tracing the connection between linguistic categories and the most fundamental abstract ideas that a person uses in interpreting experience. This focus on the conceptual level appeared throughout his writings, although often with different labels such as abstractions, categories and types, and grand generalizations (1956a, pp. 58–59, 213–16). Also consistent with this interpretation are his many references to the influence of language on an individual's or people's *Weltanschauung*, metaphysics, unformulated philosophy, cosmology, worldview, ideology of nature, and picture (or description or view) of the universe (1956a, pp. 58–61, 214–16, 221, 241–42). Such concepts may be linguistically conditioned either directly (as with time and matter in the following passage) or indirectly (as with space in the following passage) on account of their interaction with directly conditioned concepts in an overall system of thought:

There is no such striking difference between Hopi and S[tandard] A[verage] E[uropean] about space as about time, and probably the apprehension of space is given in substantially the same form by experience irrespective of language. The experiments of the Gestalt psychologists with visual perception appear to establish this as a fact. But the CONCEPT OF SPACE will vary somewhat with language, because, as an intellectual tool, it is so closely linked with the concomitant employment of other intellectual tools, of the order of "time" and "matter," which are linguistically conditioned. We see things with our eyes in the same space forms as the Hopi, but our idea of space has also the property of acting as a surrogate of nonspatial relationships.   (1956a, pp. 158–59)

Exactly how language conditions thought will be taken up in more detail shortly.

Whorf's notion of "concepts" needs to be distinguished from more direct, lower-level processes of perception. The existence of an underlying distinction in Whorf's thinking between concepts and percepts (sometimes labeled sensations, impressions, or apprehensions) emerges in the passage cited just above, wherein he distinguishes between the apprehension of space and the concept of space, between space as we see it and our idea of space. Even when discussing time and matter earlier in his discussion, he implicitly invoked a similar distinction with his references to basic experiences which underlie our understandings. For time, he mentioned the "subjective 'becoming later' that is the essence of time" and the "subjective experience" or "feeling" of temporal duration that is covered or cloaked by linguistically induced patterns (1956a, pp. 141–43). For matter, he referred to "the observable appearance" of things which, he noted, comes into conflict with linguistically induced patterns (1956a, p. 141). Throughout his writings Whorf made appeal to such direct experiences with or apprehensions of natural phenomena, implying that there is a lower level of psychic experience to which we can, on occasion, have access.

Whorf was rarely explicit about this perceptual level, especially as to whether it can be directly influenced by language or not. Appeals to this level in his accounts suggest that fundamental perceptions are not in fact actually altered. This view gains support from the following remark indicating that certain psychic experiences are not destroyed but merely given different emphasis:

What surprises most is to find that various grand generalizations of the Western world, such as time, velocity, and matter, are not essential to the construction of a consistent picture of the universe. The psychic experiences that we class under these headings are, of course, not destroyed; rather, categories derived from other kinds of experience take over the rulership of the cosmology and seem to function just as well.   (1956a, p. 216)

(See also Whorf, 1956a, p. 267 for a similar remark.) However, there are cases in which he seemed to hint at an influence on perception itself, as in the following:

The categories and types that we isolate from the world of phenomena we do not find there because they stare every observer in the face; on the contrary, the world is presented in a kaleidoscopic flux of impressions which has to be organized by our minds – and this means largely by the linguistic systems in our minds. We cut nature up, organize it into concepts, and ascribe significances as we do, largely because we are parties to an agreement to organize it in this way – an agreement that holds throughout our speech community and is codified in the patterns of our language.   (1956a, p. 213)

Although Whorf may have been referring here to the perceptual level by the phrase "cut nature up," the comment more probably refers to the way language itself as a classificatory device segments nature. In fact, most of his statements about fundamental analysis of experience are actually statements about how language "chops up," "segments," or "breaks down" experience (1956a, pp. 137, 240–41, 253; 1956b [1938], p. 8), and not direct statements about perception itself.[20] Thus the evidence that he believed that language directly influences perception is slender and inconsistent.

Whorf's position on this issue probably derived at least in part from his views on the nature of the external world. Whorf regarded the external world as essentially unstructured from the point of view of a speaker. This view is evidenced by his use of such terms as "stream of sensory experience," "raw experience," "kaleidoscopic flux of impressions," "flux of experience," "mass of presentation," "flowing face of nature," and "continuous spread and flow of existence," (1956a, pp. 55, 102, 213, 239, 241, 253; 1956b [1938], p. 8). Whorf was critical of those logicians who pick out tables, chairs, and other human artifacts as examples for their discussions of the relation of words to reality:

Man's artifacts and the agricultural products he severs from living plants have a unique degree of isolation; we may expect that languages will have fairly isolated terms for them. The real question is: What do different languages do, not with these artificially isolated objects but with the flowing face of nature in its motion, color, and changing form ... ?   (1956a, pp. 240–41)

The view that experience is so little structured probably has its origin in Whorf's encounter with a variety of languages that treat the apparently "same" reality so differently. Once established, however, the presumption of this absence of structure leads directly to the question of where the rich conceptual structures evidenced by people have their origin. Whorf's answer was that they lie in language, i.e., his very point of departure for the discovery of variation. When, however, Whorf encountered a conceptual structure that was different from his own and yet that he could understand, or when he found a nearly identical structure in several languages, he was led to postulate an underlying level of more fundamental experience (i.e., a more direct perceptual apprehension) to which he could refer his understanding or the emergence of parallel patterns in diverse languages. Thus this implicit perceptual level created by Whorf is more or less a residual category in his writings that he used to account for the absence of linguistic relativity in certain cases or at certain levels of analysis. Such perceptual regularities, if and when they exist, do not tend to be particularly significant because of the more important, complex overlay of higher-level conceptual structures which are to a large extent linguistically based. (Recall the example of 'space' cited above.) When variation *is* present, then it is viewed as a difference in the conceptual analysis, emphasis, or organization of essentially similar experience, the distinction between concepts and percepts being disregarded (or neutralized) in this context. Thus, the conclusion here is that Whorf's primary interest was in concepts and that percepts were of minor or secondary importance to his theory; the locus of linguistic influence is on conceptual structure.

It should be clear that Whorf's theory was about the content of thought (hence "concepts"), rather than process, although certainly content guides processing and in that sense is indistinguishable from it in most cases. This focus on content is often misunderstood because of Whorf's imprecise use of psychological terminology. He sometimes referred to reasoning being influenced by language when he meant only to refer to the importance of linguistic meaning (or patternment) and agreement about subject matter in forming our thought categories (1956a, pp. 73–74, 208–12). He referred to some ideas being more rational, by which he meant that discriminations of reality are used that are closer to "natural fact," that is, relatively uninfluenced by language or with language's influence partialed out by linguistic comparison (1956a, pp. 80, 85, 239). And he referred to logic when he really meant to refer to problems engendered by different premises or postulates underlying logic or discriminations about what constitutes an object in logic (1956a, pp. 59, 80, 207–209, 233, 244). On a few occasions Whorf actually mentioned thought processes, but always in a context in which he was emphasizing the importance of cultural and linguistic content in thought (1956a, pp. 65–68, 207, 218, 239). The issues involved in the content–process dichotomy are subtle and difficult (certainly more involved than can be taken up here), and Whorf probably had no well-formed view of the matter. Nonetheless, his entire enterprise can, in one sense, be thought of as an attempt to show that much of what we think of as process (and, hence, intrinsic and universal) is better regarded as content (that is, extrinsic and variable).

Further, when Whorf spoke of "concepts" he was not primarily referring to more removed specialized notions of philosophy or science, but rather to the habitual thought characteristic of average speakers of the language. He explained that this habitual thought world:

is the microcosm that each man carries about within himself, by which he measures and understands what he can of the macrocosm.   (1956a, p. 147)

Although the references to habitual thought are most pronounced in the discussion just cited, similar remarks appear throughout his writings (e.g., 1956a, pp. 69, 79, 221, 266).

In Whorf's view, specialized conceptual systems such as science and philosophy tend to be built upon such a system of everyday concepts. They arise by a specialization of the same linguistic patterns that gave rise to the more widespread habitual thought pattern:

> From each such unformulated and naive world view, an explicit scientific world view may arise by a higher specialization of the same basic grammatical patterns that fathered the naive and implicit view. Thus the world view of modern science arises by a higher specialization of the basic grammar of the Western Indo-European languages. Science of course was not CAUSED by this grammar; it was simply colored by it.   (1956a, p. 221)

Throughout his later writings, Whorf made similar statements arguing that to the extent that science, philosophy, logic, and mathematics emerge in a culture, they are dependent on (and frequently little more than) specialized extensions of language patterns (1956a, pp. 152–53, 208, 236, 246, 248, 263, 266). Although the concepts characteristic of these fields are especially dependent on language from Whorf's point of view, this should not obscure the fact that these specialized forms of thought are really secondary reflexes of the more basic phenomenon, namely that languages influence habitual everyday thought.[21]

Whorf occasionally implied that science and philosophy could go against the prevailing habitual pattern of concepts, as, for example, when he remarked that

> Monistic, holistic, and relativistic views of reality appeal to philosophers and some scientists, but they are badly handicapped in appealing to the "common sense" of the Western average man.   (1956a, p. 152)

And again this point arose when he discussed the emergence of the concept of the "field" in modern physics (1956a, pp. 241, 269). But to the extent that scientists and philosophers succeed in breaking out of their habitual language patterns, they do so by constructing "what amounts to a new language" (1956a, p. 152). However, as was emphasized earlier, Whorf tended, on the whole, to argue that Western science and philosophy are very much influenced by traditional Indo-European language categories (1956a, pp. 214, 246, 260, 263), a situation that can only be remedied by contrastive linguistics, which will reveal to people their linguistic biases.

We can summarize this discussion of Whorf's focus on the cognitive side by saying that he was interested primarily in the concepts people routinely use in interpreting their experience. He was less interested in either direct, lower-level perceptions or in more removed specialized concepts. He recognized linguistic influences on these latter two levels as well, but always via the central conceptual patterns and organizations typical of everyday life. In this focus on pattern and embeddedness in higher-level structures, we find a parallel between his linguistic and cognitive concerns; just as words are nothing without sentences (or sets of sentences), so elements of experience, percepts, and even specialized ideas (e.g., science and philosophy) are nothing without the everyday pattern of concepts within which they are interpreted. The focus of Whorf's research then is on the connections between these two pattern schemes, that of language and that of thought.[22]

Basic argument

Whorf did not present a fully developed, explicit theory of how language structure influences concepts, but rather gave a programmatic discussion based on the analysis of a few selected, interrelated examples. Underlying his analyses, however, were the outlines of an implicit theory and some indications of how he would have filled in the outlines. For discursive clarity Whorf's ideas will be extracted and presented here in schematic form as if they in fact constituted an explicit formal theory. A good part of the material on which this extraction is based either has been presented already in the discussion above or will emerge in the discussion of Whorf's evidence below.

First, Whorf argued, as we have seen, that a language can unite demonstrably different aspects of reality by giving them similar linguistic treatment. The principle for such a grouping of aspects of reality Whorf called *linguistic analogy*[23] to indicate its specifically linguistic nature (1956a, pp. 135, 137, 142, 147, 148; also pp. 70, 215), although he sometimes uses other terms (for example 1956a, pp. 36, 67–71). Every language must have some classifications (see discussion of Boas in chapter 1) and hence induce some linguistic analogies. The classifications, and the analogies implicit in them, (1) may be covert or overt or a mixture of the two, (2) are not "necessary" in that they vary from language to language and so cannot be simply "given" by experience prior to language, and (3) are potentially distinctive from other kinds of analyses of experience such as those of science or naive experience. The importance of such linguistic classifications is that *the meanings of elements that are grouped together influence each other*, that is, they are *analogically interpreted as "the same."* Further, in Whorf's grammatical examples, the direction of influence seems to exhibit internal pattern or regularity. Thus, forms with direct perceptible meanings influence the interpretation of forms with less direct, less perceptible meanings when such forms are grouped together in a linguistic classification. Likewise, complex forms in which *each part* has a directly perceptible meaning influence the interpretation of similar complex forms without such direct form–function matches as well as of simple forms with which they are linguistically grouped. All this yields a vision of language as a formal classificatory device that is both distinctively linguistic and internally interactive along lines of differential salience.

Second, Whorf argued that such linguistic analogies are used in thought as guides in the interpretation of and behavioral response to experienced reality. Whorf had no single term or expression for this process, referring variously to language "conditioning" or "shaping" thought (1956a, pp. 135–47), to thought "marching in step with purely grammatical facts" (1956a, p. 211), to language as a "program and guide for the individual's mental activity" (1956a, p. 212), to thought being "pointed by . . . grammars toward different types of observation" (1956a, p. 221), and to thinking following "a network of tracks laid down in the given language" (1956a, p. 256). In this discussion the phrase *cognitive appropriation* will be used to refer to the use in thought for its own ends of a structure of relations deriving from some other domain or, to be more precise, of a structure regimented according to some principles other than purely cognitive ones. One can imagine a number of kinds of structures that might be so appropriated: language is only one. Whorf's task was to provide evidence for *the cognitive appropriation of linguistic analogies*.

Whorf's view was, as we have noted, that the principal influence of language would be on habitual everyday concepts wherein speakers take (i.e., appropriate) language patterns as guides to the nature of reality. When using language patterns as a tool in this way, speakers involve the whole range of associations and connections implicit in the language's analogical groupings. However, speakers are unaware of this influence in two ways: in the first place they do not usually recognize that they are using language at all since the process of appropriation is largely unconscious (1956a, p. 137; also see pp. 209–14); and in the second place the very linguistic analogies themselves are usually out-of-awareness. Thus, speakers unwittingly accept much of the suggestive value of the linguistic analogies in their language even when, upon reflection, they might recognize that they are misleading. Use of language as a tool in this way involves, then, certain unintended costs. We may schematize Whorf's argument as in figure 1.

Unfortunately, Whorf did not go on to address directly the issues of when or why such appropriation of language structures occurs – for example, what the associated advantages are for individuals or social groups.[24] This is a significant omission in his discussion which relates to

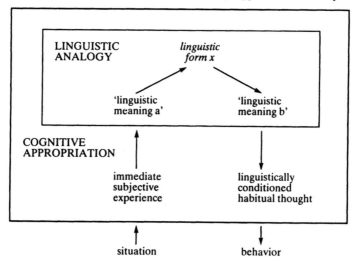

Figure 1 Diagram of Whorf's basic argument. Some aspect of a "situation" is immediately and subjectively "experienced" by a speaker of a particular language. This experience can be interpreted in terms of a 'linguistic meaning a' which corresponds to a *linguistic form x*. The *linguistic form x* also corresponds to other linguistic meanings such as 'linguistic meaning b.' By virtue of 'a' and 'b' being grouped together under *x*, they, and the experiences which they label or refer to, are seen to be analogically "the same" even though in some respects they are not in fact the same at all. This grouping of experiences via their linkage in a linguistic pattern is "linguistic analogy." If the speaker in interpreting or reflecting on his immediate subjective experience uses ("cognitively appropriates") the linguistic classification in the form of meaning 'a,' this linguistic analogy is called into play and he will respond to the experience associated with 'a' in terms of meanings properly associated only with 'b.' His subjective experience then becomes colored by his language yielding "linguistically conditioned habitual thought." If this thought is then used as a basis for some response, it should be detectable in the speaker's subsequent "behavior" – at least in certain situations.

questions that we will take up further below as to whether the process or existence of cognitive appropriation of linguistic analogies is itself shaped by the nature of the cognitive task or by the immediate or broader cultural contexts within which thought takes place. Whorf may have believed the process to be unaffected by such variables, as is suggested by some of his comments (e.g., 1956a, pp. 214, 257; also pp. 73, 85, 159, 207, 212, 235, 237). However, since he said almost nothing on this topic, it is likely that he simply did not recognize the problem of functional significance and contingency, and felt that the cognitive appropriation of linguistic analogies was a universal process.

Empirical evidence

Whorf attempted to provide evidence for his theory through a variety of examples. His basic method involved showing a parallelism between a linguistic pattern and some nonlinguistic behavior. First he established the characteristically *linguistic* nature of the language analogy. This he did by showing it either to be at odds with an analysis on some nonlinguistic grounds, usually by appeal to science or naive experience, or to be at odds with the analysis implicit in a second language, which showed that the pattern was variable by language. Second, he examined some nonlinguistic behavior to establish that the linguistic analogy had a parallel in nonlinguistic behavior and, when two languages were involved, that the parallels were distinctive. Whorf then inferred that the linguistic behavior was responsible for the nonlinguistic one. Thus, his method is essentially correlational[25] (in the broad sense of that term – Whorf, 1956a, p. 139, explicitly disavows that it is correlational in the strict sense, that is, of connecting individual features of language with individual features of culture), since without a specification of the conditions regulating the decision to appropriate linguistic analogies, true experimental manipulation is not possible. This need not be a fatal problem since correlational evidence can be relatively convincing when gathered properly, i.e., so that alternative accounts become increasingly unlikely. In Whorf's own programmatic work, however, the parallelisms or associations, although interpretively rich, were not particularly rigorous, a fact often stressed by Whorf's critics. Nonetheless, they provided an outline of a method that does in fact address the issues he was interested in. Attempts by others to infuse more rigor into such studies (see chapters 5 and 6 below) have tended to trade away both interpretive richness and relevance to the original hypothesis; for this reason Whorf's techniques warrant further study despite their deficiencies.

Lexical analogies

Whorf's first evidence of the importance of language for thought was drawn from his work as a fire inspector for an insurance company. He noticed that people act toward reality not merely in terms of the physical situation (as a fire inspector would see it) but in terms of the meaning of that situation to them:

in due course it became evident that not only a physical situation *qua* physics, but the meaning of that situation to people, was sometimes a factor, through the behavior of the people, in the start of the fire. And this factor of meaning was clearest when it was a LINGUISTIC MEANING, residing in the name or the linguistic description commonly applied to the situation.   (1956a, p. 135)

Whorf presented a variety of examples of this phenomenon. The first and most famous example involved careless behavior around what are called "empty gasoline drums," where the descriptive term *empty* tends to suggest lack of hazard.

> Yet the "empty" drums are perhaps the more dangerous [in comparison with the full drums], since they contain explosive vapor. Physically the situation is hazardous, but the linguistic analysis according to regular analogy must employ the word 'empty,' which inevitably suggests lack of hazard. The word 'empty' is used in two linguistic patterns: (1) as a virtual synonym for 'null and void, negative, inert,' (2) applied in analysis of physical situations without regard to, e.g., vapor, liquid vestiges, or stray rubbish, in the container. The situation is named in one pattern (2) and the name is then "acted out" or "lived up to" in another (1), this being a general formula for the linguistic conditioning of behavior into hazardous forms.   (1956a, p. 135)

Thus, the word *empty* has two senses, one a physically direct, more concrete sense in which a container no longer contains its intended contents, that is, has been emptied (questions of residues aside), and a more abstract, general sense meaning null and void, negative, or inert. Speakers apply the term *empty* in the first, more concrete, sense (i.e., the gasoline is all gone) and then subsequently interpret it in the second, more abstract, sense (i.e., the drums are inert, void of force, and therefore no longer dangerous). Believing the drums are not a hazard tends to lead to careless behavior such as smoking cigarettes near them. The grouping of two meanings under a single linguistic form (in this case a lexeme) creates a connecting bridge between the initial interpretation of the situation and other interpretations that are also associated with the linguistic form but that are not necessarily entailed in the situation. Whorf's argument can be diagramed as in figure 2, which is drawn so as to parallel the general pattern shown in figure 1.

Notice in this example that Whorf had presented evidence of the force of linguistic analogy without reference to comparative data from other languages. Rather, a "scientific" language, the account of physical science, is used to show the non-necessary and misleading nature of the linguistic analogy and hence, by implication, its specifically linguistic character. In each example the observable nonlinguistic "effect" is individual behavior – the ignition of a fire along with the inferred set of mental attitudes and ideas that lie behind the act leading to the fire.

Although to some this linkage may not appear distinctively linguistic, other examples in this series seem much more peculiarly linguistic, such as his discussions of materials called by the terms *limestone, waste water,* and *scrap lead,* which turn out to be combustible in certain situations despite their misleading names. Each example from his fire inspector experiences has small flaws, but the series as a whole is suggestive of one

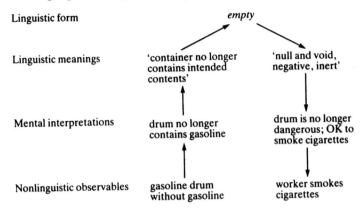

Figure 2 Diagram of one of Whorf's fire-causing examples

source of data on his hypothesis, namely the everyday ordinary confusions resulting from overreliance on a linguistic label in responding to
experience.[26] Whorf's presentation of these dramatic if somewhat
uncontrolled examples is characteristic in that he is primarily concerned
with establishing the significance of language influences.

Grammatical analogies

Whorf moved from these preliminary lexical examples to a series of five
interrelated grammatical examples which contrast English[27] and Hopi.
His first example concerns the grammatical category of number, in particular singular versus plural. He described the English pattern as follows:

In our language ... plurality and cardinal numbers are applied in two ways: to
real plurals and imaginary plurals. Or more exactly if less tersely: perceptible
spatial aggregates and metaphorical aggregates. We say 'ten men' and also 'ten
days.' Ten men either are or could be objectively perceived as ten, ten in one
group perception – ten men on a street corner, for instance. But 'ten days' cannot
be objectively experienced. We experience only one day, today; the other nine
(or even all ten) are something conjured up from memory or imagination. If 'ten
days' be regarded as a group it must be as an "imaginary," mentally constructed
group. Whence comes this mental pattern? Just as in the case of the fire-causing
errors, from the fact that our language confuses the two different situations, has
but one pattern for both. When we speak of 'ten steps forward, ten strokes on a
bell,' or any similarly described cyclic sequence, "times" of any sort, we are
doing the same thing as with 'days.' CYCLICITY brings the response of imaginary
plurals. But a likeness of cyclicity to aggregates is not unmistakably given by
experience prior to language, or it would be found in all languages, and it is not.

(1956a, p. 139)[28]

Thus, the plural category[29] applies to both perceptible spatial aggregates, as in the case of *men*, and mentally constructed, or imaginary, aggregates of cycles, as in the case of *days*. The latter can never be perceptually united into an objective spatial group. The pattern with English cardinal numbers reinforces this pattern by quantifying the amount of "time" as if it were in fact a collection of discrete entities rather than an imaginary aggregate formed out of cyclic-interval measures:[30]

> Habitual thought then assumes that in the latter the numbers are just as much counted on "something" as in the former. This is objectification. Concepts of time ... are objectified as counted QUANTITIES, especially lengths, made up of units as a length can be visibly marked off into inches.   (1956a, p. 140)

Thus "objectification" – the treatment of an imaginary entity such as "time" as if it were a perceptible object – arises in English because the patterns of grammatical number categorize two distinct kinds of experience, namely the imaginary and the objective, together as alike for the purposes of speech (i.e., by the formal machinery of English).[31] We can diagram Whorf's argument (using only the plural portion of it for the sake of clarity) as in the left two columns of figure 3. (The items mentioned under the category "Nonlinguistic observables" in this figure are explained further below in the discussion.)

Whorf showed the "non-necessary" nature of this linguistic analogy by comparing the English pattern with that of Hopi:

> In Hopi there is a different linguistic situation. Plurals and cardinals are used only for entities that form or can form an objective group. There are no imaginary plurals, but instead ordinals used with singulars.   (1956a, p. 140)

> Time is mainly reckoned "by day" ... or "by night" ... which words are not nouns but tensors,[32] ... The count is by ORDINALS. This is not the pattern of counting a number of different men or things, even though they appear successively, for, even then, they COULD gather into an assemblage. It is the pattern of counting successive reappearances of the SAME man or thing, incapable of forming an assemblage. The analogy is not to behave about day-cyclicity as to several men ("several days"), which is what WE tend to do, but to behave as to the successive visits of the SAME MAN.   (1956a, p. 148)

Thus, the grammatical pattern by which Hopi handles the phenomenon of duration is substantially different from English. The pattern "ordinal number + singular" is applied both to tensors and to nouns that refer to cases of repeated appearance, creating a grammatical bridge between the two. We can diagram the Hopi pattern as in the right two columns of figure 3. In this case, Whorf has used a comparison with a second "natural" language to show the non-necessary character of the English linguistic analogy, rather than a comparison with a "scientific" language as in the fire-causing examples. A common experience, repre-

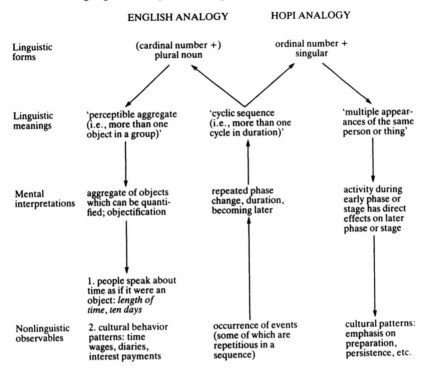

Figure 3 Diagram of one of Whorf's contrastive grammatical examples showing different English and Hopi formal analogies to similar meanings

sented by the central column in figure 3, is joined with (assimilated into) different grammatical patterns in English and Hopi and is, therefore, subject to different patterns of analogical influence in the two cultures.

Comparing this diagram with the earlier one from Whorf's fire-causing series, we find a number of changes. The linguistic analogies (the bridges between columns) are regular grammatical patterns rather than individual lexical items. Being grammatical, they cannot be dismissed as possible irregularities with localized significance, but must be recognized as integral parts of the language system. The wider range of application of the patterns is likely to lead to a greater significance in thought; the more background nature of grammatical patterning is likely to make it much more difficult for speakers to recognize or suspend belief in the ontological validity of the patterns (Whorf, 1956a, pp. 137–38). A further change in this second example is that the nonlinguistic observables giving rise to the initial mental interpretations are not clearly spelled out. Whorf did not describe the external stimuli to which people are responding, nor does he ascertain whether they are the same for both

Hopi and English speakers. He referred to the subjective experiences of becoming later and later, of duration, etc., but not to something external, and hence observable, which is the basis for this experience. This may be intrinsically more difficult for concepts such as time, but it deserves more direct attention: from what does the speaker derive the experience of duration or "becoming later" of which Whorf spoke? The problem is not inherently insoluble, and some of the kinds of external prompt which might enter the middle column have been indicated in the diagram: the recognition of similarity, of cyclic recurrence of some external events (e.g., rise and set of the sun). (Noncyclic events could then be calibrated against cyclic ones to yield the experience of duration of any event. The limits of such a calibration – in the sense of fineness – will depend on the available cross-linguistic possibilities.)

Likewise, although Whorf asserted an influence on habitual thought, he did not describe individual nonverbal behaviors to support his claims. He did cite other patterns in the language which suggest that the modes of thinking that he described are in fact present: for example, we would not say *a length of time* if we did not have an "objectified" notion of time. However, it can be argued that these language patterns should be regarded as simply other parts of the overall "fashion of speaking" of the language which as a whole influences thought and that they do not provide independent evidence of the habitual thought pattern. Whorf's positivist critics have been particularly concerned with this point, arguing that reliance on more language data to confirm the existence of habitual thought patterns makes his whole argument circular.

There is some merit to these criticisms, although the evidence is not so weak and unpromising as it might appear. Although operationally nonlinguistic evidence of habitual thought might be more elegant and convincing, overtly verbal evidence should not be regarded as unusable – indeed there may be some concepts for which verbal evidence is the only possible evidence. For such evidence to be usable, it must be a *plausible* but not a *necessary* semantic or structural derivative of the original linguistic structure. Whorf's example concerning the countability of *days* with cardinal numbers would not be acceptable independent evidence for the objectification in habitual thought of time, because we can fairly regard plurality and enumeration as *necessarily* linked in an overall system of grammatical number. Whorf's subsequent argument that our tense system grows out of the objectification of time (along with its spatialization) might be regarded as a non-necessary linkage and hence acceptable in this respect, although many would question its *plausibility*. Whorf's verbal evidence, then, is lacking, in these respects, but not all verbal evidence need be flawed in these ways. (See also the discussion of this issue by Carroll, 1956, pp. 29–30.)

Further, these criticisms of Whorf's data fail to take into account other evidence that he did provide within the overall structure of his argument. First of all, note that he has already established the plausibility of real effects on individuals in his fire-causing examples. Thus, the later assumption of such effects is not gratuitous. When he shifts to more complex patterns, it is not at all obvious what specific individual behavior would give evidence of a general view of 'time' – although the possibility of individual behavioral evidence should not be ruled out. Second, he presented a series of five interrelated grammatical examples to show the way the patterns work together to provide a systematic, coherent, yet non-necessary construal of nature (i.e., a fashion of speaking). References along the way to habitual thought are designed more to help the reader understand clearly the nature of the implications of the linguistic categories for habitual thought than to prove the existence of such thought. At the end of the series of examples, he drew together the overall implications (1956a, pp. 147–48) to make a unified statement about the probable habitual thought worlds of English (or European) and Hopi speakers as suggested by their language patterns. Concrete observable evidence for the reality and significance of the features of this habitual thought world is presented in the following two sections (1956a, pp. 148–52, 152–56), wherein he tried to show tangible cultural connections (or affinities) with the hypothesized patterns of thinking. These patterns of behavior in the culture both show the influence of habitual thought and also help confirm the underlying transfer of the linguistic pattern to thought more generally – something which is plausible given the fire-causing examples even though Whorf did not present data from individuals in this case. In short, Whorf made another shift in going from his fire-causing to his objectification examples: he substituted overall group belief, behavior, and institutions for direct evidence of individually held concepts. One pattern of this cultural evidence will be described more fully further below after we examine one final, crucial aspect of Whorf's treatment of linguistic analogies.

Analogical structures

In the examples thus far discussed, we have been focusing on the role of a single linguistic analogy in bridging between or uniting distinct kinds of experience. In looking for nonlinguistic correlates, Whorf drew connections between cultural patterns and whole sets or structures of linguistic analogies. So, before turning to the nonlinguistic evidence Whorf provided, it will be worthwhile to examine how related analogies can fit together to form an *analogical structure* linking together diverse elements of experience. The example used here illustrates, as well, how covert categories can play a role in linguistic analogy and happens, also, to concern a substantive domain that will be important in subsequent chapters and in the empirical case study reported in the companion work.

Whorf continued his discussion by examining the distinction between "individual" and "mass" nouns in English, a distinction more commonly referred to by others as the "count–mass distinction." He described the English pattern as follows:

We have two kinds of nouns denoting physical things: individual nouns, and mass nouns, e.g., 'water, milk, wood, granite, sand, flour, meat.' Individual nouns denote bodies with definite outlines: 'a tree, a stick, a man, a hill.' Mass nouns denote homogeneous continua without implied boundaries.   (1956a, p. 140)

The two kinds of nouns admit of different grammatical possibilities:[33] mass nouns do not take plurals or the singular indefinite article, whereas individual nouns do (1956a, p. 140). In other circumstances (e.g., with definite articles) there is no overt indication of the presence of one type of noun as opposed to the other. We are thus justified in viewing the distinction as reflecting a covert category (one with rather commonly occurring reactances), although Whorf did not himself label the category one way or the other.

Whorf noted that the distinction between individual and mass is more widely and uniformly drawn in English grammar than in the actual physical objects referred to:

Rather few natural occurrences present themselves as unbounded extents; 'air' of course, and often 'water, rain, snow, sand, rock, dirt, grass.' We do not encounter 'butter, meat, cloth, iron, glass,' or most "materials" in such kind of manifestation, but in bodies small or large with definite outlines.

(1956a, p. 141)

Thus, there are many circumstances in which the speaker is forced to make a grammatical distinction that would have little immediate correspondence to external reality or that would be in contradiction with that reality. The language compensates for this deficiency:

[The distinction] is so inconvenient in a great many cases that we need some way of individualizing the mass noun by further linguistic devices. This is partly done by names of body types: 'stick of wood, piece of cloth, pane of glass, cake of soap'; also, and even more, by introducing names of containers though their contents be the real issue: 'glass of water, cup of coffee, dish of food, bag of flour, bottle of beer.'   (1956a, p. 141).

Thus, Whorf argued, the [covert] individual–mass distinction has given rise to, or necessitated, a secondary [overt] pattern in the language. (The overt pattern of "individualizing" is, incidentally, one "reactance" of the covert pattern of distinguishing individual and mass nouns.)

Notice that two distinct kinds of experience – containers and body types – are brought together under a single grammatical pattern. As before, Whorf argued that this has consequences:

> The formulas are very similar: individual noun plus a similar relator (English 'of'). In the obvious case this relator denotes contents. In the inobvious one it "suggests" contents. Hence the 'lumps, chunks, blocks, pieces,' etc., seem to contain something, a "stuff," "substance," or "matter" that answers to the 'water,' 'coffee,' or 'flour' in the container formulas.   (1956a, p. 141)

So the pattern "individual noun + *of* + mass noun" covers two meanings, one with a readily interpretable perceptible correlate, i.e., a container and its contents, and another without such a correlate but which is interpreted in the same way. This parallels relatively closely the argument with perceptible and imaginary aggregates discussed above wherein the more concrete meaning influences the interpretation of the more abstract one. Thus "bodies" are thought of as being like containers that hold "contents" – substance or matter. Whorf concluded:

> So ... the philosophical "substance" and "matter" are also the naive idea; they are instantly acceptable, "common sense." It is so through linguistic habit. Our language patterns often require us to name a physical thing by a binomial that splits the reference into a formless item plus a form.   (1956a, p. 141)

We have then, in this view, an everyday basis for these philosophical notions that are so common in Western culture.

Whorf continued with an argument that this binomial pattern is extended to cover other nouns:

> the pattern of individual and mass nouns, with the resulting binomial formula of formless item plus form, is so general that it is implicit for all nouns, and hence our very generalized formless items like 'substance, matter,' by which we can fill out the binomial for an enormously wide range of nouns.   (1956a, p. 142)

Whorf was not explicit here about the nature of the grammatical bridge, but it appears to be simply categorization as a noun or a noun phrase.[34] He probably meant to restrict this argument to nouns referring to physical objects, since his next remarks indicate still another extension to nouns with more elusive referents:

> But even these [very generalized formless items like 'substance, matter'] are not quite generalized enough to take in our phase nouns. So for the phase nouns we have made a formless item, 'time' ... Thus with our binomial formula we can say and think 'a moment of time, a second of time, a year of time.'
> (1956a, pp. 141–42)

Here the container-like portion is a phase interval and the content-like portion is "time." Thus, one part of our objectification of temporal notions involves its inclusion in the general binomial pattern for physical object nouns.

Step by step Whorf has built up an analysis of a series of three interrelated analogies: body-type relator noun phrases are analogous to container-type relator noun phrases; syntactically simple physical object noun phrases, in turn, are analogous to these more syntactically complex physical object noun phrases (= relator noun phrases – especially the body-type formulas); and phase noun phrases, finally, are analogous to physical object noun phrases. This nesting of interpretive analogies is clearer if we read Whorf's sequence in reverse: phase noun phrases are interpreted like physical object noun phrases, syntactically simple physical object noun phrases are interpreted, in turn, like syntactically complex physical object noun phrases, and syntactically complex physical object noun phrases, finally, are interpreted like container-type relator noun phrases. Thus, phase nouns participate indirectly in the interpretive schema "container + contents." We can diagram the interrelations among these analogies as in figure 4. Notice how the English material from figure 3 is now embedded as one component of the larger analogical structure: Form bridge 1 and Linguistic meanings 1. That is, the Form bridge of 'cardinal number plus plural marking' is now covered by the term 'individual NP (plural),' indicating the kind of noun phrase which can take such a formal pattern. The Linguistic meanings grouped together by this formal equivalence are expressed as 'cycle (sequence)' and 'perceptible physical objects (aggregate).' By showing how the treatment of "time" in English as a homogeneously segmentable and measurable continuum is grounded in a very complex series of equivalence relations of grammatical forms, Whorf illustrated graphically the more general point that linguistic structures can link apparently diverse elements of experience together in a coherent and semantically potent way.

This example is extremely suggestive in a number of ways. First, it shows how, by serial or hierarchical grouping, a single linguistic analogy can spread its interpretive effect quite widely. Each element brought into an analogical structure thereby acquires many of the connotational values latent in the other parts of the structure. Thus, for example, when phase nouns expressing temporal duration are linked in to physical object nouns, they are not only "objectified," but they are also seen as being composed of a form plus a formless item – which view of physical objects is itself derivative of two other analogical groupings. It is this drawing together of ultimately diverse elements of experience into a single "large-scale linguistic pattern" which led Whorf to talk about a "fashion of speaking" typical of a language. Reference to the Hopi comparison shows not only different individual units in some cases but a

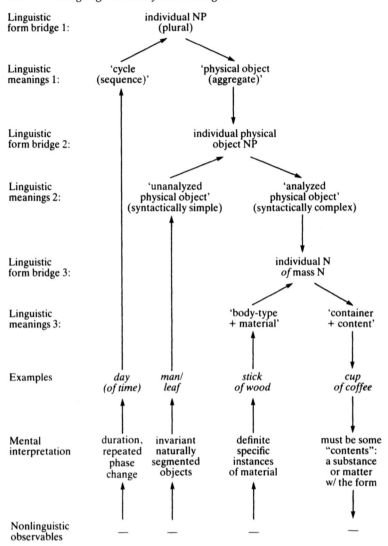

Figure 4 Diagram of Whorf's analysis of the structure of some analogical relationships among noun phrases in English

completely different pattern of overall organization which yields a distinctively Hopi system of analogical connotation or interpretation.[35]

Second, a related factor of interest is the possibility that the direction of influence is systematic. If it could be shown more generally that the concrete member of a pair influenced the interpretation of the abstract member across a wide number of grammatical[36] examples, it would allow the introduction of an a priori prediction to the investigation of linguistic analogies. Another principle of analogical effect suggested by this example is that a complex member with each part having a concrete meaning will influence the interpretation of a simple member that also has a comparable concrete meaning.

Third, some of the categories of concern to Whorf in this example are covert (see the discussion of covert categories above) – for example, the difference between mass and individual nouns in English.[37] This suggests the importance of examining these types of categories in any analysis of linguistic analogy. Although in this example, as Whorf developed it, the covert distinction serves the rather minor role of prompting the formation of an overt category whose analogical grouping is the main focus of concern, there is no reason why covert categories should not have direct effect, as Whorf himself noted on occasion (1956a, p. 69). In fact, the example could be reanalyzed focusing on the analogical grouping of "genuine contents" and "imaginary contents" into mass-type nouns, which would place the covert categorization in a more central place in the argument.[38]

Finally, the suggestion here that some portions of the grammar are compensating for unfortunate side effects of other categories in the grammar is important. On the one hand, it guarantees the Boasian premise that anything that can be said in one language can be said in any other (e.g., "mass" nouns can be used in constructions so as to determine an "individuable" extension), but, on the other hand, the need to employ additional grammatical apparatus to get the job done also guarantees the Whorfian argument that the "sense" will not be the same (i.e., the need to individualize some nouns and not others itself signals something about their meaningfulness). Whorf's argument here (as elsewhere) could have profited from an illustration that the Hopi pattern (without a count–mass distinction) set up its own referential problems for the grammar to solve. Since any grammatical category is a compromise with reality, it must generate problematic consequences and only partially appropriate solutions which in turn have their own consequences.

Behavioral effects of analogical structures

It is large-scale linguistic patterns that Whorf sought to link to cultural patterns and not, as many have assumed, each specific grammatical analogy. (And, in rejecting such local-level correspondences, Whorf remained within the main thrust of the Boas–Sapir position described in chapter 1.) At this point we have enough of his argument before us to be able to illustrate briefly the kind of cultural evidence that he developed.

We will continue with the specific example involving the "objectification" of time by English (or European) speakers. "Objectification" in the sense of treating phase nouns like nouns referring to physical objects with all that entails (e.g., the conceptualization of time as a homogeneous or formless "substance") now joins with other patterns (not described here) to yield a characteristic view of time as composed of a *linear array of formally equivalent discrete units* (i.e., like a row of identical objects). From such a view, Whorf believed, arose many of our cultural patterns involving time. The *discreteness* of temporal *units* leads to a propensity for historicity (i.e., taking a decentered or nonindexical view of events as discrete happenings rather than as artificially segmented from other events including the events of remembering, recording, or anticipating) and to a view that periods of time are somewhat like a series of equal containers to be filled as in keeping records as a function of fixed units of time. The *formally equivalent* nature of these discrete units is based on their representing equal portions of a homogeneous substance. It leads to a view that the units are in fact of equal value and hence the notion of the equivalent monetary value of time units as with rent, interest, depreciation, insurance, and time wages. Also related to this view of time are the attempts to measure time more precisely and to do things more quickly. Finally, the *linearity* of time allows us to project into the future by imagining an unending sequence of such formally equivalent discrete units; hence our attention to the budgeting, programming, and scheduling of time and our view of time as monotonous with the attendant attitudes of complacency about future events (the future will be like the past). Most of these are observable cultural practices, and in his discussion Whorf describes observable correlates of the few that are mentioned here as attitudes.

Hopi cultural patterns, by contrast, are quite different, and in ways that appear to relate to their linguistic treatment of time. Recall that in Hopi, cycles are treated like repeated visits of the "same man," hence

it is as if the return of the day were felt as the return of the same person, a little older but with all the impresses of yesterday, not "another day," i.e. like an entirely different person.   (1956a, p. 151)

With past events essentially "present" in the present, there is less incentive to be concerned with detailed recording of past events; this is supported by a more general tendency not to regard events as discrete and well bounded (1956a, p. 153). As a consequence, in Whorf's view, the Hopi fail to exhibit our tendency toward historicity. Conversely, one can act in the present to influence the future:

One does not alter several men by working upon just one, but one can prepare and so alter the later visits of the same man by working to affect the visit he is making now. This is the way the Hopi deal with the future – by working within a present situation which is expected to carry impresses, both obvious and occult, forward into the future event of interest.   (1956a, p. 148)

Whorf provided descriptions of a large number of observable correlates of this view in the form of various culturally distinctive activities of preparing: "announcing," inward and outward preparations for future events, and an emphasis in many activities on the cumulative value of persistent, incremental accumulations of effort and energy toward a goal. Note that these are not like our activities of budgeting and scheduling, but are activities in the immediate present with presumed future effect. Whorf described other practices which reflect a different view of time; and his original discussion of Hopi customs should be consulted (1956a, pp. 148–52), as it is difficult to characterize them in a few lines here. The important thing for the present discussion is that he dealt with specific cultural practices that can be observed, that appear to flow naturally from the hypothesized underlying view of time, and that are distinctive from Western European practices.

Thus, there is no shortage of nonlinguistic evidence when we take Whorf's argument as a whole, and it is incorrect to label his argument circular. By connecting the language patterns to broad cultural patterns, Whorf undoubtedly intended to demonstrate more clearly the significance he felt language had. However, the chain of reasoning from language pattern to cultural pattern is long and complex – long and complex enough to have escaped many readers entirely (hence the frequent claim that there is no nonlinguistic evidence) and to have left unconvinced some of those who in fact understood the argument. Thus, although the logic of his argument is sound, a certain degree of plausibility has been sacrificed in seeking to demonstrate significance. Whorf's case would be greatly strengthened in the eyes of many by either the demonstration of more immediate, if less dramatic, language and thought connections at the level of individual behavior or the presentation of evidence from more languages and cultures showing the same associations among these particular grammatical and cultural patterns. And where he does present evidence of effects on individual behavior, the call could be for more rigor so as to establish the distinctive role of language. Although important, all these objections to Whorf's evidence are not ultimately crippling to his thesis since, in principle, better evidence can in fact be gathered. Given the programmatic nature of Whorf's work, such problems seem inevitable.

Overview of Whorf's empirical evidence

In short, then, Whorf's evidence for his theses consisted of a series of programmatic examples that show how linguistic analogies influence thought. Some of his examples are drawn from his experience as a fire inspector and show how individual speakers are led into fire-causing errors by drawing plausible (in the sense of grammatically founded) yet situationally inappropriate inferences from lexemes that have multiple meanings. Other examples are drawn from his comparative linguistic studies of Hopi and English. Finally, some of his examples suggest that linguistic analogies fit together into more complicated structures that ultimately unite large areas of experience both formally and, hence, interpretively. He showed how speakers are led to hold certain general concepts characteristic of their cultures as they follow out the implications of their grammatical patterns. In these latter examples, the nonlinguistic evidence is somewhat indirect and in need of finer control. Although these examples do not "prove" Whorf's theory, they do show some of the kinds of evidence that would be relevant to showing both that linguistic analogies are appropriated by (or in) cognition and what sorts of effects the appropriations generate.

Ultimately, Whorf succeeded in pointing the way toward the *empirical* study of the relationship between the large-scale linguistic patterns characteristic of various languages and the habitual thought worlds of speakers of those languages. It is ironic, given the general perception of Whorf's work, that one of his most important contributions may have been to bring actual empirical evidence to bear on the very old, Romantic notion of linguistic relativity. He shifted the concern from the isolated comparison of the category content of individual sentences to the meaningful significance of the interrelation of sets of grammatical categories with "habitual" or characteristic cultural patterns.

Summary

Whorf went well beyond Boas and Sapir by exploring the language and thought problem in considerable detail. He focused on the relationship between large-scale linguistic patterns in particular languages and the habitual concepts used by speakers of those languages in interpreting reality. Implicitly, Whorf developed a model of the mechanism by which language and thought interact. Linguistic analogies associated with the linguistic classification of experience both embody conventional compromises necessary for speech and provide a locus for diverse meanings to interpenetrate and influence each other. These analogies are appropriated as guides in habitual cognitive activity such as the interpretation of external reality and result in the speaker having a linguistically conditioned habitual thought world that appears to be, but in fact is not, necessary. Whorf did not explain when or why such linguistic analogies are used in thought. Finally, he pointed the way toward the empirical study of these issues by presenting an array of programmatic examples. He shows, for example, how lexically based patterns influence individual behavior, how grammatically based patterns influence cultural belief and behavioral norms, and how such grammatically based patterns can join together into large-scale linguistic patterns with apparent internal regularity of analogical influence. In general, Whorf favored illustrations that were clear and suggestive of broad significance over those that might achieve greater control. Despite the fact that Whorf did not develop a full formal theory and systematic empirical evidence, his work represents the first significant moves in these directions.

Linguistic meaning, individual thought, and cultural pattern

Whorf broached again the possibility, rejected on empirical grounds by both Boas and Sapir, that language patterns influence cultural patterns.[39] He asked in the second part of his original question:

Are there traceable affinities between (a) cultural and behavioral norms and (b) large-scale linguistic patterns?   (1956a, p. 138)

Sensitive to the previous rejection of such connections, he appended the following parenthetical remark to his question:

I should be the last to pretend that there is anything so definite as "a correlation" between culture and language, and especially between ethnological rubrics such as 'agricultural, hunting,' etc., and linguistic ones like 'inflected,' 'synthetic,' or 'isolating.'   (1956a, pp. 138–39)

Thus, in line with Boas and Sapir (see especially Boas, 1966a [1911] and Sapir, 1949f [1912]), Whorf both rejected the notion of a highly predictive relationship between individual features of languages and cultures (as might be reflected in a "correlation"), and also rejected in particular those traditional attempts, associated with evolutionary views of culture, to relate a single very broad, general feature of the language with an equally broad, general characterization of the culture. In their place he substituted a theory of a looser, more indirect connection wherein language influences culture in some cases via its effect on the habitual thought world of speakers. Specific configurations in the grammar influence thought, which then in turn influences the development over time of particular cultural institutions.

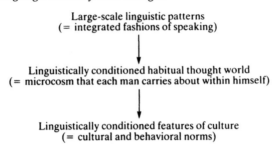

Figure 5 Structure of Whorf's argument linking language, the individual, and culture

Whorf sequenced his question and also his discussion so that he addressed first the problem of the importance of language for individual concepts. This was important for his argument since he then used the notion of an individual habitual thought world (the linguistically conditioned "microcosm that each man carries about within himself" [1956a, p. 147]) as a mediating variable or level between language and the rest of culture. Thus, at the end of his series of grammatical examples, he pulled together the various linguistic analogies that he had described to characterize habitual thought patterns for English and Hopi speakers. He argued, as we have seen, that the use in thought of various linguistic analogies (or sets of such analogies) inclines speakers to the formation of some very generalized concepts such as the "objectified" time and the "form plus formless item" dichotomy characteristic of English speakers. It is these characteristic concepts which are relevant to cultural behavior patterns:

Our behavior, and that of the Hopi, can be seen to be coordinated in many ways to the linguistically conditioned microcosm.   (1956a, p. 148)

Thus, it is this microcosm which is coordinated with behavior, and not the linguistic forms as such. We can diagram Whorf's argument as in figure 5. Only after establishing this linkage does Whorf continue with a discussion of the various cultural behavior patterns that he feels derive in part from these habitual thought world patterns. Some examples of the cultural features that he developed were presented in the discussion of Hopi and English views of time.

By the introduction of this intermediate level, Whorf was able to introduce *meaning* into the language and culture issue. It is not the existence of a particular form as such in language which gives rise to a particular pattern, or form, in culture. Rather, the use of language forms inevitably involves analogical groupings that entail *meanings for speakers*; these meanings lead to behavior patterns consistent with them.

Aspects of linguistic form that have little or no apparent connection with meaning (e.g., phonological structure, degree of inflection, etc.) would be poor candidates for generating cultural effects in Whorf's framework, until and unless some meaning value could be established for them. Likewise, aspects of culture that are very general in nature (e.g., "agricultural") are poor candidates as effects because of their potential for combining with so many meaning values; rather, more idiosyncratic cultural institutions with correspondingly more specifiable, restricted meanings fit better with Whorf's approach. In moving in this direction, Whorf implicitly discredited the notion of using a formal feature of language as an index of degree of cultural advancement and maintained his Boasian credential as an opponent of simple-minded attempts to correlate linguistic and cultural types.

Whorf was careful throughout to use words like "affinity" and "coordinate" to characterize the nature of the connection between language and the rest of culture. This is because he did not want to assert a necessary causal relation. In part this was because the connection was indirect, i.e., through the concepts held by the individual. A second factor, however, was the possibility that the language itself is responding to cultural pressures and that, therefore, any observed association might have the nonlinguistic culture as its origin. Whorf acknowledged that language and culture undoubtedly influence each other, but then continued with an argument that when a language and culture are in long historical contact, it is probable that the language plays the larger role:

How does such a network of language, culture, and behavior come about historically? Which was first: the language patterns or the cultural norms? In main they have grown up together, constantly influencing each other. But in this partnership the nature of the language is the factor that limits free plasticity and rigidifies channels of development in the more autocratic way. This is so because a language is a system, not just an assemblage of norms. Large systemic outlines can change to something really new only very slowly, while many other cultural innovations are made with comparative quickness. Language thus represents the mass mind: it is affected by inventions and innovations, but affected little and slowly, whereas TO inventors and innovators it legislates with the decree immediate.   (1956a, p. 156)

The implicit view of the nonlinguistic aspects of culture presented here, namely that they are a mere "assemblage of norms," was already under strong attack within anthropology by the 1930s even as Whorf wrote. Clearly there are aspects of both language and culture that change quickly or slowly depending in part on how integral they are to pervasive systemic patterns. Nonetheless, many would still accept the view of the language as a relatively conservative element in culture on account of the degree of its interlocking systematicity and its formal completeness (in

Sapir's sense), and Whorf's argument, likewise, may still be taken seriously. In short, although Whorf did not rule out the possible influence of culture on language, he ascribed less significance to it. It is important also that his argument was restricted to languages and cultures in reasonably long historical association; he was not considering conditions of relatively abrupt historical change which might break the pattern of connections. His argument was a conditional one. Notice, finally, that Whorf returned once more to the individual inventor or innovator even in this historical argument; this reinforces the point that it is through individuals – or, more precisely, their habitual thought worlds – that language exerts pressure on the culture as a whole.[40]

Whorf's final summary of his findings concerning the relation between language and culture brought these various points together with a special emphasis on the need for a broader focus on general patterns and their significance to people in the search for a traceable impact of language on culture:

As for our second question (p. 138): There are connections but not correlations or diagnostic correspondences between cultural norms and linguistic patterns. Although it would be impossible to infer the existence of Crier Chiefs [a Hopi institution involving announcing, or preparative publicity, which he has discussed] from the lack of tenses in Hopi, or vice versa, there is a relation between a language and the rest of the culture of the society which uses it. There are cases where the "fashions of speaking" are closely integrated with the whole general culture, whether or not this be universally true, and there are connections within this integration, between the kind of linguistic analyses employed and various behavioral reactions and also the shapes taken by various cultural developments. Thus the importance of Crier Chiefs does have a connection, not with tenselessness itself, but with a system of thought in which categories different from our tenses are natural. These connections are to be found not so much by focusing attention on the typical rubrics of linguistic, ethnographic, or sociological description as by examining the culture and the language (always and only when the two have been together historically for a considerable time) as a whole in which concatenations that run across these departmental lines may be expected to exist, and, if they do exist, eventually to be discoverable by study.

(1956a, p. 159)

Thus, Whorf believed that there are cases in which there is a relation between language and culture which is discoverable through empirical study. But he advocated an approach involving close, detailed interpretation of the right kind of case (e.g., where there is long historical association) with an interdisciplinary perspective, rather than the more traditional superficial correlation of features framed within a single disciplinary perspective. He believed that the result of such studies would show language to be the more significant factor in what is essentially an interactive situation.

General summary

Whorf advanced the arguments developed by Boas and Sapir regarding the linguistic analysis of experience. He showed that the classifications of experience implicit in each language were not limited to obvious and frequent overt categories but also involved a variety of covert categories marked only occasionally by patterns of morphosyntactic "reactance." In this way he was able to give explicit content to and to make investigable some of the more elusive features of formal coordination among grammatical categories first described by Sapir. He showed how such language categories analogically group diverse experiences, how these analogies interlock into complex structures to form a coherent interpretation of experience, and how these interpretations vary across languages. In all this he moved well beyond the comparison of isolated sentences from various languages to a consideration of the characteristic meaning structure of the grammar as a whole. He also grappled with the problems of why speakers were unaware of these language patterns and of how to compare these diverse linguistic systems in an unbiased way.

In his consideration of the influence of languages on thought, Whorf developed, albeit implicitly, a model emphasizing the unwitting appropriation of linguistic analogies – both lexical and grammatical – in habitual everyday thought. Here again, he made more explicit and investigable ideas first suggested in a much more general way by Sapir; Whorf pinpointed precise ways in which linguistic categories could introduce language-specific aspects of meaning into the interpretation of experience and showed how these patterns could be traced in the grammar. He was also the first to seek clear-cut and distinct empirical evidence for the influence of language. The most important of his arguments involved constructing an interpretation of distinctive analogical structures in two languages – Hopi and English – and postulating on the basis of this analysis a characteristic cognitive orientation which should characterize speakers of those languages. He then provided evidence for the presence of such cognitive orientations by describing specific, observable patterns of behavior in the two associated cultures. The crucial element of his argument is the emphasis on the importance of the transfer of elements of meaning within linguistic analogies for the individual interpretation of experience which, in turn, shapes specific cultural patterns of behavior. Whorf clearly rejected simple-minded correlations of the formal features of language with general cultural characteristics. He also emphasized that linguistic influences of the type he analyzed would only be operative in a context of long historical interaction between a language and other aspects of a culture. In short, Whorf not only transformed Sapir's preliminary statements about linguistic relativity into a specific and empirically investigable claim, but also provided the first evidence of the existence of the hypothesized effects.

3. Approaches in anthropological linguistics: typical ethnographic case studies

Introduction

The death of Sapir in 1939 and of Whorf in 1941 in combination with the Second World War created a brief hiatus in research. Interest was revived during the post-war period sparked in part by the appearance in 1949 of a collection of Sapir's writings (Mandelbaum, 1949) and the reprinting of four of Whorf's papers on the relation of language to thought (Trager, 1950 [1949]). Throughout the 1950s and into the early 1960s the Sapir–Whorf hypothesis was a subject of active concern for a broad range of scholars and played a crucial role in the growing recognition during this period of the importance of language in human psychological and social functioning. Despite this widespread interest, a comparatively small amount of actual empirical research was undertaken. After this period, interest in the hypothesis waned with the advent of the transformational approach in linguistics with its presumptive nativism and universalism. Only within the last decade has interest in the hypothesis revived, so it is to this earlier period that we must look for much of what little empirical work exists.

Most research on the Sapir–Whorf hypothesis during this period was developed within the fields of anthropological linguistics and comparative psycholinguistics. Most of these studies take Whorf's formulations as their point of departure whether they are building on his work or being critical of it. This chapter and the next review relevant empirical studies developed within anthropological linguistics; studies within comparative psycholinguistics are taken up in two subsequent chapters. This review emphasizes typical empirical approaches or thinking that has made an important theoretical or methodological contribution to a line of empirical work. In keeping with this focus, discussions, reviews, or reformulations not associated with empirical efforts will not be considered.

Although the studies conducted by anthropological linguistics on the linguistic relativity hypothesis cohere by virtue of their shared perspective and methods, they bear little relation to one another at the substantive or topical level and therefore do not form a cumulative tradition which can be readily characterized. In this chapter, therefore, the work of three figures – Dorothy D. Lee, Madeleine Mathiot, and Harry Hoijer – will be examined in detail and will serve to exemplify the guiding assumptions, practices, and critical problems characteristic of the discipline's earlier approach to the issues. In the next chapter, several of the more important later innovations within anthropological linguistics will be discussed.

For the most part, anthropological linguists undertook linguistically oriented ethnographic case studies to address the ideas of Sapir and Whorf. These studies were typically concerned with the relation of a single language to an associated culture or cultural mode of thought. In principle, these studies involved a detailed examination of some aspect(s) of an exotic language and a relatively direct analysis of some nonlinguistic parallel(s) in the associated culture. In practice, the overwhelming emphasis was on language materials, and nonlinguistic elements were either entirely absent or themselves essentially "linguistic." The principal positive feature of this tradition is its serious concern with complex language forms. Two striking deficiencies are the inadequate methodological control over linguistic and cultural materials and the use of language materials as "nonlinguistic" data.

Grammar as a direct reflection of culture: the work of Lee

Many studies in anthropology "read" cultural beliefs directly off linguistic forms and do not seek additional evidence for the cognitive or behavioral reality of those beliefs. Studies of this type typically *presuppose* a close linkage between language and thought with concern for establishing the nature and direction(s) of influence, that is, few of these studies are directly concerned with the linguistic relativity hypothesis as such. Nonetheless, work of this type is frequently interpreted as relevant to Whorf's ideas. Many studies could serve here as illustrations of this approach (see references to case histories in Hymes, 1964b, p. 150), but the work of Dorothy D. Lee (1959b [1944]) is the best known and, though not explicitly built upon Whorf's work, has most often been associated with it.

Lee's project was to extract from language data, both structural and textual, the worldview characteristic of a culture. For these purposes, she regarded language as reflecting the accumulated perspective of the cultural group:

It has been said that a language will delineate and limit the logical concepts of the individual who speaks it. Conversely, a language is an organ for the expression of thought, of concepts and principles of classification. True enough, the thought of the individual must run along its grooves; but these grooves, themselves, are a heritage from individuals who laid them down in an unconscious effort to express their attitude toward the world. Grammar contains in crystallized form the accumulated and accumulating experience, the Weltanschauung of a people.

(Lee, 1938, p. 89)[1]

Lee's most important studies in this vein, i.e., those based on work with native speakers, involved the Wintu language spoken by Indians in northern California.

Lee focused on the grammatical categories associated with nominals and verbals. In the noun phrase she showed the central importance of a distinction between generic and particular, a distinction which differs from and cross-cuts our English categories of number (singular versus plural) and of definiteness (definite versus indefinite) (Lee, 1959b [1944]; also 1940a, 1944). She also brought in evidence about the treatment of kin terms and possessives (Lee, 1959b [1944]; 1940b, 1959a [1950]). In the verb phrase she analyzed the complex of categories used by speakers to indicate the evidential basis for their remarks and their attitude towards their assertions (Lee, 1959b [1944]; 1938). Additional evidence is drawn from the patterns of word formation, semantic extension, and subject–predicate relations (Lee, 1959b [1944]).

Based on this detailed examination of the Wintu language Lee argued for the existence of a consistent and characteristic cultural orientation to reality which is substantially different from our own. She describes the Wintu view as follows:

A basic tenet of the Wintu language, expressed both in nominal and verbal categories, is that reality – ultimate truth – exists irrespective of man. Man's experience actualizes this reality, but does not otherwise affect its being. Outside man's experience, this reality is unbounded, undifferentiated, timeless . . .

Man believes [reality] but does not know it. He refers to it in his speech but does not assert it; he leaves it untouched by his senses, inviolate. Within his experience, the reality assumes temporality and limits. As it impinges upon his consciousness he imposes temporary shape upon it. Out of the undifferentiated qualities and essences of the given reality, he individuates and particularizes, impressing himself diffidently and transiently, performing acts of will with circumspection. Matter and relationships, essence, quality are all given. The Wintu actualizes a given design endowing it with temporality and form through his experience. But he neither creates nor changes; the design remains immutable.   (Lee, 1959b [1944], p. 121)

Lee gives a reasonably detailed explanation of how she has derived these conclusions from the specific linguistic forms she describes. Many of these analyses of individual categories are quite perceptive and, like those of Whorf, much ahead of their time in terms of subtlety of semantic analysis. However, the overall presentation is difficult to evaluate because her treatment of the grammatical forms is not systematic. Lee gives us her interpretation of the sense of a given category or morpheme, but without enough examples or details on the array of structural alternatives for us to evaluate independently whether her claims are justified.

For present purposes, the important point about this work is that it depends on strong, untested assumptions about the relation of language to thought. The only evidence presented by Lee (1959b [1944]), beyond structural semantic analyses, are analyses of myths. Other nonlinguistic "cultural" materials such as the concept of the self, kin relations, and the like are without exception derivative of linguistic analyses. In a related article on Wintu concepts of the self, Lee acknowledged as much:

The Wintu Indians of northern California have a conception of the self which is markedly different from our own. I have attempted to arrive at this conception through analysis of linguistic form and structure, as well as a consideration of biographical texts and recorded mythical material. My study is incomplete, since I have no other record of actual behavior. The ethnography of the Wintu as we have it, is an account of a dead and remembered culture. (1959a [1950], p. 131)

Thus, the entire analysis depends on structural and textual analysis. This information could, in theory, be important, perhaps even sufficient to establish such claims, if it could be assumed that language bore a reliable interpretive relationship to cognitive and cultural activity. But it is just this relation which has never been established and which remains controversial. In the absence of an assessment of nonlinguistic correlates, such a relation cannot be assumed to exist either in general or in particular. In short, studies of this sort beg the question at issue in the work of Sapir and Whorf of the relation of linguistic and nonlinguistic phenomena. Providing such nonlinguistic evidence is not a simple task, and presents recurring difficulties for all research on this problem.

Grammar as language, vocabulary as culture: the work of Mathiot

Other studies within anthropological linguistics which attempt to address the linguistic relativity issue directly recognize the importance, at least in principle, of generating some "nonlinguistic" data to contrast with the linguistic data. However, the "nonlinguistic" data often take a surprisingly "linguistic" form. Many linguists during this period sought to split structure and meaning, assigning structure to grammar and meaning to lexicon. Further, in this view, only grammatical structure was truly linguistic, while lexical content (including any order or structure in the lexicon) was essentially nonlinguistic, i.e., had its origins in cognition or culture. Thus there are studies of the relationship between language and culture which devolve into an examination of the relationship between a grammatical structure (representing "language") and a lexical structure (representing "culture"), wherein the latter is frequently a folk taxonomy derived by the methods of "ethnoscience." These attempts constitute particularly extreme cases of the lingua-centrism characteristic of this whole tradition.

As an example of this type of approach, we can take Madeleine Mathiot's (1964 [1962]) contrast of two "linguistic" variables in Papago with various "cultural" correlates. The linguistic variables were (1) the grammatical category of nominal number (i.e., singular, [simple] plural, and distributive [plural]) as indicated by morphological marking, and (2) the classes of quantifiable nouns (i.e., mass aggregate, individual, and mixed) as indicated by grammatical co-occurrence relations with certain general modifiers of quantity and by reduplication.

Mathiot focused most of her attention on the quantifiable noun categories (i.e., the second linguistic variable). She tried a variety of methods to identify "cultural" correlates of this linguistic variable. Her first procedure consisted of simple inspection of the lexemes grouped by the grammatical patterning; this yielded results in providing a unified "perceptual" group only for mass nouns. A second procedure categorized the lexeme groups by an a priori (i.e., non-Papago) framework; but this did not produce interpretable results. Finally, a third procedure involving an elicitation of a folk taxonomy based on inclusion relationships between lexemes as judged by informant(s) yielded a general association between individual nouns and living things and aggregate nouns and plants – later refined into a [±animate] distinction. The taxonomy was established by using sentences as eliciting frames, which, as can be readily seen, simply revealed another kind of linguistic relation.

She then asked what the function of this latter individual/aggregate alternation had within each individual taxonomic category. After an examination of the referential correlates of the various nouns, she concluded that the individual/aggregate alternation subdivided the taxonomy futher along "perceptual" criteria. So, she has shown that one way of subclassifying quantifiable nouns (by grammatical co-occurrence relations) correlates with another way of subclassifying these nouns (by lexical inclusion relationships), and that the interaction of the two is associated with identifiable denotational regularities. Thus, the "language and culture" issue has been reduced here to an issue of the denotational meanings associated with certain *language internal corres-pondences*. The study remains entirely linguistic.[2]

The portion of the study relating to grammatical number (i.e., the first linguistic variable) is brief but continues in the same vein. The analysis is even more disconnected from nonlinguistic cultural data, since it eventu-ally centers on a correlation between the "simple plural" versus "distributed plural" distinction with an "individual-noun" versus "any-noun" opposition. In effect, *the two original grammatical factors have been intercorrelated*.

In comparing the results of her two analyses, Mathiot was led to see an overall Papago emphasis on perceptual (versus conceptual) criteria and on gradual (versus binary) oppositions. But there is no articulated theory or contrastive cultural evidence given to make these claims persuasive. Mathiot considered these conclusions the least reliable aspect of her study, but she felt that they were amenable to further research.

In subsequent work, Mathiot (1967a,b; 1969) retained the emphasis on the distinctiveness of lexical and grammatical aspects of language, although she increasingly tended to see them as jointly responsible for semantic value. In expanding on her earlier study, Mathiot (1967a) shifted her emphasis from tracing "affinities between language and culture" generally to the uncovering of the "cognitive significance of the aspect of language chosen for investigation," which she viewed as one aspect of culture, namely the worldview of a people. But this new concept of "cognitive significance" is still essentially derived from an analysis of semantics (here operationalized as relations of denotation and connotation between linguistic sign and reality) without language-independent evidence:

In the cognitive analysis of a given aspect of language, the semantic distinctive features of that aspect are the basis for inferring its cognitive content as follows: The cognitive content of a given aspect of language is ascertained by relating the semantic distinctive features of that aspect to the concept assumed to correspond to the aspect of reality that is reflected in the aspect of language under investigation. This concept is called the *underlying concept*.

The underlying concept relevant to a given aspect of language is postulated on the basis of an examination of the range of meaning pertaining to that aspect as revealed by the naming of units of the universe of data.

(Mathiot, 1967a, p. 201)

So the "cognitive" analysis (both in theory and in practice in this study) is really a more refined analysis of meaning, and cognitive content becomes merely one level of meaning – presumably its more general, less structure-connected aspect.

Further, the development of this analysis depends on the crucial notion of "underlying concept" to which semantic features are related in ascertaining cognitive content. Yet this crucial notion is "assumed" or "postulated" on the basis of "an examination" of the range of meaning of the linguistic forms at issue – a sort of intuitive semantics – which should be highly suspect given that exactly the issue in question is the possible relativity of such interpretations. So, despite the elaborate formal mechanics of her approach,[3] Mathiot never really moved beyond language-based judgments as to the nature of Papago cognition. She did not develop nonlinguistic evidence or a theory about the relation between linguistic and nonlinguistic perspectives on cognition either in this study or in subsequent ones (Mathiot, 1969), where she more clearly acknowledged the need for such nonlinguistic evidence.

Thematic parallels between language and culture: the work of Hoijer

The best-known and most highly regarded empirical work on the language and thought problem within anthropological linguistics through the 1950s was that of Harry Hoijer (1964b [1948]; 1964a [1951]; 1953; 1954). He investigated the relation between certain grammatical categories in Navaho and general orientation was somewhat different, and we begin with a brief sketch of the intellectual context of his research.

Hoijer's view of the relation between language and culture

Hoijer's investigations of the relation between language and culture occurred in the context of a broader concern with tracing patterns of linguistic and cultural distribution in space (i.e., geographically) or change over time (i.e., historically). He differed from Whorf in that he emphasized the integrated, systemic nature of culture and rejected the view of culture as an assemblage of traits (1964b [1948], p. 457; 1953, pp. 555–56). In this he was both reflecting and advancing a view which had become more widespread in American anthropology and which, as we have seen, was present to some extent in Sapir's later work. Since he also accepted the view that language was a system, the problem of the relation of language to culture was that of the relation between two systems. Hoijer's general view of this relation was that language was a *part* of culture (1964b [1948], p. 454; 1953, p. 554).

Hoijer's view of culture as organized and integrated led to the view that in assessing the relation between cultures either in space or in time, one should focus on the covert core of the cultural system and not on more superficial overt traits which were highly subject to borrowing

(1964b [1948], pp. 455 and 457; 1953, p. 567; also 1954, p. 103). Thus he felt that the rate and extent of culture change was overestimated in traditional studies (i.e., culture was defined too narrowly by its formal and overt features), and also that, from this perspective, culture area divisions might be constructed somewhat differently. Later, he made a similar argument about language (i.e., that it is defined too narrowly) in that language groups are defined by features (usually phonological) which probably bear the least relation to the rest of culture (1953, p. 566).

In spite of these views, however, Hoijer continued to accept the basic premise that culture changed more rapidly than language. Thus, in examining the relation between language change and culture change, he looked to culture as the source of at least some linguistic change (especially in his early, pre-1948, writings). He was more explicit than Whorf as to how this came about. Cultures changed, in his view, because new needs took precedence over old habits. But once one aspect of the culture changed, its very systemic nature assured that other parts of the system, including language, could be affected (1964b [1948], p. 457).

Hoijer traced the influence of culture change on language primarily through semantics, which, in his early works, was restricted to vocabulary items: the introduction of new terms, shifts in meaning of old terms, or combinations of old terms into new compound forms (1964b [1948], pp. 450–60). However, mindful of Sapir's caution that one should not confuse a language with its vocabulary (1964b [1948], pp. 459–60; 1953; pp. 557–68), he took the additional step of trying to show how these vocabulary changes could eventually result in changes in the very system of the language. In particular, he showed how new vocabulary patterns might generate new phonetic environments and thus adjustments in the phonemic structure of the language (1964b [1948], pp. 460–61). This was another application of the principle that a change in one part of a system will have consequences elsewhere in the system. In his later writings, Hoijer specifically indicated that lexical, morphological, and syntactic patterns are all related (1953, p. 557). An important corollary of this argument was that a given cultural influence or change may have quite different effects depending on the language system it comes into contact with (1964b [1948], e.g., p. 462).

Hoijer's approach to Whorf's arguments

By 1950 Hoijer had become concerned with Whorf's specific approach to the problem of the interrelation of language and culture.[4] Hoijer felt that

Whorf had understated the degree of this interrelation, and in a series of articles (1964a [1951]; 1953; 1954) he sought to find more evidence for the sorts of connections Whorf had proposed and to place Whorf's work in the context of more general concerns within linguistic anthropology. Given his belief that other aspects of culture were just as systemic as language, he had to modify Whorf's approach. In his view both culture and language have a slowly changing, systemic, covert aspect and a more rapidly changing overt aspect, and the place to look for similarities was in the relation between the core systems.

Having rejected Whorf's argument that language must be the decisive factor in language and culture interaction because it was systematic while culture was not, Hoijer was led to seek other grounds for giving language a special place among the systems of culture. He settled on the argument that language was clearly unusual among the components of culture in that it contacted and interpenetrated every aspect of cultural life:

the dichotomy between linguistic systems and other systems in the culture is by no means so sharp as Whorf suggests. Not all nonlinguistic aspects of a culture are mere "assemblages of norms"; there are some that are also structured, perhaps as rigidly so as language and possibly, therefore, as resistant to change. The important point of difference, as between other cultural systems and language, it seems to me, is not that language is the more rigidly systemic but that the linguistic system so clearly interpenetrates all other systems within the culture. This alone might account for its larger role, if it has that, in the limiting of "free plasticity" and the rigidifying of "channels of development."(1953, pp. 566–67)

Unfortunately, this interesting suggestion that language plays a special role in culture because of its interpenetration of so many other systems within culture was not developed further by Hoijer.

Although Hoijer was somewhat more cautious than Whorf in assigning language a special role in shaping culture change, and although he made his argument for its significance on different grounds, he reached essentially the same conclusions. He emphasized, following Whorf, that language habits do not inescapably limit perceptions and thought, but rather direct perception and thinking into certain habitual channels:

It is, however, easy to exaggerate linguistic differences of this nature and the consequent barriers to intercultural understanding. No culture is wholly isolated, self-contained, and unique. There are important resemblances between all known cultures – resemblances that stem in part from diffusion (itself an evidence of successful intercultural communication) and in part from the fact that all cultures are built around biological, psychological, and social characteristics common to all mankind. The languages of human beings do not so much determine the perceptual and other faculties of their speakers vis-à-vis experience as they influence and direct these faculties into prescribed channels.

(1954, p. 94)

Hoijer thus made explicit the wide range of factors which must be considered even as he draws much the same conclusion as Whorf regarding the influence of language.

He further made explicit something left unclear in Whorf's work, namely that language operates in tandem with other cultural forces to affect thought. For Hoijer, the metaphysics of a cultural group was critical and provided the linkage between language and other aspects of culture:

> The fashions of speaking peculiar to a people, like other aspects of their culture, are indicative of a view of life, a metaphysics of their culture, compounded of unquestioned, and mainly unstated, premises which define the nature of their universe and man's position within it ... It is this metaphysics, manifest to some degree in all the patterns of a culture, that channelizes the perceptions and thinking of those who participate in the culture and that predisposes them to certain modes of observation and interpretation. The metaphysics, as well, supplies the link between language as a cultural system and all other systems found in the same culture.   (1953, p. 561)

We see here the explicit acceptance, at least in theory, of a notion akin to Whorf's microcosm mediating between various cultural subsystems. (Cf. Whorf, 1956a, p. 147.) Hoijer's overall goal then was to show that language as a structured subsystem had intimate relations with the core covert metaphysics observable in the cultural system at large.

Hoijer's empirical studies

Hoijer (1964a [1951]) sought direct empirical evidence for language and cultural interrelations in a case study of Navaho linguistic categories and their relation to the Navaho thought world. Hoijer concentrated on two detailed examples. First, he outlined the general morphosyntax of the Navaho verb and attempted to show that there is a distinctive overall "emphasis" on reporting motion and its nature, direction, and status. Unfortunately, it is not clear that all of Hoijer's evidence really indicated attention to motion. For example, the most semantically neutral motion verbs in Navaho require detailed specification of the type of object-form which is in motion. Rather than a finer specification of and attention to motion, this could be regarded as a finer specification of and attention to object-form. Similar problems of interpretation arise in the last of Hoijer's three pieces of evidence, wherein he argued that the use of an active verb in nominal function to describe an object suggests an emphasis on motion. Exactly the same pattern obtains for the static (i.e., nonmotionful) neuter verbs, so the distinctions once more have more to do with the overall view of objects than with verbs of motion *per se*.

Further, the claim that Navaho verb categories are distinctive *vis-à-vis* a broad sample of languages is not established at all.

Hoijer then sought parallels to this purported emphasis on motion elsewhere in Navaho culture. He isolates two parallels: (1) the nomadic life style of the Navaho, and (2) the motion of culture heroes in myths as they seek to perfect or repair the dynamic flux of the universe. The jump from emphasis on *kinds* or *quality* of motion (or sorts of objects in motion under my reinterpretation) to nomadism and journeys of culture heroes, which involves the *fact* or *quantity* of motion of a completely different kind, seems weakly motivated. Further, the myth data and their interpretation may be regarded as another form of linguistic data rather than a clearly nonlinguistic aspect of culture. There is no attempt to show that "motion" is a common or habitual focus of individual Navaho thought patterns in daily life or that it underlies a wide variety of specific Navaho cultural institutions.

Hymes (1961b, pp. 36, 41; 1964b, p. 149; 1966 [1964], p. 118) in his discussion of this research saw corroboration of Hoijer's assessment of the importance of motion in Navaho life in the work of other scholars, especially Reichard, Astrov, Landar, and Kluckhohn. This evidence also seems dubious. Reichard (1949), like Hoijer, based her conclusions on *linguistic* data (especially the importance, broadly, of the verb in Navaho), but noted that the pattern is characteristic of many Indian languages and hence is not distinctive of Navaho. Astrov (1950) also dealt exclusively with *myths* and their content; while stating that the Navaho are somewhat extreme in comparison with other groups, she also noted that the themes she discusses are common in many other Indian tribes. Landar (1959) reviewed the evidence to that date on Navaho motionfulness in his own study of themes in four myths, but this review of the evidence (especially from psychologists Kaplan, Suci, and Osgood[5]) is both brief and somewhat inaccurate and so adds little to the discussion. Kluckhohn (1960) based *his* analysis on Hoijer's work and so also added nothing really new to the discussion. So the purported support identified by Hymes is also derived from myths or other language analysis and tends to suggest the nondistinctiveness of the Navaho themes Hoijer identified. There are no strict nonlinguistic data of relevance beyond the nomadic history of the Navaho people mentioned by Hoijer.

In his second example, Hoijer (1964a [1951]; also discussed in 1954) outlined another aspect of verb structure which he believed paralleled nonlinguistic culture. By analyzing the Navaho pattern of subject–goal relations wherein the verb theme object–class corresponds to the *intransitive subject and the transitive object*[6] Hoijer concluded that Navaho speakers see movement and position as inherent in and specific to an object class and not spontaneously produced by an actor.[7] In Hoijer's notional characterization:

the events are reported as if object-class positions and actions existed independently and the so-called 'actors' merly [*sic*] hitched a ride on them.

(Hoijer, 1964a [1951], p. 148)

Implicit in Hoijer's interpretation was the view that concord is a sign of importance, and thus concord between verb and object of a transitive instead of with the subject of the transitive (i.e., the underlying agent) implies the peripherality of that subject. Alternatively, the syntactic equation (in case marking) of the intransitive subject and transitive object for a given transitive/intransitive verb pair implies that the introduced transitive subject (again, the underlying agent) is not significant, i.e., that they are uninvolved and "passive" in some sense. This interpretation may be correct, but it is equally likely that Hoijer's interpretation is grounded in his semantic intuitions as a speaker of English, that is, these are the interpretations that would be implied *if* such patterns occurred in English. It is another matter to show that this view is actively present for Navaho speakers, for whom these forms are routine.[8]

Hoijer's evidence that such a theme exists in Navaho culture comes from Kluckhohn and Leighton (1946),[9] who argued that a basic premise of Navaho culture is that "Nature is more powerful than man." The Navaho believe that they can control or influence nature but not master it. This evidence is unsatisfying because no concrete examples were given by Hoijer himself, and Kluckhohn and Leighton's interpretation was given simply as a summary observation and not illustrated, developed, or grounded in detail with empirical data. (See Kluckhohn and Leighton, 1946, pp. 227–28.) While the argument itself is not implausible and is probably correct, the shortage of concrete illustrations, the possibility that Hoijer (along with Kluckhohn and Leighton) has substituted his own intuition for Navaho thought patterns, and the lack of argument that the grammatical pattern and the worldview in question are at all *distinctively* related certainly make for a weak case at best. In fact, Hymes (1961b, p. 38) argues that the premise in question is widely held among American Indian groups and is not distinctive of Navaho.

Evaluation of Hoijer's work

Hoijer's writings are noteworthy for their accurate characterization of Whorf's original arguments, but his own empirical research does not meet the same standard. Most notably, the focus of his analysis is on broad thematic parallels rather than on specific interlocking structures. For language, he identified a common theme (which may, in fact, reside largely in the eye of the beholder) of "motion" in several areas of the grammar, but his argument remains a mere statement about an "emphasis" rather than developing into a demonstration of how the one component of the grammar becomes a regimenting metaphor for the grammar more generally in the fashion of Whorf's analyses. For culture, the theme is established primarily by reference to the general remarks of ethnographers about patterns of Navaho culture, remarks which use words similar to those used to describe the grammatical theme. But again, there is the simple statement of theme with very little detailed description of how specific cultural institutions reveal the theme or how they interlock into a consistent system. Further, for both language and culture, the themes expressed are very broad and, as might be expected, do not appear to be distinctive of the Navaho. This focus on themes or emphases is all the more disappointing because of Hoijer's own emphasis in his theoretical discussions on the systematic nature of the core linguistic and cultural systems. His work thus exhibits a gap between his understanding of the issues and his theoretical aspirations on the one hand and his empirical product on the other.

Nonetheless, Hoijer's work does stand out in several respects. First, he correctly recognizes (1953, pp. 564–66) that Whorf's presentation of contrasting cultural behaviors is intended to demonstrate the reality of the hypothesized microcosms. His own effort to present similar non-linguistic cultural evidence quite clearly stems from this understanding. Unfortunately, in the end, he provides substantially less empirical information than did Whorf about nonlinguistic aspects of culture and he relies more heavily on language-based data to develop what information is provided. For these reasons, his work is less satisfactory than Whorf's, even as it stands out among the other studies in this tradition in its accurate assessment of what serious empirical work would entail.[10]

Second, Hoijer saw correctly that Sapir and Whorf dealt with structural differences between languages which had semantic import:

The Sapir–Whorf hypothesis, it is evident, includes in language both its structural and its semantic aspects. These are held to be inseparable, though it is obvious that we can and do study each more or less independently of the other. The structural aspect of language, which is that most easily analyzed and described, includes its phonology, morphology, and syntax, the numerous but limited frames into which utterances are cast. The semantic aspect consists of a self-contained system of meanings, inextricably bound to the structure but much more difficult to analyze and describe. Meanings, to reiterate, are not in actual fact separable from structure, nor are they, as some have maintained (notably Voegelin 1949: 36), to be equated to the nonlinguistic culture.

(Hoijer, 1954, p. 95)

Such structural–semantic patterns might involve organized lexical patterns or grammatical categories:

Every language is made up of a large number of such structural–semantic patterns, some of which pertain to lexical sets, as in the case of the Navaho and English color terms, and others of which pertain to sets of grammatical categories, such as the distinction between the singular and plural noun in English.   (1954, p. 96)

These points needed emphasis because they stood in opposition to the widespread tendency in American linguistics at that time to separate the study of structure and meaning, to argue in effect that the study of structure without reference to meaning was the essential task of linguistics and that the study of meaning belonged elsewhere.[11] Hoijer understood that it was precisely the inseparability of structure and meaning[12] that made structural differences problematic in Whorf's view.

Third, although Hoijer presented information in his own work on only a single case (one language and culture) rather than comparative material, he recognized the importance of comparative control in investigating the language and thought problem. His contribution in this regard is taken up in the next chapter.

Summary

The most important characteristic of the case studies in this tradition is their overwhelming focus on language, what we might term a *linguacentric* approach to the problem of language and thought. The range of variation, illustrated by the three cases, ranges from complete lack of concern with providing cognitive or cultural data (Lee), to the use of language data to represent both the independent and the dependent variables, that is, both language and thought (or culture) (Mathiot), to relatively weak attempts to provide nonlinguistic data (Hoijer). In no case is the nonlinguistic portion of the study its strong point.

Even when psychological or cultural analyses are attempted, they tend to be deficient in important ways. The analysis of cultural "facts" or themes tends to be unsystematic and *ad hoc*. Other difficulties in this tradition stem from broader tendencies within anthropology such as the proclivity for focusing on single case studies, which makes it difficult to show that the description of a characteristic thought world is distinctive of the particular cultural and linguistic group. Finally, the tradition is characterized by a concern for cultural pattern rather than individual cognition. Although this follows Whorf's approach, it is subject to the same criticism, namely that such characterizations, developed directly from linguistic or other cultural data, do not necessarily provide an adequate basis for characterizing (or "reading off") individual thought.

On the other hand, most of the important advances produced by this tradition stem from insights about how better to conceptualize and investigate language. These studies are marked by detailed analyses of the complex and multiple aspects of language form and meaning which must be considered in this kind of research. They are all the more remarkable, as a group, in that the serious examination of meaning was not characteristic of their era any more than it was during Whorf's day. The next section examines some of the advances which eventually developed within or were recognized by the anthropological linguistics tradition – advances which will be important in formulating a fresh approach.

4. Approaches in anthropological linguistics: theoretical and methodological advances

Introduction

The previous chapter characterized direct empirical research on the linguistic relativity issue within anthropological linguistics. This chapter reviews later achievements within this tradition which have attempted to provide solutions or new perspectives on crucial theoretical and methodological problems in previous research. Although this work explicitly addresses Whorf's formulations, it has yet to give rise to direct empirical evaluations of the linguistic relativity issue itself. But the work does provide the foundation for such research by providing an improved understanding of the structure and functioning of the linguistic analysis of experience.

Advances have been made in three areas. First, more refined approaches to comparing the diversity of classifications across languages have emerged. This work both provides the foundation for a new empirical comparison and clarifies the way in which linguistic classifications are distinctively "linguistic" in nature. Second, the earlier interest in the diversity of linguistic classifications (structure) has been supplemented by an increasing emphasis on the diverse uses (functions) of language not only across language groups but even within a single language community. This work opens up an entirely new dimension of the relativity problem. Third, more specific content has been given to the notion that speakers have differential awareness of their various language categories. This work illuminates the process by which language categories influence thought and, in conjunction with the work on the diverse uses of language, suggests another new dimension of the relativity problem.

Controlled comparison of structural diversity

We have seen that in his linguistic studies, Whorf went beyond a simple emphasis on the diversity of language classifications to emphasize the importance of comparative analysis and meaningful cross-language generalization. He attempted, in a variety of ways, to establish a frame of comparison for linguistic analysis which would be independent of the peculiarities of any given language. But most of these ideas were not specifically applied to his work on the relation of language to habitual thought. His comparison of the English (SAE) and Hopi cases was, of course, informed by his knowledge of the structure of a wide range of languages, but it actually hinged for the most part on detailed contrasts of the two languages; no broader comparative framework was introduced to show that the linguistic patterns or the habitual thought patterns were highly distinctive of the two groups. The various anthropological case studies reviewed in chapter 3 were even less comparative, typically focusing on the structure of a single language. Again, although these studies may have been informed by the analysts' knowledge of general linguistics, the absence of explicit comparison with *any* other language, let alone with an array of languages in a more broadly based comparative framework, constituted a singular weakness of these approaches in anthropological linguistics and a movement backwards from the standard set by Whorf's own work.

Attempts were made, however, beginning in the late 1950s to take the problem of controlled comparison more seriously. These attempts converged with a general resurgence of interest during this same period in the identification of language universals and in the construction of linguistic typologies. Although these attempts have as yet had little substantive impact on research on the linguistic relativity problem, they provide essential tools for research in this area. No genuine progress can be made unless and until the differences among languages are given an adequate comparative characterization in specifically linguistic terms and these differences are then related to cognitive or cultural differences which are also given adequate comparative characterization. In this section the two principal approaches to controlled comparison which were developed within the anthropological linguistics tradition will be reviewed. One approach sought to exploit patterns of regional distribution of languages and cultures. Related languages spoken by divergent cultural groups and diverse languages spoken by similar cultural groups were identified as promising areas for controlled comparison of the relation of language and culture. A second approach involved using recently developed typological frameworks developed in the study of linguistic universals to build useful dimensions of comparison that could be applied to a large number of widely dispersed and genetically unrelated languages.

Regional approaches

Although he did not execute such a study, Hoijer explicitly emphasized the methodological need for controlled comparison to enable the drawing of sound conclusions on the language and culture question. He made the first proposal for a study which would provide such control using the Indian cultures of the US Southwest, where there are similar cultures (by traditional criteria) but diverse languages, and similar languages associated with diverse cultures (Hoijer, 1954, pp. 103–104). Figure 6 shows in schematic form the relationships among the groups he suggested comparing. By studying these peoples, it would be possible both to study the relative importance of language as against other cultural factors in shaping a thought world and to question more directly the traditional construction of culture areas upon an evaluation of overt, yet peripheral, cultural traits. (Recall that this was a major part of Hoijer's own research agenda.) In his discussion, Hoijer was not explicit about exactly how he would go about assessing the thought worlds of these various groups. Some indication of how he would have proceeded, however, is given by his own study of these issues among the Navaho, which was reviewed in chapter 3.

The Southwest Project in Comparative Psycholinguistics (Casagrande, 1956; 1960; Carroll, 1967) represented the first attempt to execute such a controlled comparison of six culture groups in the same general region, although the various groups were not as well counterbalanced for language similarity as in Hoijer's original proposal. The cultures they studied are indicated in figure 7. Unfortunately, many of the results of these studies relevant to the language and thought (or language and culture)

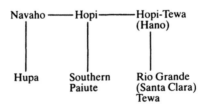

Figure 6 Hoijer's plan for comparison of thought worlds controlling for language and culture variation. Horizontal lines indicate cultural similarity. Vertical lines indicate language similarity. (Constructed from Hoijer, 1954, pp. 102–104.)

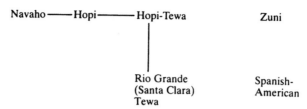

Figure 7 Southwest Project in Comparative Psycholinguistics plan for comparing culture and language groups. Horizontal lines indicate cultural similarity. Vertical lines indicate language similarity. Unconnected groups do not fit the design developed by Hoijer (shown in figure 6). (Constructed from Casagrande, 1960, p. 177.)

question were never published.[1] And those which were published addressing the linguistic relativity issue did not, in fact, take advantage of the possibilities of regional control over language and cultural group. (These studies are discussed in chapter 6 since they stress the use of psycholinguistic methods.) Apparently, Hoijer's second goal of reconceptualizing culture areas through such a study was not seriously considered.

Several years later, Bright and Bright (1965) conducted a study in northwestern California, an area in which there is "cultural identity" and "linguistic diversity," in another attempt to achieve a controlled comparison. (Unfortunately, this study used just the sort of traditional classifications of language and culture areas which Hoijer had criticized.) Since new data on the nonlinguistic aspects of these cultures were not readily available any longer, Bright and Bright resorted to an analysis of taxonomic naming structures in the vocabulary as an index of nonlinguistic culture – an approach similar in some respects to Mathiot's. In particular, a handful of general class names (for example, "bird") were examined for each cultural group. These were assumed to match aboriginal views of the physical world closely and to be primarily cultural rather than linguistic phenomena (Bright and Bright, 1965, pp. 69, 71–73) – an assumption that the authors acknowledged was controversial. So the study ultimately devolved into a study of the relation between the structure of a small set of lexical items and language family membership. On the basis of the content of the terms, they interpreted the taxonomies as showing cross-linguistic similarity of culture which, they argued, did not fit the Sapir–Whorf hypothesis. On the basis of the number of terms in each language, which they felt correlated with the degree of looseness or rigidity in syntactic structuring in the languages, they concluded that there may be a relation at this level between language and nonlinguistic culture.

As should be clear, the conceptual problems in this study are considerable, to say the least. The nonlinguistic variable is patently linguistic (i.e., vocabulary content and structure), and the linguistic variable is purely formal without consideration of associated meaning values. It is unfortunate that one of the few studies to have addressed seriously the problem of methodological control over cultural and linguistic variation is so problematic on these other methodological grounds.

Typological approaches

Typological approaches involve the characterization or grouping of languages on the basis of structural similarities rather than on the basis of purported historical or genetic relationship. The groupings can operate at many levels, such as similarity in technique of word formation, similarity in word order, or similarity in the semantic structuring of a category such as grammatical number. Observed similarities are presumed to derive from and, therefore, to give evidence of common yet independently operating formal-functional tensions intrinsic to languages as functioning semiotic devices. Thus typological approaches are central to the investigation of the nature of languages and the establishment of linguistic "universals." In fact, some of the observed similarities may result from the languages having an actual historical relationship, but this possibility is typically minimized by intentionally selecting a sample from language families known to be widely separated.

The search for linguistic universals

The search for wide-ranging linguistic generalities has long been a part of linguistic study. During the middle part of the century these concerns crystallized into a renewed search for linguistic universals, that is, empirically grounded assertions purportedly valid in some decidable way for all known languages.[2] The primary focus of these studies was on universals of phonological and syntactic (including morphotactic) structure, rather than "semantic" structure (that is, patterns of meaning) (for example, Greenberg, 1966b [1963]).

Even though this work was not explicitly directed toward the significance of linguistic diversity for thought, the empirical results of the research have inevitably had their influence on the evaluation of the linguistic relativity hypothesis. The basic argument has been that the observed commonalities among languages demonstrate the existence of common cognitive and semiotic processes at work in all known languages. A marked relativity in conceptual worldview simply can not be sustained, the argument goes, in the face of this evidence.

This argument is misguided in a number of respects. A degree of commonality among languages in no way establishes the position that the remaining differences are in fact negligible – either from the point of view of linguistic theory or from the point of view of a consideration of the nonlinguistic significance of linguistic forms. As we have seen, Whorf himself was interested in establishing valid cross-language generalizations, and this was not in conflict with his assessment of the significance of differences.

Further, the vast majority of these linguistic universals take the form of implicational statements. That is, many of the relevant universals are not statements about absolute commonality among languages but rather statements about constraints on the pattern of variation. Thus, rather than absolute statements that all languages have feature X, these universals consist of statements that if feature X. is characteristic of a language, then it will in general be the case that feature Y is also characteristic of the language (Greenberg, 1966a; 1966b [1963]; 1978b; Comrie, 1981). As such, these statements in no way deny the fact of significant patterns of variation, but rather simply seek to grasp such variation within a unified framework.

The argument for typological control

It is this attempt to grasp variation within a unified framework which makes this research relevant to research on the significance of linguistic variation. To characterize one meaning structure as different from another (or many others) one needs to be able to say the languages are different "in some respect" – that is, that there is in fact *a common dimension in terms of which they differ*. Differences cannot, in fact, be discussed in any serious way without some theory of commonality. Thus typological patterns developed from work on linguistic universals can provide the sort of framework within which meaningful differences can be characterized in a principled manner.

The argument for typological control in the investigation of linguistic relativity has been made by Hymes (1961b).[3] He argued that the typological approach could be of as much importance for understanding the semantic (i.e., meaningful) aspect of language as it has been at the levels of phonology and grammatical form. He advocated the use of the term *cognitive style* to characterize semantic patterns, remaining neutral, however, both with respect to whether or not the meanings at issue are represented in grammar or vocabulary and with respect to various theoretical positions about the origin of the patterns (1961b, p. 22).[4]

Hymes (1961b, p. 23) divided the range of possible studies of cognitive style into four groups ("sectors of interest") generated by crossing two axes of contrast. The first division was on an axis of *form* and *content*; our interest in the present case is with the analyses of the content of cognitive styles. The second division was on an axis of *specific* and *general* (or manifest and latent). A typology of *specific contents* of cognitive style in language would involve looking at individual grammatical categories as they vary across languages. A typology of *general content* of cognitive style in language would involve looking at whole grammatical configurations.

Hymes felt that the extant and still growing body of descriptive works concerned with semantic issues would provide a basis for the construction of adequate typologies at the level of *specific content* (1961b, pp. 30–31, 41). His chief example of how such work could both be used for and profit from a typological perspective was Jakobson's (1971a [1957]) analysis of the categories of the Russian verb.[5] In this work Jakobson attempted to describe the principal grammatical categories of language (for example, gender, number, tense, aspect) in formal terms based in part on the underlying dimensions of the speech event. He then illustrated each category and showed how the Russian verb utilized a selected subset of the verbal categories. The semantic value of any given category stems in part from the set of categories of which it is a member. The set of categories as a whole can also be thought of as representing a significant, and therefore meaningful, selection from the array of possibilities, but this point is not emphasized by either Hymes or Jakobson. In the end, typologies of specific content have been conceived of and developed as linguistic descriptions. Their implications for thought or culture have been little considered.

At the level of *general content*, that is, contrasting languages on the bases of pervasive emphasis, theme, or "fashion of speaking," Hymes discussed the work of Lee, Hoijer, and Whorf (Hymes, 1961b, p. 36). Hymes expressed considerable concern about the difficulty of discerning a linguistic worldview. He mentioned first some traditional problems characteristic of such studies, including the

pitfalls of circularity (linguistic differences as the only evidence of psychological differences which language is said to determine or reflect), anachronism (reading contemporary significance into dead metaphors), translation meanings, and taking grammatical terminology literally.   (1961b, p. 36)

Even if these problems were solved, Hymes still doubted that a grammar (or lexicon) could be said to *contain* a worldview – apparently meaning by this that the *structure of the language alone* does not embody and cannot be a sure guide to a worldview. The structure of language is only one of several factors contributing to a worldview. Although this is certainly true, taken to its limit, Hymes's statement seems to preclude even asking about the relationship between linguistic worldview and general worldview: one can only ask about the relationship between a linguistic "cognitive style" and general worldview. Such a conceptualization seems to ignore the force of Sapir's (1964 [1931]) important observation that each language is a self-contained, formally complete symbolic system able to encompass all possible experience and, in this sense, establishes a general orientation to the world.

Hymes continued his discussion of general content by emphasizing the necessity for nonlinguistic evidence to test for broader significances (i.e., connections to a broader worldview) and the difficulties of gathering such evidence (1961b, pp. 36–37). And later (in his summary) he returned again to this issue:

> The significance [of general or latent cognitive style] has often been taken as that of world view, or metaphysics, e.g. Whorf and Lee in various writings ... A major concern has been with significance as a determinant of behavior. It is clear in general that linguistic habits, including those involved in typology of cognitive styles, do influence non-linguistic behavior, especially habitual behavior. At the same [time] it is clear that such influence is partial and complex in its manifestations, rather than complete or easy to discern. The analysis of such influence requires experimental test; in other words, the import of a linguistic cognitive style for contemporaneous behavior can be investigated for only a portion of the languages which can contribute to a typology of such styles.   (1961b, p. 41)

> In short, the relationship between the elements of a cognitive style in a language, as discovered from the usual content of linguistic descriptions, and the contemporary or subsequent behavior (and thought) of those who speak the language, is problematic in principle and determinable only by empirical test. For many languages of the world, the relationship will remain unknown.
>
> (1961b, p. 42)

Even in asserting the importance of research on cognitive style for linguistics, Hymes was sobered by the difficult prospect of gathering comparable information on nonlinguistic cognitive or cultural dimensions. Given the requirements for experimental (or at least well-controlled) tests, the relationship must necessarily remain unknown for many languages.

This argument about the difficulty of acquiring nonlinguistic evidence applies equally well to single case studies and to comparative studies. But to undertake contrastive studies, Hymes argued, a typological framework is essential. By typology in this instance, Hymes apparently meant the explicit application of some general comparative framework to the data. Ultimately, all studies concerning the general content of a cognitive style need to be approached from this point of view:

> There is an additional problem of validity and reliability with regard to determining cognitive styles of the more general sort, and this problem is precisely a typological one. Although most recent work in these sectors has been within some individual language, some work, such as Whorf's, has raised the question of

contrast in type between languages, and it is necessary to view all such work in that perspective, as raising questions of the place of the particular language in a general typology of linguistic cognitive styles.   (1961b, p. 37)

With this remark, Hymes directly addressed a central problem in Whorf's work, that is, the lack of a controlled comparative framework for language. (This is paralleled by a need for some analytic control over the nonlinguistic variable as well. Although Hymes himself did not draw this conclusion, his warnings on the difficulties of assessing nonlinguistic behavior comparatively suggest the importance of selecting critical cases on the basis of systematic sampling of other aspects of culture as well.)

An important advantage of applying such a typological framework is that it can provide some control on those studies which trace themes within a language. It is easy in tracing out such themes in a language to assimilate more and more material, subsuming ever more tenuous elements into the pattern and ultimately watering down the semantic content at issue. This occurs because there is no intrinsic limit on our interpretive power. Typological control – a comparative framework – can be important in providing constraints on this process:

> The typological perspective has methodological consequences . . . It should be possible to state what cannot fit and why . . .
> In sum, there is needed a framework for contrastive perspective, for control and delimitation of the evidence for a cognitive orientation or style. In part this is a matter of the sharpening of knowledge that comes from detailed comparison . . . In part this is a matter of providing heuristic help – types of phenomena to look for and among which to place what is encountered – and such should be connected with operations for determining the presence of a type.   (1961b, p. 37)

Thus, a comparative framework should not only allow us what can and cannot fit but also should suggest what *should* fit into a configuration, leading us to new questions and insights (1961b, p. 37). (This, of course, addressed directly the weakness of Hoijer's thematic approach: it lacked any analytic constraints of this sort.) Hymes closed his discussion with the caution that the style attributed to a language still might not be distinctive of the culture if the characterization is made at the wrong level (1961b, pp. 36–38).

Hymes did not give any indications, however, of what the outlines of such a comparative framework at the level of general content might look like. He suggested, somewhat indirectly, that the closer the attested argument was tied to specific linguistic and cultural details the more patent validity a contrast might have, but nothing more. Instead, he indicated that such a typology must be built from whatever cases we happen to have, and so he proceeded to develop an illustrative case from Chinook to add to the extant sample.[6] Thus Hymes diagnosed the problem and indicated in a global way the desirable solution, but he did not give specific directions to guide future research.

Hymes's difficulty in this case may stem from not recognizing the true nature of the comparison present in Whorf's analysis. Whorf did not construct the "fashions of speaking" for Hopi and English from a single grammatical category (a factor of specific content of a cognitive style), but neither did he assimilate material freely from *all* aspects of the grammar (for a true characterization of overall general content). Rather, he explored in some detail rather delimited, clearly interrelated domains of the Hopi and English grammars. In particular, he focused on the expression of quantity in the noun phrase and tense in the verb phrase.

Although it does indeed seem unlikely that a single grammatical category (of unknown structural significance) extracted from a language will bear a measurable relation to behavior, the whole grammar is not the next logical level of attack. Rather, as Whorf's work illustrates, there are subsections of the grammar bearing definable interrelations with each other which are candidates for comparison – specific enough to permit the establishment of meaningful typological controls and yet general enough in their import to have implications for general cognitive activity and behavior. The next few sections review works which give some indication of how we might proceed in this direction – building medium-scale typological frameworks up from a conjoining of several specific typologies of individual grammatical categories.

The selected cases approach to the construction of typologies

The most significant problems in any typological study are the validity of the tentative comparative categories used to sort cases and, equally importantly, the justification of the placement for any given language (or rather its patterns) into a given category. Immense as these problems are for phonology and syntax, they are even more problematic in the area of "semantic" structure. A command over the meaning of forms is often more difficult to guarantee than is an accurate description of the formal devices themselves.

A solution has emerged within linguistics for handling this problem, namely the use of a small set of selected cases, often chosen for their diversity, over which the investigator has substantial control by virtue of extensive experience with the set of languages. This is then supplemented by insights derived from written descriptions of other languages which have particularly rich documentation on the dimension in question or which appear to represent critical variants of the dimension. This approach avoids the twin poles of restricting one's attention to a single case where one has relatively complete control – typically the investigator's native language – or, alternatively, of attempting a comprehensive global survey which, although broader in scope, lacks interpretive depth.

A recent example which makes this approach explicit is Friedrich's (1974) study of the category of verbal aspect (one of several *universal categories* of the sentential predicate), for which he identifies (proposes) three *basic features* sensitive to syntactic context.[7] Friedrich begins with an extensive examination of the aspect system in a particular language, Homeric Greek. He then frames this analysis cross-linguistically, identifying and ordering the basic features of verbal aspect, by reference to a detailed study of the aspect categories in three other languages – a procedure he labels "quadrangulation" because it is based on four languages. This analysis is then placed in a still larger framework of languages by the use of selected materials written about other languages. He describes the approach and its background as follows:

What follows is limited to some tentatively axiomatic, cross-linguistic propositions that all tie in with Homeric Greek. As for wider evidence, I have limited myself to "quadrangulating" from Homeric Greek to Tarascan, English, and Russian, plus some patterning from a half dozen other systems, particularly Yokuts. So I stand between the monolingual "Cartesian" extreme and the "anthropological" kind of typology exemplified by Hockett's *Manual of Phonology*.   (1974, p. 34)

The methodology of such "quadrangulation" has more general implications (for culture as well as linguistic studies), which have never been adequately developed. For the concept of "quadrangulation" I stand indebted to Ralph Linton who used it creatively in reaction against both the "single tribe" and the "world sample" bases for generalization. Linton felt that the soundest basis for generalization was three to six empirical structures for which the scientist had some close analogue of native intuition but which were typologically diverse with respect to the theoretical problem.   (1974, p. 34, n108)

This methodological stance is extremely important. An analysis built from a single case can neither ground its categories (i.e., establish the frame of analysis as having a status independent of the particular object of analysis) nor make any meaningful claim for generality. An analysis built on a world sample necessarily ends up being mostly statistical when what is needed, at least in establishing a case for a typology of semantic structures (or "cognitive styles"), is an interpretation in categorial-structural terms; also, such analyses often, though not necessarily always, share the problem of grounding the comparative categories, since the analyst's own culture and language tend to dictate the comparative categories. Some form of more limited typological approach, exemplified by Friedrich's "quadrangulation," would appear to be an essential middle step in building a comprehensive (i.e., world-wide) typology in any semantic domain.

The cognitive implications of typological patterning

What remains is to show how such middle-range typological work can be used to gain a greater degree of methodological control in the investigation of the linguistic relativity issue.

Universals and variables

Each semantic typology consists of two mutually related components. First, there is a common substantive dimension (a universal category, in Friedrich's terminology) which relates diverse structures as the "same" in some respect, typically in terms of "solving" some universal semiotic problem.[8] Second, this substantive dimension can be broken down into a set of basic features which, in their various formal[9] configurations, articulate the major alternative systems for representing the basic substantive dimension. The substantive dimension specifies the unity underlying the various specific configurations of basic features. Any given language can then be characterized as handling a given substantive semantic problem with a certain formal arrangement (a specific configuration) of the basic features relevant to that substantive dimension.

Cognitive implications can be drawn from such a typology in two ways. One can focus on the cognitive implications of the substantive commonality, that is, the unifying element "underlying" or "common to" the diverse systems exhibited by languages. The focus, then, is on the universals of language and thought interactions. Or one can focus on the cognitive implications, if any, of the various formal alternatives themselves, that is, the diverse ways the "same" substantive dimension can be handled. The focus, then, in the latter case is on certain specific language and thought relations and, potentially, on possible relativities based on using one particular formal alternative instead of another. The crucial point, for whichever of these two foci is selected, is that the two perspectives are intimately related: proper understanding of the common dimension is built from a comparative base, abstracting across instantiated alternatives; proper understanding of each individual case depends on placing it within the framework of the whole set of alternatives, which reveals its larger significance. In this sense, the investigation of the relation between Language and Thought and between languages and thought (in the sense of these terms set out in the introduction) are necessarily part of a common enterprise.

There has been no research on the language and thought problem fully incorporating such a dual perspective, although there are two close approximations. First, there is the research building on the work of Berlin and Kay (1969) concerning the cognitive bases or the underlying ("universal") structuring principles of the typological regularities exhibited by sets of "basic" color terms. And second, there is the research done by Silverstein (1973; 1976a; 1977; 1980; 1981a; 1987) concerning the cognitive implications of some of the underlying ("universal") structuring principles involved in case-marking systems. In both instances the analyses recognize a finite range of cross-linguistic variation for the aspect of grammar at issue and attempt to account for this variation within a single overarching system of ordering principles. But the primary cognitive concern in both cases is on the implications of the *universal* pattern and not on the significance for thought of the variations. The research on sets of color terms will be taken up in chapter 5 along with related psycholinguistic research on color and color terms. Silverstein's approach will be described here to give an illustration of what is involved in deriving cognitive implications from typological linguistic data. Since the linguistic issues involved are complex and require, for full understanding, some mastery of a technical terminology, only a brief, partial sketch can be developed here, outlining the logic of the approach. Additional details of this approach are presented as part of the linguistic analysis in the companion volume to this work.

The typological pattern[10]

Silverstein's immediate goal was to give an account of the regularities underlying the diversity of case-marking systems in languages. His more general goal was to indicate a general strategy for linguistic comparison. Case marking involves indicating by means of formal devices the grammatical function of noun phrases in sentences, that is, the underlying relations of arguments to their predicates and of arguments to one another. Thus, for example, in English the principal noun phrases in an active declarative sentence[11] can be marked to show whether they are in the nominative or accusative case. The "object" (in traditional terms) of a transitive verb is marked in the accusative, and both the "subject" of a transitive verb and the "subject" of an intransitive are marked in the nominative. The actual marking may take a variety of alternative forms: morphological (for instance, nominative *he* versus accusative *him*), word order (nominative position before the verb versus accusative position after the verb), etc.

The languages of the world contain a wide variety of very intricate ways of indicating syntactic function in this way. One particularly striking characteristic is that some languages show several *different* case-marking systems depending on the kind of noun phrases being marked. The most commonly encountered "alternative" to nominative–accusative marking is ergative–absolutive marking. In this latter type of marking, the "subject" of a transitive sentence is marked in the ergative case and both the "object" of a transitive sentence and the "subject" of an intransitive sentence are marked in the absolutive case – that is, this system cross-cuts our familiar nominative–accusative pattern. These differences are somewhat more easily conceptualized if we distinguish the three *principal* case roles which must be marked in intransitive and transitive sentences: Subject (S) = "subject" of an intransitive; Agent (A) = "subject" of a transitive; Patient (P) = "object" of a transitive. Nominative–Accusative systems thus treat Subjects and Agents alike as distinct from Patients. Ergative–Absolutive systems treat Subjects and Patients alike as distinct from Agents. This can be graphically portrayed as in figure 8. Some languages apply nominative–accusative marking to some kinds of noun phrases and ergative–absolutive marking to the remaining kinds of noun phrases. Such a language is said to have a "split" case-marking system and, following Silverstein (1976a), is often called a "split ergative" language.

One of Silverstein's principal goals was to give an account of such splits, that is, where they occur (i.e., which noun phrases are treated in one way and which in another) and why (i.e., what the underlying logic of such systems is). Silverstein showed that if we take a comparative, typological point of view, such split systems show certain regularities. Thus, in a given language, to take a simple example, noun phrases with a certain feature of referential meaning such as [+ animate] will take a pattern of nominative–accusative marking, whereas other noun phrases will take ergative–absolutive marking. We can say that a single referential feature [± animate] governs (or allows us to predict) the case-marking split in the language. A very small set of ordered features appears to govern the case-marking splits in a wide variety of languages.

More generally, the noun phrases in a language can be classed into *types* on the basis of asymmetries of syntactic distribution (patterns of markedness or neutralization) in the utterances of that language. Semantic and pragmatic referential *features*[12] of the type just mentioned can then be identified which describe the patterns differentiating these various noun-phrase types in a language. Every noun-phrase type in a language then represents a particular configuration or "bundle" of such

Figure 8 Contrast of nominative-accusative and ergative-absolutive case-marking systems

features which govern the array of grammatical categories which can be applied to that noun-phrase type.

Once identified, the set of operative features for a given language can be ordered one with respect to the other by relations of relative markedness: by degree of referential specificity for *semantic* features and by degree of extensional inclusiveness for *pragmatic* features. Thus, for example, whatever categories are applied to nouns specified as [+ animate] will also be applicable to nouns specified as [+ human], but not necessarily vice versa, and so on. Feature systems of this type from a variety of languages show a great many similarities and can be superimposed (intercalating nonmatching features in any instance) to form a composite, cross-linguistic "hierarchy of features" arranged in a linear order. Such a hierarchy is thus a statement (or expression) of a linguistic generalization pertaining to the operative features and their ordering across languages. Evidence for every point in the ordering of features may not be present in every language, but it will generally be the case that there is at least one language which reveals the relative ordering of each adjacent pair of features. More importantly, all languages will be consistent with the ordering, that is, no exceptions to the ordering will occur.

Having once developed such a feature hierarchy, one can work backwards to give an order to the various noun-phrase types from which the features were derived in the first place. That is, whatever grammatical categories apply to a given noun-phrase type will also apply to types higher in the ordering. The ordering itself should generalize across languages. Again, no given language may provide sufficient evidence for the entire ordering of noun-phrase types, but aggregately a large sample of languages provide such justification on the basis of the composite feature ordering. This ordering of noun-phrase types can then be used to provide a framework for the interpretation of a number of typological patterns.

To return to the above example, the features which govern the splits of case marking correspond to those in the hierarchy of features produced from the general analysis of the inherent lexical content of the various noun-phrase types.[13] Many of the most important cross-linguistic generalizations for case marking can be stated in terms of implicational statements grounded in the ordering of noun-phrase types generated from the full hierarchy of features. For example, it can be stated that if a given noun-phrase type X takes an accusative case marking under certain syntactic conditions, then all noun-phrase types "higher" in the ordering than X will also take accusative case marking under those same syntactic conditions.

The cognitive implications

Silverstein then took up the cognitive implications of this typological patterning, focusing on the significance of the universal referential continuum suggested by the ordering of features and noun-phrase types.[14] He first characterized the nature of the ordering of the noun-phrase types in terms of their relation to the event of speaking:

> It is possible to interpret the universal ordering in terms of principles of an hierarchy of inclusiveness that centers on the event of speaking in which the noun phrase types are used, so that use of language itself is at the basis of an *analogical regimentation* of reference.   (1980, p. 1)

This means that those noun phrases which inherently refer to some aspect of the event of speaking itself (however implicitly) perforce stand in a more privileged position ("higher" in the ordering) than those which do not. Thus, the event of speaking serves as the presupposable standard against which is measured how "natural" it is for various noun phrases to occupy certain propositional roles. And particular case-marking patterns essentially signal various sorts of deviations from this presupposable standard.[15]

   This ordering can be interpreted as a measure of the psychological salience of a given noun-phrase type to serve in a particular propositional role relation (for example, as agent of a transitive clause):

> The universals of case-marking treat this [setting of the features governing the application of various case marks] as the dependent variable, with both propositional role (case-relation) of the referent, and the inherent lexical content of the noun phrase type used for reference, as the independent variables. We may interpret the universal as saying something about the *universal asymmetries of salience* of the various combinations of noun phrase type and propositional role. That is, we may see this as a correct formulation of the *"naturalness"* of various types of referents in what are coded as Agent-of and Patient-of-case-relations. Although no language has a case-marking system that directly gives evidence about all of the asymmetries of salience, nevertheless there is considerable

psycholinguistic evidence that we can induce these asymmetries even for strongly accusative or strongly ergative languages.   (1980, p. 2)

The relevant psycholinguistic evidence shows that the underlying features and their ordering established by cross-linguistic analysis (e.g., $[\pm\,\text{human}] \geq [\pm\,\text{animate}]$) can in fact be shown to have psychological reality (or force) for speakers of a language which does not itself show any case-marking split for noun phrases with those features.[16] This reinforces the claim that the hierarchy of features (or ordering of noun-phrase types) represents a universal which is somehow "present" even when not explicitly indicated in categorial asymmetries of grammar in a particular language.

This leads, in turn, to the suggestion of the fundamental psychological status of the inherent lexical content hierarchy:

The conclusion that we are led to in this particular functional realm is that there is a fundamental, perhaps "innate" character to the inherent lexical content hierarchy, insofar as we interpret it to tell us something about the cognitive bases for referring and predicating.   (1980, p. 5)

Two facts are important about this claim. First, it is crucial to realize the importance of the final phrase, that is, that these are claims about the fundamental cognitive bases "for referring and predicating" – not cognition in general. Second, the hierarchy as a whole is not instantiated, as such, in any single language. It is a fact established on the basis of comparison of multiple languages. It is unlikely that such cognitive bases could be discovered on the basis of a single language's structure. Although psycholinguistic experimentation may produce evidence for the psychological salience of some elements of the hierarchy not actually operative in the grammar of a particular language, it is unlikely that they would ever be properly interpreted without an understanding that their salience derives precisely from the fact that they can potentially serve as a critical juncture in the act of referring and predicating – a fact revealed only by contrastive research on other languages.

Silverstein thus showed that an adequate approach to an understanding of the psychological substratum of language must be built on a comparative base. The focus, from the psychological perspective, was on how certain of the psychological saliencies (degrees of "naturalness" for serving certain roles in referential speech) associated with various noun-phrase types operate as a grid for the erection of a variety of particular linguistic systems. He was not concerned, at least in this substantive area, with the general cognitive implications of the use of language nor with the significance of a particular implicational regularity built on such psychological asymmetries. More importantly, he was not concerned with the significance of the fact that any given speaker (or group of speakers) typically operates within only one such system from among many that could be built on the same foundation, that is, he is not concerned with Whorf's problematic.[17] Nonetheless, his work provides a model of how to compare languages in a manner that reveals how their cognitive underpinnings lie in the use of language itself.

The structure of linguistic categories

No detailed discussion has been undertaken here concerning Boas, Sapir, and Whorf's first observation, namely that languages classify experience. The outstanding issue that must be resolved in this area is the sense in which a linguistic classification is specifically "linguistic" in nature. Can linguistic classifications be reliably characterized so as to distinguish them from classifications which are not linguistic? Subsequent work on the linguistic relativity problem has not seriously grappled with this issue to date. An adequate treatment of the problem will depend on developing a general account of human classificatory activity.

However, the trajectory of Silverstein's analysis of noun-phrase categorization as outlined above suggests that at least some linguistic categories (typologically characterized) take the nature of speech (or speaking) itself as their fundamental organizing principle. Linguistic classifications are developed historically for use in social acts of communication and ultimately take this social fact as their point of departure in organizing experience into categories. Other social and psychological activities having differing functional goals and organization may ground themselves in some other way. It should eventually be possible to specify points of divergence between differing classificatory modes, differences that can then be applied to distinguishing a specifically linguistic influence on thought. Other work which might profitably be brought to bear on this problem includes marking theory (see Lyons, 1968), the role of metalinguistic activity (discussed below) in shaping categories, and Sapir's (1949b [1944]) distinction among logical, psychological, and linguistic points of view. This problem will be dealt with again in the context of interpreting the empirical findings in the companion volume to this work.

Conclusion and summary

Regional (or geographic) approaches depend completely on locating a naturally occurring appropriate array of linguistic and cultural combinations – which may be no simple task. No well-developed version of this approach has ever been implemented successfully. If the proper conditions were found, the approach would offer the advantage of providing relatively precise control over nonlinguistic cultural variables.

Typological approaches, by applying principles developed from cross-linguistic studies of phonological and syntactic structures to the arena of structures of meaning, offer an alternative method of achieving some control over the characterization of the nature of linguistic variability. From one point of view, by drawing on a much larger pool of languages, such studies can be more readily undertaken than can regional approaches. However, despite the great control they offer over linguistic variables, they present considerable difficulties on the nonlinguistic side given the tremendous range of associated cultural patterns which must be considered. To some extent the use of selected cases studied in some detail can mitigate these difficulties.

The majority of studies using the typological approach to date have been concerned with the cognitive implications of typological regularities or "universals." It should be possible to reverse this emphasis and use typological data as a framework for studying the significance of differences. Under this approach, a pattern of commonality across languages serves to insure that a common domain is involved across the diverse languages; variation in the pattern indicates differing possible linguistic codings of the common semantic/cognitive domain. The question is whether the differing linguistic codings bear any relationship to thought.

Diversity in the cultural uses of language

Whorf assumed that language was essentially referential in nature, that is, that it primarily fulfilled a referential function. Further, he assumed that all languages had more or less the same effects on, or functional relation to, habitual thought. At times he is explicit about this:

We [have seen] . . . that, in linguistic and mental phenomena, significant behavior (or what is the same, both behavior and significance, so far as interlinked) are ruled by a specific system or organization, a "geometry" of form principles characteristic of each language. This organization is imposed from outside the narrow circle of the personal consciousness, making of that consciousness a mere puppet whose linguistic maneuverings are held in unsensed and unbreakable bonds of pattern . . .

And now appears a great fact of human brotherhood – that human beings are all alike in this respect. So far as we can judge from the systematics of language, the higher mind or "unconscious" of a Papuan headhunter can mathematize quite as well as that of Einstein; and conversely, scientist and yokel, scholar and tribesman, all use their personal consciousness in the same dim-witted sort of way, and get into similar kinds of logical impasse.   (1956a, p. 257)

In these assumptions, Whorf did not differ significantly from his contemporaries in Boas's circle. Typically, when Whorf wrote about "cultural" influences on language, he was vague about the mechanism of cultural influences on language structure and assigned such influences a secondary status. He did not indicate that the processes of interaction themselves might be variable.

Only once did he explicitly suggest that the functional relationship between language and thought might itself be shaped by or contingent upon specific cultural or linguistic configurations.[18] In one of his last essays he wrote:

All this is typical of the way the lower personal mind, caught in a vaster world inscrutable to its methods, uses its strange gift of language to weave a web of . . . illusion, to make a provisional analysis of reality and then regard it as final. *Western culture has gone farthest here, farthest in determined thoroughness of provisional analysis, and farthest in determination to regard it as final.*

(1956a, p. 263, my italics; cf. p. 244)

This sense that there may be something different about the use of language in the West, or at least about the relation among language, ideology, and reality in the West, has received very little attention (but see Rumsey, 1990; Friedrich, 1990, and references therein). Such a claim would radically contextualize Whorf's own argument (see Lucy, 1985a).

In this section we review developments within anthropological linguistics which suggest that differences in the use of language are indeed a problem. The problem can be thought of from two points of view: quantitative, whether a language category is actively used in thought, and qualitative, how a language category is used in thought.

The quantitative dimension: active use of categories

Hoijer emphasized that understanding the use of the structural–semantic patterns of a language must be an important factor in the analysis of their effects.[19] Mere presence or absence of a specific grammatical category alone is not a sufficient basis for inferring a possible influence on thought. To be relevant for habitual thought, the language patterns at issue should be in active use:

every language includes a number of active structural–semantic categories, lexical and grammatical, which by virtue of their active status serve a function in the everyday (nonscientific) analysis and categorizing of experience. It is the study of these categories, distinctive when taken as a whole for each language, that yields, or may yield, significant information concerning the thought world of the speakers of the language.

One further point requires emphasis. Neither Sapir nor Whorf attempted to draw inferences as to the thought world of a people simply from the fact of the presence or absence of specific grammatical categories (e.g., tense, gender, number) in a given language.   (Hoijer, 1954, p. 98)

Hoijer followed with a citation of Whorf's remarks on "fashions of speaking." While all this is present in Whorf's writings, Hoijer made the argument somewhat more directly and clearly, probably because of the attempts by others to suggest tests for Whorf's ideas that hinged on the presence or absence of this or that particular lexeme or grammatical fact. Hoijer argued essentially that for the study of linguistic relativity the focus should be on linguistic patterns in active or frequent use so as to guarantee their *cognitive* (or cultural) *salience*.

This concern re-emerged, in slightly different form, some years later in Hymes's work, where he tried to indicate the cognitive salience of a linguistic pattern by reference to its relationship to recent historical change. In his paper "On typology of cognitive styles" (1961b), he developed an example from the Chinookan language family spoken aboriginally in the Columbia River Basin area of North America. He noted that one set of dialects (Wishram and Wasco) contain a set of initial tense–aspect prefixes and case-like postpositions not shared by the other dialects (1961b, p. 39).[20] Distinctions are made within both sets which seem to indicate direction between or a relation of motion between two terminals or poles. Hymes speculated that both of these patterns emerged quite recently in the dialects (within the last few hundred years or, more probably, the last few generations). He discussed other patterns in the language which also characterize phenomena in terms of polar oppositions: a pattern in kinship terminology, derivation of verb themes (especially those for mental activity) from simple verb stems, derivation of nouns from verbs, and a diminutive–augmentative contrast[21] for some lexical items. Several of these additional patterns show evidence of active use within recent historical periods in the incorporation of loan words into the dialects (1961b, pp. 39–40).

Hymes saw a common cognitive orientation underlying these patterns, and took the facts of recent innovation into the language and of current productivity as signs of an active cognitive style in the dialects:

In sum, a number of different developments in Wishram and Wasco Chinook seem to exhibit a preference for expressing relationships between two terminals. The exposition has been cursory, and lacks the methodological safeguards of seeking contrary explanations and negative instances, and of detailed contrast with other cases. But since the material is part of the recent changes in the language, there is prima facie evidence that something real and significant is being dealt with. Recent changes in the development of a language may be diagnostic of the presence of cognitive orientations. When several changes exhibit a similar orientation, it seems justifiable to speak of the presence of a cognitive style.

There are cultural analogues of the linguistic style, but to discuss these would divert attention to the problems of determinism, causality, prediction of behavior and the like. For the present, I want simply to argue that the analysis of the recent semantic drift of languages may be the fruitful way of amassing relevant cases of a preliminary typology of linguistic cognitive styles. (1961b, pp. 40–41)

Thus, for his notion of "cognitive style" Hymes emphasized the importance of demonstrating the *contemporary productivity* of a pattern. This differed somewhat from Hoijer's concern with active or frequent use of a pattern, but remained fundamentally a concern with demonstrating the *cognitive* (or cultural) *salience* of a given linguistic pattern.

The qualitative dimension: differing use of categories

There is another, more qualitative, dimension to the problem of usage, namely how languages, or language categories, can be used differently in thought. There has been little direct work on this issue within anthropological linguistics. The most relevant material concerns variations in the *cultural uses* of language. Although this work is cast in terms of differences in cultural use, rather than more specifically cognitive use, it grapples with the essential problem, namely that diverse cultural groups in fact use languages in distinctive ways and that this fact poses a problem for the comparison of structural effects of the type proposed by Whorf. We may then distinguish this as a concern with *functional relativity*, relativity based on the different uses of language, as opposed to Whorf's concern with *structural relativity*, relativity based on the different grammatical patterns of language.

In line with the Boasian interest in stressing the common functional value of the world's languages, despite their structural diversity, Whorf's arguments tended to take as an assumption that various languages were related to and influenced their associated cultures in much the same way everywhere. Beginning in the early 1960s and continuing to the present there has been an increasing interest in the "ethnography of speaking" (or "ethnography of communication") as a focal problem in anthropological linguistic studies (Hymes, 1962; Gumperz and Hymes, 1964; Gumperz and Hymes, 1972; Bauman and Sherzer, 1974). The focus in these studies is on the diversity of the uses of language in various cultures.

In a seminal paper Hymes (1966 [1964]) articulated the relevance of this orientation to the linguistic relativity issue. He began by elaborating the contrast of his position and Whorf's:

LINGUISTIC RELATIVITY is a notion associated, via Whorf (1940), with the structure of language. To my knowledge, Whorf first proposed the term, using it to call attention to differences in linguistic structure, and to their importance for experience and behavior. Less studied, but I think, theoretically prior, is a relativity that has to do with the use of language. The notion of a second type of linguistic relativity calls attention to differences in cultural pattern, and to their importance for linguistic experience and behavior.

The first kind of linguistic relativity is associated with inference from linguistic data to other aspects of culture. I propose to show that the second kind can be associated with inference from ethnographic data to functions of language.
(1966 [1964], p. 114)

The essential contrast is clearly drawn: Whorf is concerned with the implications of "differences in linguistic structure" for "experience and behavior" (language structure → culture), and Hymes is interested in "differences in cultural pattern" for "the use of language" (culture → language use). Hymes places this shift of emphasis in historical perspective and lays out the range of possible interactions of structure and use, uniformity and diversity, both within and across cultural patterns.

This reversal of interest affects the validity of Whorf's approach. Hymes went on to clarify the connection:

As linked to the Weltanschauung interest, the emphasis [in Boasian linguistics] upon structural diversity had to assume functional uniformity. The very contrasts drawn in structure between, say, Hopi and English, presupposed for their cognitive and behavioral significance that the paired languages each played much the same role in the respective cultures. THE INFERENCE OF DIFFERENTIAL EFFECT ON WORLD VIEW ASSUMED EQUIVALENT ROLE IN SHAPING WORLD VIEW . . .
Here lies the crux of the relationship between the two types of linguistic relativity. What if two languages do not have equivalent roles? It is the contention of this paper that the role of language may differ from community to community; that in general the functions of language in society are a problem for investigation, not postulation . . . If this is so, then the cognitive significance of a language depends not only on structure, but also on patterns of use.
. . . My contention is that people who enact different cultures do to some extent experience distinct communicative systems, not merely the same natural communicative condition with different customs affixed. Cultural values and beliefs are in part constitutive of linguistic reality.   (1966 [1964], p. 116)

Thus, because the cultural shaping of the use of language alters the potential for the structural patterns to connect with thought, it ultimately frames, or relativizes, Whorf's question as being dependent on the existence of certain functional interrelations of language and thought.

It is important to realize, however, that Hymes was not asserting that the structural effects suggested by Whorf do not in fact exist. He was asserting, as a both logical and empirical problem, that the findings depend on establishing some prior commonalities of use. It is possible that usage varies so significantly that no claims for structural relativity, as such, can be independently established. It is also possible that sufficient commonality of usage exists between certain languages (Hopi and English might or might not qualify) such that structural effects can be reasonably assessed. It is also possible that there is sufficient commonality of use (at least from a cognitive perspective) in all languages to assure some general language structure and thought interactions everywhere. The best candidate in this latter case would no doubt be a claim (or argument) that the universality of the referential function minimally assures such interaction. (This is one implication of some of Silverstein's 1979, 1981b, work on awareness reviewed below.) But Hymes's point was that, to an important degree, it is an empirical problem which of these possibilities obtains and one that has not yet been adequately investigated.

Hymes continued (1966 [1964], pp. 116–23) with a more complete discussion of the problem of the various ways to fuse these two relativities into a single theory. He focused on establishing three steps (or levels) in which research on the linguistic relativity issue should be handled. First, there is the description (or depiction) of the language and the culture as exhibiting a distinctive pattern. This does not entail taking positions on significance (other than the generic assumption that some significance exists), on the degree of similarity (if any) between the patterns, or on the direction of dependence (if any). Hymes emphasized that this step really amounts to little more than standard linguistic and ethnographic practice and that it is not especially controversial. (This is hardly the case, as will be made clear in a moment.) He also felt that relativity of use is not really at issue at this step. It would seem, however, that a description of patterns of use should necessarily be included in the description of each language so as to be able to entertain questions about relativity of use.

Second, there is the assignment of a specific place to the linguistic traits or patterns, an assessment of their fit with the rest of culture. This specifically raises the question of the functional role or place of language in the culture:

The place assigned may be among any and all aspects of culture and social life: conscious or unconscious metaphysics, values, aesthetics, enculturation, productive activities, type or stage of culture, thought, behavior; or, the place may be one of effective autonomy. Whatever the case, assignment, though it may be implicit, is unavoidable. To take what is depicted linguistically as isolated from other aspects of culture is still to assign it a place within culture as a whole.

(1966 [1964], p. 118)

Hymes's last point is especially important, that is, that any account must place language *somewhere* with respect to the broader culture. It is this fact which makes his separation of these first two steps so problematic. The notion that language and culture can be given autonomous descriptions without a consideration of their functional relationship to each other privileges one conceptualization of the relationship. Hymes wants to stress that any given descriptive account is compatible with a variety of functional connections; but ultimately, his own argument makes this questionable. An adequate description would have to take account of such functional relationships in the very formulation of the structural description.[22]

Hymes tended to characterize the possible functional differences in terms of differential distribution and hierarchical relationship among a more or less constant set of functions:

Given a view of language that recognizes that it serves a number of functions, whose hierarchy may vary from case to case, it is not surprising to find one language serving predominantly aesthetic roles, and another language serving predominantly cognitive needs, or to find different aspects of the same language serving each.
. . . Scholars . . . have argued that the total range of conceptual functions served by a language may be generally the same . . . and that the differences among languages consist in the fact that the hierarchy and mode of implementation of such functions is not universally the same . . . So also for the total range of communicative functions served in a community. The range may be generally the same (types of function being universal), but the hierarchy and mode of implementation is not universally the same.[23] What is a matter of one sector for one language may be a matter of another sector for another language; what is a matter of one language for one community may be a matter of another language for another community – even though the same language may be found in both. Further, language is but one semiotic system among others, and what is a matter of language for one community may be a matter of gesture, plastic art, ritual, for another . . . In particular, metaphysical intuitions and assumptions may or may not be expressed in a language, depending upon the role the language plays in the community.   (1966 [1964], p. 122)

The place of genuinely culture-specific functions remains somewhat vague here, although in principle they can be incorporated into such a framework.

Hymes's third step concerns explanation, that is, the interpretation of "the nature and direction of dependence" between language and the rest of culture. The goal is

to interpret or explain the relationship between the data depicted (step 1) and the cultural place and fit found for them (step 2), as due to a particular kind of dependence between the two.   (1966 [1964], p. 120)

Hymes indicates that there are a number of dimensions on which an explanation in terms of dependence can be, and has been, further subdivided. He extracts four basic standpoints that may be taken as to the ways in which (or directions by which) influence can move between language and the rest of culture:

(1) language as the primary (source, cause, factor, independent variable, etc.);
(2) the rest of culture as primary;
(3) neither as primary, the two being seen as jointly determining;
(4) neither as primary, the two being seen as determined by an underlying factor (such as world-view, *Volksgeist*, national character, etc.).

(1966 [1964], p. 120)

These four standpoints can then be applied in two ways – following Whorf – to the development of culture and to the development of individuals:

The Whorfian hypothesis comprises, not one, but two sets of relationships between language and that which language may determine. One set concerns the development of a culture, and another set concerns the development of an individual. In other words, there are both culture-historical (phylogenetic) and life-historical (ontogenetic) dimensions and the standpoint taken on one dimension can be independent of the standpoint taken on the other.

(1966 [1964], p. 120)

Hymes then discusses the placement of some of the traditional treatments of the problem within this grid of possibilities.[24] He further notes that the same set of distinctions as to degree and shape of linguistic determinism apply whether one is concerned with linguistic diversity (hence relativity) or linguistic uniformity (hence universals).

Hymes himself felt that the relativity of use pointed most clearly toward the importance of culture as a determinant of language ([2] in the schema). However, he concluded that all the four types of directional influences are possible and that only a theory which embraces this fact will prove adequate:

the cultural structuring of the use of language may be seen as generally controlling [from above] the role of language structure (standpoint 2); but the content of language may condition use [from below], and on occasion decisively (standpoint 1) ... Sometimes it will be desirable to recognize language use and cultural patterns as both controlled by an underlying factor ... (standpoint 4); and on some occasions, no useful purpose will be served by recognizing other than an interdependence (standpoint 3). In sum, with use, as with structure, a monolithic position is not tenable; an adequate theory must coordinate several standpoints.   (1966 [1964], p. 123)

Hymes did not explicitly argue for a theoretical ordering of importance (or priority) among these dimensions, nor does he suggest in what sequence they should be investigated.

In discussing the direction of influence, especially how to assign weight

to the relativities of structure versus use, Hymes placed considerable
emphasis on the process of cultural transmission as the locus of effects.
Thus, the age at which various aspects of the culture are encountered or
acquired is very important:

the direction of the dependence between a language and an aspect of culture may
vary with the age at which linguistic competence is achieved in regard to the
aspect of culture; or, if the aspect of culture is not transmitted primarily
linguistically, the relation between the age of general linguistic competence and
that at which the aspect of culture is experienced. Different sectors of culture are
in general differentially involved with language, verbal art vs hunting, for
example; the degree to which language enters into socialization, ritual, etc. varies
crossculturally [*sic*]; beliefs, values, and practices as to communication with
infants and children vary; the scheduling of use of language varies in terms of
setting and occasions for communication; etc. All the empirical conditions which
govern whatever opportunity language has to play a role with regard to an aspect
of culture may be found to vary cross-culturally. Explanation of the connection
between linguistic pattern and the rest of culture cannot be abstracted from its
ethnographic, sociolinguistic base.   (1966 [1964], pp. 122–23)

Given the continuous, multidimensional nature of enculturation, the
practical problem of isolating an "aspect of culture" and the time of its
acquisition by the child is no small task. Hymes also seemed to feel that a
linguistic structure would have an influence only if explicitly employed in
a certain functional way. When we consider habitual thought, as Whorf
did, such assumptions do not seem especially crucial. Nonetheless,
Hymes pointed to an important problem, namely that the concrete locus
of psychological effects is in the individual, and it is at this level that
questions of causal mechanism and direction must be addressed if they
are to be addressed at all.

The remainder of Hymes's discussion of the relativity of use consisted
of three empirical examples showing the relation of cultural values to the
place and use of language. The first example discusses the differential
valuation and use of languages in situations of bilingualism and accultur-
ation. Hymes showed how the retention of native languages in situations
of language contact relates to the function of languages as markers of
group boundaries and group pride. The second example explored the
differences between two historically related language groups in the way
they use language to explicate culture. One group makes more complex
(i.e., more inventive, rational, and systematic) use of their linguistic
resources in the construction of cultural ideologies; the other uses its
linguistic resources more simply, and shows a corresponding freedom
from or indifference to elaborate secondary interpretations of cultural
life. The third example consisted of an extended analysis of the patterns
of language use among Wishram Chinook culture. Hymes described a
general valuation of the discursive use of language, showed how certain

speech events are constituted as formal discursive uses of language, and showed that across several domains of such discursive uses (disclosure of spirit visions, conferring of personal names, and narration of myths) there exists a common pattern that a speaker should disclose only what he is sure of ("disclosure depends on certainty"). This corresponds to what Hymes called a "perfective" attitude in the grammar, namely patterns of using verbal aspects forms such as the perfect or imperfect and using certain future verb forms only if the reported event could be presumed to be nearly certain.

These examples successfully illustrate some of the dimensions one would want to consider in studying the significance of language use. They also serve to illustrate various axes of analysis such as cross-linguistic comparison, use of "genetically" related languages, and intra-cultural comparison. Ultimately, however, the examples stand as ethnographic accounts of cultural *attitudes* toward language use and do not indicate how such differences might then feed back to influence culture. Further, Hymes did not demonstrate the individual psychological significance of these patterns. And in each case he must rely on broad ethnographic characterizations of the correlates of the linguistic facts, most gathered without explicit reference to the hypothesis at issue. Hymes was aware of these problems (see, for instance, 1966 [1964], pp. 157, 165), but could not address them; in this respect, that is, from an operative point of view, he remained close to the anthropological linguistics norm of lingua-centrism.

In overview, Hymes's various distinctions clarify some important dimensions of the linguistic relativity problem which traditional approaches ignored for one reason or another. Ultimately, however, Hymes lacks a specific theory of the interrelation of language with thought, whether at the level of the individual or of the cultural group. He did claim that questions of functional relativity must be addressed before those of structural relativity and, somewhat less strongly, that attention to the development of the individual represents the sphere in which many of these questions can best be explored. But these are very global suggestions. Thus, despite his considerable contribution to the correct articulation or categorization of the problems in this area of research, he contributed relatively less to its solution. This weakness shows up in his remark at one point that there is, in his view, simply too much variability to allow for a general account. This perspective seems to stem from inadequately pursuing two themes: first, whether there is some general role of language in culture which could serve to ground a comparative theory of cultural functions even if not all functions can be so encompassed, and second, whether there is any general role of language in thought which could serve to ground a comparative theory of cognitive functions, again, even if not all functions can be so encompassed. Both of these problems are briefly raised by Whorf and considerably clarified by Hymes, and yet are not satisfactorily resolved. Hymes moves us closer to a contextualized account of the language and thought problem, but as yet he has no theory about the continuities of context that would make comparative research possible. Theoretically, a unified conception of these dimensions is necessary; empirically, a typology of cultural and cognitive functions must be built.

Several other lines of research are relevant to exploring a possible relativity of use (or function), although this work will not be reviewed in detail here. One line has emerged from the study of subcultural differences in language use. Most of this work draws its inspiration from Vygotsky's (1978 [1930–34]; 1987 [1934]) argument that the social institution of formal education, conceived of as a specialized verbal practice, plays a central role in moving a child (and, ultimately, the society) from spontaneous to higher forms of thought. Within sociology, Bernstein (1971) and others have argued that the various social classes in Western society use language differently and that this difference has effects on educational success. It remains unclear whether and to what extent these differences stem from actual cognitive effects of the linguistic practices or from social prejudices of other types (cf. Bourdieu, 1984; Bourdieu and Passeron, 1977; also Labov, 1975). Similar arguments and disputes have developed with regard to literacy (see, for instance, Cole and Scribner, 1981; Goody and Watt, 1968) and technical-bureaucratic language (see, for example, Havránek, 1964). Most of this growing body of research has not been linked theoretically to the linguistic relativity issue or empirically to serious cognitive assessment. For programmatic statements regarding the linkage and its relevance to cognition, see Bernstein (1971, esp. ch. 7), Hymes (1980), Lucy (1985a,b; 1989), Lucy and Wertsch (1987), and chapter 7 below.

A second line of research pertinent to the relativity of use has arisen regarding the implications of adopting one or another language as an official state language. If one regional or ethnic language is adopted, speakers of other languages often feel their culture has been slighted or jeopardized. (For a recent review and case study, see Woolard, 1989.) Similar, but somewhat more dramatic concerns arise when non-European countries consider adopting a European language as a national language. Use of a European language is often seen as advantageous because it is useful in international affairs, neutral relative to the languages of competing regional and ethnic groups, and well developed in terms of having a script, a technical-bureaucratic vocabulary, etc. Offsetting such advantages are concerns about importing an alien, colonial European worldview – conceptual, stylistic, or both. Most of this research on establishing a national language is only of indirect interest here because it has not been related to the linguistic relativity hypothesis, let alone been used to test or investigate it in any serious way. Laitin (1977) provides the most complete discussion of the possibility of linking such research on the adoption of a national language with concerns about linguistic relativity. His own empirical research in the Somali Republic indicates that bilingual speakers differ in their expressions of identity, relations to authority, bargaining style, and invocation of religious values as a function of whether they are responding in English or Somali to the tasks he poses. Note that the structural characteristics of the two languages play virtually no role in his argument – his is a claim about the significance of the use of a particular code for other patterns of verbal interaction. Alisjahbana (1986) reviews the Indonesian experience in creating a national language from Malay, emphasizing the necessary transformations in both conceptual structure (i.e., addition of new vocabulary) and patterns of use.

A third line of research relevant to patterns of use focuses on literary language. Among many others, Sapir (1949e [1921], ch. 11) argued that certain literary works were more difficult to translate because they depend heavily on the specific genius of the language. Friedrich (1986) has recently developed this view further in a synthesis of the linguistic relativism issue with the concerns of general poetics. He argues that individual imagination (the ability to integrate experience) is massively influenced by the poetic potential of language – rather than by its logic or basic patterns of reference: "Poetic language . . . is the locus of the most interesting differences between languages and should be the focus of the study of such differences" (1986, p. 17). When Friedrich invokes the poetic potential of language, he follows Jakobson (1960) in regarding all natural language use as having a poetic dimension, a dimension which is functionally foregrounded in "poetry" in the narrower sense. Thus, the impact of the relativism he proposes is meant to be general and yet, also, to be especially potent in explicitly poetic uses. It is important to note that Friedrich does not believe his assertion of the primacy of poetic effects is provable; thus his work begs the issue at stake in the present discussion, namely how the relativity issue can be empirically evaluated. However, Friedrich's approach does suggest the importance of focusing on the poetic function of language in future work.

These three bodies of research on various uses or functions of language suggest how fruitful it would be to attend more seriously to the whole range of functions in language. And the need for an improved treatment of the usage question will emerge again in the review of the psycho-linguistic tradition undertaken in the next two chapters. But an adequate theory in this area will require a systematic investigation and typologizing of the varieties of language use with an eye toward their cognitive significance. Such a systematic investigation has yet to be undertaken, hence the present review and the research in *Grammatical categories and cognition* remain focused on structural differences in everyday patterns of reference.

The reflexive dimension: cultural origins of the linguistic relativity hypothesis

A final dimension of this problem deserves explicit mention, although it will not be developed here. We noted at the outset of this section that Whorf was sensitive to the extreme interest the West has taken in using its languages as final guides to reality. In this respect, Whorf's concerns with the impact of language forms upon thought are especially relevant to our own society. His claims constitute the natural, polar opposite of the widespread belief that language is a faithful map of reality and can be relied upon as a sure guide to it. It takes our culturally specific language forms as reflecting universals of human thought. Whorf called this assumption of universality into question. But in calling it into question, he tended to universalize his own insights. That is, he frequently assumed that all people everywhere use their languages (in particular, use them to guide thought) in the same ways that we do. This is not a necessary assumption (as he himself seems to sense at times), and is the ultimate point of Hymes's argument.

Recognizing this situation, we can ask about the origin of this view of language in our own cultural history. Although Hymes noted some of the dimensions along which there have been shifts in the view of language and thought relations (1966 [1964], pp. 114–16), he did not explore the reasons for the shifts. What is required here is a detailed history of the uses and understandings of language in the European tradition, one which traces the connections between such shifts and broader social patterns. Such a study would provide the ground for understanding the salience and significance of the linguistic relativity problem as Whorf described it as our problem – the generality of which for others has yet to be established. A somewhat longer, though still preliminary, development of this argument is given in Lucy (1985a). Friedrich (1986, ch. 2) sketches the history of the more general tension between determinism and indeterminacy in Western philosophical thought about language. Haugen's (1977) contrast of a tension between rationalism (favoring universalism) and romanticism (favoring relativism) in European (especially German) thought could also be developed in this direction (cf. Shweder, 1984).

Susceptibility to awareness of language structure and function

Boas, Sapir and Whorf all argued that speakers typically use linguistic categories without conscious awareness of them. Sapir and Whorf emphasized in addition that speakers lack awareness of the influence of their language on their thought. However, as we have seen, there was no well-developed argument for the uniqueness of language in this regard as opposed to other highly automatic, background behaviors. However, Whorf's work suggested that there are regularities in the way speakers apprehend language categories.

Whorf's insights and suggestions were not seriously explored subsequently within this tradition until the mid 1970s in a series of papers by Michael Silverstein (1976b; 1979; 1981b; 1985b). Silverstein was interested in accounting for the relationship between native speaker awareness of language and the actual use of language. He argued that the ease or difficulty speakers had in becoming "aware" of various aspects of their language seems to depend on certain general semiotic properties of the actual form and function of the language signs in question. Silverstein specifically tied his argument to Whorf's work and suggested that this differential susceptibility to awareness could help provide a principled basis for an account of the interrelation of linguistic structure, function, and ideology.

Silverstein's project and terminology

Silverstein's (1976b) general project is to provide a comprehensive social anthropology of linguistic use, that is, to provide an account of speech as meaningful social behavior. In the service of this project, he has introduced a series of terms which need to be explicated before turning to his specific arguments about awareness. His approach centers on those elements of speech, *indices* or *shifters*, whose meaning "always involves some aspect of the context in which the sign occurs" (1976b, p. 11). Examples of common shifters in English include the personal pronouns and indications of verbal tense. Computation of the referential value of these forms always depends on having knowledge of the specific context of utterance. To give an account of the relation of speech signs to contexts more generally, that is, to state regularities of contextualized use and to see speech as effective action in specifiable cultural contexts, is to give a *pragmatic* analysis of speech behavior. Such an approach contrasts with accounts of language completely in terms of decontextualized referential meaning, that is, in terms of the *semantic* dimension of language.[25] Notice that Silverstein defines semantics somewhat more narrowly than most linguists. He is able to do this, in part, precisely because he recognizes other kinds of meaning and does not need, therefore, to assimilate all meaning into a single category of semantics. In principle, semantics represents an asymptote of pragmatics, where the relevant features of the nonlinguistic (non-"code") context to which the sign must relate are reduced to a minimum and the linguistic code itself (its grammatical and stereotypic meaning values) become the only operative context.

One of Silverstein's principal aims is to elucidate the ways in which actors' partial awareness of and ideology about the structure of action ultimately shapes and is shaped by action itself (Silverstein, 1979). In particular, he is concerned with the systematic relationship between a speaker's understanding of the nature and uses of speech and the actual structure of speech as revealed by "scientifically" grounded formal-functional analyses:

I should clarify that ideologies about language, or linguistic ideologies, are any sets of beliefs about language articulated by the users as a rationalization or justification of perceived language structure and use . . .
    . . . I want to develop here some aspects of the subject that will, I hope, show the relationship between ideology and structure in the realm of language to be much the same as in any other realm of social life, a phenomenon of no little significance for the practice of linguistics.   (1979, p. 193)

In doing this he hopes to "generalize Whorf's penetrating insights from the plane of reference to the whole of language function" (1979, p. 194).

As a referential medium, speech can refer to any aspect of experience and, therefore, unlike other forms of social action, it includes the possibility of reference to itself. Speech can serve as its own *meta-language*. Such self-reflexive speech events provide crucial evidence about native speakers' understandings of speech. Speech events about the semantics of language are termed *metasemantic* referential speech events (for example, glosses of the meaning of a lexical item in terms of other, complex phrasal forms in the language); speech events about the pragmatics of language are termed *metapragmatic* referential speech events (for instance, explanations of when and how to use a certain form). Metasemantics is a particular kind (a special case) of metapragmatics, that is, speech about the meaning value of speech when the only context taken into account for use-specification is the code itself (i.e., in this sense, the "decontextualized" semantico-referential dimension of speech). This reflexive power of language is not perfect, however, and not all aspects of language form and functioning are susceptible to native description with equal ease. One part of Silverstein's concern with the relation of ideology to structure is cast, then, in the form of an investigation of the limits of (meta) linguistic awareness and the role such limits place on the cultural constitution of speech events (see Silverstein, 1992; Lucy, 1992).

The limits of awareness

Silverstein characterizes his claim as follows:

> the point I wish to make is that it is extremely difficult, if not impossible, to make a native speaker take account of those readily-discernible facts of speech as action that he has no ability to describe for us in his own language.
> (1981b, p. 1)

So speakers cannot accurately take account of some aspect of speech as social action unless they can describe the relevant aspect in their own language. Their ability to describe those facts is, however, bounded by the limits of speakers' metapragmatic capabilities. Silverstein formulates the following general hypothesis about these limits:

> For the native speaker, the ease or difficulty of accurate metapragmatic characterization of the use of the forms of his own language seems to depend on certain general semiotic properties of the use in question. That is, the basic evidence we have for awareness of the pragmatic dimension of language use, susceptibility to conscious native testimony, is universally bounded by certain characteristics of the form and contextually dependent function of the pragmatic markers in speech . . . we will be interested in seeing why native speakers are able or unable to characterize the contextual appropriateness of speech, and to manipulate it for the investigator. (1981b, p. 2)

His claim is, therefore, that the ease and accuracy with which speakers can characterise language pragmatics, as indexed by susceptibility to conscious native testimony, is bounded in certain predictable ways.

Silverstein's more specific hypotheses as to the factors limiting characterizability (i.e., susceptibility of a signal to conscious native testimony) center on the formal and functional properties of the descriptive signal and the described signal. Initially Silverstein identified three dimensions of linguistic signals which govern whether or not native speakers can accurately characterize them metalinguistically (1976b, pp. 49–50; see also pp. 29–36; elaborated more fully in 1981b). Silverstein later (1981b, 1985b) added two more relevant dimensions concerning how speakers treat the forms in metapragmatic discourse.[26]

The first three dimensions (as refined in Silverstein, 1981b) deal with those properties of the pragmatic signal to be described which govern how adequately they can be described. (1) Speakers can more readily become aware of and describe speech signals which have a high degree of *unavoidable referentiality*, that is, forms which, along with their pragmatic value, at the same time are segmentable as signs contributing to the speech function of referring (or describing). Signals which do not contribute to reference as part of their pragmatic value (for example, certain markers of regional or class affiliation signaled by pronunciation differences) are more difficult for speakers to describe correctly. (2) Speakers can more readily become aware of and describe speech signals which are *continuously segmentable*, that is, which form a coherent sequential unit in speech. Meanings conveyed by discontinuous forms (for instance, present progressive marking in English verbs) or nonsegmentable forms (for instance, modification of only some features of a typical phoneme bundle) are more difficult to describe correctly.[27] (3) Speakers can more readily become aware of and describe speech signals which are *relatively presuppositional*, that is, which are linked to independently verifiable contextual factors (for instance, the demonstratives *this* and *that* in English). Forms that are not so linked, that is, those that can bring the contextual factor into focus of interaction by the fact of their implementation (for example, using a familiar pronominal form in various European languages) are more difficult to describe correctly. (Dimensions (1) and (3) are closely related but distinct: unavoidable referentiality has to do with the signal's relation to reference without regard to the nature of the context of utterance; relative presupposition has to do with the signal's relation to context without regard to whether it is referential or not.) Any specific signal can be characterized on these dimensions so as to predict its susceptibility to accurate native speaker awareness – both in the sense of how readily it can be characterized and in the sense of how accurately it can be characterized.

The two additional dimensions (as introduced in Silverstein, 1981b) deal with exactly how native speakers are able to treat pragmatically effective forms in reflexive (metapragmatic) discourse. (4) *Decontextualized deducibility* concerns the speaker's greater ease in stating the decontextualized implications of an utterance containing the form at issue, that is, what the use of the form typically presupposes in context and, therefore, in the absence of any specific context, what its use will be taken in general to entail. In general, speakers are less likely, less able, to state the context-specific creative effects of an utterance as the meaning of a form, but rather describe it in terms of a propositional form the truth of which is entailed by the use of the form in question. (5) *Metapragmatic transparency* concerns the degree of formal similarity between any pragmatic form and the utterance used (metapragmatically) to describe the pragmatic value of that form. If the form of the describing utterance closely matches the form of the described utterance, then the described utterance is metapragmatically transparent. The degree of metapragmatic transparency characteristic of an utterance in contrast to other similar utterances can sometimes serve itself as a social index (for example, of perceived "indirectness" used in the signaling of "politeness"). Any specific description will be influenced by the extent to which its decontextualized implications are readily deducible and its form is metapragmatically transparent.

Application to the linguistic relativity issue

Silverstein's arguments are preliminary and still in the process of being developed. Further, the evidence in favor of them at present is largely anecdotal. However, those familiar with the realities of linguistic fieldwork should require little convincing that limitations exist in native speaker awareness of their own languages. And these analyses reveal that the reasons for and the ways in which linguistic categories are "out-of-awareness" should be one critical focus of research on the linguistic relativity problem.

Two general claims underlie Silverstein's arguments. First, the processes limiting or governing metapragmatic awareness are common across all languages. At this level they guarantee that natural language categories and functions will be, to a degree, "misapprehended" by native speakers whatever the language. Further, the directionality of misapprehension is systematic (Silverstein, 1979, pp. 100–103; 1981b, pp. 19–21). Silverstein argues that referential, segmentable, and presupposing forms are the most obvious to native speakers and that accurate accounts of them can be more readily given. Among the items maximizing these criteria are those lexical items which have clear referential value. So we can expect lexical items of this type to be the focus of naive accounts about language form and function. Silverstein observes that this is just the case in our own tradition:

Just as we would expect, our Western philosophical theories of language . . . have traditionally started from word reference, in particular from proper names, which native speakers feel to be concrete, pointing out an absolute reality "out there." Such theories have tried to generalize the notion of how language means from this maximally aware metapragmatic sensibility.   (1981b, p. 19)

One would expect this emphasis on word reference to be a common or universal element of naive understandings of language – although not necessarily always embedded within a formal philosophical tradition.

Second, the substantive outcome of such reflections will be skewed differently depending on what particular categories and functions happen to be favored in their susceptibility to awareness in a given language. Thus, the universal factors that limit susceptibility to awareness, by operating on differing linguistic structures and uses, will produce different patterns of substantive awareness (for example, different elements will appear in word form). This process can be illustrated by the attempts within our own intellectual tradition to understand the nonreferential functions of speech:

ordinary language philosophy with [the philosopher John L.] Austin ... discovered certain lexical items – segmental, referential, presupposing, deducible, maximally transparent forms – called "performatives," that seemed to be a key to the non-referential functions of one's own language. It is not by chance that these performatives, such as promise, christen, dub, etc. were discovered first by the linguistically naive native speakers of Oxford; they satisfy all our criteria. But unfortunately, accurate though they may be for certain of our more transparent speech functions in English, they cannot merely be treated as a universal set to be ferreted out by inaccurate translation techniques in the most remote corners of the globe ... Indeed, they represent only a tiny fraction of the functioning of our [own] language, though a fraction that is easily susceptible of native awareness. The further we get from these kinds of functional elements of language, the less we can guarantee awareness on the part of the native speakers.

(Silverstein, 1981b, pp. 19–20)[28]

Similar examples and arguments concerning the partiality of native understanding and the limitation of generalizing to other languages or to "reality" can be made for naive understanding of language categories. For example, Silverstein (1985a) provides an extended case study of the interaction of general cultural factors, native ideologies of speech, and general linguistic constraints to determine jointly certain patterns of gender marking in English. And Rumsey (1990) suggests that the Western conception of the relation between words and things is itself latent in the structure of English.

If we broaden the notion of awareness to include differences in salience (or intuitive awareness), then perhaps a related account of the directionality of analogical influence can also be given. Since languages differ as to what features of meaning are lexicalized, so too must the particular substantive (meaningful) elements susceptible to speaker awareness. Note here that an understanding of indexical (pragmatically based) signs can help clarify how two languages can have equivalent referential power without having identical categories (Jakobson, 1971a [1957]; Silverstein, 1976b). Languages differ in how they parcel out referential meaning into semantic and pragmatic categories:

A very large part of the Whorfian œuvre (1956[a]), in fact, can now be seen as a first attempt to draw out the Boasian implications of how pure referential (semantic) categories and duplex (referential–indexical) ones combine differently from language to language to accomplish ultimately isofunctional referential speech events. What one language accomplishes in utterances with a single referential index (for example, tense), another accomplishes with a combination of semantic category plus referential index (for example, aspect + status[29]).

(Silverstein, 1976b, p. 25)

This sets the stage for different analogical formations in the two languages. The argument can be extended to include giving interpretive priority to expressions with a one-to-one match of segmentable form with referential meaning. Recall here Whorf's example of the priority given to container + contents expressions in the interpretation of expressions referring to body-type + material and unanalyzed physical objects in English. In this case, however, the argument is for interpretive salience and not conscious awareness.

Silverstein's approach thus lays the groundwork for a more complete and adequate understanding of the relation between language and thought. However, a number of problems and ambiguities need to be resolved before the potential contribution can be realized. First, the implications of this argument for the relevance of language form and function to thought need to be drawn out in detail. Silverstein himself remains firmly within the general pattern of lingua-centrism character-istic of work in anthropological linguistics on this issue by trying to account (at least implicitly) for the cognitive impact of linguistic forms by reference to facts about languages – namely the extent to which they can adequately describe their own functioning. If these limitations are ultimately cognitive, then they need to be articulated as part of a coherent cognitive theory about the ways in which and degrees to which any phenomenon, including language as a special case, can be appre-hended, and, as well, how those limitations come into play as an influence on thought generally. If the limitations are specifically semio-tic, then the relevance to a general claim about cognition needs to be articulated. And if the limitations have to do with a specific interaction of the cognitive interpretation of speech-as-action via a reflective (meta-) level apprehension which itself involves speech, then it needs to be shown why this occurs and how it is unavoidable. In short, the discussion as it stands bypasses the issues of when and why language becomes involved in thought and, therefore, exactly how such "limits to awareness" operate to affect that involvement. Silverstein's focus throughout remains on an improved conceptualization of language and its functioning. When he takes up Whorf's concerns, he does so not so much in terms of differences in habitual thought so much as in differences in conscious construals of reality.

A related problem arises on the cultural side in that Silverstein focuses almost entirely on common (universal) processes limiting awareness and gives little consideration to possible cultural variation in the constitution of metalinguistic activity. He discusses the articulation of the factors limiting awareness with specific linguistic forms and the interrelation of these linguistic forms with cultural beliefs and practices, but he pays little attention to the ways in which and to what extent the very processes of apprehending language may themselves be shaped by specific cultural activity. When he has dealt with the possibility of cultural diversity in awareness, he has focused either on the cultural motivations for ideological reflection on language (Silverstein, 1985a) or on broad implications of certain sorts of attitudes toward language (Silverstein, 1979).

This universalizing orientation shows up in Silverstein's interpretation of Whorf's term "objectification." As we noted in chapter 2, Whorf used the term "objectification" to characterize a specific tendency in English as contrasted with Hopi, a tendency to treat imaginary entities as if they were perceptible concrete objects with all of their attributes. This culture-specific formulation becomes universalized in Silverstein's interpretation as a general principle of *objectification* (1979, pp. 201–203). Thus, what Whorf takes as a specific substantive pattern in English, Silverstein interprets (perhaps correctly) as a universal formal process valid for all languages. What is needed is a typology of attitudes toward language and modes of apprehending them which could yield both more detail on universal processes and some picture of important variations.

Further, Silverstein equates objectification with the term *referential projection* throughout his discussion. This latter term is apparently drawn from Whorf's (1956a, pp. 261–63) use of the term "project[ion]" (borrowed from psychology) to discuss the tendency to "see" or "find" in reality evidence supporting a given linguistic analysis – one which is patently erroneous. His point is to emphasize that a secondary, extraneous linguistic pattern can be so powerful that it will induce people to alter their very perception of reality. But these need not always involve "objectifications" in the sense of treating an imaginary entity like a tangible entity. To take one of Whorf's most vivid examples, the lexical combination *Coon cat* is analyzed by some speakers as a compound of *racoon* (abbreviated to *'coon*) and *cat*, rather than as a sort of cat introduced into New England by a certain Captain Coon, hence a *Coon cat*. Whorf's point is that local lexical meaning is dependent on grammatical pattern and that if speakers appropriate the wrong pattern, they will misapprehend reality. He elaborates:

In more subtle matters we all, unknowingly, project the linguistic relationships of a particular language upon the universe, and SEE them there, as the good lady SAW a linguistic relation (Coon = raccoon) made visible in her cat.

(Whorf, 1956a, p. 262)

In particular, a possessive form is misinterpreted during metapragmatic reflection as being an adjectival form and the adjectival form is then read into (is deduced as being present in) reality. This insight on Whorf's part is close to the argument Silverstein makes in his discussion. It is important, however, to separate the general linguistic process (refer-

ential projection or decontextualized deducibility) from the language-
(or culture-) specific illustration (objectification). An interesting question is the extent to which the two interact, that is, to what extent a strong
tendency toward "objectification" in a culture facilitates or amplifies the
universal tendency toward "[referential] projection" or to what extent
the most prevalent form of projection is, in fact, "objectification" –
which is what Silverstein seems to suggest.

A second general problem area concerns the proper application of the
concept of "awareness" to the linguistic relativity problem. Silverstein's
argument is that there are certain common (universal) processes limiting
metapragmatic awareness which, when applied to any given language,
will differentiate among the various signals of that language as to their
susceptibility to metapragmatic awareness. In his development of the
dimensions of awareness he deals almost entirely with the native's ability
consciously to focus on and to provide accurate metapragmatic characterization of the use of the forms of his own language. The basic
evidence for awareness of the pragmatic dimension of language use is
"susceptibility to conscious native testimony." By dealing primarily with
susceptibility to explicit awareness in his argument and evidence, Silverstein cannot really account in a principled way for the impact of
differential salience operating outside of these explicit instances or even,
for that matter, establish a definitive relationship between susceptibility
to testimony and actual awareness. In more recent work, Silverstein
(1986b; 1992) has begun to deal more substantively with the relative
explicitness versus implicitness of metalinguistic activity, but this work
has not yet been used to rethink the issue of intuitive or tacit awareness.

Whorf too dealt with awareness in several different senses. He refers
to speakers lacking conscious awareness of the influence of language on
thought, to speakers believing or having an ideology that language is only
a vehicle for thought, and to speakers finding various aspects of language
structure and meaning relatively more salient in their analogical formations. It seems reasonable that the degree of susceptibility to
conscious testimony should play some role in these different areas, but it
needs to be clearly articulated.[30]

A third problem emerges in Silverstein's discussion when he attempts
to link the phenomena of differential awareness and referential projection to Whorf's analysis of overt (cryptotypic) versus covert (phenotypic)
categories:[31]

[Whorf] invented the notion of a "cryptotypic," or, as we now say, "deep" or
"underlying" semantic structure that lies behind the overtly segmentable forms
of speech. This cryptotypic structure of referential categories constituted the real
'rational' classification of the sensory modalities implemented in fully propositional speech, the highest function of language to the Boasian way of thinking

... But, the native speaker ... is hopelessly at the mercy of so-called "pheno-typic," or as we now say "surface" lexicalized forms of the language. The native speaker tends to reason from the misleading surface analogies of forms to which, in piecemeal fashion, he attributes true referential effect in segmenting the cultural universe.   (1981b, pp. 18–19)

There can be little question that Whorf is concerned with misleading analogies drawn from the surface forms of language. But, as we have seen, covert categories always operate in tandem with overt categories to jointly produce meaning (or an "underlying semantic interpretation" in Chomsky's, 1965, p. 16, sense), so it is somewhat misleading to equate cryptotypic categories with underlying semantic structure and pheno-typic categories with surface structure.[32] And, although covert categories tend to be more "rational," they still represent a source of misleading influence on thought from the point of view of another language. Finally, recall that the covert/overt distinction is not invoked at all in Whorf's later (post-1938) writings on the relation of language and thought.[33]

The central question is the extent to which Whorf's argument about analogical influences hinges, albeit implicitly, on the covert/overt distinc-tion. The distinction can be most readily applied to his "habitual thought" paper (1956a, pp. 134–59), where equivalent formal "surface" representations appear to have different "underlying" semantic inter-pretations. Whorf does not try to show that the two interpretations which have been merged in surface representation are in fact distinguishable by reference to a covert category revealed by syntactic test. Rather, they are shown to be distinct by reference to a second language. His emphasis is on how two aspects of *experienced reality* are lumped together, not on how distinct covert linguistic categories are lumped together.[34] Nor does his argument hinge on something about one of the patterns being overt and the other covert.

The overt/covert distinction can also perhaps be applied to some of Whorf's later examples (for instance 1956a, pp. 258–63), which, in fact, more closely approximate cases of relative speaker awareness of and testimony about certain linguistic elements as opposed to others. In these examples Whorf tried to show that the referential value of a given lexeme depends for its interpretation on the particular grammatical pattern into which it is put and that a lexical unit can be quite differently interpreted depending on the interpretation of the grammatical frame, as in the *Coon cat* example mentioned above. The examples do not show, and are not designed to show, that overt categories as a group override covert categories as a group in speaker awareness or interpretation. Rather they show the importance of which covert category is selected to interpret an overt category.

Interestingly, Silverstein's summary of Whorf's argument in terms of the dimensions of awareness he has explicated also does not need to make any explicit appeal to the overt/covert distinction:

> [Whorf] claims that insofar as reference is concerned, the native's awareness is focussed on continuously-segmentable ("lexical" in his terms) units, which presuppose the existence of things "out there" that correspond to these units one-to-one on each referential use of speech. Of course, the native is only partially correct, and is generally inaccurate in his "awareness." (1981b, p. 19)

The overt/covert distinction, as a claim about ubiquity of formal representation, cross-cuts the question of the specific nature of the formal representation, that is, whether it is continuously segmentable or not. And both claims about formal representation cross-cut the issue of substantive analogical groupings. From this perspective, Silverstein's arguments should not be seen as a clarification of Whorf's ideas but rather as a further development of them.

Summary

It is important, in summary, to recall Silverstein's original goals. Silverstein is interested in accounting for the difference between the accounts of a language given by native speakers and those which could potentially be given by trained linguistics and, ultimately, in exploring the implications of such differences for language functioning, linguistic theory, and linguistic practice. He is interested in how the unique reflexive property of natural language plays a role in the functioning of speech as meaningful social action. Silverstein sees his work as drawing on, or inspired by, Whorf's in important ways:

> What we have done here is to generalize Whorf's observation [about the referential function of speech] for the whole range of functions of speech, reference being just one function that is clearly at the center of the whole ethno-linguistic system. We have claimed that we can best guarantee native speaker awareness for referential, segmental, presupposing functional forms in his language. And we can bound the kind of evidence the native speaker can give us in terms of deducible referential propositions about functional forms maximally transparent to description as speech events.   (1981b, p. 19)[35]

This accurately accounts for the significance of Whorf's work for Silverstein's project, but not vice versa.

Whorf, by contrast, emphasized the influence of linguistic patterns on interpretations of nonlinguistic reality. Silverstein's observations constitute the first real progress in accounting for two crucial components of the linguistic relativity problem: how it is that speakers can remain unaware of the importance of linguistic categories for thought and why it is that certain linguistic forms have greater salience than others in the operation of linguistic influences. For Silverstein's arguments to play a crucial role in an account of the relation of language and thought, however, there needs to be a more direct application of them to Whorf's specific project. This will necessitate spelling out the relationship of the limits of awareness to a general theory of cognitive and cultural functions, the development of a more refined conceptualization of the different types of "awareness" at issue including separating general processes from culturally (historically) specific ones.

General summary

The approaches described in this chapter grapple with important questions concerning the functioning of language and its cultural nature. First, they suggest techniques for incorporating multiple languages (and cultures) into a coherent framework for comparison. And some of the developments in this area also point toward the possibility of conceptualizing how linguistic categories are specifically "linguistic" in their structure and functioning. Second, they indicate that variation in the way languages are used in different speech communities comprises an important variable. Extending the concern with the social uses of language to the question of the uses of language in cognition, we can say that the extent to which linguistic classifications (the traditional focus of concern) can be expected to have effects on thought is necessarily contingent on the degree to which and manner in which those classifications are actually brought into play as a matter of cultural practice. And third, work reviewed here provides promising suggestions as to why the linguistic analysis of experience tends to remain out of awareness and how naive attempts to become conscious of language structure and function have predictable characteristics.

On the whole, work in the tradition reviewed here remains lingua-centric; virtually no new developments occur in the conceptualization of nonlinguistic variables. In part this is because some of these ideas, while relevant to Whorf's work, were developed for other, purely linguistic, purposes. But mostly, the effort simply has not been made. The crucial need is to bring these theories and methods to bear in a renewed empirical assessment of Whorf's questions, an empirical assessment which attends to possible cognitive and cultural outcomes.

5. Approaches in comparative psycholinguistics: experimental studies on the lexical coding of color

Introduction

The relationship between language diversity and thought did not receive a significant amount of research attention from psychologists until the 1950s, with the emergence of the subdiscipline of psycholinguistics. Although this increased interest in language within psychology can be traced in large part to Whorf's work,[1] actual studies of the cognitive significance of linguistic diversity have represented a relatively small portion of the total research effort. This is consistent both with a general tendency on the part of psychologists to avoid intercultural comparison and with a specific reluctance to cope with the full complexity of linguistic structure and diversity. The tradition is also marked by a strong concern with experimental assessment of individual cognition, and all the studies in this tradition compare some feature of one or more languages with the behavioral patterns of a sample of speakers on tasks designed to reveal cognitive processes.

These psycholinguistic studies can be divided into two broad groups: those involving the significance of lexical codability – to be dealt with in this chapter – and those involving the significance of some aspect of grammar such as form classes or logical relators – to be dealt with in the next. By far the majority of the studies fall into the lexical group, and the majority of these, in turn, concern the significance of color terms for cognition. These studies of the lexical encoding of color will be the focus of this chapter.

The studies involving color have been unified over the years by a more or less consistent methodology. The basic procedure involves presenting speakers with samples of colors in two tasks. The first task involves naming or describing certain of the color samples. These responses are then used to construct a "linguistic" measure for each color, for example a measure of how readily each color can be lexically encoded or described. In these studies, then, language is represented by lexical items

127

functioning denotationally. The second task involves performing some other "nonlinguistic" activity with the same colors. Most often a perceptual recognition memory task has been used; typically this involves asking subjects to recognize from memory certain colors from within a large array of colors. Thought, then, is taken to involve a set of cognitive "processes" which can be examined by means of a methodologically rigorous experimental assessment of individual nonlinguistic behavior; the cultural "content" of thought is not of concern. The results are analyzed to see whether there is any relationship between the two types of responses ("linguistic" and "nonlinguistic") that could be taken as evidence for or against some specific hypothesis concerning the relationship between language and thought.

From a conceptual point of view, the tradition concerned with color codability has evolved through two major periods: one (1953–68) in which language was seen as determining thought and one (1969–78) in which language was seen as reflecting thought.[2] The major studies from each of these periods will be discussed. But despite these differences in orientation, certain crucial theoretical assumptions are common to both periods. The first section of this chapter will examine these assumptions in considerable detail. The analysis will show how the assumptions of the first period both precluded any meaningful test of Whorf's ideas and made the emergence of the second period with its reversal of emphasis virtually inevitable.

The psycholinguistic approach to the relativity question

The intellectual and methodological approach dominating psycholinguistic work was developed and articulated by Eric H. Lenneberg[3] (Lenneberg, 1953) in collaboration with Roger W. Brown (Brown and Lenneberg, 1954) and John M. Roberts (Lenneberg and Roberts, 1956[4]). Lenneberg's central task, as outlined in the first part of this section, was to reformulate the relativity problem so as to make it amenable to traditional psychological concerns and methods. The most important component of his reformulation, taken up in detail in the subsequent parts of this section, was the development of a procedure for objectively characterizing and comparing language categories in terms of their denotational referents.

Lenneberg's reformulation of the problem and his critique of Whorf

Emphasis on individual processing potential

Lenneberg sharply redirected the focus of interest:

> The republication of Benjamin L. Whorf's articles ... has aroused a new interest in this country in the problem of the relationship that a particular language may have to its speakers' *cognitive processes*. Does the structure of a given language affect the thoughts (or *thought potential*), the memory, the perception, the learning ability of those who speak that language? ... The present paper is an attempt to lay bare the logical structure of this type of investigation.
>
> (1953, p. 463, my italics)

First, notice that Lenneberg's concern was with cognitive processes, not with the shared content or interpretive categories of thought which had been the focus of the anthropological linguists. These processes included perception, memory, and learning capacities, which were never directly considered by Whorf or other anthropological linguists. Second, notice Lenneberg's reference to thought potential. By contrast, Whorf's central concern was with habitual thought and not with intellectual potential, a concern which paralleled his interest in what a language routinely did refer to, not what it potentially could refer to. In short, Lenneberg psychologized the hypothesis by redirecting concern to processing potential. The subtext, as will become clear, was to make the investigation "scientific" by searching for universals by means of objective methods.

Emphasis on mechanism connecting language to thought

Having reconstructed the problem in this way, Lenneberg criticized previous approaches – Whorf's in particular – from this perspective in the first part of his discussion. He presented three arguments. He first criticized Whorf's underlying assumption that there was a relationship between language and thought:

> Underlying all of Whorf's theoretical work is the fundamental assumption that the individual's conception of the world (including perception, abstraction, rationalization, categorization) is intimately related to the nature of his native language.   (1953, p. 463)

Lenneberg's claim that Whorf *assumed* a relation between language and thought ("conception of the world" in this case) seems strange when we consider that the point of several of Whorf's articles was precisely to *demonstrate* that such a relationship existed. Lenneberg's criticism is comprehensible only if we construe it to be about the specific mechanism of connection. He was criticizing Whorf for not specifying *how* it is that language connects with thought. Whorf provided partial answers with his argument about analogical influences, but Lenneberg never referred to this argument, and we can assume he did not recognize it. But Whorf's argument was incomplete in that he did not give an account of why cognitive appropriation occurs, that is, of the utility of using linguistic categories in thought, or an analysis of which specific cognitive processes are affected. Thus, Lenneberg did identify an important underdeveloped aspect of Whorf's theory. Unfortunately, Lenneberg never was able to answer these questions either.

Lenneberg did clarify what was required, from his point of view, to demonstrate such a relationship:

a demonstration that certain languages differ from each other suggests but does not prove that the speakers of these languages differ from each other as a group in their psychological potentialities. To prove this, *it would be necessary to show first that certain aspects of language have a direct influence on or connection with a given psychological mechanism, or at least that speakers of different languages differ along certain psychological parameters.*   (1953, p. 463, my italics)

This makes clear that Lenneberg's concern was with the specific nature of the connection between language and thought. From one point of view, he was claiming that the general relationship between Language and Thought (or speech and thought) needs to be established *before* the question of differences can be addressed. Such a demonstration of Language and Thought connections did not in principle have to be comparative (i.e., cross-linguistic), but rather merely needed to show that in principle Language and Thought can be linked.

But he also mentioned an alternative approach in this passage: one could show a psychological difference corresponding to or correlating with a linguistic difference – without specification of mechanism. Presumably at least some of Whorf's research would meet this second criterion, were it not for Lenneberg's own tacit assumption that a "psychological parameter" must involve processes such as attention and memory revealed through standard experimental assessment of individuals rather than content such as categories and interpretive frameworks revealed through observation and ethnographic analysis. The problem with Whorf's approach, then, was not so much that the logical structure was inadequate but that Lenneberg did not accept the terms of Whorf's psychology. This is particularly disturbing since the underlying force of the Whorfian argument was that much of what we consider to be process in psychology can perhaps be better understood as content, and, in particular, content which derives its structure from language forms.

Lenneberg then considered Whorf's fire-causing examples, in particular "the empty-gas-drum case" (which we reviewed in chapter 2), as examples of the few instances in which Whorf considered individual (rather than comparative) data. However, Lenneberg did not accept them as evidence:

I cannot accept this as evidence for the assumption that behavior is influenced by language. Clearly, English is capable of distinguishing between a drum filled with an explosive vapor, one that contains only air, and one which is void of any matter. This very sentence is my evidence. The person who caused the fire could have replaced the word *empty* by *filled with explosive vapor*. His failing to do so (as well as his careless behavior) points to a lack of experience with explosive vapors, perhaps complete ignorance of their existence. The linguistic – or rather stylistic – fact of the occurrence of the word *empty* in the individual's insurance report would indeed be interesting if Whorf could have shown at the same time that this man had had plenty of contact with and knowledge of the explosive vapors which form in emptied gas drums. This Whorf did not try to do. In short, the basic assumption that language affects non-linguistic behavior derives from an inspection of linguistic facts. Therefore nothing is added to such an hypothesis by referring back to the same or similar linguistic facts. (1953, p. 464)

Here Lenneberg has extended the concern with potential (rather than habitual) behavior to language forms themselves. Whorf was not discussing what *can* be said in English, but what typically *is* said. Lenneberg's theoretical concern with the "potential" rather than the habitual stemmed from his own disciplinary concerns and assumptions, which are in no way privileged on logical grounds and, in practical terms, seem less compelling. The force of this argument is further weakened by the fact that his *own* subsequent empirical research will exclude from consideration a good deal of what *can* be said about color in favor of a focus on the most frequently used terminology across subjects (Brown and Lenneberg, 1954, pp. 458, 459; Lenneberg and Roberts, 1956, pp. 20, 25).

Further, the argument that the use of the word *empty* suggests a lack of prior knowledge about explosive vapors essentially attempts to reverse Whorf's argument and to claim that use of the linguistic form usually derives from, or reflects, individual experience rather than shapes it. This was Lenneberg's own tacit assumption, and he felt that Whorf needed to disprove it for his argument to go through. There is some merit to the argument that Whorf's analysis of this example was incomplete – he could have done more to show how language (or the particular forms of English) played a distinctive role in this case.[5] But Lenneberg never showed why his assumption that language use merely indexes thought should be privileged over Whorf's. Further, even if Lenneberg's specific assumption was accepted (i.e., use of the word *empty* indexes prior ignorance of danger), it fails to address the deeper question as to why such thought patterns come into being in the first place: why doesn't the original association of danger with full gasoline drums "naturally" carry over to the used drums? In short, Lenneberg has dismissed too much: an influence of language on interpretations of *new* situations would itself be of considerable psychological significance. The focus on what one *should* know about a situation is, at root, simply another variant of the concern with potential knowledge rather than actual situational knowledge. Lenneberg did not show how such potential thought (i.e., what could be said) is more relevant to actual behavior than is habitual thought.

Emphasis on lexical denotation

Lenneberg's second set of criticisms concerned the difficulty with using evidence from translation meanings, or "the translation method." His central objection is that we cannot equate the meaning of an utterance with the sum of the general meanings of its individual elements. This led him to object to Whorf's illustration of how referentially equivalent utterances can have substantially different semantic substructures. Whorf's example involved showing how the English phrase "it is a dripping spring" would be rendered in Apache; he presented a morpheme-by-morpheme analysis of the equivalent utterance and claimed that the resulting phrase would be something like "as water, or springs, whiteness moves downward." Lenneberg's response to this example was first to illustrate that a morpheme-by-morpheme gloss of English would sound just as odd. Perhaps this argument held some rhetorical force in 1953; it seems less compelling today in light of similar efforts by those interested in generative semantics to provide exactly this sort of analysis of English utterances. And, the fact that a scientific description sounds odd does not amount to a substantive criticism.

But there were other bases of Lenneberg's discomfort with this approach:

> It makes no sense to equate the global meaning of an utterance with the sequence of abstracted, general meanings of the morphemes that occur in that utterance. To translate the Apachean statement *it is a dripping spring* appears no less reasonable than to translate it *as water[,] or springs, whiteness moves downward at a place* (or, *the place is white, clear; a clearing; a plain* – which, I gather from Whorf, is the synthesis of the elements); for what we translate are equivalent verbal responses to particular stimulus situations, and the Apachean response to the natural phenomenon in question corresponds to our response *it is a dripping spring*.   (1953, p. 465)

Three aspects of these remarks are noteworthy. First, Lenneberg misread Whorf's text. He took Whorf's two examples, showing how differently the semantic value of the verb *ga* ('be white, be clear') emerges depending on syntactic construction, and conflated them into a single example. He thus missed seeing how structurally different the Apache constructions are. Second, although one would not want to *restrict* the meaning of an utterance to the sum of its semantic values, Whorf was not doing anything very unusual here in claiming that this general meaning (categorial meaning as a function of structure) is one aspect of the meaning of an utterance – and he wanted to emphasize its importance. When Lenneberg subsequently argued that "what we really want to know is how the Apachean structure of syntactic categories differs from the English one," he was articulating Whorf's point exactly. Whorf was not merely "translating," as Lenneberg would have it, but rather was showing how essentially different elements combine in a distinctive way. (This point is developed more rigorously, of course, in Whorf's professional articles than in this example, drawn from an article written for MIT alumni.) Third, and most significantly, Lenneberg argued that it really makes no difference how we translate these other languages. Our own rough gloss, 'it is a dripping spring,' will serve as well as ("appears no less reasonable than") one which captures the Apache forms more precisely. Lenneberg claimed that such an approach was a matter of one's translation philosophy. This represents the core of Lenneberg's view: he ruled out Whorf's approach because he preferred another. Lenneberg ended up arguing for functional equivalence in terms of giving primacy to pragmatic (referential) equivalence: this is *what we would say* in this context, so it serves as an adequate translation of *what they are saying*. This approach essentially dismisses the question at the very core of the debate, that is, exactly how important *are* differences in syntactic and semantic structure? Is the *same thing* really being said? In short, Lenneberg's alternative represented a dismissal of the significance of semantic structure without any real argument. One suspects that, at least implicitly, Lenneberg did not really want to be bothered with the details of Apache grammar or that of any other language. He could avoid such difficulties by focusing on the potential for referential equivalence. From this point of view, observed structural differences only affect relative efficiency, not substantive message.

Lenneberg continued with four other arguments against the translation method which, in some ways, represent spin-offs of this basic argument against using general meanings. (1) He objected to using our glosses for the terms of their utterances and then comparing them with our own utterances, as this results in our comparing our way of thinking with itself. This argument only makes sense if we interpret it as a complaint about the adequacy of our theoretical metalanguage. As we have seen, Whorf, for one, was fully aware of the problems here and worked to help build such a metalanguage free of the bias of any one language. And as we will see shortly, Lenneberg made his own attempt to construct a metalanguage, an attempt which makes precisely the error he cautions against here. (2) He objected to taking metaphorical items literally when there is no evidence of current cognitive salience. Of course, it is exactly the occasional cognitive (and ultimately behavioral) significance of the unintended implications of such supposedly dead metaphors that Whorf was attempting to demonstrate with his fire-causing examples. (3) He argued that we need to look at associations with situations, not just general meanings. This is another way of saying that he wanted to lay emphasis on the pragmatic referential (denotional) function of language (or on the extensionalizable aspect of meaning) in his approach to the problem. This is certainly one important aspect of meaning, but it hardly exhausts it. In fact, Whorf was attempting to show that very general semantic structures also play a role precisely by linking together diverse elements of experience analogically. (4) He complained that we can't explicate specific contexts and associations for language forms because they vary so widely by culture. This seems less an argument against Whorf than against Lenneberg's own denotational emphasis. There may in fact be more comparability at the general level of grammar than there is in specific referential situations. All these arguments reflect Lenneberg's own view of language as fundamentally denotational and sidesteps Whorf's problematic.[6]

Emphasis on controlled assessment

Lenneberg's third area of criticism consisted of a short statement against *ad hoc* theories of language and thought relations:

Turning to ethnolinguistic literature we find an abundance of working hypotheses where it is difficult to see how they might contribute to a universally valid and useful theory of language (such that language is related to non-linguistic behavior), because the facts underlying such working hypotheses cannot be generalized so as to fit more than a single language. I am not saying that such hypotheses are right or wrong; many have been proposed by experts on specific cultures, by scientists of undisputed merit. I am merely pointing to the difficulty, if not impossibility, of deducing from these hypotheses, if they are sound, general and verifiable laws. A common means of validating hypotheses has been barred from the beginning in these cases, namely cross-cultural verification. This, however, does not exclude the possibility that the investigators may have intra-cultural evidence for each individual hypothesis proposed.

(1953, pp. 466–67)

Certainly Whorf's work contrasting Hopi and English was not *ad hoc* in this sense. No doubt Lenneberg had in mind here the work of the various anthropological linguists who dealt with case studies of a single language and culture. We have seen how these case studies (reviewed in chapter 3) were indeed *ad hoc* and that the recognition within the tradition of the possibility and desirability of comparison was rarely realized in practice. The irony, as we shall see, is that many of the studies in the tradition inaugurated by Lenneberg's approach eventually devolve into little more than a single *ad hoc* case study of just the sort he criticized – namely the analysis of the speech and behavior of English-speaking Americans.

Summary

In summary, the first half of Lenneberg's 1953 paper reversed two key assumptions in Whorf's approach: he emphasized cognitive process rather than conceptual content and he emphasized cognitive potential rather than habitual thought. These reversals set the stage for his three criticisms of Whorf's work. First, Whorf merely presupposed a mechanism connecting language and thought, whereas he wanted to see the connection made theoretically explicit and empirically demonstrated. This turns out to be more an expression of Lenneberg's preference for looking at processing potential rather than habitual concepts rather than a logical necessity – as his own comments make clear. Second, Whorf relied too heavily on translation meanings. In fact, Whorf relied principally on comparative structural analysis in his most important pieces. What appears to lie behind Lenneberg's argument was a desire to focus on pragmatic referential equivalence rather than a full assessment of meaning which would include semantic and structural contributions to meaning. Such an approach essentially discards the original problem. Again, the issue is one of preference, not substantive argument. And third, much previous work on this problem area was *ad hoc* in nature in that it involved factors unique to a particular language or culture. This criticism did not apply to most of Whorf's work with Hopi, but, as Lenneberg noted (1953, p. 467, n7), it does aptly characterize much of the subsequent work in anthropological linguistics. Lenneberg's dissatisfaction with previous methods led him to develop a more systematic comparative method (to be described next) which represents one of his most important contributions. In sum, Lenneberg's reformulation and criticisms stem in large measure from his disciplinary orientations. These orientations will turn out to be inimical to the fair assessment of the relativity hypothesis.

The objectification of meaning: Lenneberg's intra-cultural method

The second half of Lenneberg's 1953 paper outlined a general method-ology for investigating language and thought relations intra-culturally, a method which was meant to meet his goal of looking at processing potential while circumventing the three criticisms he has just made of previous research. The method involved assessing within one language the degree of *codability* of some referential domain. The concept of codability provided a mechanism by which language and thought are related. The use of a referential domain to calibrate linguistic responses fulfilled the aim of emphasizing the pragmatic denotional aspect of meaning, and avoided thereby the problems of the translation method. And the focus on codability allowed some value to be derived from well-controlled studies of a single language; the need for comparative studies was reduced since they were not essential to investigating codability itself but served instead only as a check on over-generalization.[7] Lenneberg illustrated the intra-cultural method with a study of the relation of color terminology to cognition. We are concerned in this section with explaining Lenneberg's rationale for his method.

Anything can be said in any language (or, the irrelevance of messages)

Lenneberg began his argument by noting that the linguistic maxim that anything can be expressed in any language implies that the problem at issue is not one of content or subject matter of utterances. Differences must be at the level of ease and facility.

> Now, if we believe, as we do, that we CAN say anything we wish in any language, then it would seem as if the content or subject matter of utterances does not characterize or, indeed, give us any clear information on the communicative properties of a language. Thus we are led to the somewhat banal conclusion that *the only pertinent linguistic data in this type of research is the HOW of communi-cation and not the WHAT . This HOW I call the codification; the WHAT I call the messages* ... meaning can be excluded entirely from our research, at least theoretically, and we have therefore an assurance that we are actually studying aspects of codification.   (1953, p. 467, my italics)

This reformulation is problematic in a number of respects. Lenneberg has side-stepped the issue of what is habitually said or what must be habitually expressed; he continued emphasizing what potentially can be said. The intended force of the linguistic maxim on which his analysis was based is that all languages, as semiotic systems, are equally adequate as referential devices and not that individual utterances (or expressions) from different languages can be or usually are equivalent. Lenneberg drew too neat a line here between code and message; Whorf's point was that the HOW and the WHAT interact in important ways.

A little further on, Lenneberg acknowledged that some aspects of meaning are relevant to codification:

Unfortunately, however, it is not always equally easy to decide whether a phenomenon is pertinent to codification or not. Many assertions about language which derive from semantic observations, or at any rate, which include elements of meaning, nevertheless seem to be relevant to codification. Most obvious in this connection is the fact that a language always selects for codification highly specific aspects from the physical and social environment . . . There can be little doubt that these considerations, though clearly of a semantic character, have a bearing on the problem of codification. Hence, the distinction between codification and messages is not the same as between syntactics and semantics or between form and meaning. All those observations about meaning are relevant to codification which refer to an aspect of speech behavior which is forced upon the individual speaker by the rules of his language and where infringement of the rules would result in defective communication. For instance, an individual reporting about a given event is forced to stipulate very definite conditions, aspects, and relationships if he wants to be understood.[8] . . . Whatever information is optional in his communication is message.   (1953, pp. 467–68)

So Lenneberg wanted to include only those aspects of meaning which are relevant to codification, that is, those aspects which are obligatory. In this he appeared to present a view which is similar to Boas's point that certain meaningful distinctions are obligatory in the very use of a code. However, the significance for cognition of differences among these obligatory, ultimately structural aspects of meaning clearly was not the focus of Lenneberg's concern, and he did not deal with the problem again.

On the contrary, Lenneberg wanted to escape considering this structural dimension of meaning altogether. Although he could not deny its significance in theory, in practice he worked to avoid the subtle considerations of meaning involved in the "translation method." He did this by ignoring linguistic form and relying entirely on efficiency of denotional reference at his index of codability. He claimed that

the [intra-cultural] method dispenses with the necessity for translation, or the exact equation of linguistic data between one language and another. For what will be compared are CORRELATIONS OF SPEECH BEHAVIOR WITH RECOGNITION BEHAVIOR, not linguistic forms . . . *The intra-cultural method . . . objectifies the intuited meanings of forms by carefully relating them to stimuli of the environment.* Thus it is possible (at least in some instances) to specify meaning by referral to the physical properties of those stimuli.   (1953, pp. 470–71, my italics)

This objectification of meaning,[9] that is, the reduction of meaning to entities and properties to which one could make ostensive reference, was a central aim of Lenneberg's approach. And the proposed method "works" precisely by washing out variation in structural meaning, that is, by attempting strictly to separate code and message.[10]

Any one language can serve for all (or, the irrelevance of differences among codes)

Lenneberg's "intra-cultural approach" was also ostensibly designed to solve a problem of the lack of comparability across languages and the associated *ad hoc* nature of earlier research:

Ethnolinguistic research based on cross-cultural comparison must endeavor to isolate data, both on codification and on cognition, that are general enough to have comparable equivalents in at least two different languages and cultures; otherwise comparison would be meaningless. It is not infrequent, however, that a working hypothesis relates a certain cognitive datum to some phenomenon pertinent to codification which appears to be unique, lacking entirely a parallel in any other language. There is a simple way of studying this situation; I call it the intra-cultural approach, because it reduces [the need for] cross-cultural comparison to a desirable but not indispensable expansion of investigations.

(1953, p. 468)[11]

One can hardly disagree with the main argument here that comparison must be between equivalents of some sort. But the fact that cross-cultural approaches sometimes present problems in the development of such equivalents does not constitute an argument for intra-cultural designs unless the question at hand is amenable to such approaches. Lenneberg did not show that this is the case. (That, in fact, the contrary is the case will be made clear in the discussion of the inter-cultural method which follows.) But the rhetorical structure of Lenneberg's 1953 article makes it *appear* that Whorf's questions could be addressed by this approach.

Lenneberg's whole line of argument can only make sense if it is seen as an argument about the study of the mechanism of Language and Thought relations, that is, how language and thought interrelate in functional terms. The notion of codification has been transformed here from the original concern (cited above) with specific formal peculiarities of encoding forced on a speaker by the rules of his particular language into a concern with general processes of encoding forced on a speaker by using any Language. This general process of codification can be equally well addressed using any specific language. This interpretation is borne out in Lenneberg's examples.

As one example of how codification might be studied, Lenneberg discussed the codability of colors. He described a procedure to examine descriptions of colors given by a sample of speakers of a language to determine which colors are highly codable – highly codable being operationalized as easily named. This ease of naming can be indexed, for example, by unanimity in response (1953, p. 469). He argued that

some colors have the property of eliciting a homogeneous response from English-speakers, whereas other colors elicit a heterogeneous response. This is to say that linguistic communication in English is more efficient when some colors are referred to than when others are. There are cogent reasons to assume that the distinction made here between the colors is a purely linguistic one, and that there are no physical properties in the colors or physiological ones in the eye which would elucidate the difference in response made by English-speakers to these colors. (1953, p. 469)

(See also Lenneberg and Roberts, 1956, pp. 20–21.) No explanation is given for several important claims: that homogeneity of response should be considered more "efficient," that this task relates to the efficiency of communication of colors in general (i.e., outside of this task context), or that the response pattern has nothing to do with the colors themselves or properties of the human visual system (vague allusions to "cogent reasons" for believing this notwithstanding). Lenneberg, however, tended to conceptualize the various colors as equally salient, context-independent elicitors, so that any patterns of differences must stem from the language code. In fact, of course, subjects are responding to particular colors not only using a specific language but in a specific task context. For example, experimental subjects were first shown an array of colors from which the to-be-named colors were to be drawn. This effectively indicated to the subjects the level of description and range of contrasts with which they were to operate.[12] "Efficient" codification in this task context need not be so elsewhere. By focusing on the various colors as equivalent, autonomous elicitors in this way, Lenneberg ignored some important variables such as the intrinsic psychophysical properties of the sample colors or the relationship of the sample colors to the neighboring samples in the array. These variables (and others) provided the grist for thirty years of subsequent reinterpretation of the significance of this approach.

More importantly, Lenneberg's discussion of the color research example makes it clear that he was not interested in the impact of structural differences among diverse language forms, but in the functional interrelation of one language's set of forms with other forms of behavior. This becomes clear, for example, in the following passage about the relevance of comparative work to codability findings:

Suppose now that this entire color research were repeated in a different culture where a different language is spoken. If our predictions about recognition, based on previously determined facts of codification (which vary of course from language to language), should not be borne out in this other language, the argument advanced in the first experiment would be seriously weakened. Conversely, if the results should be confirmed, this would fortify the argument. In either case, however, VALIDATION of the basic hypothesis is independent of cross-cultural comparison. The cross-cultural comparison merely adds or sub-tracts weight. It is very important to realize that the validation itself is the result of intra-cultural correlation of two sets of recognition behavior on the one hand ... with two sets of English speech behavior on the other hand (efficient and not so efficient linguistic communication).   (1953, p. 470)

So, the specific characteristics of English *as* English are not at issue. The argument which would be weakened or strengthened is the general notion of codability, *not* the particular effects of English. If Lenneberg were to find the same pattern in another language – a link of codability and recognition memory – what would be supported is the notion of codability; any actual difference in codability is a secondary concern, even though it may have motivated the original analysis! Thus, although Lenneberg began his analysis with a discussion of Whorf and the relation of diverse languages to thought, he eventually shifted (in line with his earlier criticisms) toward a concern with generic relations between Language and Thought (or speech and cognition).[13] Nearly all sub-sequent psycholinguistic research has followed his lead. The intra-cultural method is not meant to and can never apply directly to the sort of issue Whorf was concerned with.

The crux of Lenneberg's argument seems to be that establishing the significance of codability as a general fact about the way Thought relates to Language would make linguistic relativity (of a certain sort) a straightforward deduction; hence, the focus of research attention should be shifted to establishing this sort of relation. But if this shift is associated with the reliance on the intra-cultural approach, it can only work (i.e., yield meaningful results) if factors such as linguistic codability can be shown to be *the* explanation of the pattern of nonlinguistic behavior:

It is necessary that the codification criterion should be the ONLY criterion by which the stimuli can be grouped in this way.   (1953, p. 471)

Without this assurance, the correlations in the single language could be due to some other variable. But the principal (perhaps only) way to check that there is no other variable accounting for the observed pattern is to see that the pattern is in fact systematically different in some other language. To repeat, the best evidence that a pattern is a distinctively *linguistic* pattern lies in the evidence of cross-language variation. (It could be argued that it can rightly be called "codability" in the first place only if it meets this condition.) So, we are led to conclude that the use of codability as a theoretical construct ultimately depends in important ways on the availability of inter-cultural evidence of diversity. And, more

generally, the establishment of Language and Thought relations ultimately depends on cross-linguistic evidence, since it must be established
that the patterns of functional interrelations are everywhere the same (cf.
discussion in chapter 4).

Summary

In sum, Lenneberg suggested that Whorf's ideas could be addressed by
studying codification by means of the inter-cultural method. His argument involved first drawing a distinction between message and code, thus
immediately minimizing the importance of code–message interactions of
the sort Whorf sought to emphasize. Second, by reference to the premise
that differences in what can be said do not distinguish languages, he
argued that Whorf's problem cannot be about messages but must be
about codes. Finally, he interprets the question of codes in terms of
different ways of handling the same messages, or, as we might say, the
same reality. Since this effectively shifted the focus of research to how a
language (any language) encodes reality, Lenneberg was able to argue
that the general process or mechanism of codification can effectively be
studied in a single language. If it can be established that the pattern
codification in one language is relevant to nonlinguistic behavior, then it
follows, he claimed, that where codification differs, so must the nonlinguistic behavior. Of course, the differences in codification can now
only be quantitative, not qualitative, since a common reality is presupposed. This effectively reduces the problem of languages and thought to
one of Language and Thought. The relativity question has now become a
question of how a single language treats "objective" reality. The
possibility that a language plays a role in *constituting* a speaker's reality is
essentially dissolved.

   It should be emphasized that this methodological argument was
completely in harmony with Lenneberg's theoretical critique. He
emphasized the investigation of the mechanism linking Language and
Thought, avoided the translation method by turning to denotation, and
circumvented the potential difficulties of cross-cultural comparison. He
also eliminated any possibility of addressing the original hypothesis.

Objectified meaning as a metalanguage for comparison: Lenneberg's inter-cultural method

In a subsequent article Lenneberg (Lenneberg and Roberts, 1956) took
up the problem of doing comparative research. He now argued that there

were certain problems which are amenable only to an inter-cultural (or, cross-cultural) method, namely those cases in which the whole language is taken as an instance (Lenneberg and Roberts, 1956, pp. 4–5). The typical case would be where the relevant linguistic parameter involved some general structural property of the language. This, of course, was exactly Whorf's concern. In theory, this represented a return by Lenneberg to the question of the specific form of codification and the obligatory meanings conveyed by a code structure. In practice, as we will see, Lenneberg continued to avoid a direct consideration of actual structural (grammatical) differences.

Lenneberg felt that the comparability of data across languages represented one of the major problems in the field of language and cognition studies (Lenneberg and Roberts, 1956, pp. 5, 32–33). He argued that cross-cultural approaches must involve linguistic parameters which, although they vary among languages, can nonetheless be characterized as the same in some respect:

Verification [of a hypothesis] requires that we know *what* we are varying, which, of course, is not the case [in the examples] here. We have no terms in which to make a comparison of the [linguistic conditions] or, in other words, there are no parameters that describe pertinent qualities of the [linguistic conditions] involved. The problem of comparability is of paramount importance in this kind of research.   (Lenneberg and Roberts, 1956, p. 5)

The principal theoretical task in Lenneberg's subsequent discussion was to explicate exactly how to go about developing such comparability for linguistic data. In theoretical terms, he was seeking a descriptive metalanguage.

Three criteria for developing comparable language data

Lenneberg presented "three criteria for the choice of language data" for cross-cultural research (Lenneberg and Roberts, 1956, pp. 6–7). The three criteria are applied only to lexical forms. First, the referents (in the extensional sense) of the lexical items must be completely *universal*, that is, present in every culture. The universality of the referents guarantees, as it were, the comparability of the linguistic forms making reference to them. The referents, then, serve as the "objective" metalanguage for analysis and comparison. Second, the linguistic condition (i.e., the array of forms [= lexical categories] extending the universally available referents) must show some *variation* across languages. If the linguistic variable were everywhere identical, we would have no reason to expect any differences in associated nonlinguistic cognitive behavior to be a product of language. Third, the parameters for describing the referents must exhibit a certain *simplicity*. Lenneberg felt that we must select a referential domain whose parameters are simple enough to be readily described. The more complicated the domain and the more parameters it entails, the more difficult will it be to conduct effective comparison. He felt that although there are many language variables which meet the first two criteria, the last criterion is difficult to meet.

Lenneberg's restriction of interest to lexical denotation was not merely an instance of formulating the issue too narrowly. A deeper problem is involved here, one which goes to the heart of the difficulties with Lenneberg's approach to comparative research and all subsequent work which emulates it. The emphasis on lexical denotation stems from a view of language which is fundamentally opposed to the possibility of linguistic relativity, for, as was suggested earlier, it contains within it the assumption of the inverse hypothesis, namely that languages merely reflect (inventory) reality and so can be adequately characterized by reference to that reality and in disregard of language internal structural patterning. Thus, even though the method was devised in an attempt to test the hypothesis of an influence of language on thought, it inevitably led (both logically and historically) to the rejection and reversal of the hypothesis. How this is so will become clearer if we work through Lenneberg's specific argument for focusing on the "language of experience."

The language of experience

Lenneberg argued that "one realm of words" satisfies his three criteria, the language of experience:

By *language of experience* we mean the words and morphemes that refer to the most elementary forms of experience such as the sensation of temperature, of humidity, or of light . . .

It is not difficult to see how the language of experience satisfies the three criteria for the selection of data. The world over man is equipped with the same sensorium even though he may not always make precisely the same use of it. The sensory mechanisms are always present and the basic sensory stimuli are available everywhere to man. It can be assumed that it is possible to refer to elementary sensations in every language, and it is quite immaterial to this assumption whether or not languages differ in their linguistic treatment of the referents . . . The criterion of variability is also met by the language of experience if we may judge by the ample literature on the subject.

(Lenneberg and Roberts, 1956, pp. 7–8)

Although the claim here is purportedly about language (or at least "one realm of words"[14]), it is so in a very unusual sense. This can be seen if we consider the three criteria.

First, the claim about universality is mostly a claim about nonlinguistic facts – certain universals of perceptual experience and of environments,[15] quite aside from any considerations of language. It is a claim about language only in that "it can be assumed that it is possible to refer to elementary sensations in every language." Thus, to the extent that the claim is about language, it is not a claim about lexical or grammatical structure at all. Rather than comparing specific language structures, only the global variability in handling a specific denotational problem is compared, for which, it should be noted, the only cross-linguistic unity lies in the ostensive referents (the "objective" meaning). The universality criterion, then, is not met under this formulation by a linguistic parameter – at least in any meaningful sense of the term linguistic. That it even appears to be linguistic at all derives from the assumption that we are talking about "words" in various languages.

Second, although no doubt there *is* "variability," it is not clear how it can be specified linguistically, for the approach lumps together morphological forms and complex phrases, habitual usages and rare (but situationally appropriate) occurrences, precise specifications and general indications, all into the same bag as somehow *characterizing a language*. That this was Lenneberg's intent is clear in this remark about color classification:

After asking a sufficient number of English speakers what name they would give to the various shades [of color], we can then determine where the boundaries of the English response classes are in the intensity continuum. Thus we learn how English classifies various kinds of light stimuli. If this procedure is repeated with speakers of a language other than English, the two kinds of grouping arrangements can be compared and we may thus determine whether or not there is a difference between them. Should we find that a difference exists – and the odds are in favor of it – we would have observed a "code phenomenon." A "code phenomenon" is a characteristic feature of a specific language.

(Lenneberg and Roberts, 1956, pp. 8–9)

This "code phenomenon," this "characteristic feature" of a language, need not correspond to any well-defined formal unit-type of a single language (such as a lexeme), let alone the same formal unit across languages. Nor need it consistently correspond with any common functional element (noun, adjective, etc.). All we have is a statement about statistically frequent verbal responses to particular referential tasks. Linguistic structure (language as such) is not directly at issue.

This problem is somewhat concealed by Lenneberg's diagrammatic illustrations of the problem. He portrayed the problem in terms of a single linear stimulus continuum (for instance, hue) which can be calibrated psychophysically. Language I divides this continuum into two terminological classifications (A and B), and Language II divides the same continuum into three terminological classifications (a, b and c). The presentation suggests that the "classifications" are actual categories of the languages I and II – but in fact they need not correspond to any regular structural or type level elements in those languages. (Specifically, they need not correspond to lexemes in the two languages.) Even where such a correspondence can be guaranteed in one of the languages (by definition), it cannot be assumed for others. The presentation further suggests that the forms making up these "classifications" both refer to and divide up the given stimulus continuum in the same way, that is, that the differences are only quantitative, not qualitative. In fact, the language forms may not refer to the same things at all (even as they effectively discriminate among the same stimuli), and they may have other significant elements of meanings.[16] The argument seems plausible as a general comparative strategy only if readers follow Lenneberg in assuming that the categories correspond to lexical items which refer essentially to the stimulus continuum as *we* conceive of it. But this cannot, in principle, be guaranteed.[17]

Freed from the emphasis on lexical denotation, Lenneberg's first two criteria can be combined into a single general prerequisite for meaningful, controlled comparative work, namely that linguistic reference must show a pattern of *constrained variation*. In other words, the languages must show a pattern of variation, but the variation must be well bounded enough so that an argument can be made that the variation is in fact over the "same" domain. It does not seem necessary, at the outset at least, to insist on absolute universality in the sense that a specific referent be available in every culture, since useful generalizations may be drawn across significant subsets of languages. Nor does denotational reference provide the only means for generating a theoretically adequate description of the language patterns. Nonetheless, in the characterization of the desirable logic of interrelation of universals and variations in language and thought studies – what has been called here a pattern of constrained variation – Lenneberg has identified a crucial feature that all comparative studies must exhibit. In this respect, his analysis represents an historically important contribution.

Lenneberg next considered the simplicity criterion:

> The criterion of simplicity of the referent is easier to satisfy in the case of the language of experience than for most other words with determinable referents. This is due to the fact that the stimuli of sense perception can in most cases be ordered in systematic ways, and the *ordering systems* provide frames for description.
>
> (Lenneberg and Roberts, 1956, p. 8)

These ordering systems would include, for example, an ordering of thermal stimuli on the dimension of intensity. Some stimuli, such as colors, are best ordered relative to multiple psychophysical dimensions.

This ordering also serves to ground the psychophysical calibration necessary to make the essentially quantitative comparisons across groups mentioned in the previous paragraph. So what makes the language of experience "simple" is not some fact about the linguistic aspect of these forms, but rather that the psychophysical characterization of their referents appears to be relatively "simple" (at least to us – developing a cross-cultural standard of simplicity would not be an easy task). In short, the simplicity has to do with the characterization of nonlinguistic stimuli, not language.

Summary

In sum, the "three criteria for the choice of language data" for cross-cultural research turn out not to have much to do with *language*, but rather represent a set of criteria for selecting good *referents* to use in psychological testing.[18] Such referents should be universally available, should be treated differently by different languages, and should be simple to describe. Lenneberg's essential approach was to work from referents to their encodings, from "reality" to "languages." This inevitably suggests that reality is the primary phenomenon in the interaction and that language classifications are secondary, merely encoding "it" in diverse ways. But since the reality is in fact conceived of here as the raw sense data of perception, and perception is ultimately taken as an unproblematically prior part of the cognition, this leads irresistibly to the conclusion that it is cognition that is being encoded by language and cognition that is, therefore, ultimately shaping language. This neatly inverts the main thrust of the Whorfian argument, instantiates a common folk view, and leaves the ontological status of the "perceptual" reality unquestioned. Whorf's questions were precisely about the problematic nature of taking our own categories (linguistic or cognitive or perceptual) as a universal metalanguage; Lenneberg's proposal for a comparative method, despite a numer of positive aspects, makes just this mistake: it uses our categories as the metalanguage for "objectively" describing the nature of referents purportedly independently of any language. The irony is that it is done in the service of attempting to verify Whorf's proposals.

Aside on Lenneberg and American psychology

It is symptomatic of American psychology that the only acceptable bases for behavioral regularities must lie "out there" in objective reality, or "inside" as biological dispositions. There is no room in this disciplinary tradition for socially constituted regularities. This made it difficult for psychologists such as Lenneberg to deal in a sophisticated fashion with cultural and linguistic variation. Within the parameters of his approach, as set out in the previous two sections, discovery of genuine linguistic or cultural relativity was simply not possible. The problem stems from his conception of language as "mapping" objective reality, that is, linguistic meaning as essentially consisting of denotational reference to reality "out there." Forced, some years later, by the weight of linguistic and philosophical argument to give up this view, Lenneberg moved to the only other acceptable option within psychology: a "Neo-Kantian" (as he termed it) claim that concepts (including linguistic concepts) derive from ordering "impinging physical stimuli in a predetermined and species-specific way" (1962, p. 105). And in his later work, Lenneberg (1967) turned, quite naturally, to a consideration of the biological bases of language, that is, to a consideration of how thought (now biologically conceived) influences language.[19] Within the course of his career, then, Lenneberg presaged the historical shift on psychological research on Whorf's proposals from an emphasis on external objects to an emphasis on internal mind as giving rise to language form.

The English lexicon as metalanguage for describing objective meaning (and reality)

The crucial move in Lenneberg's intra-cultural approach was the construal of meaning in terms of stimuli in the environment, what I have termed the objectification of meaning:

> The intra-cultural method ... objectifies the intuited meanings of forms by carefully relating them to stimuli of the environment. Thus it is possible (at least in some instances) to specify meaning by referral [*sic*] to the physical properties of those stimuli. (Lenneberg, 1953, p. 471)

The central task in implementing this objectification was to adequately describe or define "the stimuli of the environment." How was this done? Where did Lenneberg get his description of reality? In his original (1953) discussion, the issue was not directly addressed. Lenneberg presented an illustration (or demonstration) of the use of the method using color stimuli but without attempting to motivate this choice of stimulus domain or its descriptive characterization.

In the following year, Brown and Lenneberg (1954) published the specific results of their research on color codability with English speakers. Again, the selection of stimulus domain was left basically

unmotivated. However, some insight into their approach can be gleaned
from their commentary on one of Whorf's examples. What this example
made clear was that the English lexicon was the covert ground for their
description of reality, that is, English was the metalanguage for describing objective meaning. This interpretation was later confirmed more
explicitly in Lenneberg and Roberts's (1956) discussion of the language
of experience and of color in particular.

Three kinds of "snow"

Brown and Lenneberg's introductory discussion centered on Whorf's
example (apparently drawn in part from Boas 1966a [1911], pp. 21–22)
of differences between Eskimo and English expressions for what we call
"kinds of snow."[20] In their account, the English word *snow* was
transformed into the comparative term "snow," which is *what the two
languages are really referring to*. Brown and Lenneberg's discussion
constantly assumed that there really is a common "something" called
"snow" which comes in three varieties and which both groups are equally
able to perceive but treat differently:

The Eskimo's three "snows" are sufficient evidence from which to infer that he
discriminates *three varieties of snow* ...
   What can be said of the English speaker's ability to distinguish *the same three
kinds of snow*? ... Consequently the fact that English speakers do not have
different names for *several kinds of snow* cannot be taken to mean that they are
unable to see the differences.
   Whorf himself must have been *able to see snow* as the Eskimos did since his
article describes and pictures the referents for the words ...
   Although *the three kinds of snow* are namable in both Eskimo and English,
each of them requires a phrase in ordinary English, whereas single words will do
it for the Eskimo.   (1954, p. 455, my italics for phrases with *snow*)

All these phrases essentially presuppose both the existence of something
called "snow" (which comes in several varieties) and that the various
linguistic forms in the two respective languages merely divide "it" up
differently.
   Whorf challenged exactly this sort of use of our own categories as
scientific metalanguage, and he was more careful in his usage of the
English term *snow*. He discussed the English/Eskimo contrast in two
places. His figure 10 (Whorf, 1956a, p. 210) *pictured* the referents
without labels and claimed that English *classifies* these referents with one
word, whereas Eskimo uses three words. (And Whorf was specifically
contrasting this example of what we group under the label *snow* with an
inverse one wherein Hopi speakers have a single noun *masa'ytaka* to

cover what we would call [flying] insects, airplanes, and aviators – but not birds.) Later in his discussion Whorf argued that our class 'snow' would seem too large and inclusive to an Eskimo:

We have the same word [*snow*] for falling snow, snow on the ground, snow packed hard like ice, slushy snow, wind-driven flying snow – whatever the situation may be. To an Eskimo, this all-inclusive word would be almost unthinkable; he would say that falling snow, slushy snow, and so on, are sensuously and operationally different, different things to contend with; he uses different words for them and for other kinds of snow.   (1956, p. 216)

So, even when forced to use the term *snow* in his discussion, Whorf took pains to indicate that the word (and the classification it implied) was "almost unthinkable" to the Eskimo.[21]

It might be argued that the use of the word "snow" in this way by Brown and Lenneberg was necessary (or convenient) for presenting the argument to English readers – just as it was for Whorf. There is some merit to this argument, but this was not the essential motivation, as is shown by two factors. First, Brown and Lenneberg argued at some length that English speakers can and do make the same distinctions the Eskimo make by using phrases (for example, "good-packing snow and bad-packing snow"). What they clearly did not grasp is that for the English speakers these referents remain *varieties of snow*, whereas there is no evidence at all that the Eskimo regard these three referents as varieties of the same thing. The only way it can make sense to argue that the Eskimo are making the same distinctions is to constrain the possible meanings of the Eskimo lexical forms severely, that is, to equate their "true" (here, denotational) meaning with the objective reality corresponding to the English forms and to equate their structural (semantic) meaning with the underlying phrase structure of the comparable English forms. Second, Brown and Lenneberg's empirical study of color codability operated with the same implicit assumptions. More importantly, the analysis of "color" by Lenneberg and Roberts (1956) made these orientations and presuppositions completely explicit.

Many kinds of "color"

The rationale for working with color

Brown and Lenneberg's experiment investigated the relation within English between the linguistic codability of various colors and recognition memory for those same colors. The decision to focus on color referents was partially motivated in that it offered several advantages:

Color categories differ from such categories as snows in that they have boundaries that can be plotted on known dimensions. Color categories, furthermore, are continuous with one another, sharing their boundaries.

(Brown and Lenneberg, 1954, p. 458)

However, the reason for choosing color as opposed to any other domain was never made clear.

Lenneberg's general claim was that the choice of domain had something to do with language:

Knowledge of a given language will usually determine which kind of sense-perception terminology one wishes to study. One may be struck by a peculiar vocabulary in the area of smells, of touch, or depth-perception.

(Lenneberg and Roberts, 1956, p. 11)

But no indication was ever given that color terms constitute a structurally distinctive part of English or, for that matter, of any language. The selection of referential domain was not, in fact, motivated by the structure of English grammar either taken alone or in contrast with some other language. The only fact about English that could possibly have motivated the selection of this domain is the existence of the English lexeme *color*, which suggests that there is a referential experience that has some unity for English speakers. Under this criterion, most of the lexical forms of English would constitute potential comparative categories. This is not a useful criterion, nor does it seem to be the sort that Lenneberg would have wanted to advocate. The selection of referential domain was arbitrary from a linguistic point of view.[22]

In recent years it has become common to view the choice of the color domain as unfortunate in light of later work suggesting that in this area perceptual physiology determines language structure (see, for instance, Brown, 1976, Kay and McDaniel, 1978; Hardin, 1988; Rosch, 1987). As should be clear from the course of the argument here, the problem does not lie with color, *per se*, but in the entire way of conceptualizing the problem. Simply choosing another domain will not solve these conceptual problems. Consider, for example, the various studies within cognitive anthropology of kin terms, botanical terms, etc., which historically have shown many of the same problems in defining the domain of inquiry and developing an unbiased metalanguage.

The objective characterization of color

Once this referential domain was selected, it had to be characterized in some way:

Whatever the choice [of sense-perception terminology], it is essential that the researcher familiarize himself with the most important psycho-physical variables of the stimulus material. (Lenneberg and Roberts, 1956, pp. 11–12)

The goal here was to develop an objective, language-independent characterization of the referents against which to calibrate the patterns of linguistic and nonlinguistic data (within one language for an intracultural study or across several languages for an inter-cultural study). This objective psychophysical characterization was to serve, then, as the metalanguage for the description of the referents and the activities performed with respect to them:

The speech events (color terms) and the behavioral events (recognition) were related to these stimuli. The specifications of the physical properties of the stimuli served as a metalanguage, so to speak, for the description of both types of events. (Lenneberg, 1953, p. 471)

This passage also makes clear that the metalanguage for describing the referents, and thereby the events related to them, is not induced in any way from formal linguistic analysis. It is rather derived from the scientific categories we have developed to describe "color," that is, the referents of our term *color*.

The category of "color" is defined as being composed of three psychophysical dimensions: hue, brightness (or value), and saturation (or chroma). If we try to order color samples in a meaningful way

we would discover that if the surface or conditions of reflectance are held constant for all colors, three criteria must be used in assigning every single color (chromatic and achromatic) a logical place in a system or catalog. The three necessary criteria correspond to the three perceptual attributes of color: hue, saturation, and brightness ... An objective definition of these attributes is difficult since they are phenomenal variables lacking perfect correspondence with one single physical property of the stimulus.
(Lenneberg and Roberts, 1956, p. 12)

Several assumptions are packaged into this brief passage. Surface conditions are partialed out without explicit justification; one can only assume that we do so because it is not part of what we as speakers of English consider to be "color." In fact, some languages appear to fuse reference to surface reflectance with some of our color dimensions. Conklin (1955) describes lexical items in Hanunóo which refer both to hue and reflectivity. Such forms are often translated into English by the terms 'wet,' 'shiny,' 'dry,' and 'dull.' The three (remaining) criteria necessary to characterize colors adequately "correspond to the three perceptual attributes of [our scientific notion of] color." The implication was that the three attributes exist in and exhaustively account for "color" and all we have done is (re-)discover them. (The difficulties of giving an objective definition of these dimensions should provide the clue that these categories are more problematic than might first appear.) But most importantly, the decision as to what dimensions are necessary to describe "color" adequately depends ultimately on what one understands "color" to be. The normative understanding in this case has clearly been drawn from English.

Color as a comparative category

No demonstration was given that the concept "color" provided a valid comparative category for languages.[23] Brown and Lenneberg did hedge on the universality of specific color categorizations:

> It does not follow that people everywhere either see or think of the color world in the same way. Cultural differences probably operate on the level of categorization rather than controlled laboratory discrimination.   (1954, pp. 457–8)

However, as this passage illustrates, and all subsequent work within this tradition (both comparative and otherwise) confirms, "color" itself and its tripartite dimensional composition are not at issue; they are presupposed. Only variations in the manner of dealing with what we conceive of as "color" are ever at issue. This replicates exactly the treatment earlier in their discussion of the category "snow," where the English lexeme was taken as the guide (the metacategory) for characterizing the objective referential domain.

In Lenneberg and Roberts's study, which was explicitly comparative, the problematic status of "color" as a comparative category was more directly raised, but was still left unanswered. Here, as we have seen, the attempt was made to justify the use of "color" by first generating a more general argument for working with the "language of experience." (It seems likely that the general argument was in fact developed some time after the decision to use the color domain.) The same disposition to use English lexical categories emerges in the arguments for working with the language of experience.

Lenneberg and Roberts first emphasized that the "language of experience" met the criterion of universal availability:

> It can be assumed that it is possible to refer to elementary sensations in every language, and it is quite immaterial to this assumption whether or not languages differ in their linguistic treatment of the referents. Nor does it matter here whether some languages have so-called "abstract" or universal terms such as our word *green* or whether instead they have one word referring to the green color of plants and another that is used only for green paints or green objects. In both cases there is a language of experience with common referents, thus meeting the requirement of universality.   (1956, p. 8)

What, then, is the language of experience? It is any form or set of forms in a language referring to "elementary sensations,"[24] that is, to a certain set of "common referents." What are these "common referents," and how can they be characterized? In some cases we can certainly point to them (or produce them before a speaker), but this works only if we ourselves first know what to point to (or produce), that is, if we already know what the referents are. How do we get a relevant set? Will any random assortment of referents do? How are we to know what they are – or choose what they shall be? Lenneberg's example gives us the solution: we can use an English word ("green" in the example, "color" in the larger study) to describe a set of referents and their variations (i.e., kinds of green, kinds of color). Such a word essentially picks out and characterizes a relevant set of referents for us.

This may help *us* determine what the target referents are, but will it help someone using another language? This seems unlikely. Perhaps we can point to the referents. For example, we can use "green" to describe the referents to ourselves so that *we* know what they are – what to point to (or present) – and then we can point to (or present) the referents so *they* (speakers of whatever language) will know what the referents they are supposed to describe (or respond to) are. But will speakers who are asked to describe (or respond to) the referents we are pointing to going to know what we are pointing at? Pointing alone seems unsatisfactory. (Imagine someone simply pointing to many examples of the referents encompassed by a foreign lexeme meaning "green color of plants." What sorts of descriptions are they likely to get from us?) Perhaps we can eliminate competing possibilities as to our intended referent when we point by putting our referents in a context where there can be no mistake about our intent, that is, we can take our referents from their usual contextual embeddedness and put them in situations where they only contrast with other similar referents. (Lenneberg and Roberts, 1956, p. 12, introduced their discussion of color in just this way: "If we were given a large number of color samples and asked to arrange them in a systematic fashion . . .") This guarantees by design that every response – ours or theirs, verbal or nonverbal – pertains to "color" as we have conceived of it. The assumption of universality is self-validating, since the entire universe of the task, both conceptual and operational, is defined and structured with reference to our lexical category. There is little or no room for any other category system to reveal itself, and no possibility of recognizing its appearance within the preset interpretive framework. Lenneberg made this explicit:

Our aim is to study how words relate to objects. But we cannot study the behavior of *words* unless we keep some control over the objects. We must do everything we can so as to bring some order into physical "reality." We have chosen phenomena that can be measured and ordered with respect to each other. The color space is simply an ordering device that allows us to assign every possible color a specific position or point. The entire world of color is encompassed in the color space. Our next step now is to discover how the color words of a given language, say English or Navaho, fit into this space ... Obtaining replies to this type of question will be called *mapping color terms into the color space*. Naturally, every language is likely to have somewhat different maps; but the color space, which merely describes the psychophysical properties of colors, is constant for all of mankind.   (1967, pp. 338–39)

All this merely formalizes the implicit logic of the "snow" example.

Regarding the second criterion of variability, Lenneberg and Roberts remarked that

The criterion of variability is also met by the language of experience if we may judge by the ample literature on the subject.   (1956, p. 8)

However, they never really discussed this variability in general terms. Turning specifically to color, they did, of course, present considerable data on Zuni color terms, but, as has been shown, the very formulation of the category "color" already shapes the data. Lenneberg and Roberts asked informants to "recite all the color words they can remember" (1956, p. 20; see also p. 23); what this question involved in practical terms is not clear, since there appears to be no general term meaning 'color' in Zuni. They then asked informants to map these color words onto a color array (1956, pp. 25–27). The Zuni results differed at a few points from the English results, but nothing truly unusual arose – or could have arisen. (These Zuni results are discussed further below.)

Further evidence for the tacit use of English as a metalanguage emerges, finally, in the discussion of how the language of experience meets the simplicity criterion. Lenneberg and Roberts argued that the parameters for describing stimuli constitute a frame for description:

the stimuli of sense perception can in most cases be ordered in systematic ways, and the *ordering systems* provide frames for description.   (1956, p. 8)

This makes it appear that these ordering systems are language independent and solve the problem of description of the referents. But notice that they have already presupposed the segmentation of some set of stimuli to which this ordering system applies. The ordering systems must order something, and it is that something that is problematic. Consider another remark:

description of the referents or range of referents of the words *hot, sweet, loud* can sometimes be accomplished with a single parameter and very often with as few as two or three.   (1956, p. 8)

This makes it absolutely clear that the ordering systems apply to (or operate on) the "referents or range of referents of the words" of English.

Consider, now, the ordering system for color in particular:

Since we are proposing to use the three perceptual dimensions [hue, brightness, and saturation] as a metalanguage in terms of which the referent of any color term can be described, we might pause to ask to what extent the coordinate system arising from the use of these dimensions might itself be culture bound. Two questions are involved: the first is whether the dimensions (hue, brightness, and saturation) are universally applicable; the second is whether the calibration of these dimensions is reliable. For the time being, we may leave the first question unanswered, recognizing, of course, that there is nothing "natural, logical, or necessary" in these dimensions. For our purposes, they are measuring sticks which can be conveniently used in describing cross-cultural similarities or differences.   (Lenneberg and Roberts, 1956, p. 14)

What has been left "unanswered" here is exactly the central issue of concern: the validity of using the categories of one language, however refined scientifically, as the metalanguage (or measuring stick) for comparison with others. The entire approach guarantees that one will not find interesting and truly novel category differences, for one can only encompass descriptively (or measure quantitatively) what the metalanguage allows. The fact that we can precisely characterize the English category in scientific, psychophysical terms does not and cannot justify the use of the category comparatively. As Lenneberg and Roberts concede, it may be that "there is nothing 'natural, logical, or necessary' in these dimensions" insofar as we are concerned with natural language. In fact, even though the formal scientific characterization is derivative of English (or the Western European languages more generally), it can obscure the true nature of the native language categories as actually used by speakers. Arguments can be made, for example, that specific English color terms commonly refer only to *hues* (as opposed to saturation and brightness) and that black and white are not color terms at all. Consider, for example, the third use of the word *color* in the following passage:

Standardized color stimuli were used in conducting the research. These consist of a set of 329 color chips ... The set is composed of 320 color chips ... and nine chips of neutral hue (white, black and greys).   (Berlin and Kay, 1969, p. 5)

Summary

The essential problem with this whole approach is that at some level Brown, Lenneberg, and Roberts really did accept the naive view which they questioned at one point in their discussion, namely that languages are "itemized inventories of reality" (Brown and Lenneberg, 1954, p. 454). Categories of English can be and were used as the metalanguage for describing this objective reality. Then, once this version of objective reality is presupposed, the relation both of language forms and of nonlinguistic behaviors to "it" can be assessed. The nature of reality itself (that is, its linguistic and cultural constitution) is never taken as problematic in this approach or in the entire tradition built on it. The categories of the English are transparent windows to reality. And, since the referential value of the forms in other languages are pre-regimented in terms of the English, the structures of reference in these languages never contradict the presuppositions of the metalanguage, but merely re-represent (re-present) the universe of denotata it allows in some new divisions.

There is a place, to be sure, for preliminary notional characterization of common referential value of similar forms in diverse languages, but such characterizations should build from the similarities among language structures (i.e., the grammatical categories) to commonality in typical referential value. Unlike Lenneberg's methodology, such an approach is systematically vulnerable to reconceptualization in light of the different languages at issue.

It is clear that some metalanguage for description is necessary. By contrast to the work in anthropology reviewed in chapter 3, Lenneberg's emphasis on this must be regarded as a significant advance even if his specific solution is unsatisfying. Theoretical languages in the physical sciences are created to describe physical phenomena, and hence they are tested against the world of physical phenomena – objective reality – which provides the feedback whereby they are developed and refined. But our theoretical language in this case is not describing the world of physical phenomena but languages, or, perhaps more correctly, language–world relationships. (It is this fact of language describing language that makes it a *meta*language that we need.) In this situation we cannot simply test or refine our theoretical (meta)language against the world of physical phenomena as expressed in our language; rather, it must be tested against the observed structure of languages, or language–world relationships, whatever this might involve in terms of additional social and psychological factors. No simple appeal to the world of physical reality can ever capture these other dimensions – especially when the categories of one specific language are privileged in the very description of that physical reality. A major task in the companion case study will be to develop a metalanguage for characterizing the differences between languages or language–world relationships which includes, but is not limited to, an appeal to typical referents.

Linguistic structure as a determinant of color cognition

The first major period (1953–68) of research on linguistic relativity using the color domain corresponded with the rapid post-war development of psycholinguistics as a subfield at the intersection of psychology and linguistics. During this period, the operative hypothesis was that linguistic structure was a determinant of color cognition, and the major immediate goal was developing a methodology for investigating this hypothesis which would be consistent with traditional psychologic assumptions and interests. The previous sections of this chapter hav described the approach to language characteristic of this tradition. Th section will recount how the investigation of the relation of language t thought was operationalized.

The concept of codability: the work of Brown and Lenneberg

The principal empirical study employing Lenneberg's methodology wa reported in Brown and Lenneberg (1954; see also Brown, 1956, pp. 308–9; 1958b, ch. 7). This study has served as the prototype for nearly all subsequent research purporting to study Whorf's ideas within the discipline of psychology. The study used color as the objective referential domain upon which both language (lexical denotation) and thought (perceptual recognition memory) operated.

Lexical categories and objective reality

Brown and Lenneberg began by characterizing the naive, or common-sense, view of language as a simple itemized inventory of reality and by contrasting this with Whorf's argument that

the world is differently experienced and conceived in different linguistic communities and . . . that language is causally related to these psychological differences.
(1954, p. 454)[25]

The rest of the preliminary discussion elaborated on the possible meaning of and evidence for these two points.

Brown and Lenneberg claimed that Whorf's evidence for the first point, that there are in fact cognitive differences, "is entirely linguistic" (1954, p. 455). This argument was introduced to indicate the significance of their own study, which attempted to provide the crucial nonlinguistic evidence. As should be clear, however, their claim ignored both the ethnographic (or "cultural") evidence which Whorf provided and the anecdotal evidence of individual behavior from the fire-causing examples which Lenneberg (1953) had criticized. Brown and Lenneberg divided this "entirely linguistic" evidence into two types: lexical features and structural features.

A reinterpretation of Whorf's lexical examples

Their discussion of lexical features of language centered on Whorf's example of the differences between Eskimo and English expressions for what we call "kinds of snow." Their argument had two characteristics which are already familiar from the earlier discussion but which warrant brief reiteration.

First, on the linguistic side, lexical meaning was reduced to denotational reference:

Words are used meaningfully when they are selectively employed with reference to some kind of environment – whether physical, social, or linguistic. The linguist in the field may discover the referent of a term by noting the pattern of its usage.
(1954, p. 455)

As we have already seen, this conceptualization effectively washed out the importance of structural relations among forms in a language as constituting a significant part of the meaning of a lexical item. This was coupled, of course, with the use of English lexical categories as the metalanguage for describing referents.

Second, on the cognitive side, their original characterization of Whorf's views as having to do with the way the world is "experienced and conceived" was rearticulated as having to do with a problem of "perceptual discrimination," which in turn was operationalized as being "consistently able to respond differently to distinctive stimulus situations" (1954, p. 455). This made the claim more amenable to treatment by certain traditional psychological techniques, but also transformed the problem in two important ways. A question about what a person habitually does or regularly experiences became a question about what one is *able* to do, and a question about concepts became a question about a perceptual response.

The dismissal of Whorf's structural examples

Brown and Lenneberg considered structural features of the grammar (as opposed to lexical features) only briefly. Their basic criticism of Whorf's arguments was that he assumed that such structural elements (for instance, nouns, gender, etc.) are "symbolic categories," that is, that they have referential meaning. Thus,

When [Whorf] finds structural differences in languages he concludes that there are parallel cognitive differences ... When the structural class has ... obvious semantic properties, Whorf's conclusions have a kind of plausibility.
However, very few structural classes have such clear and consistent meanings.
(1954, p. 456)

It appears here that Brown and Lenneberg mean to refer to form classes in Bloomfield's sense and not grammatical categories in Whorf's sense (following Boas and Sapir). Even given this shift in focus, it seems unfair to say that Whorf would take *any* structural fact and convert it directly into a cognitive meaning – Brown and Lenneberg have merely caricatured him here. Whorf's point was rather that some formal categories do in fact have such meaningful correlates and that many more can serve as bridges for the analogical flow of meaning. For the latter reason, even if some structural feature did not have "meaning" in Brown and Lenneberg's sense, this would not seem to warrant ignoring its possible significance.

Implicitly recognizing this, they extended their argument one step further by saying that even if such meanings could be established by an analyst, this does not mean that they are present for speakers:

Even where the ethnolinguist can discover consistent structural meanings, it does not follow that these meanings are present to the native speakers of a language ... No safe inferences about cognition can be made on the basis of the simple existence of the structural classes described by Whorf.   (1954, p. 456)

Of course, the exact same argument can be made about lexical items, and, therefore, about Brown and Lenneberg's own claim about color terms. Their comments merely restate the obvious, that at some level the problem is an empirical one, not a logical one. The underlying message here is perhaps that structural facts are harder to comprehend within Brown and Lenneberg's framework, or, what is more likely, that for some reason lexical items seem more clearly "meaningful" and "relevant to cognition" to them. We may have here a striking illustration of the limits of awareness discussed in chapter 4. When their disregard of grammatical structure is coupled with the use of English lexical categories as the metalanguage for comparative work, there is no room for discovering the sort of variance of interest to Whorf.

Codability: linking language and thought

Brown and Lenneberg attempted to give an account of why differences in terminology such as those between Eskimo and English exist. They formulated their account in terms of the notion of *codability* (later called "name-determinacy" by Lenneberg, 1967, p. 342). Their argument was based on Zipf's (1935) empirical observation that within a given language more frequently used lexical items tend to be shorter than less frequently used ones, whether this length is measured in phonemes or syllables. Brown and Lenneberg generalized this observation:

> Suppose we generalize the findings even beyond Zipf's formulation and propose that the length of a verbal expression provides an index of its frequency in speech and that this, in turn, is an index of the frequency with which the relevant perceptual judgments of difference and equivalence are made. If this is true, it would follow that *the Eskimo distinguishes his three kinds of snow more often than Americans do.*   (1954, p. 455, my italics)

Three distinct steps are packed into this generalization. First, a relationship between frequency of use and relative word length has been generalized to a relationship between frequency of use and relative "length of a verbal expression." This allowed Brown and Lenneberg to go beyond comparing words and apply the principle to comparisons between words and whole phrases, which they needed to do to deal with Whorf's "snow" example. They ignored the fact that many words are longer than phrases if measured morphologically or phonemically.

Second, the relations of length within a single language have been generalized to comparisons across languages. There was nothing in Zipf's account to justify such a cross-language comparison. Zipf's claim was about a common relation of length to frequency within any given language – presumably because it is questionable to compute relative length across different phonological and grammatical systems and frequency of use across different universes of discourse. Brown and Lenneberg's reformulation amounts to an evaluation of what the significance of the difference would be if it were an internal characteristic of English. Further, to say that the Eskimo have lexicalized what for us are complex noun phrases (because they use them so frequently) essentially presupposes that they *originally had* complex noun phrases of the same type as we have, that is, with the unified conceptual content shown in the common noun phrase head "snow." This cannot be presupposed. Only if one can guarantee such substantive unity can specific formal differences be taken as significant. Without other information about the languages, the line of reasoning from word length to psychological salience *across* languages simply cannot be grounded.

Third, frequency of use is assumed to have some relationship to frequency of perceptual judgment. Although this may be a reasonable inference in specific cases, it seems problematic as a general principle. The problem is that some extremely frequent formal elements with perceptual concomitants (for example, *to* denoting locative relation) need not always implicate the perceptual concomitant when they are used (for example, *to* signaling indirect object, infinitive verb, etc.). Notice that Zipf makes no claim about content.

Notice also that language structure has already been made into a dependent variable. The Eskimo are not distinguishing "kinds of snow" more often because the structure of their language makes this easy or obligatory (although such an argument could be made), but rather, the structure of their language springs from differences in attending to "snow." This becomes clear in the ensuing discussion, and Brown and Lenneberg emphasized that:

Such conclusions are, of course, supported by extralinguistic cultural analysis, which reveals the importance of snow in the Eskimo's life.   (1954, p. 456)

There is nothing inherently wrong with such a formulation in itself, but finding this conceptualization of language as a dependent variable within the logic of a formulation supposedly attempting to test for the effects of language as an independent variable is surprising. It suggests just how deeply embedded this view of language is.

Further, this approach renders all nonlinguistic evidence ambiguous, since it can equally well be "determining of" as "determined by" language. For example, Brown and Lenneberg next proposed that frequency of perceptual categorization indexes general psychological salience:

We will go further and propose that increased frequency of a perceptual categorization will mean a generally greater "availability" of that category . . . We think, really, that more namable [i.e., lexicalized] categories are nearer the top of the cognitive "deck." (1954, p. 456)

So high frequency of use of a form should generate high psychological salience of the category it encodes. But, following the argument embodied in the generalization of Zipf's law, it could equally well be argued that the "availability" arises from general cultural salience, which is merely indexed by speech.

Figure 9 displays the logic of Brown and Lenneberg's application of this generalization of Zipf's law to lexical items graphically, using as an example the inter-cultural comparison of the codability of "kinds of snow." Words are relatively "short" forms. This implies that the categories encoded by words are frequently used and that they have high psychological salience. Thus, all things being equal, categories namable (intra-linguistically) by a lexical item are more salient than those which are not so namable (i.e., which require several words to describe). Applying the same reasoning comparatively (inter-linguistically) yields the implication that if one language uses a phrase where another uses a word, then the category is more psychologically salient in the latter. It is

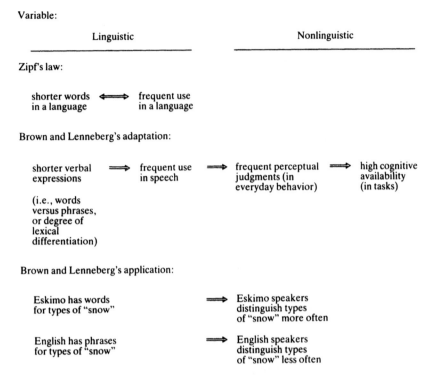

Figure 9 The inter-cultural case: operationalization of the linguistic and nonlinguistic variables linked with Zipf's law in Brown and Lenneberg (1954). (⟸⟹ to be read as "correlates with"; ⟹ to be read as "indexes.")

this concept of relative namability, later called "codability," which is the basis for the experimental work.

The codability of colors and color cognition in English

Brown and Lenneberg's actual experimental study concerns the relation within English between linguistic codability of various colors and recognition memory for those same colors. The general rationale for working with the color domain has been outlined in earlier sections.

Operationalizing codability

Having settled on color as a domain, Brown and Lenneberg's first task was to operationalize and measure the linguistic codability of various colors. They selected a set of 24 colors to serve as stimuli; the 24 both sampled evenly from a larger array of 240 colors and included those colors which are the best exemplars of the eight most frequent English color words.[26] Then subjects were presented with the colors one at a time and asked to "name" them with the word or words one would usually use to describe the color to a friend. Several measures were then drawn from this task: number of syllables in the name, number of words in the name, reaction time from presentation of the color to uttering a response, interpersonal agreement on the name, and intrapersonal agreement (i.e., over time) on the name. These five measures, under statistical analysis, yielded a single common factor – labeled "codability" – which accounted for most of the variance in the naming of the 24 colors. Notice that "codability" was defined as a property of the *color stimulus* when presented *in isolation* from other colors. Relative codability involves the relation of one color's typical encoding in English to the general pattern of encoding among the 24 other colors. But the other colors are not copresent for naming. The interpersonal agreement measure showed the largest factor loading and was used for all subsequent comparisons with cognitive behavior.

There has been considerable slippage here in the concept of codability. First it had to do with lexical versus phrasal encoding, then it became an abstract "variable" for which lexical encoding was only one among several indices. This "variable" is never really defined by Brown and Lenneberg. And now for the subsequent experiments it will be represented by degree of interpersonal agreement. The original relation to linguistic structure (however weak) has now been completely lost. Lenneberg and Roberts later defined codability as follows:

Codability is a measure of the efficiency with which either a color or another sensory experience may be transmitted in a given language code.
(Lenneberg and Roberts, 1956, p. 20)

The problem is that efficiency can be a function of many variables other than linguistic structure (Lenneberg, 1967, p. 352). This notion of efficiency, literally construed, will re-emerge some years later in the concept of communication accuracy.

The relation of codability to recognition memory

The next step was to compare this "linguistic" measure of codability with "nonlinguistic" recognition memory performance. Experimental subjects were briefly shown 4 color samples at a time, and then after a thirty-second delay asked to identify the colors from among a larger array of 120 color samples.[27] These "nonlinguistic" results were scored

Variable:

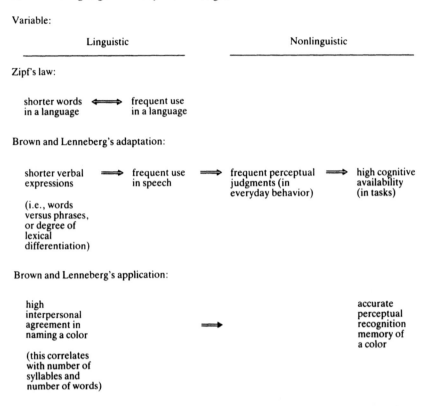

Figure 10 The intra-cultural case: operationalization of the linguistic and nonlinguistic variables linked with Zipf's law in Brown and Lenneberg (1954). (⟸⟹ to be read as "correlates with"; ⟹ to be read as "indexes"; ⟹ to be read as "predicts [under hypothesis]".)

and then compared with the "linguistic" codability scores and found to correlate positively. Thus the "linguistic" and "nonlinguistic" responses were correlated. The result was not, however, statistically reliable – although Brown and Lenneberg did not point this out. The overall logic of the operationalization and experimental design for this intra-cultural case is shown in figure 10.

The problem of perceptual discriminability

At this point Brown and Lenneberg introduced a new dimension of the problem, namely that there might be differences in perceptual discriminability:

There is, however, another variable that influenced recognition. The 120 colors used are not perceptually perfectly equidistant. The manufacture of equidistant color chips is technically difficult and expensive and, indeed, above a certain level of saturation, impossible. Since we were unable to control experimentally the variable "discriminability," we must ask whether or not our findings were due to a positive correlation between codability and discriminability. Could it be that our codable colors were so distant, perceptually, from their nearest neighbors that their superior recognizability was actually due to these better discrimination conditions? (1954, p. 460)

Notice that "discriminability" is a property of a *color stimulus* when presented *in the context of a particular stimulus array*. It is the relation of the distinctiveness of a color from its neighbors to the general pattern of distinctiveness of other colors in the same array. It is different than "codability," which is a property of the color taken in isolation from an array.[28]

Brown and Lenneberg then constructed a measure of relative discriminability and recalculated their results controlling for this factor. They found that codability and discriminability correlated negligibly and that controlling statistically for the effects of discriminability revealed a slightly stronger correlation between codability and recognition memory. This corrected value, unlike the original value for the codability–recognition correlation, was statistically reliable. For some reason Brown and Lenneberg failed to point out that the level of the discriminability–recognition correlation was even higher, that is, that differences in perceptual discriminability accounted for more of the variance in recognition memory than did linguistic codability. The more balanced conclusion would be that recognition memory for a color can be predicted by (correlates with) two factors: its linguistic codability and its perceptual discriminability relative to other colors in the array within which it is to be distinguished. A composite factor such as "contextualized codability" (or "strategic codability") would probably provide the best predictor.

A mechanism by which the correlation between codability and memory might arise was suggested by informants' replies ("in trial runs") as to

how they managed to retain the four colors in memory after they were removed from sight. Most *Ss* reported that they named the colors when they were exposed and "stored" the names. (1954, p. 460)

From this Brown and Lenneberg argued that

It seemed likely, therefore, that those colors that are quite unequivocally coded would be most likely to be recognized. When a color elicits a considerable range of names, the chances of recovering the color from the name would be reduced. (1954, p. 460)

This inference that unequivocal coding should yield high recognition is not warranted. What matters (by their own evidence) is the effectiveness of that encoding relative to the array within which the color must be recognized.[29] This may bear no simple relationship to homogeneity of response.

Nonetheless, Brown and Lenneberg administered several variants to their task to try to manipulate the difficulty of "storage." They argued that as the storage demands increase, codability (the "linguistic" independent variable) should become a more important factor relative to perceptual discrimination (the "nonlinguistic" independent variable), which should stay the same or diminish. The correlation of memory with codability does indeed rise with task difficulty, but the relationship between discriminability and recognition shows no such simple linear relationship. The possible interactions of the two factors are not considered. In all, the analysis of "difficulty" seems too inadequately developed to establish much about the relative importance of linguistic codability versus perceptual discriminability as factors in recognition memory – although any account would clearly profit by successfully incorporating such a factor.

Comparative results with Zuni speakers

As should be clear this study did not, in itself, address Whorf's basic questions about the significance of differences *between* languages. In part, as we have seen, this was because Brown and Lenneberg (1954, p. 458) believed that inter-language comparison was not necessary to investigate Whorf's proposals. Nonetheless, they turned in their discussion section to a brief description of a comparative study with Zuni Indians using similar methods and apparatus. Lenneberg and Roberts ·(1956) later provided a fuller report on the Zuni work. The latter report was quite thorough in presenting linguistic details – in fact, more thorough and more informative than the account of the English results in Brown and Lenneberg.[30] However, neither study fully reported on Zuni recognition memory results.

Brown and Lenneberg presented the following information about the Zuni study:

The Zuni color lexicon codes the colors we call orange and yellow with a single term. Monolingual Zuni *S*s in their recognition task frequently confused the orange and yellow colors in our stimulus set. Our English-speaking *S*s never made this error. It is a distinction which is highly codable in English and highly uncodable in Zuni.   (1954, p. 461)

(Notice that the Zuni can be seen as "confused" and in "error" only if one accepts that the categories exemplified by the stimulus set are different, and this entails accepting the experimenters' description of reality, that is, the English-based metalanguage of description.) Lenneberg and Roberts did not provide much additional information, apparently because the Zuni monolingual sample was elderly,[31] small ($n = 4$), and not strictly comparable to the English-speaking sample. This is the information they *did* provide:[32]

In one respect, however, the repetition of the recognition experiment with Zunis was truly amazing. In English, orange and yellow are the most sharply defined color-categories, and, accordingly, their foci scored highest in recognition by Americans. But monolingual Zunis do not distinguish at all between orange and yellow. The entire region is occupied by a single category. It is striking that not a single monolingual Zuni [$n = 4$] recognized correctly either orange or yellow thus completely bearing out the expectations based on the hypothesis. (1956, p. 31)

Putting these statements together, we learn that English speakers differentiate the colors "orange" and "yellow," define the lexical categories *orange* and *yellow*, referring to them quite narrowly, and do not confuse the colors "orange" and "yellow" in recognition. Zuni speakers do not differentiate the colors "orange" and "yellow," define the lexical category *lhupz/inna*,[33] referring to them quite broadly, and make errors with (confuse?) the colors "orange" and "yellow" in recognition.

One problem with this comparison with the Zuni lies in the ambiguous use of the term codability. The operational usage of Brown and Lenneberg (1954, p. 458) called a color highly codable to the extent it was invariably named by the same name, that is, elicited high interpersonal agreement. The expectation, comparatively, was that different colors would show this unanimity of response. In the absence of specific information on uniformity of naming, one has to rely on the original generalization of Zipf's law as with the "snow" example, namely that short length of utterance and frequency of use correlate inversely:

So long as the data collected are of the usual linguistic variety, this difference of codability will be manifest in only one way – environmental distinctions expressed lexically in one language are expressed with word combination in another language. (1954, p. 458)

A number of objections were raised earlier to the cross-linguistic use of this relation of length and frequency when one has no information about within-language patterns. And the relation between frequency and "unanimity in response" (Lenneberg, 1953, p. 469) or "reliability of naming response from person to person within the linguistic community and from time to time in one person" (Brown and Lenneberg, 1954, p. 462; also p. 459) seems beyond assessment without specific data on the language.[34]

Another problem is the degree to which the Zuni "color" terms correspond to our terms in the sense of referring to the same domain composed of the same three perceptual dimensions. This is a problem which has been mentioned repeatedly in this discussion. There are two principal problems. First, does a conceptual notion of "color" as a domain actually exist for the Zuni? And second, if so, do the parameters of that domain correspond to our own? Lenneberg and Roberts gave no clear answers to these issues. Although it does appear that the informants could in fact refer to the color samples without great trouble, a separate study by Hickerson (1975) concluded that there is no general term for "color" in Zuni. Further doubts about these Zuni data are raised, however, by some additional information (actually cited by Lenneberg and Roberts) which illustrates concretely the various parameters which can be involved in what appear to us to be "color" terms. Linguist Stanley Newman provided the following information concerning two Zuni terms which can be used to refer the "color 'yellow'":

As an example of discriminated meanings, Zuni has two lexemes expressing the literal notion of the color "yellow." Lexeme A would be used in contexts such as "yellow shirt, yellow paint." Lexeme B is employed in combinations such as "yellow skin, yellow leaves." The difference is not one of hue. Rather, lexeme A covers many shades of yellow characterizing an object, while lexeme B refers only to an object that has become yellow (or a related hue, which might be translated by English "pale" or "rusty") as a result of ripening or aging. In itself such a distinction has no wide significance, except perhaps to suggest that an investigation of color terms must recognize that such terms may express discriminations other than those involved in the color spectrum.

The semantic range of lexeme B, in various morphological combinations, indicates the manner in which certain concepts are linked in terms of Zuni cultural associations. In its singular form lexeme B refers to any ripened or aged yellow object. In the plural it is specialized to refer to pollen or corn meal, a culturally important linkage for other related meanings of this lexeme. When it is preposed to an element meaning "stretching across," it forms the prayer term for "road" and, by extension, "the road of life." Reference here is to the ceremonial sprinkling of corn meal to form a path, symbolizing the sacred road.

(Newman, 1954, pp. 87–88)

In a comparison of the morphological status of the various color terms Hickerson (1975) reached a similar, although more general, conclusion about Zuni terminology, namely that there were two basic kinds of terms with color reference: broad abstract terms deriving from verbs and specific terms deriving from substantives (nouns and particles):

The verbs [referring to color] deal, ultimately, with processes of change or 'becoming'; most of the actual forms indicate an apprehended verbal state. Nouns and particles refer to intrinsic color, specific to a substance or object, and unchanging. In other words, these two types of terms – verbals and substantives – seem to reflect to basically different types of experience.

(Hickerson, 1975, p. 328)[35]

The assumption that the categories (lexical or otherwise) of another language which show some extensional overlap with our own also correspond in intensional terms is unwarranted.

Other cases could be given of the multiple perceptual or conceptual values which can be coupled with terms referring in part to hue. For example, there are many English lexical forms which also blend reference to hue with other meaning values. Most such forms have (or had historically) special reference to humans (for instance, *blond, brunet/ brunette*), other animate entities (for instance, *palomino, appaloosa, bay, sorrel*), or socially significant objects (for instance, *scarlet, maroon*). Such forms are common in many languages where "color" terms may contain as a central element of their meaning reference to person- or body-types, to socially significant objects such as domesticated animals, edible plants and plant products, and ritually significant minerals, or to state changes and stages in sequences (see, for example, Conklin, 1955; McNeill, 1972; Kuschel and Monberg, 1974; Bolton, 1978; Turton, 1980). Such linguistic patterns, that is, cross-linguistic regularities in the ways languages elaborate descriptions of the appearance of referents, are bypassed in the psychophysical conceptualization of color-term meaning. Any truly *linguistic* universals having to do with reference to what we call "color" will have to be built up from a careful analysis of actual language patterns rather than imposed on them by an a priori scheme.

Summary

Brown and Lenneberg's study provided the blueprint for the main features of this tradition. The linguistic variables of interest to Whorf were altered in significant and characteristic ways, including the focus on lexical forms rather than grammatical ones, the reduction of lexical meaning to denotational meaning, the use of evidence from a single language to draw inferences about a fundamentally cross-linguistic question, the use of the denotational value of English lexical items as the metacategories for comparative work, and the equation of lexeme use in an experimental context with language use more generally.

The understanding of thought was also transformed in important ways, including a concern with how cognitive processes "in" the individual intersect with cultural category content. This represented the addition of an important perspective to research on the linguistic relativity problem. However, the value of this shift in focus is somewhat undermined by the emphasis on relatively perceptual processes like short-term recognition memory rather than more conceptual processes like logical memory and reasoning, on behavior in artificially contrived experimental contexts with unknown relation to habitual everyday thought, and on global quantitative correlation rather than on more qualitative assessment.

Despite these various problems, the attempt to introduce methodological control into research on linguistic relativity represented an important step. In this respect, the whole approach developed within the comparative psycholinguistics tradition is in sharp contrast to the work in anthropology, where, on the one hand, the topical foci are not theoretically motivated and hence vary widely and, on the other hand, the research methods tend to lack even minimal levels of control if they are specified at all. The challenge is to retain some of this methodological rigor without sacrificing so many of Whorf's insights.

From codability to communication accuracy

Replications, extensions, and problems

Over the next decade most textbooks in psychology, anthropology, and linguistics presented (and still present) differential lexical segmentation of the color domain as the quintessential example of the way in which linguistic relativity might operate. But the actual amount of subsequent empirical work using the basic elements of Brown and Lenneberg's approach was very, very small.[36] There were three classes of studies. First, there were replications of the basic finding (for instance, Van de Geer, 1972 [1960]). Secondly, there were extensions of the Brown and Lenneberg approach to relating codability to recognition memory beyond the domain of color to photographs of faces (Frijda and Van de Geer, 1961), other pictures (Stefflre, 1958, cited in Lantz and Stefflre, 1964), figures (Glanzer and Clark, 1962), binary numbers (Glanzer and Clark, 1963), and nonsense syllables (Stefflre, 1963, cited in Lantz and Stefflre, 1964). And, finally, there were a series of developments in the research on the domain of color centering around variations in the stimulus materials and experimental tasks.[37]

The problematic for the subsequent studies on color stemmed from research by Burnham and Clark (1955) which examined hue memory using a different array of colors: the Farnsworth–Munsell array. This array contains only moderately saturated colors separated by uniform psychophysical increments. Lenneberg (1961) was able to compare the results of this memory experiment with naming data which he had collected on the same array. He found that with this array codability and recognition memory were negatively correlated. Lenneberg concluded that the original results were restricted in their validity to the Brown–Lenneberg array. He proposed an alternative theory to account for the two sets of results in terms of subject-generated linguistic anchor points for each array.

Development of the communication accuracy measure: the work of Lantz and Stefflre

A more satisfactory solution emerged from the work of Lantz and Stefflre (1964),[38] who proposed using a new measure of codability which they called communication accuracy. They argued that memory was like communication with oneself over time. To the extent that this intrapersonal communication is like interpersonal communication using language, it should be possible to approximate it and investigate its functioning by studying such interpersonal communication:

We will view memory as though it were a situation in which an individual communicates to himself through time using the brain as a channel. This communication process can be approximated by having individuals communicate with other people. Items accurately communicated interpersonally would then be predicted to be more accurately communicated intrapersonally as measured by the usual memory tests. And, pairs of items confused in interpersonal communication would tend to be confused in tests of memory.

(Lantz and Stefflre, 1964, p. 473)[39]

(See also Stefflre, Castillo Vales, and Morley, 1966, p. 112). Communication accuracy was assessed by having some subjects encode the colors "using the word or words you would use to name it to a friend so that he or she could pick it out" of the array (which they were shown before beginning the task) (Lantz and Stefflre, 1964, p. 475). Then a second group of subjects decoded these descriptions by trying to find the original color in the recognition array; each decoder worked with a subset of actual encodings counterbalanced so as to equalize the effect of any given encodings on the overall score.

This proposed measure of codability – communication accuracy – was superior to previous measures in two respects. First, it more directly simulated the hypothesized cognitive activity, unlike the more indirect measures such as intersubject agreement and length of utterance. Subjects actually used the encodings to find the chips, thus giving a direct measure of the relative effectiveness of the encoding. Second, the measure was context-sensitive, that is, it allowed the linguistic variable to respond to specific details of the task context. This is extremely important in allowing the measure to work effectively across a variety of stimulus arrays and task procedures:

The nature of the context in which a color – and presumably any other sensory stimulus – is found is very important in determining what kind of verbal measure will successfully predict nonverbal behavior in regard to it ... the communication accuracy measure reflects the effects of context on ease of recognition, while naming agreement does not. If the nonverbal measures obtained on a given item can be radically altered by context – as recognition can – then the verbal measure from which we are trying to predict should also have this property, as communication accuracy does.   (Lantz and Stefflre, 1964, p. 480)

Thus, for example, naming agreement across subjects will be a less efficient predictor if there are multiple names for a color, each of which is equally effective, or if there are many alternative colors in the recognition array to which a given name, however apt, could apply. Communication accuracy as a measure escapes these problems by allowing the subjects to tailor their descriptions to the particular array and by permitting all the descriptions for a given color to be used even if they are quite diverse.

The experimental work showed that communication accuracy not only predicted the memory results better than any other measure of codability previously used, but it also predicted memory equally well on both of the two stimulus arrays. This effectively resolved the extant contradictions within this tradition and firmly established at least one language and cognition relationship.

A cross-cultural study of communication accuracy: the work of Stefflre, Castillo Vales, and Morley

Two additional studies soon followed using the communication accuracy measure on different populations. Both of these studies are highly significant. The first, a cross-cultural study by Stefflre, Castillo Vales, and Morley (1966), assessed the relationship between communication accuracy and recognition memory using the Farnsworth–Munsell array in two additional languages: Yucatec Maya and Mexican Spanish. It is worth emphasizing that this was the only cross-linguistic study within this entire first era that presented the results of comparative cognitive assessment.[40] Stefflre *et al.* found that communication accuracy and recognition memory correlated within each language group but that speakers of the two different languages found different colors easy to communicate and easy to remember. They also asked speakers in each language to identify the color samples most typical of each of their descriptions. Further analysis then revealed that the recognition memory errors tended to lie in the direction of the colors identified as typical of the descriptions. From the perspective of this tradition, both of these findings were striking confirmations of the linkage of language and thought. Unfortunately, this study has received surprisingly little attention. (But see Lucy and Shweder, 1979, and Lucy, 1981.)

One difficulty with the communication accuracy measure appears in this comparative work, namely that the predictor bears a very ambiguous relationship to the lexical or grammatical structure of a language. This is true both in practice and in theory. In practice, Stefflre *et al.* (1966) presented no information on the structure of color expressions in Yucatec and Spanish. The whole experiment was presented without a shred of linguistic description. Thus, although they tell us that the two languages differ in their communication accuracy scores, they do not tell us what the linguistic expressions actually are or how they differ (if they do) in any significant way. Yet, if such a difference is to be called a linguistic difference, one should presumably be able to show that the observed effects stem from, or at least correspond to, some facts about the structural patterning of the two languages. But "language" as represented by communication accuracy remains a black box from the point of view of this experiment.[41] It is difficult, therefore, to tie the results to any facts about the languages as such and to rule out the possible influence of some third variable.[42]

The ambiguity also exists at the level of theory. Lantz and Stefflre carried the tacit assumptions of this tradition to their logical conclusion. For language, they have maximized the focus on the denotational (or extensional) potential of languages regardless of structural means: how well can the languages get a given referential job done given a certain task? From this point of view, it does not really matter how, specifically, speakers communicate the colors. Lantz and Stefflre viewed this as an advantage:

The kind of formulation presented here of relations between language and behavior emphasizes the productivity of language – new descriptions may be formed spontaneously and function to encode stimuli effectively ... Any description of the relations between language and behavior or language and thought that does not take this into account and emphasizes only the role of dictionary words and/or grammatical categories will find it difficult to deal with the facts found in a particular experimental context. (1964, p. 481)

This was worded as an additional consideration (i.e., one shouldn't be limited to the dictionary and grammatical categories), but it made explicit all the assumptions latent in Lenneberg's emphases on the functional equivalence of languages as denotational devices – the irrelevance of specific messages and of code differences. Yet in one sense, it should have been surprising to Lantz and Stefflre that there were any cognitive differences, since the principle that anything can be said in any language coupled with total freedom of expression on a specific task ought to insure potential equivalence at this level.

Second, in terms of the theoretical view of the relations between language and thought, they argued that it is denotationally adequate utterances (or encodings) that actually correspond to how Language is used in Thought. The approach is reminiscent of the claim that thought is a form of inner speech. Ultimately this approach shifted the focus still further away from the significance of patterns of structural organization as subtle guides for and influences on habitual patterns of thought. But, more significantly, the original Brown and Lenneberg conceptualization that colors (or any aspect of experience) codable with a lexical item (or structurally minimal unit of some form) would be better remembered (more "available") was simply dropped from further consideration. This was the last remnant of "linguistic structure" in Brown and Lenneberg's approach. And Whorf's questions about the analogical suggestiveness of structural patterns continued to be completely bypassed.

To recognize these difficulties does not necessarily imply that either the practice or the theory is incorrect or unmotivated, but only that there has been substantial movement away from original concerns and conceptualizations. The Lantz and Steffle formulation represents, in some ways, the logical outgrowth of a number of underlying tendencies in this tradition. First, there was the inadequate treatment of language, reflected, on the one hand, in the persistent reluctance to engage in the difficult task of comparative linguistic analysis and, on the other hand, in the strong emphasis on the denotational aspect of language. These tendencies account for the original concern with a narrowly denotational interpretation of lexical items of English, the emphasis on what can be said in a language, and the continuing acceptability of research with no report of descriptive linguistic data. This combination of an emphasis on denotation and what can be said, in a context of indifference to significant structural differences, assured, over time, an increased concern with the responsiveness of language to task- and immediate context-defined ends rather than a concern with the general significance of structural means and meaning.

Second, there was the constant focus on psychological mechanisms, that is, how language is actually used in thought. This was reflected primarily in the continual concern with the relation of Language to Thought. It interacted with the conception of language just mentioned to produce the initial concern with the relative psychological salience of surface lexical items. Later this was expanded to include larger stretches of speech. This expansion was a natural outgrowth of the emphasis on what can be said, rather than on what habitually must be or is said. And the eventual development, in line with this process-oriented interpretation, into a loose theory of inner speech merely makes overt what has been assumed from the outset, namely that the actual surface forms of language are involved in thought. All that has been changed is that chunks larger than lexical items are now considered to be cognitively relevant.

Third, the emphasis on experimental methodology led, again, almost inevitably, to the discovery that certain experimental procedures and assumptions were instrumental in creating the specific results. Thus, this tradition, like so many others in experimental psychology, turned into a study of "the experiment":

> It has been our experience that any modification in an experimental procedure that alters the way subjects describe the situation to themselves may alter the results of the experiment. (Lantz and Stefflre, 1964, p. 479)

Thus, it is no accident that Lantz and Stefflre's research was concerned with solving problems that had arisen with earlier experiments. It solves these problems by bringing the actual experimental design into line with the implicit assumptions of the tradition.

Communication accuracy in the deaf: the work of Lantz and Lenneberg

The second significant subsequent study, one involving several contrasts among deaf children, deaf adults, hearing children, and hearing adults using the Farnsworth–Munsell array, was reported by Lantz and Lenneberg (1966). The results basically show that communication accuracy predicts memory performance for the two groups (deaf and hearing), but that the pattern of communication and memory errors differ for the two groups. On the recognition task the children as a group made more errors than the adults, and the deaf as a group made slightly more errors than the hearing; however, there was no statistically reliable difference in absolute number of errors between the two adult groups (hearing and deaf), even though their patterns of recognition were quite different. What is important for present purposes is that both adult groups were operating with the same "language" from a structural point of view:

> The difference in Communication Accuracy between the deaf and hearing adults is particularly interesting because, after all, both groups use English. The incongruence between the performances indicates that Communication Accuracy reflects not only the semantic properties of a natural language but also the particular use that a group of speakers makes of the language. The deaf when communicating to each other or to themselves apparently make a different use of English than the hearing population. (Lantz and Lenneberg, 1966, p. 777)

This raised for the first time in the work on color the problem of a relativity of use.[43] The case was particularly salient because language structure was held constant (at least in theory), so the results could not be due to a difference in language structure *per se*; the rate of recognition accuracy was comparable, so the results could not be due to a difference in cognitive ability or in the supposed effectiveness of language in aiding cognition; and yet the two groups differed in their error patterns in ways predictable from their communication accuracy.

Results for the children were more difficult to compare because the deaf children made significantly more errors than the hearing children, but Lantz and Lenneberg observed:

> Much of the work in the language–thought hypothesis has been based on the belief that possession of a verbal label (especially possession of a commonly agreed-upon label) underlies the ability to perform various cognitive tasks more effectively. The fact that some of the deaf children in this study possessed the same names for the colors as the hearing children, but were far inferior to them on ability to remember the colors, makes it clear that the mere possession of a verbal label does not necessarily affect cognitive behavior. Apparently the hearing children used their verbal descriptions in some kind of intrapersonal communication system – that is, communicated to themselves across time – and the deaf children did not make this kind of use of their verbal descriptions.
>
> (Lantz and Lenneberg, 1966, p. 778)

This represented a potential quantitative difference in use between the two groups quite aside from any qualitative differences of the sort found for the adults. This concern with the differences in the cognitive use of color language represented a significant new insight, one which, unfortunately, has yet to be seriously explored.[44]

Summary

The concern with color codability gave way in time to a concern with communication accuracy. This development was a joint product of two forces: the discovery that the original findings linking codability and recognition memory were task- and stimulus-specific, and the inclination to a model that hypothesized internal processing mechanisms more directly by looking at external efficiency of encoding. The new measure proved effective in detecting cross-cultural differences – perhaps related to structural differences between languages – and in detecting differences between the hearing and deaf – probably related to differing patterns of language use in the two groups. The development of the communication accuracy concept condenses into a single measure the essence of the psycholinguistic tradition: it operationalizes both the theoretical concern with cognitive process and the theoretical indifference to questions of language structure.

Color cognition as a determinant of linguistic structure

A second major period (1969–78) of color research was inaugurated by the appearance of a study by anthropological linguists Berlin and Kay in 1969.[45] They were interested in contesting the claim "associated in America with the names of Edward Sapir and B. L. Whorf" that "the search for semantic universals is fruitless in principle" because "each language is semantically arbitrary relative to every other language" (1969, p. 2). They maintained that they had refuted this view by showing the existence of a semantic universal[46] precisely in the area of research typically used to exemplify linguistic relativity: "the alleged total semantic arbitrariness of the lexical coding of color" (1969, p. 2). Their study questioned the fundamental assumption of previous color research, namely that colors form an even perceptual continuum, and, building on this revision, they ultimately reversed the directionality of language–thought interaction to claim that the human visual system sets constraints on the range of variation in semantic structure.

Basic color terms and focal colors: the work of Berlin, Kay, and McDaniel

"Basic color terms"

Berlin and Kay (1969, pp. 5–7) first provide the criteria for identifying a "basic color term." The criteria are largely intuitive, that is, the notion of "basic" is given little formal theoretical justification. The general aim was to discover the terms in each language which have specialized reference to what English-speaking researchers would call colors. A mix of criteria was then created to exclude everything that was not wanted in this set. The criteria included formal qualities (i.e., monolexemic status), substantive values (i.e., breadth of signification relation to other terms, range of denotation), and behavioral responses (i.e., tendency to occur at the beginning of elicited lists of "color" terms). Applying these criteria (in conjunction with some subsidiary criteria) yields the English set of basic color terms. The intuitive appeal of this approach for English speakers is apparently so great that it has been widely accepted despite the obvious circularity of the procedure, the lack of coherent theoretical grounding for the criteria, and the inconsistent application of the criteria even to the English case. The conclusions of the study depend, of course, both on accepting these criteria and on their proper application.

different structural alternatives (for example, having three terms instead of five) necessarily alters the meaning of each term. But, in the end, the meaning *is* the denotation and the denotation *is* the focal color, and therefore the focal color *is* the semantic meaning of the "basic color terms."

These problems were treated somewhat more seriously in later work by Kay and McDaniel (1978, pp. 615–17), but even there, where the argument is considerably more sophisticated, in the end the semantic universals "are based on pan-human neurophysiological processes in the perception of color" (1978, p. 644). This emphasis on the shaping role of the color stimuli themselves was, as we have seen, an inevitable outcome of the original assumption that forms are fundamentally to be understood as denotational classifications of reality. In this respect, Berlin, Kay, and McDaniel continued the general pattern of development in this tradition by bringing the explicit theoretical understandings into line with the implicit assumptions which had always underlain the whole approach.

They also continued to verify these denotational values with an experimental task using a specific Munsell array. Even accepting a denotational approach, this significantly constrained the potential for detecting significant denotational variation. The impact of the task situation and materials themselves on the findings were not investigated[49] either by direct manipulation[50] or by the introduction of additional nonexperimental materials. The impact of such factors on the results is difficult to judge, but given the history of difficulties with different stimulus arrays in this tradition (recall Lantz and Stefflre, 1964), such effects are likely. In short, even in challenging some of the principal explicit assumptions of the color research tradition, certain tacit assumptions and methodological limitations have been left intact.

Typological approaches

One positive feature of the Berlin and Kay approach was the explicit introduction of a comparative, almost typological, perspective. Their work is not strictly typological in the sense that it built up from a comparison of linguistic descriptions to some general statements about linguistic regularities. That is, they did not identify the presence of a widespread formal–functional linkage by means of comparison. Rather, they regimented the comparative linguistic data in terms of a set of pre-established, intuitive criteria.[51] Ideally a comparative framework would be theoretically grounded and independent of the categories of any single language. Since the notion of "basic color term" is largely intuitive and fundamentally based on English (however much it may have been formalized), these criteria have not been met. Nonetheless, such a schema does effectively provide a framework within which any given language can be placed relative to any other. Development of such comparative linguistic frameworks will be necessary to conduct adequate psychological comparison if the findings of specific differences are to have some general import. For example, a comparison of a language with three color terms with one with four terms has, at least in principle, something to say about the larger sample of languages with three and four terms. The absence of such an overarching framework was characteristic of previous work both in anthropological linguistics, where it led to the production of isolated case studies showing a single language–culture parallelism, and in comparative psycholinguistics, where it led to black-box comparisons showing the mere existence of a difference. Despite its many problems, the development of such a framework represented the first substantive attempt to achieve a goal long recognized by both major traditions.

Focality and recognition memory: the work of Heider

Research by Heider[52] (1972b) took the logical next step and tried to show that focality (i.e., the unevenness in the perceptual salience among the color stimuli) would also account for both the codability patterns and the recognition memory results found by Brown and Lenneberg (1954). This would effectively establish that the correlation of codability and recognition memory was an artifact produced by the covariance of both of these variables with focality in the Brown and Lenneberg array. Heider's results were generally supportive of this contention. She essentially gave an account of one of the ways in which the Brown and Lenneberg array was perceptually biased in favor of certain colors – a fact which had already been of concern in this tradition and which Lenneberg had come to refer to as the effect of the color context (1967, pp. 351–54). However, Heider, following Berlin and Kay, did not conceptualize the problem in terms of a specific array, but rather in terms of focal colors *per se* regardless of the contexts in which they occurred. The focal colors should, in theory, be the best recognized and remembered regardless of what other colors are in the array since they derive their special salience from universal psycho(physio)logical factors and not from any task or array context. Thus, she did not seriously consider either the earlier work which tried to cope with such array-specific patterns by constructing a context-sensitive measure of communication accuracy (Lantz and Steffire, 1964),[53] or the later work which showed cross-cultural differences in communication accuracy with a more well-controlled array (Steffire *et*

G

al., 1966).[54] These were crucial omissions: Heider ignored the most powerful available measure of codability and did not show that her own alternative account of the earlier results would also work for different arrays.

Focal colors versus communication accuracy: the work of Lucy and Shweder

Lucy and Shweder (1979) took up the significance of these oversights in Heider's work and showed that many of her findings could be attributed to the fact that focal colors were more perceptually discriminable (i.e., perceptually more distant from their neighbors) than were nonfocal colors in the specific Berlin–Kay array.[55] With an array corrected for these differences in discriminability (i.e., accidental inequities between focals and nonfocals in the stimulus array[56]), focals were not remembered any better than nonfocals, while communication accuracy continued to provide a good predictor of memory performance, suggesting that the specific verbal descriptors used in a language are in fact used to aid color memory. These results also suggested that the original Berlin and Kay findings might also depend heavily on characteristics of the specific array they used, although there is some evidence that this is not always the case (Collier, 1976).

In a cross-linguistic study replicating the Lucy and Shweder study, Lucy contrasted communication accuracy with focality as predictors of recognition memory in American English, Mexican Spanish, and Yucatec Maya using the Lucy–Shweder array (Lucy, 1981; Lucy, Gaskins, and Castillo Vales, 1990). Communication accuracy remained the best overall predictor in each language, but focality emerged as a good predictor for some male subgroups. Differences between language groups and among subgroups – men and women – within languages were interpreted as relating to differential patterns of use of perceptual versus linguistic strategies for remembering. This study indicates that focality may be a good predictor of memory performance for some groups. The combined work of Garro (1986) and Lucy and Shweder (1988) indicates that the absence of incidental conversation during the memory task will increase the likelihood that speakers successfully use focality as an aid to memory. These subsequent studies show the importance, once more, of further investigation of characteristic patterns of the use of language in thought for different groups and different task conditions.

Category boundaries and perceptual judgment: the work of Kay and Kempton

The vast majority of the work on color stemming from the Berlin and Kay formulation has been concerned with verifying or challenging the proposed universal or the proposed evolutionary sequence of color-term development. By comparison there has been almost no research taking advantage of this quasi-typological framework to examine the relativity question. One recent study by Kay and Kempton (1984) attempts to initiate work in this direction.

Kay and Kempton compared two languages that differ in color terminology: American English, which contains the terms *green* and *blue*, and Tarahumara (a language of northern Mexico), which contains a single term *siyóname*, which refers to 'green' or 'blue.' Their question is whether the linguistic difference will produce a difference in subjective distance between colors which lie on the category boundaries.[57] Specifically, they ask whether English speakers will *exaggerate* the differences since they have terms which distinguish the colors lexically, whereas the Tarahumara will not because they do not distinguish the colors lexically. Notice that this inverts Whorf's approach, which would emphasize that the Tarahumara are *overlooking* an available discrimination which English speakers recognize. The two formulations yield the same prediction when only the responses to the boundary colors are compared. However, once the contrast is framed in terms of other possible comparisons among colors as it is by Kay and Kempton, then the specific prediction does matter. Kay and Kempton's data appear to be more consistent with Whorf's formulation than with their own.

Subjects (English $n = 5$, Tarahumara $n = 4$) were then presented with triads of color samples and asked to judge which of the three was more different from the other two. Results were consistent with an interpretation that English speakers exaggerate the psychophysical distance between colors on the category boundary between *green* and *blue* in comparison with Tarahumara speakers. The implication, given the cross-linguistic regularities formulated by Berlin and Kay, is that similar perceptual differences obtain for other languages where differences among color-term systems exist.

This study can be criticized on a variety of methodological grounds (for instance, small sample size – especially in light of the size of some of the differences, shift from an emphasis on category foci in defining the language differences to an emphasis on category boundaries in defining perceptual differences, etc.). But the difficulties of this particular study should not obscure the potential value of conceptualizing linguistic differences in this way as showing patterns of constrained variation. The very same (quasi-)typological framework which presents a linguistic universal and suggests hypotheses about cognitive universals (for example, the work of Heider) can be used as a comparative grid for asking about the significance of linguistic variation for cognitive functioning.

Summary

In short, this second era of color research is characterized by continuity with the first era at the theoretical level in its conceptualization of language, at the substantive level in its use of the color domain, and at the methodological level in its use of mapping procedures to discover category foci and boundaries. However, it reverses the overall emphasis toward the view that both language structure and cognitive structure (i.e., perceptual recognition memory) are determined by underlying perceptual regularities – specifically, by focal colors. And, since the appearance of this work, this view has prevailed. Nonetheless, despite this overall orientation, there is evidence generated within this era that language (as communication accuracy) is more important than focality in determining recognition memory patterns and that language (as lexical categories) can have an influence back on perceptual processes. Further, there are serious conceptual problems with regarding the formulation of the linguistic universal on which the new tradition rests.

Aside on cognitive anthropology

Berlin and Kay's research and the studies inspired by it form part of a large body of work in anthropology on the relation of language and cognition. Very little of this work deals directly with the linguistic relativity issue, although Whorf's work is sometimes invoked (for example, Dougherty, 1985, p. 4). Begun in the 1950s, the research joined together the use of the formal methods and concepts of linguistics with a view of culture as a set of individually held cognitive rules and categories ("whatever it is one has to know or believe in order to operate in a manner acceptable to its members," Goodenough, 1964[1957], p. 36). Most work in this tradition equates cognitive and linguistic categories and then "reads" cognition directly from language. In this respect, the whole line of work begs the issue of the relation of language and thought. For representative collections and reviews of this research see Tyler (1969), Spradley (1972), Casson (1981), and Dougherty (1985); for more recent efforts, see Holland and Quinn (1987).

Although this tradition was developed to provide rigorous methods for deriving another culture's cognitive categories, during the 1960s a significant number of researchers reoriented their attention toward discovering cognitive universals. To find cognitive universals using the evidence of language structure and use, one must first find linguistic universals. Thus, a great deal of effort has been expended to identify linguistic universals, particularly in lexical structure. Often, as in the case of Berlin and Kay's work, such research is assumed to be relevant to or even to refute the linguistic relativity hypothesis. Three characteristics of this shift toward identifying universals undermine such claims. First, there has been a tendency to narrow the linguistic focus dramatically, in part to facilitate comparison. The whole enterprise centers increasingly on the denotational value of isolated lexical items, and a language's grammatical formations and patterns of signification are ignored. Second, the emphasis on common patterns leads to inattention to the possible cognitive and cultural significance of the differences which do exist. Rarely is there any test for an influence of language variation on cognition. Finally, perhaps most significantly, once a possible cognitive universal has been identified, many researchers immediately begin looking for the source of such universals in constants of the human organism or the physical environment. This exactly parallels the pattern in American psychology described above and exemplified in the trajectory of Lenneberg's thinking on the color issue; language becomes the dependent variable. The assumption of an isomorphism between language and thought in conjunction with these three tendencies – narrow linguistic focus, de-emphasis of the implications of variation, and treatment of language as the dependent variable – make most of this later work on universals tangential to the linguistic relativity issue, and it will not be reviewed further here. However, as should be obvious, the critique developed here for research on color universals should raise serious questions about the validity of much of the work in cognitive anthropology.

General Summary

In overview, two general characteristics dominate the comparative psycholinguistic research on the lexical encoding of color. First, the research is characterized by *a theoretical vision of a decontextualized "natural" word–object relationship*. On the one hand, lexemes are privileged over other forms and then are studied without reference to their grammatical properties, including their relations with other lexemes. Thus, significant structural differences among languages are washed out. On the other hand, "color" is privileged as a perceptual indubitable and conceived of as separable from co-occurring features of the environment. Thus, significant cross-cultural commonalities in the association between colors and other features of experience – both perceptual and otherwise – are systematically ignored. Finally, the word–object connection itself is conceived of from a functional point of view as primarily that of explicit classification (or "mapping") – that is, as a socially decontextualized individual act, a natural categorization of nature. The fact that these classifications are part of a structure established for the purposes of speech in a particular social world is lost to view. The *use* of color terms in ordinary, communicative (hence social) speech is first backgrounded, and then some of the implicit classifications produced by such speech are foregrounded as the central and defining functions of the forms. The differences in usage of "color" terms among groups or across contexts neither can be nor are examined. The structure, function, and social context of the forms is never seriously examined and cannot, therefore, ever enter into the investigation.

Second, this psycholinguistic research tradition is characterized by *methodological assumptions and approaches consistently at odds with its own research objectives*. The original goal was to test whether differences among languages affected thought – understood initially as habitual conceptual interpretations of reality. Thought was reformulated as having to do with processing potential, thus effectively screening out any possibility of detecting the habitual conceptual patterns suggested by the original hypothesis. Then language was construed in terms of the methodological procedure of objectifying meaning. This tacitly assumed that reality can be unambiguously characterized in advance of linguistic comparison, thereby locking out the possibility of detecting significant structural differences by declaring which meanings will count and which will not. (Specifically, only the denotational value of color terms with respect to hue, brightness, and saturation will be considered.) All languages will look alike under this procedure, as they are being sifted in terms of this a priori category. The situation was doubly confounded in that the tradition then relied, again tacitly, on English to characterize the objective reality, thereby locking in the English worldview as natural and necessary. (Specifically, only the denotational value of *our* color terms as *we* reflectively understand them will be considered.) With this refinement, all languages will look like English. Then the language–thought relationship was consistently operationalized so as to make language structure the dependent variable wherever possible. The original formulation (codability – generalizing Zipf's law) tacitly assumed a causal priority of patterns of frequency of use over formal structure rather than vice versa. The revised formulation (communication accuracy) continued the trend by focusing on efficiency of use and dropping any consideration of formal structural means. The final formulation (focality) completed the transformation by postulating that the utility of certain referents (focal colors) gives them a privileged status in determining the shape of linguistic structures (basic terms). At every juncture, then, the operationalization of the hypothesis forces the conclusion that thought (i.e., unmediated apprehension of reality) determines language structure and that differences in language structures are mere quantitative variants of a common universal pattern. One can see how the "discovery" and widespread acceptance of current theories about universals of color terminology was all but inevitable within this tradition.

6. Approaches in comparative psycholinguistics: experimental studies on grammatical categories

This chapter reviews the balance of the work in psycholinguistics directly concerned with the linguistic relativity issue. Unlike the color research and related work on codability reviewed in the previous chapter, these studies are few in number and do not all cohere as a tradition; they consist of relatively isolated efforts at addressing Whorf's questions. Most of them are directly concerned with cross-linguistic comparison of grammatical differences, and all use experimental approaches to individual assessment. These studies are important because they bring the cognitive and methodological concerns of the psychologists together with the linguistic and comparative concerns of the anthropologists. They identify the sorts of category differences that can be meaningfully compared, they show how psychological hypotheses can be developed from such comparisons, and they illustrate some of the specific ways such hypotheses can be tested. Unfortunately, the experimental tasks often bear no clear relation to everyday behavior or to a general theory of cognition. Further, none of these studies employs a systematic linguistic approach: neither the structural nor the functional position of the categories within one language or across languages is adequately addressed. Without a precise linguistic characterization, the psychological hypotheses become meaningless and the experimental results uninterpretable.

Form classes and habitual classification

The first group of studies, all from the late 1950s, have a methodological focus. They attempt to devise experimental techniques capable of detecting whether grammatical categories have effects on individual cognition. The categories of concern are conceptualized as form classes, that is, distributional regularities emerging from grammatical analysis that also have a general referential meaning value. Evidence for cognitive effects is sought in distinctive patterns of individual nonlinguistic responses to a set of stimulus materials in an experimental context. The experimental observations are presumed to index everyday behavior. These studies are of special importance here because several of their substantive concerns and methodological techniques will be used in the empirical research reported in *Grammatical categories and cognition*.

The psychological reality of the parts of speech: the work of Brown

During the 1950s many linguists attempted to describe word classes such as noun, verb, etc. purely in formal distributional terms and without reference to "semantic" considerations, that is, to meaning. Among the more important reasons for this reluctance to invoke meaning was the poor fit between the distributional facts and the various proposed meanings; for example, nouns do not always name "substances" or refer to "persons, places, or things." So, for linguists, terms such as *noun* came to be used to label a distributional pattern rather than a basic meaning. And as long as such grammatical classes were characterized in such purely formal terms, they did not readily suggest important cognitive differences between languages. This general orientation accounted for much of the resistance to Whorf's work among linguists during the 1950s, since his claims depended on form and meaning being intimately related.

These linguistic concerns did not hold as much force for psychologists in the emerging subfield of psycholinguistics, because psychologists had traditionally worked with probabilistic associations (Brown, 1956, pp. 259–63; 1957, p. 1; 1958b, pp. 244–47). As Roger Brown reasoned, even loose relationships of form and meaning might be psychologically significant:

the layman may operate in this area as in so many others with probabilistic as well as invariable attributes. The existence of a correlation, though it is less than perfect, between grammatical functions and semantic attributes would surely be discovered by native speakers if it could be of any use to them.

(1958b, pp. 244–45)

In particular, he hypothesized that such relationships might play a useful role in language learning:

It may be that nouns *tend to have* a different semantic from verbs, and that the native speaker detects this tendency while he is in the process of learning the language. (1957, p. 1)

Brown undertook several studies (1957; 1958b, pp. 243–53) to see whether there were, in fact, such associations between form classes and meaning during language learning. He hoped "to show how one kind of grammatical practice, the allocation of words to one or another part of speech, does affect cognition" (1957, p. 1).

In several respects which will be detailed below, these studies by Brown did not directly address the linguistic relativity issue, but they deserve attention here nonetheless. First, Brown's work was stimulated by the relativity question, and he conceived of the results as directly relevant to it. Second, his work represents the first attempt in any of the traditions under review at controlled assessment of the relationship between a grammatical category and individual behavior. Third, the work is indirectly relevant to the relativity issue because of its implications for language development.

Brown first observed the speech of pre-school children (ages three to five) in their classroom interactions. On the basis of these observations he concluded that "the nouns and verbs of children were more nearly consistent with the usual semantic definitions than are the nouns and verbs of adults" (1958b, p. 247). This led Brown to hypothesize that "as the form classes grow larger they decline in semantic consistency" (1958b, p. 247). He checked this in a second study by comparing standardized word frequency lists[1] for adults with those of first-grade children. Both the nouns and verbs of children were closer to the classic definitions of the parts of speech:

children's nouns are more likely to name concrete things (in the sense of naming narrow categories with characteristic visual contour and size) than are the nouns of adults ... The common notion that verbs name actions seems to be truer for the vocabulary of children than for the vocabulary of adults.   (1957, p. 2)

Brown concluded that "the nouns and verbs used by children have more consistent semantic implications than those used by adults" (1957, p. 2). However, this material did not directly address the question of whether the children were aware of these semantic implications.

Brown then undertook a third, experimental study to see whether children showed sensitivity to the grammatical (i.e., word-class) differences between nouns and verbs, and between mass nouns (i.e., those naming substances) and particular nouns (i.e., those naming objects),[2] in their interpretations of new words. He presented children a series of pictures each showing an *action* being performed on a *substance* in a *container*. Each picture was then introduced by the experimenter using one of the nonsense words *niss*, *sib*, or *latt* as a verb, a mass noun, or a particular noun. So, for example, when the nonsense item was serving as a verb, the child was asked

Do you know what it means to sib? [In principle the child answers "no."] In this picture you can see sibbing. Now show me another picture of sibbing.[3]

(1957, p. 4)

Whereupon the child was shown three additional pictures to choose from: one with the same *action*, one with the same *substance*, and one with the same *container*. The expectation was that the child would be sensitive to the grammatical clues and select an appropriate alternative. So, in the example just given, the child should select the picture with the same action. Brown's expectation was confirmed: in each case the children strongly favored the grammatically appropriate choice. He concluded that "in this language, at least, the semantic implications of the verb, mass noun, and particular noun are discovered by native speakers" (1957, p. 5).

Brown argued that this discovery of these semantic implications was functional for the language learner in providing clues to the meaning of newly encountered words:[4]

If a part of speech has reliable semantic implications it could call attention to the kind of attribute likely to belong to the meaning of the word ... The part-of-speech membership of the new word could operate as a filter selecting for attention probably relevant features of the nonlinguistic world. (1958b, p. 249)

One problem with this interpretation, of course, is that it assumes that the primary source of new words for the child is the speech of other children, where the form classes will in fact have these "reliable semantic implications." By Brown's own analysis, new words encountered in conversation with adults will not have such reliable implications.[5] However, if we accept his interpretation, Brown has shown one way in which a "grammatical feature of a language affects the cognition of those who speak the languages" (1957, p. 5).

Brown connected his finding to the linguistic relativity issue by pointing out that the grammatical categories of various languages differ quite markedly:

It now seems quite probable that speakers of other languages will also know about the semantics of their grammatical categories. Since these are strikingly different in unrelated languages, the speakers in question may have quite different cognitive categories. It remains to be determined how seriously and how generally thought is affected by these semantic distinctions.   (1957, p. 5)

He made the further point that speakers need not be consciously aware of such semantic implications for them to have effects:

Even though form-class semantic is used in the language learning of both children and adults it probably drops from consciousness as language skills become smooth and rapid ... However, it does not follow that form-class semantic is inoperative in the accomplished speaker. Like other sorts of meaning it may exist as a disposition ... It is not that people are always thinking in terms of gender or substance or round objects, but that they are disposed to think in these terms.
(1958b, p. 253)

Brown closed by emphasizing that such dispositions will probably be more significant in affecting certain activities which are less context- or situation-dependent. Demonstrating a relation between language and thought, or language and culture, will require studying such nonlinguistic behaviors:

> The different dispositions should come out in problem solving, poetry writing, painting, and creative thought in general. The effect of form-class semantic cannot be demonstrated with linguistic data alone but requires the study of extralinguistic behavioral data.   (1958b, p. 253)

To the extent that these less context-dependent activities are culturally specific, Brown was touching in an indirect way on a possible functional relativity of such structural effects.[6]

Nonetheless, despite these arguments, Brown's study failed to address the relativity question directly. First, from the point of view of language, his study lacked a comparative dimension. Although he was ahead of his time in recognizing the potential scope and significance of language variation, he provided no evidence for his claim of variation in regard to the specific grammatical forms at issue: count noun, mass noun, and verb. Without an examination of the structures of other languages, there are no grounds for asserting that the particular categories are language-specific (this is certainly problematic with nouns and verbs) or that the pattern of responses is distinctive of the language group (perhaps children everywhere would show similar patterns of response on the task, even with different language categories). The point is not that the categories or behavioral responses are *not* language specific, but only that this conclusion cannot be justified on the basis of the evidence provided. Second, from the point of view of thought, the "nonlinguistic" behavior which was supposedly being influenced by language actually had to do with *language learning* in a task where linguistic cues were patently salient. On this evidence alone there is no reason to believe that there will be influences on thought or "nonlinguistic" behavior more generally. What Brown has actually shown is that the meaning values of the grammatical categories are "psychologically real" during language development·– but not that they have any effects on adult behavior generally. Despite his discussion of the problem, then, Brown's study as it stands did not really address the linguistic relativity issue. And his more recent work on language and thought (for example, Brown and Fish, 1983) continues to omit a comparative dimension and a clear nonlinguistic variable.

Brown's specific conclusion about the probable significance of form-class meaning for language learning seems more justified. Modified versions of his approach have been and still are being used in the study of language development to address questions about the role of universally given "semantic" content versus language-specific "syntactic" form in the development of grammatical categories (see, for instance, Gordon, 1985, and references therein). When comparatively framed, data of this sort on the referential content of categories can be relevant to the linguistic relativity issue.

Brown's work is also important in that it distinguishes between the requirements of grammatical analysis and those of psychological analysis. As he noted, the formal characterization of a language category typical of linguistics may not be the most appropriate for identifying cognitive effects. In particular, the probabilistic characterization of a language category typical of psychologists may suggest "notional" regularities underlying diversity. This raises the broader question of how to characterize language categories and the relationship between language categories and "thought" or "reality" for the purposes of comparison.[7]

Comparative studies of the functions of language classifications in behavior: the work of Carroll, Casagrande, and Maclay

During the late 1950s a group of anthropologists, linguists, and psychologists collaborated on the Southwest Project in Comparative Psycholinguistics and devoted part of their efforts to testing experimentally whether different language categories had effects on the nonlinguistic behavior of individual speakers (see chapter 4). One study conducted by Carroll (Carroll and Casagrande, 1958) dealt with semantically complex lexical categories rather than with "the language of experience." Studies conducted by Casagrande (Casagrande, 1960 [1956]; Carroll and Casagrande, 1958) and by Maclay (1958) dealt directly with grammatical category differences – the only studies of this sort to be developed and published since Whorf's death. They are closely related in method and content and will be treated here as a group.

Common orientations

These studies shared a basic approach to the linguistic relativity issue. On the linguistic side, as with Whorf and the anthropological linguists, Carroll and Casagrande's (1958, pp. 19–20) central premise[8] was that a continuous world of experience[9] must be fitted into discrete linguistic categories – both lexical and grammatical[10] – for there to be efficient communication about it. Although they did not rule out the possibility of grammatical universals, they emphasized that there is substantial variation across languages and that even where there is apparent similarity, there may be differences in semantic implication that can make exact translation equivalence difficult to establish.[11] And, although any concept can be expressed in each language, there will be differences in what concepts are obligatorily expressed:

> in general, any grammatical concept found in one language can be expressed somehow in every language, even if the expression is a little awkward or periphrastic. Languages do differ remarkably, however, in the grammatical concepts which are mandatory: for example, the use of the singular–plural distinction is said to be mandatory in English but completely optional in Chinese.
> (Carroll and Casagrande, 1958, p. 20)

This clarifies the type of grammatical category that interested them: differences in obligatorily expressed concepts.

On the psychological side, like those working in the color tradition, Carroll and Casagrande (1958, pp. 20–22) posed their basic question in terms of individual behavior and thought:

> Is the behavior of a person (aside from his language behavior) a function of the language he happens to speak? Granted that languages differ in the ways we have described, what effects will these differences have on the way a person thinks, the way he deals with other people, or the way he deals with his environment?
> (1958, p. 20)

Unlike Lenneberg, however, they did not emphasize potential thought over actual habitual thought, nor did they so sharply separate process from content, preferring to speak more globally of "the way a person thinks," "modes of thinking," or "modes of categorizing experience."

In line with their psychological orientation, they emphasized experimental methodology.[12] Maclay made this explicit:

> The point at issue [in this study] is whether accurate predictions about relatively concrete and specific behavior in an experimental situation can be derived from the examination of language structure. The present study thus differs from most earlier work in three major respects: (1) the method of investigation is experimental rather than observational; (2) the predictions are made from present language to future behavior [i.e., in new situations]; (3) the behavior studied consists of specific instances rather than large scale patterns.
> (Maclay, 1958, p. 220)

The crucial task was to identify a precise correspondence between a specific linguistic phenomenon[13] and a specific "nonlinguistic" response (Carroll and Casagrande, 1958, p. 21). For Maclay, a nonlinguistic response was any behavior not involving the oral production of speech, and although his task instructions were given verbally, the responses themselves did not require speech. Maclay also made an effort "to prevent subjects from realizing that the experimental task had any connection with their language" (1958, p. 222). Carroll and Casagrande (1958, p. 21) decided to consider a response nonlinguistic if it was neutral with respect to the special symbolic system against which it was being tested. Thus, they felt comfortable with giving the subjects verbal instruction and in receiving verbal answers and explanations from their subjects. So, nonlinguistic behavior is defined residually: they have no overarching view of cognitive process or structure within which certain activities (for instance, remembering) can be defined as essentially nonlinguistic and for which language can play a specific role. A similarly direct approach assured that the nonlinguistic task actually involved classification: they simply designed tasks explicitly consisting of sorting or grouping, rather than looking for evidence of implicit classification in some other activity (for example, remembering).

The crucial linkage between language categories and nonlinguistic behavior was made via specific referents. That is, the prediction was that if a language category grouped specific referents together, then subjects should also group them similarly in nonlinguistic behavior:

a convenient basis for prediction lies in the well-known fact that languages categorize the universe and further that referents united in one language are separated in another. This being the case it should follow that referents classified together linguistically are likely to be classified together non-linguistically.

(Maclay, 1958, pp. 220–21)

This is quite similar to Lenneberg's basic approach of using colors as referents and talking about their grouping in language and in some nonlinguistic response. However, unlike Lenneberg, these three investigators did not attempt to provide a framework (or metalanguage) for describing the referents.

In sum, these three experiments fused some elements of the two traditions under review. In harmony with the anthropological linguists they emphasized variations in what is obligatorily expressed by radically different languages. In harmony with other psycholinguists they emphasized eliciting an individual nonlinguistic behavioral response under controlled experimental conditions.

Individual studies

The specific findings of these experimental studies are ambiguous and, for the most part, not too interesting from a contemporary perspective. Therefore, in summarizing these experiments, the focus will be on the logic of the designs and their adequacy for testing for linguistic relativity rather than on details of procedure or results. The analysis of these early experimental designs directly motivates portions of the empirical work reported in *Grammatical categories and cognition*.

Carroll: Hopi lexical meaning and preferences in picture sorting

Many Hopi lexical verbs referring to physical activities have a semantic structure different from corresponding English verbs. To see whether these semantic differences would correspond to differences in non-linguistic performance, Carroll created a triads sorting task using line drawings. Each of the 17 items in his task consisted of a set of three drawings (A, B, C): two (A, C) could be referred to by the same verb in Hopi, two (B, C) could be referred to by the same verb in English, and two (A, B) formed a neutral combination. Adult speakers of English and of Hopi[14] were asked to indicate which two pictures went together and to explain why. To clarify the items and procedure Carroll described one item in detail. Picture A showed a woman closing a lidded box, picture B showed a woman covering a sewing machine with a cloth, and picture C showed a woman placing a wicker plaque over a box of food:

> The linguistic basis for this item resides in the fact that in Hopi there is a verb *'u'ta* which means "to close an opening," and this is the verb normally used for placing covers on open boxes, closing lids, closing holes in tubes or walls, etc.; in contrast, placing a cover on something for protection against dust or damage is represented by the verbs *na:kwapna* or *nönöma*. In English, however, we tend to use *cover* regardless of whether we are covering an opening or not, and we tend to reserve *close* for the situation where an opening can be more or less exactly fitted with a lid or other special stoppage (also for special cases like *closing a book*). On this basis it was hypothesized that Hopis would tend to put together pictures A and C, while Anglos would tend to put together pictures B and C.
> (Carroll and Casagrande, 1958, pp. 23–24)

To introduce the task to the subjects, there were six pre-test items

> designed to reveal whether the subjects understood the task and to make it clear that they were to respond on the basis of the action or type of action represented rather than incidental features of any objects depicted.
> (Carroll and Casagrande, 1958, p. 22)

Performance on the task, then, did not necessarily represent spontaneous responses to the pictures. Speaker's choices were scored as being consistent with Hopi, with English, or with neither. Overall the results were in the predicted direction, but did not appear to be statistically reliable.[15]

The explanations given by speakers for their choices revealed great diversity in the bases of response. Using these responses in conjunction with a re-examination of the purely linguistic data, Carroll was able to weed out items that had gone "sour," that is, that were not in fact testing the original hypothesis at all. Using only the subset of "good" items, Carroll found a much stronger trend in the predicted direction, a trend that appeared to be statistically reliable.[16]

Carroll concluded that his technique was a promising one for studying the linguistic relativity hypothesis. He made three suggestions for future work: (1) pre-test the drawings to see how subjects are interpreting them; (2) use monolinguals rather than bilinguals; and (3) ask subjects to choose which of two pictures (A or B) go with a fixed third picture (C). Although Carroll was not explicit, the goal of these improvements would presumably be to make the test more sensitive by reducing the influence of extraneous factors ("noise") so that the patterns of interest would show more clearly.

Despite some obvious weaknesses, this is an extremely important study. It is the first psycholinguistic study under review that has actually taken seriously the differences between two languages. Significantly, the patterns of difference between the two languages were used to generate the relevant triad configurations. Carroll first selected a point of referential equivalence or overlap between expressions in the two languages. He then asked what other referents one language would include that another would not, and vice versa. Next he tried to show how differences in what is grouped together linguistically affect the subsequent nonlinguistic behavior toward that referent. Although the approach depends on using a point of referential equivalence to establish a basis of comparison, it does not restrict in advance what other factors might be included as relevant dimensions of meaning difference. The study thus avoids the approach typical of the color tradition, namely the construction of an a priori model of an optimal or "correct" interpretation of reality within which both languages' categories must be fitted.

The principal weakness of the study from a linguistic point of view is that the comparison was between an *ad hoc* assortment of lexical items. Carroll did not show that the lexical items form a systematic structural or functional part of each language or, therefore, that the differences between languages stemmed from regular patterns characteristic of the two languages as languages.[17] This makes it difficult both to judge the importance of the differences between the two languages and to generalize the specific findings to other parts of these two languages or to other languages. In this sense the comparison is *ad hoc*, not unlike the case studies of the anthropological linguistics tradition.

From a cognitive point of view, the study represents an important attempt to generate well-defined predictions about nonlinguistic responses for *both* groups – an essential step in any meaningful comparison. Unfortunately, the relationship of the responses in the experimental task to habitual behavior generally remains somewhat murky. No general claim was made about the relation of cognition to language or about the relation of the specific task to everyday behavior. Thus there is no way to predict when such language classifications will be used in thought or how important their use might be. The situation was exacerbated by the pre-test training procedures and the explanations elicited after each selection, both of which may have elicited responses to the stimuli that exaggerated the linguistic meanings at issue. Further, since the construction of the test triads was motivated by *ad hoc* lexical comparisons, no general characterization of the referents seems possible either. From a comparative perspective, the absence of any principled description of the referents precludes the efficient selection of materials for further comparisons with other languages.

Casagrande: Navaho classifiers and shape preference in object sorting

To refer to certain events, the Navaho language requires using distinctive verb stems which indicate the "form" of the object being acted upon.[18] Casagrande characterized and exemplified this grammatical pattern as follows:

> It is obligatory in the Navaho language, when using verbs of *handling*, to employ a particular one of a set of verbal forms according to the shape or some other essential attribute of the object about which one is speaking. Thus, if I ask you in Navaho to hand me an object, I must use the appropriate verb stem depending on the nature of the object. If it is a long flexible object such as a piece of string, I must say *šanléh*; if it is a long rigid object such as a stick, I must say *šantį́į́h*; if it is a flat flexible material such as a paper or cloth, I must say *šanitcóós*, and so on.
> (Carroll and Casagrande, 1958, pp. 26–27)

Thus the various nouns and their associated referents are effectively classified by such verbs into a small number of sets. Since these noun classes are not overtly marked on the nouns themselves, they constitute covert categories in Whorf's sense:

> The groups of words in Navaho which together regularly take one or another of these verb stems . . . carry no linguistic [i.e., morphological] marker of their class membership. They comprise what Whorf has called a covert class . . . Nor, in the absence of native grammarians, are there any terms in Navaho for these categories themselves. This like many another grammatical rule operates well below the level of conscious awareness. (Carroll and Casagrande, 1958, p. 27)

Thus the linguistic variable in this study was an out-of-awareness covert grammatical category.

American and European psychological research available at that time had shown that children first sort or distinguish among objects on the basis of size and color and only later on the basis of form (Carroll and Casagrande, 1958, pp. 27, 30). Since Navaho children as young as three use the verb stem signaling "form" differences correctly, Casagrande hypothesized that the presence of this obligatory category might have an effect on the emergence of form as a basis for the classification of objects during child development and that the ordering observed in the West might be an artifact of the languages spoken (Carroll and Casagrande, 1958, p. 27). Casagrande's specific hypothesis was that Navaho-speaking children would attend earlier to form as a basis of classification than would comparable English-speaking children:

> The hypothesis was, then, that this feature of the Navaho language would affect the relative potency, or order of emergence of such concepts as color, size, shape or form, and number in the Navaho-speaking child, as compared with the English-speaking Navaho children of the same age, and that Navaho-speaking children would be more inclined than the latter to perceive formal similarities between objects. (Carroll and Casagrande, 1958, p. 27)

In short, speaking Navaho in childhood should alter the developmental emergence of preferred bases of classification.

To test this hypothesis, Casagrande created a triads sorting task with ten items.[19] Casagrande described the items and their administration as follows:

> Ten pairs of objects (colored wooden blocks, sticks, and pieces of rope) were used, each of which differed significantly in two respects, e.g., color and size, color and shape, size and shape, or shape and Navaho verb-form classification. These pairs of objects were arranged before the child, one pair at a time. After being presented with a pair of objects, the child was shown a third object similar to each member of the pair in only one of the two relevant characteristics, but of course matching neither, and was asked to tell the experimenter which of the pairs went best with the object shown to him. For example, one of the pairs consisted of a yellow stick and a piece of blue rope of comparable size. The child was then shown a yellow rope, and the basis of his choice could be either color or the Navaho verb-form classification – since different verbal forms are used for a length of rope and a stick. (Carroll and Casagrande, 1958, pp. 27–28)[20]

This task was administered to Navaho children aged three to ten divided into two groups according to whether they were language-dominant in English or Navaho.[21] The expectation was that the Navaho-dominant group would favor "shape or form"-based choices overall and at an earlier age in line with their grammatical pattern. It was hoped that by using Navaho children throughout, the variables of race, culture, and environment might be controlled (Carroll and Casagrande, 1958, p. 30).

Results were in the expected direction for the contrasts pitting verb-form against color and pitting shape against size: Navaho-dominant children preferred verb-form and shape as a basis of classification, whereas English-dominant children did not. These results appear to be statistically reliable.[22] Results for the contrasts of shape with color and of size with color showed both groups favoring color. When the subset of seven items contrasting shape or verb-form against color were analyzed by age, there was a strong, consistent tendency for the Navaho-dominant children to prefer "shape or form" as a basis of classification earlier than the English-dominant children and to maintain an edge throughout the age spectrum – although both groups showed a steady increase in such preference.[23]

The same task was later administered to two groups of non-Navaho English speakers. The first group consisted of white American middle-class children in the Boston metropolitan area (Carroll and Casagrande, 1958, pp. 28–31)[24] and the second group, reported some years later (Casagrande in Fishman, 1960, p. 335, n4), consisted of a group of Harlem schoolchildren.[25] As mentioned above, on the basis of published reports, Casagrande expected white English-speaking children to favor color and size over form. Contrary to this expectation, his results revealed that on the seven key items, they favored "shape or form" over color and size – exactly as had the Navaho-speaking children. And although their preference for "shape or form" at the earliest age appears to be slightly weaker,[26] they exceeded the Navaho in every subsequent age group. This embarrassing result demanded some explanation. Since the results conflicted with earlier studies, the most economical conclusion would have been that the various results – and perhaps even classificatory "preferences" in general – are task specific.

However, Casagrande sought an explanation instead in the cultural experience of these upper-middle-class white children: specifically "practice with toys and other objects involving the fitting of forms and shapes, and the resultant greater reinforcement received from form-matching" (Carroll and Casagrande, 1958, p. 31). Casagrande cited evidence that even within white society preference for form correlates with social class, thereby accounting for the difference between his results and those of others. This analysis is apparently confirmed by his subsequent work with the Harlem schoolchildren. This group's performance was "very close to the English dominant Navahos and . . . the same age trend shows up" (Casagrande in Fishman, 1960, p. 335, n4). So Casagrande drew the conclusion that language can encourage a tendency to classify in certain ways but that other cultural influences during childhood also matter:

The tendency of a child to match objects on the basis of form or material rather than size or color increases with age and may be enhanced by either of two kinds of experiences; (a) learning to speak a language, like Navaho, which because of the central role played by form and material in its grammatical structure, requires the learner to make certain discriminations of form and material in the earlier stages of language learning . . .; or (b) practice with toys and other objects involving the fitting of forms and shapes, and the resultant greater reinforcement received from form-matching.   (Carroll and Casagrande, 1958, p. 31)

In short, and not surprisingly, obligatory linguistic categories are only one source of effects on behavior.

This study was the first psycholinguistic study to attempt to assess the impact of a specific grammatical difference on individual nonlinguistic behavior. It successfully generated an experimentally testable hypothesis about nonlinguistic behavior from the analysis of an "exotic" grammatical pattern. Conceptually, it united Brown's concern for the sensitivity of children to grammatical patterns with Carroll's concern for the effects of language differences on nonlinguistic behavior. The ambiguous results should not obscure the historical significance of this attempt or its utility as a reference point for the design of further studies.

From a linguistic point of view, the study is deficient in two respects. First, in a crucial sense, the study was not really comparative. Only Navaho was analyzed; there was never any explicit analysis of English. Thus the comparison was not between two well-defined patterns, a pattern in English and a pattern in Navaho, but between one pattern in Navaho and its absence in English. There was never any statement as to how Navaho and English treat "form" distinctively relative either to one another or to some larger array of languages. Perhaps English favors "form" just as much or more than Navaho in some of its categories.

Second, the analysis of Navaho itself was very weak. No information was given about the significance of the grammatical pattern in the overall structure of the language (is it a structurally important grammatical category or a minor, peripheral one?) or in the use of the language (is it used frequently or only rarely?). No attempt was made to show that the language as a whole exhibits a bias toward "form," that is, that the specific verb-stem pattern is part of a "fashion of speaking" cutting across categories in the language. Finally, it is clear from Casagrande's own text that the meaning of these verb-stem classes is not adequately captured by the labels "form" or "shape." This makes the linkage to "form" as a general classificatory dimension in childhood somewhat tenuous.[27] These weaknesses raise questions about the likelihood that this Navaho pattern could ever affect nonlinguistic behavior as hypothesized.

There are also problems from a cognitive point of view. First, as in Carroll's study, no attempt was made to assure that the task simulated or represented everyday habitual behavior. Further, the hypothesis had to do with a transient aspect of child development, rather than with an enduring disposition of adult speakers. Even if the hypothesis had been clearly confirmed, the results would be ambiguous from the point of view of the traditional debate over the linguistic relativity issue.

Second, the experimental hypothesis was not specific enough. As Casagrande eventually concluded, there were many factors that could plausibly determine an early preference for "form." This common problem with correlational studies was exacerbated by using a single, global hypothesis about preference for form. The global prediction could become more persuasive if embedded within an array of supporting results. A more distinctive, specific hypothesis (for example, about the relative ordering for each group of all the dimensions such as form, size, color, material, etc.) could help rule out competing interpretations and provide more convincing results. As it stands the prediction is too general to bear the interpretive weight placed on it.

In his discussion of Casagrande's ambiguous results, Fishman (1960, pp. 335–36) quite correctly noted that they raised questions about the relative importance of language as opposed to other factors in influencing behavior. He suggested that even though there may be a genuine linguistic relativity, it may not be a very important factor in behavior.[28] This may indeed eventually prove to be the case, but such a conclusion should be based on a larger and more reliable body of evidence. Unfortunately, very little further research has been done, and Casagrande's work remains one of the few prototypes available of an experimental approach to the linguistic relativity issue.

Maclay: Navaho classifiers and form preference in object sorting

Maclay (1958) tested for nonlinguistic effects of the same Navaho verb-stem classes as Casagrande.[29] He characterized these categories as having to do with the physical characteristics of objects and relabeled the categories to reflect the dimensions he believed were important: 'slender-flexible,' 'slender-rigid,' and 'flat-flexible.' Maclay argued that this might influence nonlinguistic behavior by encouraging attention to "form":

> In his verbal behavior a Navaho is thus in the position of having made very frequent distinctions among objects on the basis of their form. He should, therefore, make these distinctions more readily in his non-verbal behavior than will a native speaker of a language not containing such obligatory distinctions.
>
> (1958, p. 222)

Notice that the formulation washes out such distinctions as rigid versus flexible which have to do with the material composition and dynamic properties of an object.

Maclay worked with a substantially different subject pool than Casagrande. Maclay's subjects were mostly adults. In addition to Navaho speakers, he included both white ("Anglo") English speakers and Pueblo Indian groups whose languages are unrelated to Navaho (Athapascan). The Pueblo group was added to the minimum two-way contrast of English and Navaho "in order to ensure that the results gotten would not merely reflect an Anglo versus Indian or majority–minority difference" (1958, p. 223).

Maclay's classification task involved twelve items each consisting of four objects to be grouped into two pairs.[30] Items were constructed so that groupings could be made on the basis of "Form" (the operationalization of the Navaho verb categories), "Function or Material,"[31] or "Color."[32] After the task, subjects were interviewed about their language background in some detail and an index of language experience was developed. Finally, a follow-up interview was conducted with one Navaho subject to get "his reaction to the experiment and his interpretation of the whole situation" (1958, p. 225).

Maclay developed a number of specific predictions about the expected patterns of sorting for each group, about latency in response times between groups and between types of items, and, for the two Indian groups, about correlations between language experience and pattern of response. No statistically significant differences emerged among the three groups either in pattern of sorting or latency of responses. In particular, Navaho and English subjects performed very much alike both in terms of sorting and in terms of latency. Maclay concluded that his hypotheses had to be rejected:

The direct comparison among the three groups with respect to both sorting and latency failed in every case to produce the expected differences . . . given a known linguistic category, it cannot be reliably predicted that non-linguistic behavior will correlate with it. (1958, p. 228)

There were, however, some positive results with the language experience index: Navaho form-based responses correlated reliably with degree of exposure to the Navaho language. Further, as expected, the correlation value for the Pueblo Indian group whose languages should not encourage form-based responses was significantly smaller than that of the Navaho.

Maclay interpreted his results in terms of the multiplicity of possible classifications for any two objects in a language (1958, p. 228). It became clear during the detailed follow-up interview with the one Navaho subject that the verb categories were not the only way of classifying the objects. In particular, two items sometimes had the same name in Navaho and "could thus be said to be classified together linguistically on a lexical basis" (1958, p. 229). Maclay concluded:

If every object and event participates in a number of intersecting linguistic categories one can never make the absolute statement, "Navaho does it this way," as if the language systematically cut the universe up into neat and mutually exclusive segments. (1958, p. 229)

Maclay proposed a way to handle this problem of language flexibility by distinguishing between "Language and Speech" or "language structure and language behavior":

A structural description ... consciously ignores certain aspects of language behavior such as frequency of occurrence ... In the case of experimental investigations relative frequency will probably be an even more important variable; perhaps the single most significant factor. This suggests that experimentation should be preceded by a thorough investigation of actual usage on the language behavior level. (1958, p. 229)

In short, from a psychological point of view, the frequency of use of a form may be as important as its structural value. This is reminiscent of Brown's point about the different concerns of psychologists and linguists.[33]

This study, appearing in the same year as Casagrande's,[34] represents, then, a second attempt to assess the impact of a specific grammatical difference on individual nonlinguistic behavior. Although it dealt with exactly the same Navaho grammatical pattern, the hypothesis, the subject populations, and the specific experimental task differed from Casagrande's study. The hypothesis was that the language differences produced an enduring response preference among adult speakers, rather than just a transient preference during child development. In addition to the Navaho and English subjects, there were also Pueblo Indian speakers to provide further information relative to minority-group status. Finally, more sorting options were available in each test item and a new dimension for grouping was provided ("Function or Material"). Despite these various differences, the English and Navaho responses were again quite similar, suggesting that Casagrande's finding of similarity between these two groups was not accidental.

From a linguistic point of view, Maclay's study suffered from the same comparative and descriptive difficulties as Casagrande's. Although Maclay claimed that "the verb categories under consideration were obligatory in Navaho but not in any of the other languages represented" (1958, p. 223),[35] he provided no descriptive data on English or the Pueblo languages to show that these languages did not also favor form.[36] Although it was reasonable to have assumed that his readers had some familiarity with English, there can be no justification for lumping together nine Pueblo languages without providing any analysis of their common traits or suitability as a comparison group. With regard to the analysis of Navaho, Maclay apparently accepted the traditional descriptive label of these classes as having to do with "form" even more uncritically than did Casagrande. This simple characterization eliminated from consideration other properties of objects that might have been relevant to the application of the verb stem and guided the construction of a stimulus set restricted in the same way. Further, he made no attempt to indicate the structural or functional significance of the verb-stem classes in the language or to discuss the grammatical treatment of the other dimensions (i.e., color, material) presented in his tasks. In fact, Maclay (1958, p. 220) explicitly eschewed looking at large-scale patterns.

Maclay's only initial linguistic concern was that the specific verb-stem classifications were obligatory in Navaho and not in the other languages. When this narrow structural approach failed to produce a reliable prediction, he recognized its inadequacy and raised the general problem of how to link linguistic analysis with a cognitive prediction and specifically how to generate a meaningful prediction if every "language has a variety of alternative ways of classifying stimuli" (Maclay, 1958, p. 229). This is partly a practical problem: when working with speakers of a different language, adequate pre-testing can help detect unforeseen problems with the interpretation of the stimulus materials. However, the problem also lies partly in the particular formulation of the problem. If the relativity hypothesis is operationalized in terms of a specific linguistic category engendering a specific nonlinguistic grouping of stimuli, then the problem is intrinsic, for there will always be many ways to refer to a stimulus, each occurring with a differing frequency and potentially producing a distinctive "grouping" of stimuli. Under this formulation the only solutions are to configure the experimental context more tightly and/or to work in terms of probabilities of response. Put another way, one must control or assess the likelihood that a given syntactic category will actually be invoked and then appropriated in a given behavioral context. This conceptualization in terms of frequency of use is the solution that Maclay advocated. However, such an approach raises serious questions about the significance (and generality) of the effects attributed to any structural pattern. It would appear that this situation is exacerbated by focusing on stimulus groupings emerging from the application of little used, structurally peripheral categories, and minimized by dealing with the interpretation of stimuli stemming from frequently used, structurally central patterns. Maclay ultimately did not see that the weakness and partiality of his own structural analysis of Navaho made the issue of frequency especially potent.

From a cognitive point of view also, the problems encountered by Casagrande of a global hypothesis and weak link to everyday behavior re-emerge. Despite the absence of an argument for a link to habitual behavior, however, Maclay's approach was closer to traditional concerns than was Casagrande's in that he predicted that language differences lead to enduring behavioral dispositions in adults. However, in the end, Maclay was unable to formulate an experiment that would effectively distinguish among the groups: all three sets of speakers performed remarkably alike on his task. The difficulty lay partly with the imprecision or absence of a linguistic analysis – he had no prediction for two of the three groups. Casagrande solved this problem by referring to a baseline pattern of dimensional preference found in previous psychological research. Maclay, by contrast, provided no such baseline for his predictions. He made predictions about differential response among the three groups without any information about what pattern of responses might be expected from two of the groups.[37]

Common problems

The studies reviewed in this section shared two common goals: (1) assessing individual nonlinguistic behavior experimentally in order (2) to identify influences on behavior stemming from differences in linguistic structure. In each case, the results were ambiguous in part because of the specific way these goals were met.

The goal of individual experimental assessment was met operationally by all three studies: nonlinguistic classification behavior was assessed by having subjects overtly "classify," that is, sort or group, objects without speaking. But the relation of behavior in experimental tasks to habitual thought or to everyday behavior remained very unclear. There was no attempt, for example, to model the specific experimental sorting tasks along the lines of some everyday practice. Nor, in contrast to the color tradition, was there any general argument about the functional relation between language and cognition analogous to the arguments about codability. In fact, no mention was made of cognitive processes such as attention, memory, or reasoning. Because he was only dealing with a mixed assortment of lexical contrasts, Carroll simply could not make a general argument about habitual behavior. Likewise, because he dealt with a transient developmental difference, Casagrande could not draw conclusions about everyday adult thought. Maclay, by contrast, could have made a general argument but settled instead for the simplest correlational formulation: if referents elicit the same linguistic response, they will elicit the same nonlinguistic response. The very generality and looseness of this prediction make its verification difficult, as Maclay discovered.

The studies also met the second goal of language comparison operationally, that is, they each worked with speakers from more than one language and dealt with differences between those languages. But the linguistic comparisons were not substantive. On the one hand, there was simply no description of some of the languages involved, so that the comparison was between the "presence" of a specific obligatory category in one language and its "absence" (or some other unknown status) in the comparison languages. On the other hand, even for the languages where there was some description, there was no analysis of the structural or functional place of the category in the language as a whole. Thus, although Carroll dealt with complex lexical semantics, we have no idea whether the differences stem from some more fundamental, general differences between Hopi and English or whether they represent isolated instances. And, although both Casagrande and Maclay dealt with a Navaho grammatical category, we have no idea how significant this category is in terms of the structure of Navaho or in terms of frequency of use. It is not even entirely clear what the meanings of the different verb-stem classes actually are.

In short, the structural outlines of a meaningful approach to empirically exploring the linguistic relativity problem can be seen in the goals and general approach of three studies. And throughout there are promising ideas and interesting techniques. In the end, however, the outline is never quite filled out with real substance and the promise of the approach is, therefore, not realized.

Summary

The studies dealing with form classes broke new ground in bringing together the psycholinguists' concern for experimental assessment of individual behavior with the anthropological linguists' concern for differences between the obligatory grammatical categories of languages. In particular, they showed how testable hypotheses can be generated from the analysis of complex lexical and grammatical categories and they developed an array of techniques for addressing those hypotheses. They thus point the way toward dealing with more complex, conceptual linguistic categories. However, the studies also showed a common set of weaknesses. There were few explicit arguments linking the experimental tasks to general cognitive processes or to everyday behavior. The linguistic analyses were weak in that they were typically confined to a single language (yielding, then, only a contrast between "presence" and "absence") and failed to characterize adequately the structure and use of the categories at issue.

Perhaps the most important by-product of these efforts was the further evidence they provided on the importance from a *psychological* point of view of understanding the pattern of use of a linguistic category. Brown's study showed that the linguists' precise distributional characterization of form classes might not be as useful as a characterization of the typical use of a category. Carroll and Maclay's studies revealed the importance of understanding the application of linguistic categories to the specific task and materials used for nonlinguistic assessment. Maclay emphasized that a description of the use of a category was an important part of its adequate characterization. Casagrande's study showed the importance of considering nonlinguistic influences on task behavior and the difficulty of developing a hypothesis capable of differentiating among multiple influences. In a variety of ways, then, these studies emphasized the importance from a psychological standpoint of going beyond a simple structural analysis and assessing the way in which and how often a category is actually used. However, the significance of these valid and important issues is perhaps exaggerated in these studies because of the weakness of their structural analyses of language and the absence of any real psychological models of the interrelation between language and thought.

Logical connectors and formal reasoning

There is virtually no psychological research on linguistic relativity dealing with aspects of language other than lexical items and form classes. This section describes two such studies. Both deal primarily with the significance of logical connectors for formal reasoning. Nearly the entire section is devoted to a study concerning Chinese counterfactual reasoning and to related research stimulated by it. A second, less significant study of the relationship between logical operators and logical reasoning among the Yucatec Maya is also briefly described. Both studies illustrate the importance of distinguishing analytically between the structural features of a language and the characteristic patterns of use of those features.

Chinese counterfactual reasoning: the work of Bloom

Within the field of psycholinguistics the most recent research on linguistic relativity aside from the continuing work on color is Alfred Bloom's work comparing English and Mandarin Chinese (1981). Bloom identified a constellation of linguistic patterns in English which he claimed encouraged a mode of hypothetical, counterfactual, and theoretical thinking among English speakers. Both the linguistic patterns and the associated mode of thinking are only marginally present in Chinese. Bloom linked these linguistic patterns both to individual performance in experimental tasks and to broad cultural patterns in the two societies. He also developed a preliminary theoretical account of the mechanisms by which languages influence thought.

Bloom's theoretical orientation

Bloom argued that Whorf's ideas had been rejected in the past by behaviorist psychologists (for instance, Watson), language philosophers (for instance, Frege, Russell, Wittgenstein, Quine), and American structuralist linguists (for instance, Bloomfield) because entertaining these ideas would have entailed violating one or more of the principal substantive and/or methodological tenets of their theoretical paradigms. This argument has merit so far as it goes, but Bloom's review lacked balance in that it did not consider in any detail either Whorf's own work or subsequent work in psychology, anthropology, and linguistics that has directly addressed Whorf's ideas.[38] Thus Bloom failed to address the deeper question of why even research sympathetic to Whorf's ideas had fared so poorly in the past. And therefore, in the end, despite approaching the relativity question in a substantially different way, Bloom repeated many of the same errors as his predecessors.

Bloom built his new empirical approach to the linguistic relativity question on the "cognitive structuralism" of Piaget and Chomsky. He felt that the emergence of the cognitive structuralist paradigm had changed the research situation radically because there was no need to violate the basic theoretical or empirical tenets of this paradigm to address Whorf's questions.[39] He seemed unconcerned that the dominant cognitive structuralists he mentioned, Piaget and Chomsky, were in fact committed to identifying universals with a strong undercurrent of biological nativism. Bloom characterized cognitive structuralism as assuming that there is a separate realm of thought or cognitive structure that develops in interaction with the environment and underlies language and other behavior. The existence of this cognitive realm separate from language sets the stage for asking about interactions between realms:

it seems . . . reasonable to suppose that if there exist cognitive structures separate from language, then just as those structures might affect and hence be reflected in language, so might language affect and hence be reflected in them. The Cognitive Structuralist paradigm, in other words, lays the theoretical infrastructure necessary for serious consideration of Whorf's claims. (Bloom, 1981, p. 11)

Bloom's central goal using this paradigm, then, was to show that the question of linguistic influences is worthy of consideration by demonstrating that it can be productively addressed. Notice, however, that most of the research on Whorf's question has tacitly assumed the existence of cognitive structures separate from language.

Bloom's central argument

Bloom (1981) began his argument by describing how he initially noticed that Chinese speakers had difficulty with counterfactual questions. From these observations he developed a hypothesis that traced the difficulty to the structure of the Chinese language. He then provided anecdotal and experimental evidence supporting this analysis.

Initial observations and formulation of the problem

While administering a questionnaire designed to measure levels of abstraction in political thinking to residents of Hong Kong, Bloom found that respondents had difficulties with questions framed as counterfactuals. When presented with a counterfactual statement such as "If the Hong Kong government were to pass a law requiring that all citizens born outside of Hong Kong make weekly reports of their activities to the police, how would you react?" subjects consistently responded with statements such as "But the government hasn't," "It can't," or "It won't." Bloom pressed subjects further and got responses such as "We don't speak/think that way," "It's unnatural," or "It's unChinese." By contrast, American and French subjects responding to similar questions never seemed to find anything unnatural about the questions and readily indulged in the counterfactual hypothesizing the questions were designed to elicit.

Bloom found these Chinese responses especially interesting because they correlated with the absence in the Chinese language of "structures equivalent to those through which English and other Indo-European languages mark the counterfactual realm" (Bloom, 1981, pp. 13–14). This led him to ask:

Could having or not having a counterfactual construction in one's language play a significant role in determining how inclined one will be to think in counterfactual terms?   (Bloom, 1981, p. 14)

His subsequent research attempted to answer this question.

Under Bloom's analysis,[40] the English counterfactual consists of an implicational sentence, often of the form:

If [clause 1], (then) [clause 2],

in which the main verb in the first clause is in the past or past perfect (or contains the form *were to*) and the verb phrase in the second contains the forms *would* or *would have*:

If he ran faster, he would win.
If he had run faster, he would have won.

By contrast, for Chinese speakers to establish a counterfactual, they must either rely on an implicit, pragmatic negation of the premise in the speech context or make an explicit, semantic negation of the premise by a prior statement. So, for example, to express the meaning equivalent to the English counterfactual

"If John had come earlier, they would have arrived at the movies on time (but didn't)"   (1981, p. 19, slightly altered)

a Chinese speaker would have to say

"If John come + past [time marker[41]] earlier, they arrive at the movies on time."
(1981, p. 19)

The counterfactual interpretation only obtains for the Chinese if the addressee already *knows* that John was late. If the addressee does not know that John was late, then the sentence would typically have a simple implicational (perhaps hypothetical but not necessarily counterfactual) interpretation equivalent to the following English sentence:

"If John came earlier, they arrived at the movies on time."   (1981, p. 19)

To clarify ambiguous situations, the Chinese speaker can explicitly state the necessary premise:

John is + past [time marker] late. If John come + past [time marker] earlier, they arrive at the movies on time.

In short, counterfactuals in Chinese depend for their interpretation relatively more on knowledge or interpretation of the immediate context of speaking, whereas those in English depend relatively less on the immediate context because they are more explicitly marked.

In addition to his initial observation and linguistic analysis, Bloom provided a number of other pieces of informal evidence to bolster his argument that there is in fact some significant difference in the use of counterfactuals by Chinese and English speakers. He mentioned that counterfactuals are rare in Chinese written texts, that it is difficult for Chinese speakers learning English to master this part of English grammar, that the difficulty in working with counterfactual expressions persists even after practice with them, and that native speakers usually judge the counterfactuals negatively and prefer other forms of expression (Bloom, 1981, pp. 17–18). The linguistic analysis coupled with the informal evidence suggests that Chinese speakers are able to think and speak counterfactually, but that in the absence of a distinct marking for the counterfactual they do so much less often than do English speakers.

In light of this further analysis Bloom refined his hypothesis:

> let us suppose that a language, by whether it labels or does not label any specific mode of categorizing experience, cannot determine whether its speakers will think that way, but can either encourage or not encourage them to develop a labeled cognitive schema specific to that mode of thought.
>
> (Bloom, 1981, p. 20)

As should be obvious, this is a variant of the familiar codability hypothesis: the crucial difference between language groups does not lie in their concepts as such but rather in which concepts are labeled and therefore more cognitively salient (see Brown and Lenneberg, 1954, p. 457). Further, the existence of a label can help speakers constitute or develop a corresponding cognitive category (Bloom, 1981, pp. 20–21, 61–86; 1984, pp. 275–76). Bloom's argument in terms of what a language does or does not "encourage" was also reminiscent of earlier approaches.

However, Bloom's formulation was also distinct from previous work in two ways. First, he shifted from emphasizing the coding of external reality to the coding of a particular conceptual structure. He believed that language influenced abstract conceptual thought more strongly than the perception of reality and that the effect of a pre-existing label would be much greater for less perceptually based categories. (For an early statement of much the same view, see Fearing, 1954.) But in making this shift, Bloom gave up the objective metalanguage which was so crucial to the color tradition and which was also used, although less explicitly, in the studies of form-class differences.[42] He then needed to devise some other unbiased standard for description (or calibration) of cognitive schemas so as to assure that subjects in his experimental tasks were presented with the "same" cognitive opportunities. But Bloom did not develop any such standard, nor, for that matter, did he seem to understand the need for one. The situation was further complicated by his reliance on language texts as stimuli, where equivalence was established only by means of translation. Such judgments of equivalence are always subject to question and alternative interpretation, and, not surprisingly, Bloom's findings have been repeatedly criticized as artifacts of his Chinese stimulus materials. (These criticisms are discussed in detail further below.)

What Bloom's critics have not recognized, however, is that the problem is deeper than the specific inadequacies of his translations; the real difficulty is that his approach to language description lacked a comparatively based and referentially grounded framework against which alternative claims about the language could be resolved.[43] A comparatively based description characterizes a grammatical pattern in a neutral fashion by placing it within a range of types where the parameters of variation among types serve as the metalanguage of description. Without such a comparatively based description, the grammar of one of the languages at issue (i.e., Chinese) will tend to be judged as inferior ("deficient") with respect to the one being used as the tacit standard (i.e., English). A referentially grounded framework (in the present case) is one that makes some appeal to the observable non-linguistic context of utterance. Without a referential ground, disputes over translation become inevitable and irresolvable because both sides can plausibly claim to have the superior ("correct") description of the linguistic facts.

Second, in a related move, Bloom shifted to a concern with a "specific mode of categorizing experience" (1981, p. 20) and away from more traditional concerns with cognitive categories or with cognitive processing potential. As will become clear further below, this formulation of the relativity question shifted the focus away from a structural relativity (wherein the structured category content of language influences the fundamental content or process of thought) and toward a functional relativity (wherein certain ways of using language in specific cognitive activities support or encourage those activities). A correct understanding of this transformation of the problem is crucial because Bloom focused exclusively on an area of cognitive activity where English speakers exhibit an ability that Chinese speakers do not – another example of a "presence" versus "absence" approach to differences. Accepting Bloom's formulation inevitably leads to the conclusion that the Chinese language lacks something structural that English has and that Chinese speakers think less well than English speakers because of this structural deficit. When Bloom's data are recast in functional terms, not only does this question of structural superiority dissolve, but also a more coherent and powerful argument emerges about the potential interaction of linguistic structures and functions.

After a brief review of Bloom's evidence, these two points will be developed further in two subsequent sections.

Experimental evidence

Bloom put his hypothesis about counterfactuals to several experimental tests. The first task, developed by Bloom (1981, pp. 22–31) over a period of several years, involved presenting three versions of a story to different samples of speakers and following the presentations with questions about the content of the stories. The stories used the following formats:

[English:] X was not the case, but if X had been the case, then Y would have been the case, Z would have been the case, and W would have been the case, etc. . . . [Chinese:] X was not the case; but if X was, then Y, then Z, then W, etc.

(Bloom, 1981, p. 22)[44]

Notice that the explicit statement of the initial negative premise reproduces the Chinese pattern used outside of the more usual concrete situational contexts (Bloom, 1981, p. 22), but that only the English explicitly signals a counterfactual in the subsequent clauses.

After the presentation of the stories, subjects were questioned to see if they understood the counterfactual nature of the stories, that is, whether "the final consequent or consequents of the series of implications presented refer to things that have happened or rather to things that have not" (Bloom, 1981, p. 23). The expectation was that the English speakers would have no problem:

English speakers equipped with counterfactual schemas might be expected upon seeing the words "if he had . . . would have," to shift promptly into the counterfactual mode of processing and hence to understand in an almost self-evident manner that, of course, the consequents are to be interpreted as counterfactual . . .   (Bloom, 1981, p. 23)

Chinese speakers, by contrast,

might be expected . . . to encounter greater difficulty . . . in recognizing . . . that the paragraph is about the realm of the might-have-been; and . . . to encounter greater difficulty . . . in holding a counterfactual perspective in mind as a stable point of mental orientation from which to analyze the series of consequents presented.   (Bloom, 1981, p. 23)

English subjects consistently outperformed the Chinese subjects in their ability to correctly identify counterfactual statements in the stories as counterfactual.[45] Further, bilingual Chinese speakers generally did better than monolinguals and, when given both English and Chinese versions of the stories, tended to do better on the English versions. This bilingual evidence was crucial because it suggested that language rather than some other cultural factor might be the source of the behavioral difference. Bloom also administered different versions of the Chinese stories, varying the degree of explicitness of the counterfactual content. The Chinese performance was enhanced on the more explicit versions, again suggesting that language structure was the critical factor in task performance.

Bloom administered a second experimental procedure involving counterfactual questions. Chinese and English speakers were presented the following question written in their respective languages:

"If all circles were large and this small triangle '▲' were a circle, would it be large?"   (Bloom, 1981, p. 31)[46]

Most Chinese speakers answered "no," whereas most English speakers answered "yes." This result was consistent with the hypothesis that the Chinese speakers have trouble working with the counterfactual mode.[47] Bloom also reported that whenever the same question was given orally, even to highly educated speakers (for instance, to Hong Kong University faculty members), most Chinese responded with the following sorts of remarks:

"No! How can a circle be a triangle? How can this small circle be large? What do you mean?"   (Bloom, 1981, p. 31)

Some subjects elaborated further, as did one who said:

"I know what you Westerners want me to do, you always want me to assume things, even when they don't make sense. But we Chinese don't do that."
                                                                (Bloom, 1981, p. 31)

By contrast English speakers never raised these sorts of objections.

Bloom concluded his discussion of counterfactuals by recognizing that other factors could account for these differences:

One could . . . argue that rather than reflecting the impact of language structure on thought, the evidence reflects the existence within Chinese society of a general cultural proclivity against counterfactual thinking which is responsible for both the lack of an explicit marking of the counterfactual in the language and the reluctance of Chinese speakers to venture into the counterfactual realm.
                                                                (Bloom, 1981, p. 32)

Unfortunately, Bloom's only response to this possibility was simply to assert without argument that there "must be" a language influence:

the very fact that the English-speaking child from the outset hears thoughts expressed in an explicitly counterfactual way and by early adolescence is expected himself to become master in both concrete and abstract contexts of explicit counterfactual speech, while his Chinese counterpart does not share this linguistic experience, *must affect* importantly the relative facility each develops for this mode of speech and thought – particularly so, moreover, for even though the rudiments of counterfactual thinking may predate language development, further development of a facility for counterfactual thought *must take place* within a language and hence be subject to whatever influence that language exerts.   (Bloom, 1981, pp. 32–33, my italics)

Needless to say, simply asserting the argument in this way cannot substitute for some evidence that language is the decisive influence. Bloom took for granted precisely what he intended to prove. And, as will be made clear below, he eventually conceded that the existence of a proclivity for or against counterfactual reasoning in a culture has more to do with the history of that society than with linguistic structure as such.

A closer examination of Bloom's tasks reveals that they failed to provide a diagnostic test of his hypothesis because they essentially assessed language comprehension. On the one hand, the results could not demonstrate clear "nonlinguistic" consequences, since the tasks were completely language centered. On the other hand, the results could not demonstrate convincingly that language structure was the causal factor, because any manipulation of the texts could also alter comprehension. So, for example, the improved performance of Chinese bilinguals when working in English and of all Chinese speakers when working with the stories containing more explicit counterfactual content could reflect improved text comprehension rather than any shift into a different mode of reasoning. Ideally, any experimental procedure simplifies or controls actual situations so as to reveal more clearly the relationships among variables that are confounded or conflated in their natural or everyday state. Bloom's experiments did not do this; they merely demonstrated that what he suspected was generally characteristic of the patterns of language use of the two groups did in fact show up in specific instances.

Summary

In sum, there are three general problems with Bloom's approach which will reappear throughout the discussion in the following two sections. First, he lacked a comparatively based, referentially grounded framework for language description. This is one factor underlying the debate over his characterizations of Chinese counterfactuals described in the next section. Second, he emphasized the cognitive effects of certain specialized uses of grammatical structures rather than the effects of everyday patterns of use on habitual thought and behavior. This leads to a variety of problems having to do not only with whether his experimental findings can reasonably be linked to general patterns in Chinese and American culture but also with whether his findings have anything to do with the structure of Chinese and English. Third, many of his experiments are not diagnostic of anything. On the one hand they do not clearly demonstrate the effect of language on nonlinguistic behavior. On the other hand they do not clearly establish that language rather than some other cultural factor underlies the observed behavioral differences.

The Bloom–Au debate

The chief critic of Bloom's work has been Au (1983; 1984). She both criticized his experimental procedures and attempted, unsuccessfully, to replicate his results. In turn, Bloom defended his original work and argued that Au did not properly replicate his experiments. The debate is reviewed here not so much to evaluate the substantive facts of the case, but rather to indicate the difficulties that arise in resolving such disputes when the relativity problem is framed in the way Bloom framed it. Particularly important are the lack of a comparatively based, referentially grounded framework for linguistic description, which underlies the debate over whether Chinese is "deficient" and whether Bloom has characterized the counterfactual "correctly," and, secondly, the failure to differentiate analytically between effects due to the presence of a grammatical structure (as it is ordinarily used) and its use in a specialized mode of discourse. The debate also foregrounds two other more specific design problems: the difficulties of interpreting the responses of bilingual subjects and those of using linguistic stimuli to demonstrate nonlinguistic effects.

Au's initial criticisms of Bloom

Au began by summarizing Bloom's linguistic analysis and citing his conclusion that "the Chinese language has no distinct lexical, grammatical or intonational device to signal entry into the counterfactual realm" (Au, 1983, p. 157). She did not disagree with this claim, but argued that it made no difference because "In the real world ... Chinese speakers use counterfactuals with little ambiguity" (1983, p. 157) and because counterfactuals are "as explicit to Chinese speakers" as English counterfactuals are to English speakers (1983, p. 158). Bloom, of course, never claimed that Chinese speakers could not express counterfactual utterances, and he described in some detail the grammatical patterns used to do so. Au herself referred to exactly the same constructional possibilities. Rather, his claim was that despite this capability to express counterfactuals, the difference in explicitness of marking did seem to be important:

On the one hand, Chinese certainly do, within certain situations, think and speak counterfactually; on the other, the lack of a distinct marking for the counterfactual seems ... to be associated with significant cognitive consequences.

(Bloom, 1981, pp. 19–20)

In short, Au did not initially express any substantive disagreements with Bloom's linguistic analysis. Her claim was simply that the formal grammatical differences didn't matter in practice.

Au then summarized Bloom's experimental work. She characterized Bloom as starting with the language difference and then developing an interpretation in terms of the different cognitive effort required to think counterfactually in the two languages. Significantly, her account ignored the fact that Bloom began his research in the first place because he saw a behavioral difference between Chinese and Americans in dealing with counterfactual arguments. The linguistic analysis in terms of overt marking, the cognitive interpretation in terms of inclination and effort to think counterfactually, and the experimental tasks designed to provide "a more objective test" for these preliminary interpretations all stemmed from his initial, informal observations. By ignoring this observational starting point, Au both obscured the original purpose of the experiments (i.e., to verify the informal observations) and made it appear that Bloom's claims depended entirely on the experimental results.

Au then turned to a discussion of Bloom's experiments, which she found "difficult to interpret" because of his "quasi-experimental design" wherein he "assigned each group, but not each subject, to an experimental condition" (Au, 1983, p. 160). This made it difficult to separate out the language difference from other, unknown characteristics of the groups. (On the confounding of language and culture by Bloom, see also Cheng, 1985, p. 918.) There is merit to this criticism, although the special problems involved in providing control for cultural factors by using bilingual subjects (who can be assigned to each condition randomly) should not be underestimated, as will become clear below.

Au then singled out for specific criticism the crucial experiment in which Bloom had a single group of Taiwanese subjects work with both a Chinese and an English version of the story. These bilingual subjects gave significantly fewer correct interpretations of a counterfactual story when working in Chinese than when working in English some three months later. Au criticized Bloom's procedure because he had not counterbalanced the experiment: he gave all the Chinese versions before all the English ones. This confounded the effect of the language switch with the effect of repeated exposure to the story and may have affected subjects' response to the task:

they may have suspected that there was something tricky they perhaps missed the first time. The 'experienced' subjects may therefore have been cautious, and tried much harder this time.   (Au, 1983, p. 160)

Thus, what appeared to have been an effect due to switching to English may in fact have been due to the second exposure to the task.

Au saw confirmation of this interpretation in the fact that Chinese university student subjects working only with the English version did not show the same markedly superior score. These university student subjects gave roughly equivalent responses when working in either language. Bloom explained this in terms of a higher degree of bilingualism in English among the university student subjects. It is not clear how this would possibly explain why these subjects were *less* accurate in English than the nonstudent subjects. It would be more reasonable to argue that the Chinese only do as well as English speakers on Bloom's task if they work in English *and* if they are especially motivated or careful.

Au's initial criticisms made it appear that her objections to Bloom's procedures were technical ones (i.e., counterbalancing of subjects and stimulus presentations) rather than substantive ones.[48] And she characterized her work as an attempt to sort out possible confounding effects in his original study. However, there are reasons to believe that Au was fundamentally unhappy with Bloom's conclusions (see, for instance, Au, 1983, pp. 157, 182; 1984, p. 289). As Hatano (1982, p. 819) observed in reviewing Bloom's book, the formulation invited a "deficit" interpretation for the Chinese language and people because there was no equivalent analysis of a bias in English. Unable or unwilling (at least initially) to disagree with the linguistic analysis or the cognitive theory, she was forced to argue that the specific linguistic difference didn't matter and that Bloom's findings must have been due to some error in procedure. However, if Au had only been interested in the counterbalancing issue, she could have simply replicated Bloom's experiment with an equivalent sample and a counterbalanced design. She did neither, and we never do learn whether repeated exposure to the task affects the results. Instead, she developed a new counterfactual story for use with a different sample.

Au's empirical studies

Au conducted several studies of her own using an "experimental" design. The first study examined whether bilingual speakers differed in their inclination to reason counterfactually depending on whether they were speaking English or Chinese and whether the difference "could be attributed to memory overloading or to the absence of a linguistic construction for the counterfactual *per se*" (Au, 1983, p. 161). Au's concern was that

When we compare the English and the Chinese versions of [Bloom's] story, we can see that every implication is marked in the English versions with a counterfactual cue (*would have*), but there is no corresponding cue in the Chinese versions. This means that Bloom's English-speaking subjects were reminded of the counterfactuality by every *would have*, whereas the Chinese-speaking subjects were not. It was therefore hypothesized that memory overloading might help to account for the comprehension problems that Bloom's subjects had with the Chinese versions of [Bloom's] story.   (Au, 1983, p. 161)

Notice that this was *exactly* Bloom's claim: differences in the manner and systematicity of the linguistic marking of counterfactuals affect the ability to effectively adopt and sustain a counterfactual point of view. However, in this passage, Au wrote as if the number of cues in the story was somehow an experimentally introduced artifact, independent of the languages as regularly used. In Au (1984) this claim became even more explicit.

Au created a new counterfactual story for her study because she felt that, from the point of view of native speakers such as herself, Bloom's Chinese texts were not very idiomatic (1983, p. 161; also pp. 167, 181–82). Although introduced offhandedly, this was a crucial new argument by Au, and it eventually became the focus of her criticism (Au, 1984). Au carefully checked the various versions of her new story for idiomatic construction. The different versions were designed to test her hypothesis of "memory overloading" by systematically manipulating language, the number of counterfactual implications, and the number of counterfactual cues.[49]

Au found that bilingual Hong Kong secondary-school students nearly all interpreted her new story correctly regardless of the variations in language, number of implications, or number of cues. She concluded that "Chinese bilingual subjects had little difficulty in understanding the counterfactual story, whether written in Chinese or English" and that her findings "contradict[ed] Bloom's findings" (Au, 1983, p. 166). Au found her results "surprising" and speculated that the failure to replicate Bloom's findings might have resulted from the change of story or from the characteristics of her new subject pool.

A major problem with Au's experiment was that subjects performed nearly perfectly. This suggests that the story was too easy to interpret to be of diagnostic value and that her results showed a "ceiling effect." Bloom's story and question (grossly simplified) took the following form:

1.1 X could not read Chinese,
1.2 but if X had been able to read Chinese,
1.3 X would have discovered and been influenced by $Y_{1,2,3}$.
1.4 X would then have done $Z_{1,2,3}$.
1.5 Indicate what contributions (i.e., Zs) X made to the West.

Au's story and question, by contrast, took this form:

2.1 X did not understand the language spoken by the natives;
2.2 if X had been able to understand the language spoken by the natives and not fled so quickly,
2.3 X would have learnt $Y_{1,2,3}$.
2.4
2.5 Indicate what things (i.e., Ys) X knew about the natives.

Notice that Au's story was considerably simpler in terms of overall structure and counterfactual complexity. Further, her question was about a different and much simpler logical element in the story: whereas the Y elements she asks about are actual facts not known by X, the Z elements Bloom asked about never actually happened.

To test for an effect due to the stories themselves,[50] Au conducted a study using her story and the most idiomatic version of Bloom's story with Chinese–English bilinguals. Again, the subjects "revealed very little difficulty with the counterfactual logic in either story in either language" (Au, 1983, p. 168). In particular, although the scores for Bloom's story were significantly lower than those for Au's, they were also higher than he had originally found and roughly the same in both languages.[51] In short, Bloom's results showing a difference among Chinese bilinguals depending on whether they were using English or Chinese were not replicated using his own materials.

Au now suggested that the failure to replicate Bloom's result might be due either to details of experimental procedure or to differences in the subject groups – in particular, ability with English. She noted the latter possibility could not be tested because Bloom's subjects were no longer available. To shed some light on this problem, however, Au conducted two additional studies varying subject characteristics.

The first study attempted to replicate Bloom's findings with English-speaking American subjects using both Bloom's and her original stories and some additional unidiomatic translations of each from the Chinese versions. The results using her own story were replicated, but Bloom's results with American subjects were not replicated. Au found a lower rate of counterfactual responses than Bloom had found with English subjects in his original experiment or than she had found with the Hong Kong bilinguals. The additional unidiomatic translations reduced performance – but not significantly – on both stories. Au suggested that the failure to replicate Bloom's American results might have had to do with the fact that her sample was of high-school students, whereas Bloom's was of college students.

The second additional study varying subject characteristics involved a younger sample of Chinese schoolchildren who had had less exposure to English. Au first tested to be sure the children did not have full command of the English counterfactual construction. Then she tested for comprehension on her story. She found that the accuracy rate shifted at about age twelve from about 75 percent to about 100 percent. Unfortunately, she did not also administer Bloom's story, and therefore this study sheds no light on Bloom's results and why they were not replicable.

Au concluded that there was no evidence of a difficulty with counterfactual reasoning among Chinese speakers. Bloom's original story had presented subjects with more difficulty than hers, but she attributed this to the unidiomatic quality of Bloom's story. Au also emphasized that her

Hong Kong bilinguals did better in English than did the American English-speakers. As she noted,

The major question raised by, and not answered in, the first four studies was whether or not the high counterfactual response rates of the Hong Kong sample were due to the subjects' mastery of the English subjunctive.

(Au, 1983, p. 182)

Au (1983) felt that her final study with children less experienced in English resolved this problem. But since she only used her own story, which was structurally different and consistently easier to comprehend than Bloom's, this conclusion does not seem warranted.

Fittingly, Au closed her discussion by emphasizing, as had Lenneberg many years before, the importance of idiomatic translations, that is, the use of functional equivalents rather than literal or structural equivalents. The latent assumption of this position is that structural differences do not really matter.

Bloom's reply to Au (etc.)

In a reply to Au, Bloom claimed that Au made three incorrect assumptions in her studies.

Sample population.   First, he argued that her subject pool had a different linguistic background:

My subjects were college students and adults whose education, with the exception of foreign language courses, had been fully in Chinese and who were immersed principally within a Chinese psycholinguistic world. Hers, by contrast, were all students in the Anglo-Chinese track of the Hong Kong educational system which instructs primarily in English and which prepares students for entry into English universities. They were subjects, in other words, who were thoroughly immersed in an English psycholinguistic world.   (1984, p. 280)

In short, Bloom's subjects were more immersed in a Chinese language world than were Au's.

Regarding the performance of Au's subjects, Bloom made reference to his earlier argument (Bloom, 1981, p. 32) that Chinese-speaking subjects who have been deeply acculturated into English are likely to attach a counterfactual interpretation as a second meaning to their Chinese labels for "if . . . then" and so transform those labels into direct, though ambiguous, signals of both counterfactual and implicational thoughts:

At that point, these bilingual Chinese-speakers come to have Chinese labels for counterfactual thoughts and thus can be expected to respond directly, just as English speakers do, to invitations into the counterfactual realm.

(1984, p. 280)

Bloom originally made this argument about highly bilingual subjects in an attempt to account for the fact that Chinese university student subjects tended to perform about the same in both Chinese and English. He did not point out that these same highly bilingual subjects were *less* accurate with English counterfactual stories than the nonstudent subjects – a fact which completely undercut his argument: either the students who knew *less* English did *better* or, if this group's results are discounted (i.e., if he concedes Au's point that the difference might have been due to the effects of repeated exposure to the task for the nonstudent group), there was no difference between languages for bilingual subjects. In spite of this, it is fair to say that differences in the subject populations used by Bloom and Au presented a possible source of differences in their findings. Also, neither one provided a good argument or supporting body of research to buttress his or her arguments about the expected performance of bilinguals of various types.

Bloom (1984, pp. 283–85) also criticized Au's two studies aimed at exploring differences in subject characteristics. Regarding Au's American subjects, Bloom seized upon her suggestion that the difference in results might be due to the educational background of the subjects. Bloom claimed that "intellectual sophistication" is crucial in interpreting his stories. But if this age or educational difference does matter with American English-speaking subjects, then it suggests that Bloom's results did not really have to do with language structure *per se* but with a specialized use of language associated with higher education. Any linguistic relativity would lie at least as much at the level of language use as at the level of language structure. (Certainly most American high-school students can be considered fluent speakers of English from a structural point of view.) The claim would be that the structural factor only operates as a significant factor in special task contexts, that is, in special uses. The alternative interpretation is that Bloom's results with American college speakers were not reliable.

Bloom argued that Au's results with younger Chinese schoolchildren were consistent with his position because the materials were so simple:

What Au has shown in this part of her work is simply that Chinese-speakers, in the absence of specific counterfactual labels, do arrive at counterfactual interpretations in response to a single negated premise followed by a simple implicational statement based upon it – one of the fundamental premises of my work. In such a simple task ... the effect of having or not having counterfactual labels cannot be expected to emerge.   (1984, p. 285)

Thus, Bloom attempted to undercut Au's evidence about subject characteristics by criticizing the stimulus materials they worked with. Au (1984) replied that one of her other original samples was "nearly monolingual" (see Au, 1983, pp. 177–81). What she did not point out was that these subjects worked with her story, which Bloom also criticized as too simple. (This is discussed further below.) And, in her reply to Bloom, Au (1984, pp. 300–1) did not improve the situation, because her further work again failed to use his original story but rather worked with a more "idiomatic" version of it. But Bloom's emphasis on the need for the counterfactual stories to be complex and difficult foregrounds the fact that he is not dealing with habitual thought engendered by language but with specialized skills linked to age and education.

A later study by Liu (1985) replicated some of Bloom's and Au's tasks using a sample of essentially monolingual Chinese elementary- and high-school-aged children living in Taiwan. With this sample, which met Bloom's criterion of living in a Chinese psycholinguistic world, she found counterfactual reasoning patterns more similar to Au's than to Bloom's. Compared with Au's adults, Liu's high-school sample had slightly lower counterfactual scores on each of the narrative tasks. These findings effectively rebutted Bloom's argument that Au's results were due to the language environment of her subject population. It should be noted that Liu's high-school students were exposed to English in school, but apparently less so than Bloom's own Taiwanese sample. Although Liu (1985, p. 253) dismissed the result, it is worth mentioning that her sample shows a notable jump in counterfactual performance, and a drop in comprehension errors generally, in the eighth grade, when they are first taught the English counterfactual (see figure 1 and table 2 in Liu). It remains unclear how much exposure to English is enough to make a difference in performance. By using both Bloom's and Au's original materials, Liu was also able to show that the development of counterfactual skills was real and not an artifact of the shift in assessment materials, as suggested by Bloom. It remains unclear whether it is age or education that is more important in this change.[52]

Idiomatic Chinese.   Au (1983) had criticized the Chinese version of Bloom's story which she had used for not being idiomatic, but she was not specific. In his reply, Bloom (1984) defended his Chinese versions. First, he argued that they were in fact idiomatic:

it should be stressed that the Chinese versions of my stories were all written by native Chinese-speaking professors at the National Taiwan University and judged by them to be in grammatical, acceptable and comprehensible Chinese.
(1984, p. 283)[53]

Second, he argued that Au's results with bilingual subjects confirmed the interpretability of the counterfactual content of the Chinese stories since 86 percent of her bilingual subjects gave such interpretations. Of course the fact that Au (1983, pp. 171, 174–75; 1984, pp. 297) consistently showed that Bloom's materials could elicit counterfactual interpretations was at odds with his major claim, hence the importance of his argument (discussed above) that her subject pool was not equivalent. And third, he noted that Au's attempt to make his story more idiomatic in fact made it "markedly less counterfactual in content" (1984, p. 283).[54] It is also worth noting here that Bloom had originally reported that his grammatical analysis, on the basis of which the stories were constructed, was "confirmed by interviewing of both Chinese monolingual speakers and native Chinese, Chinese–English bilinguals" (1981, p. 15). And, in a review of Bloom's book, Jordan found "the Chinese protocols colloquial except where his theoretical framework predicts that they cannot be" (1982, p. 747).

In a reply to Bloom, Au (1984, p. 291) elaborated her objections to his texts, asserting that "Bloom has misanalyzed the counterfactual construction in Chinese" (1984, p. 291). Au claimed that her objections were shared by others. Cheng (1985, pp. 919–20) has made similar arguments about the unidiomatic quality of Bloom's Chinese texts. Cheng (1985, n2) also consulted with college-educated native speakers of Chinese, including two instructors of Chinese at the University of Michigan.

There is probably no easy way to resolve the deeper issues involved in this dispute. Certainly, both sides can cite authoritative support, and it is obvious that there is no consensus among speakers of Chinese as to what is required to express a counterfactual. Some of the differences here may have to do with how much English influence there has been not just on the subjects, but on the experimenters and critics themselves. It is likely that Bloom's critics, for example, operate in the English psycholinguistic world, as Bloom defined it. Even if a consensus could be forged by polling a large number of Chinese speakers, it would not necessarily accurately reflect Chinese speakers' actual behavior. A body of data on actual patterns of speech would provide the most convincing evidence. But actual behavior cannot be meaningfully observed unless a regular environmental condition (thing, event, situation, etc.) can be found with which to elicit "counterfactual" speech reliably. This difficulty highlights the most striking difference between Bloom's approach and that of all earlier studies: there is no comparatively based, referentially grounded anchor for his comparisons. Without such an anchor, it is difficult to appeal to "what speakers habitually say." Moreover, this absence of a referential (denotational) ground is intentional, since Bloom is trying to move away from working with perceptually bounded research domains toward conceptually more complex abstract domains. Ironically, because of this orientation, it may be impossible to "prove" Bloom's claim in any satisfying way, even if he is right.

Complexity of story.   Bloom criticized Au's story as too simple and argued that his paragraphs were generally more complex and abstract:

> My paragraphs involve rather abstract, intellectually demanding content and . . . limit factual statements to the original premise . . . casting all subsequent implications as counterfactuals, presumptions as to what would have happened if. Au's, by contrast, involve more concrete, less intellectually demanding content, and relate as facts not only the original observation . . . but all of the subsequent implications as well . . . In fact, the only aspect of Au's story which is counterfactual is that the explorer [i.e., X] did not know these facts, but would have if he had been able to speak the language and had stayed around.
>
> (Bloom, 1984, p. 281)

In short, Bloom didn't feel that Au's stories were difficult enough to be diagnostic of a cognitive difference. Bloom further criticized Au for having focused only on his simplest, most explicitly counterfactual Chinese text; he argued that another of his texts was more complex and a more reliable measure of counterfactual thought.

Unfortunately, Au (1984) did not respond directly to the criticism of her stories, and it remains a major weakness in her argument. Instead, she tried to show that the effects Bloom reported were due not to complexity but to the unidiomatic quality of his stories. In particular, Au (1984) said that she had not used Bloom's more complex Chinese story because it was not, in fact, written in the counterfactual mode (i.e., it was strongly unidiomatic). She argued that it did not include certain verbal auxiliary forms that would usually be obligatorily used in such contexts. (Cheng, 1985, p. 919, put forward the same argument.) She proposed that this might be more important than any difference in complexity.

Au conducted a new experiment using Bloom's "more complex" version of his story and a modified version of it including these verbal auxiliaries. She showed that response rates in both the Chinese and the English languages were a function of whether counterfactual markers were included or deleted from the story. Au argued that the inclusion of these markers was the crucial difference between Bloom's two versions and not, as he had argued, any difference in complexity. But, from another point of view, this study confirmed Bloom's general claim that the presence of overt counterfactual markers is a crucial factor in performance. And, in the end, the study did not resolve the basic disagreement about which text constitutes idiomatic Chinese: the story with the counterfactual markers or the one without.[55]

Once again, Liu's (1985) study provides some relevant evidence. In her replication of Bloom's and Au's work, she included Bloom's original story, Au's more idiomatic version of it, Au's original story, and a less idiomatic version of it designed by Liu herself. In the analysis of her results, Liu did not find statistically reliable differences in counterfactual reasoning between the more idiomatic and less idiomatic versions of the two stories. Although this result cannot resolve the deeper dilemma of how to characterize and compare idiomatic language patterns, it does indicate that translation differences were not the prime source of the difference between Bloom's and Au's findings. Liu's results also indicate that Bloom's story is indeed harder than Au's. This difference is statistically reliable and is probably due to the difference in complexity discussed above.

Finally, Bloom (1984) also criticized Au for not dealing with his inference problem involving the circle and the triangle. Au again responded by criticizing the Chinese translation and conducted a new study comparing performance using Bloom's translation and her suggested alternative. Bilingual subjects were also asked to translate a brief counterfactual text. There was no difference between the two versions of the inference problem. However, Au's subjects did do significantly better than Bloom's Chinese subjects, which again raised the question of sample population differences. Au's translation task involving a counterfactual text was used to divide her subjects into two groups: those who could produce a correct counterfactual translation from English and those who could not. Au showed that both groups were equally successful on the circle and triangle task, suggesting that the mastery of the English counterfactual played no role in performance. And, in a final study, she showed that a group of bilingual[56] subjects who were unable to translate her counterfactual text correctly were able to correctly interpret the counterfactual implications of her more idiomatic version of Bloom's story. This suggests that speakers who are not adept at the English counterfactual can nonetheless interpret counterfactual stories correctly.

Liu (1985) also replicated Bloom's circle and triangle inference problem. She generated a new translation of it, created other versions with different content, and presented them in different formats to her sample of school-aged children of different ages. She found that age of the child, content, and format all affected subject performance. Her results suggest that both the content and the form of Bloom's problem were especially difficult. And, perhaps most importantly, she once again replicated Au's findings that the Chinese could indeed reason counterfactually with this problem at approximately the same rate as English-speaking Americans. Unfortunately, Liu does not attempt to account for the great discrepancy between Bloom's findings and those which she and Au report.

Summary

It is not clear at present that any solid conclusions can be drawn about Chinese counterfactual thinking. First, there is considerable disagreement about the structural facts of Chinese.[57] Since the division in expert opinion may have to do with normative differences between speech communities with different exposure to English and Western modes of thought, the presentation of some empirical data as to how Chinese speakers from different groups actually speak, that is, how ordinary speakers respond linguistically in a common situation, would help. The problem is not merely to get idiomatic Chinese but to get equivalent situations which provide fair opportunities for both groups. It is not clear that such cross-linguistic equivalents can be established without some appeal to reference (or, more broadly, to some theory about the relation of language to nonlinguistic context) and without first characterizing the comparative difference in neutral terms rather than in terms of deficit. A further question concerns the use of the language structure: the presence of a structural option does not assure that it is either obligatory or even frequently used. If it is used only in specialized contexts, then the problem of general relevance must be addressed. Again, data on actual performance would be helpful.

Second, even if the structure and use of the relevant aspects of Chinese were clarified, there would be a problem with using bilingual subjects without first having a clear picture of monolingual response patterns. The strongest patterns should emerge with functionally monolingual speakers, and a baseline of this sort is needed to assess the English influences on Chinese. Bloom only weakened his position by bringing in the bilingual data without exploring the whole issue of bilingualism and biculturalism more carefully. Certainly the differences between Bloom's results and those of Au and Liu seem substantial enough to warrant caution about what is characteristic of Chinese speakers and about what accounts for any differences that are observed.

Third, there is a problem with the stimulus materials and what constitutes a sufficiently difficult counterfactual story. Au's story was clearly much simpler than Bloom's; it neither provided a fair replication of his study nor, apparently, did it offer opportunity for differentiating degrees of ability with counterfactuals. Bloom's stories were more complex overall and did show differences, but when he varied the complexity of the Chinese stories, he also varied the linguistic markers, thus confounding, from Au's point of view, idiomaticity with complexity. Finally, if the complexity of a story makes a difference, then a whole host of influences on behavior other than explicit morphological marking become relevant. Bloom can no longer claim that exposure to relatively overt marking of the counterfactual during child development is sufficient to encourage counterfactual thinking. The clearest evidence that this is not the case comes from Au's American high-school students, who did less well than American college students even though they were fluent in English and presumably used counterfactual forms in speaking English. Rather, Bloom must argue for an interaction of structural potential with functional needs. The core of his difficulty is that he did not distinguish which factor was crucial: the availability of the structural option, the presence of the functional need, or both. This ambiguity in his analysis will become even more obvious in the following section. The main points for the present are that his experiments simply could not distinguish among these alternatives and that his whole approach to the relativity question depended heavily on translation judgments of just the sort that so concerned Lenneberg thirty years earlier.

Bloom's supplementary arguments: convergent patterns in Chinese

Bloom argued that the counterfactual pattern in English was part of a larger linguistic worldview. His evidence for this larger worldview will be reviewed here primarily because it illustrates crucial differences between China and the West in the cultural use of language and confirms the specific functional interpretation of Bloom's counterfactual data proposed above. This additional evidence is marked by thinness of linguistic analysis, absence of further comparative data, reliance on entirely language-oriented experiments, and weakly substantiated global generalizations about Chinese and Western culture. Although the work on counterfactuals suffered from these same weaknesses, they were not emphasized in the above discussion so as to highlight the main lines of the existing debate. In any event, these problems become much more evident in this section.

Bloom claimed that use of the counterfactual in English and other Indo-European languages formed part of a distinct, larger set of patterns that *give rise to* thinking in terms of theoretical abstractions:

the counterfactual differs from most other linguistic elements in that it seems to constitute a member of a special set of English and, more generally, Indo-European linguistic devices that lead speakers to develop cognitive schemas specifically designed to enable and encourage them to shift ... to projecting and operating with theoretical extractions from [their] baseline models [of reality]. And not only does the Chinese language not have any structures equivalent to the counterfactual but neither does it have structures equivalent to the additional members of this special set.   (Bloom, 1981, pp. 33–34)

Bloom's attempt to establish the existence of a broader linguistic worldview differed from Whorf's in two striking ways. First, in contrast with Whorf's belief that many or perhaps all meaningful language forms can interrelate structurally to suggest a worldview, Bloom apparently believed that this set of linguistic devices is "special." Second, and more importantly, the various linguistic patterns as they were described by Bloom do not form the kind of integrated analogical structure that Whorf proposed. In fact, closer examination reveals that the crucial, albeit implicit, tie that bound these various forms together in Bloom's discussion was a functional one, that is, they are all used in a characteristic linguistic register and mode of thinking. In short, these various linguistic forms constitute a functionally rather than structurally defined unity. And, as will become clear shortly, Bloom really articulated a functionally rather than structurally based linguistic relativism.

The generic concept

Bloom first described a special use of the definite article *the* in English to indicate a "generic" entity. He began by characterizing the ordinary uses of *the* first acquired during a child's development

to refer to a particularly determined object only if . . . [it] is either one of a kind . . . or if there is some reason for the child to presuppose that his listener has some familiarity with the object.   (Bloom, 1981, p. 34)

Subsequently, the child acquires the more specialized "generic" use:

[with singular, concrete, count nouns] "the" acts not to direct attention to a particular object but acts instead to direct attention to a generic concept conceptually extracted from the realm of actual or even imaginary objects.
                                                                              (Bloom, 1981, p. 34)

So, use of the definite article with a singular, count noun without a presupposable referent establishes a shift to "generic" meaning. For example,

if [an English] speaker talks of "the kangaroo" in the absence of any actual kangaroo or previous mutual familiarity with one, "the" will no longer be interpreted as entailing reference to any particular kangaroo, but will rather be interpreted as a signal of the generic kangaroo – as a signal to the listener to direct his attention to a theoretical entity extracted from the world of actual kangaroos.
                                                                              (Bloom, 1981, p. 34)

In sum, these specialized uses trigger a shift to a new interpretation.

Although Bloom implied that the creation of a generic interpretation in English requires the co-occurrence of a category of count nouns with the definite article *the*, generic concepts can also be signaled using mass nouns without *the* (for example, *blood* rather than *the blood*) and with nouns which are not exclusively count or mass (for example, *cake* as well as *the cake*). Bloom only briefly mentioned the existence of such alternatives[58] and did not discuss their significance. In general, he did not discuss in detail the grammatical prerequisites of this usage, that is, the larger set of structural options (for instance, singular versus plural) on which the generic interpretation hinges. In short, he neither characterized the structural features of English accurately nor explained precisely *how* they were being exploited.

Second, Bloom did not recognize that the shift to generic reference involves a reflexive dimension whereby *the language code is used to refer to its own typical use and meaning.* For example, in using the phrase *the kangaroo* to make generic reference, a speaker essentially refers to that set of referents which would typically be referred to by the lexeme *kangaroo.* This structure is transparent in Bloom's experimental task described below, which involves just such a reflective judgment about word meaning. The extent to which this reflexive use relates to thought (habitual or otherwise) is not obvious. If such reflective judgments are relevant to cognition, the cultural encouragement and significance of such judgments is probably at least as important as the linguistic structure of the object of judgment. (This is even clearer for more socially oriented referents of terms such as *success.*) It would seem that the actual process of making generic reference has less to do with the structural potential of a language and more to do with a particular way of using language, less to do with a distinct way of marking than with a special use of an existing means of marking.[59] Actual instances of generic reference amount to manipulating the code to achieve reference to/ through an already available cultural/linguistic category – itself no more "theoretical" than any other cultural entity. Bloom's analysis, and others like it, can be regarded as a form of meta-folk-intensionalization of implicitly available pragmatic categories in which he has interpreted the pragmatic effects achieved by such a tactical move in semantic terms – in particular, as designating attributes of conceptual objects, hence a "generic" kangaroo.

Bloom then contrasted the English pattern with Chinese which he claimed does not offer the possibility of generic reference because, for example, the unmodified form *kangaroo* would be used where we would use *a kangaroo, the kangaroo, kangaroos,* and *the kangaroos.*[60] Bloom asked a sample of Chinese speakers about their interpretations of the lexeme *taishu* ('kangaroo') when used in a sentence where it occupied the [+ definite] position (i.e., before the verb) but had no immediate contextual correlate.[61] Speakers were asked whether the sentence in addition to referring to an actual kangaroo, to some actual kangaroos or even to all actual kangaroos, might have an additional interpretation, for example, as a conceptual kangaroo.   (Bloom, 1981, p. 36)

Only about one-third said that it could, and most of these had had extensive exposure to English. Bloom concluded that the distinct way of marking the generic concept in English may play

an important role in leading English speakers ... to develop schemas specifically designed for creating extracted theoretical entities ... and hence for coming to view and use such entities as supplementary elements of their cognitive worlds.
                                                    (Bloom, 1981, p. 36)

Since Bloom did not provide corresponding English data, we do not know that the Chinese response is in any way distinctive. Second, speakers' judgments hinged on their understanding of what is meant by a "conceptual kangaroo," and it is not clear what this question meant to Chinese speakers or what it would mean to English speakers. Does a negative response imply that a speaker cannot refer to the species generically, that is, *qua* species?

Entification of properties and actions

Bloom next examined a process he labeled *entification* in English: the use of suffixes such as *-ity*, *-ness*, *-ance*, *-tion*, *-ment*, *-age* to convert properties and actions (i.e., adjectives and verbs) into entities (i.e., nouns). For example, English speakers can convert *sincere* (an adjective) into *sincerity* (a noun). Bloom argued that such derivations are similar to counterfactuals in that they signal

movement from description of the world as it is primarily understood in terms of actions, properties and things, to description of the world in terms of theoretical entities that have been conceptually extracted from the speaker's baseline model of reality and granted, psychologically speaking, a measure of reality of their own.   (Bloom, 1981, p. 37)

Besides being "conceptually extracted" and "theoretical," such forms also "entify," that is, convert properties and actions into things. An English speaker

talks of properties and actions as if they were things; he converts in effect what are in his baseline model of reality characteristics of things and acts things perform into things in themselves – and by means of such entification, ascends to a more conceptually detached way of dividing up the world.
                                                    (Bloom, 1981, p. 37)

This is an extremely sweeping claim, especially given that many languages permit similar derivation among the basic parts of speech and that others do not distinguish them morphologically in the first place. Further, Bloom himself noted that some derivations, those referring to the means or results of actions, do not refer to conceptual abstractions or have the status of entifications (Bloom, 1981, p. 37). Unfortunately, he gave no general criteria for distinguishing such false "entifications" from actual ones.

Bloom (1981, p. 38) claimed that Chinese does not have any mechanism to entify properties or actions, but can express roughly the same ideas in various ways. For the cases where an actual noun is required, Chinese tends to provide a separate lexical item. Otherwise, verbs or adjectives are used in alternative constructions. Bloom provided the following examples of Chinese equivalents for English nominalizations:[62]

English Expression	*Chinese Equivalent*
Mary's sincerity . . .	Mary is sincere
Mary's sincerity cannot be doubted	Mary is so sincere, (you) cannot doubt (her)
Sincerity is a virtue	Sincere is a virtue
	(i.e., being sincere or acting sincerely, since adjectives and verbs are not distinguished here)

Bloom argued that the recent emergence in Chinese of derivational suffixes similar to those existing in English confirmed this analysis. Although these suffixes are not yet fully productive and speakers find them foreign sounding, their very existence has probably been stimulated by contact with English and suggests that traditional Chinese grammar did not provide any means to signal the English meanings (Bloom, 1981, p. 3, citing Weinreich, 1968).

Entification of conditions and events

Bloom extended his argument about entification in English to more complex syntactic structures. The processes of converting a sentence describing a condition or an event into a noun phrase is another form of entification, because on a cognitive level the speaker is

moving from the description of a condition that is the case, may be the case, or is not the case, to an extraction of the idea of the condition as a purely theoretical entity . . . for the mere utterance of the nominalized expression . . . does not commit him to any condition that is or is not the case, but only to the idea of the condition, the notion of it, extracted from the world of actual, imaginary, or potential happenings.

Similarly, in discussing events rather than conditions . . . [he] moves from the description of an event that has happened, is happening or will happen to an extraction of the idea of the event as a purely theoretical notion.

(Bloom, 1981, p. 40)

Bloom argued that the English speaker creates

a model of the world in which these characteristics and happenings have been explicitly transformed into things in themselves, have gained a degree of ontological status independent of the things or people who possess them or the actors who perform them.   (Bloom, 1981, p. 41)

In short, when these constructions are converted into nominal form, Bloom interpreted this to mean that their referents had been construed as theoretical entities. But he never made clear whether all nominalizations imply the creation of theoretical notions, nor did he discuss any of the syntactic and discourse functions served by nominalization in English. Bloom basically generalized one possible meaning of nominalization to all cases of nominalization. What he needed to show – but did not – is that other speakers of English make this same generalization.[63]

Bloom regarded this abstraction of theoretical entities as similar to the processes involved in creating generic concepts and counterfactuals. Recall, however, that no structural element connects entification with generic concepts and counterfactuals. Nor do the two sorts of constructions Bloom regarded as entifications result from the same process, since one involves lexical derivation and the other clausal embedding. The linkage among all these linguistic elements lies not in the form of the elements but in their common use in the discourse pattern Bloom has identified.

Bloom then argued that, by contrast, the Chinese language does not provide Chinese speakers with "the specific structural means and thus the motivation to entify conditions and events into truth-commitment-free ideas" (Bloom, 1981, p. 41). Chinese speakers can only express an approximation of the English sense. So, for example, the English expression

"The acceptance of that measure depends on the approval of the subcommittee's report"   (Bloom, 1981, p. 41)

can be expressed by the rough Chinese equivalent

"Whether or not that measure is accepted depends on whether or not the subcommittee's report is approved."   (1981, p. 41)

These various Chinese equivalents can differ substantially from the English in their implications. But we cannot evaluate the Chinese, because Bloom has focused exclusively on replicating the English sense rather than on characterizing typical Chinese patterns for handling the syntactic functions associated with English nominalizations.

Once again Bloom (1981, pp. 41–44) discussed relevant changes in modern Chinese apparently stemming from contact with Western languages. Contemporary Chinese contains a construction using the form *de* (or *ti*) to entify conditions and events into truth-commitment-free ideas. *De* signals that the material to the left of it modifies the noun to its right. Constructions using *de* are generally considered to be nonstandard and Westernized. Although they are used to translate many English expressions, the difficulties involved in interpreting the multiple left embeddings required with complex *de* constructions limit their practical usefulness.

Bloom also developed an experimental task in order to "gain some insight into the cognitive underpinnings of these linguistic facts" (1981, p. 44). Chinese and English speakers were presented two model sentences in their native languages, one describing an action and one ascribing a property to an object. Next to each sentence was a nominalized variant, as in the following example:

This thing is important → The importance of this thing.

Subjects were then shown three additional sentences in their native languages and asked to transform them using the principle exemplified. Nearly all of the English-speaking subjects transformed the sentences "correctly," whereas many Chinese-speaking subjects did not. Bloom interpreted these results as evidence that the English speakers have developed "entification schemas," while Chinese speakers have not. However, notice that the Chinese were at some disadvantage since they were apparently working with "nonstandard" constructions using *de*. Further, this task, like the one used for generic reference, centered on a metalinguistic skill: the speaker's abilities to manipulate language forms explicitly. Given these facts, the relationship of performance on Bloom's task to habitual speech and behavior remains very unclear.

Entification and the construction and manipulation of theoretical frameworks

Bloom's discussion of entification concluded by connecting the English linguistic pattern to the widespread use of theoretical frameworks in the West. He suggested that entification is done partly in the service of theory construction since it facilitates the construction and manipulation of theoretical frameworks:

one reason[64] . . . why English speakers entify conditions and events is that by so doing the conditions and events can be transformed into individual conceptual units, which can then be fitted, as individual components, into more general theoretical/explanatory frameworks ... the entified English sentences convert the subject/predicate descriptions of conditions or events into individual noun phrases and then insert those noun phrases into single subject/predicate frameworks, thereby in effect subordinating the conditions or events to the relationships that link them to one another. The hearer or reader is no longer led to consider the conditions or events on their own terms, but to consider them only as a function of the role they play in the relationships under discussion. The relationships themselves take on a reality of their own, a law-like quality, which derives from the fact that they are understood, not merely as descriptions of observable or imaginable real-world phenomena, but as examples of *a different domain of discourse altogether*, as theoretical explanatory frameworks designed to provide a clarifying perspective on the world of actual conditions and events and their interrelationships, while at the same time maintaining a certain cognitive distance from the speaker's or hearer's baseline model of that world.

(Bloom, 1981, p. 46, my italics)

So entification (i.e., productive nominalization) allows a speaker to subordinate descriptions of properties, actions, conditions, and events so as to permit a focus on the relationships among them. This is useful, Bloom argued, in the construction and manipulation of theoretical frameworks, because entire series of events or conditions can be woven together so that the focus is on the role each plays in the theoretical structure rather than on the "actual" logical, causal, or temporal order of the series. When speaking in Chinese, by contrast, one is forced to follow the logical, temporal, or causal sequence in which events actually fall, and the same opportunity to construct theoretical frameworks does not arise. Interestingly, Bloom (1981, p. 48) concurred with his Chinese informants that the Chinese versions of his examples were "more accessible and straightforward."

Bloom then claimed that the linguistic pattern gives rise to the cognitive pattern (1981, p. 48). This conclusion appeared to conflict with the suggestion just made that linguistic entification serves culturally specific cognitive functions and, therefore, plausibly arises in response to those needs. This tension is resolved in his subsequent theoretical discussion, where he argues that cultural pressures give rise to the language patterns historically but that languages then influence individual thought during development. This, of course, is not what is generally meant by linguistic relativity, where, even in an interactive model, language has some priority. The crux of the problem is that Bloom dealt not with the influence of diverse language structures on thought but, as will be discussed further below, with the presence in English of "a different domain of discourse altogether."

To provide controlled tests of his interpretations of the relation of entification to the ability to manipulate theoretical frameworks in terms of relationships among variables, Bloom (1981, pp. 48–51) administered some experimental tasks to English and Chinese speakers. First, subjects were presented with two paragraphs concerning some of the factors conditioning how much pollution affects health. The first paragraph was written in terms of conditions and consequences, and the second in terms of relationships among variables. Subjects were asked to answer an inferential question based on the paragraphs by selecting from four proposed responses. The prediction was that Chinese-speaking subjects should find the second version more difficult because their language has not encouraged them to develop schemas for transforming conditions and events into entified component elements of theoretical frameworks and to operate with them as a function of the roles they play in such frameworks. By contrast, English-speaking subjects should do about as well on the first version as Chinese-speaking subjects and should not find the second version appreciably more difficult than the first, because their language has encouraged them to develop schemas specifically suited to transforming conditions and events into entified component elements of theoretical frameworks and to operate with them as a function of the roles they play in such frameworks (Bloom, 1981, p. 50). The prediction was confirmed: English speakers performed equally well on both versions; Chinese speakers performed at the same level as English speakers on the first version but showed a drop in performance on the second.

Takano (1989) criticized this study on the grounds that a minor error in wording in the second version allows additional correct answers that Bloom did not recognize – thus calling into question Bloom's interpretation of the results. Using the original materials, Takano was able to replicate Bloom's results with a sample of Japanese and American university students. In doing so, however, Takano noted that the whole difference between the two groups was due to the natural science students in the Japanese sample. This suggested that students with more sophisticated analytic skills might be noticing unintended alternative answers to the second version. In further studies, Takano was able to show that the same pattern held for natural science students in an American sample if they had sufficient mathematical training. Takano concluded that the drop in Chinese and Japanese performance in Bloom's second version of the pollution story was probably due not to a language difference but rather to superior mathematical training. More generally, Takano concluded that Bloom's methods are incapable of distinguishing communication failure from thinking failure. Takano's conclusion seems plausible, although it does not, in fact, establish that Bloom's conclusions would not be sustained using a corrected second version.[65]

A third, more complex paragraph (Bloom, 1981, pp. 51–52) was administered concerning the relation of various climatic and dietary conditions to how comfortable a certain individual feels. The task in which this paragraph was employed was more difficult than the previous one in several respects. First, whereas the previous two paragraphs involved two variables and one relationship, this one involved one variable and two relationships. Second, correct solution of the question posed about the paragraph required choosing two of five alternatives. Third, Bloom argued that there was no way to answer the question unless one had constructed a theoretical model of the data presented in terms of relationships, because the last line of the paragraph asked the subject to reverse relationships implied but not directly expressed in the text.[66] The task was difficult for both groups, but, as expected, English speakers did much better than Chinese subjects. Bloom recounted that Chinese subjects expressed the sense that the question was overly complex, overly abstract, and blatantly unChinese. Bloom reported that under follow-up questioning, when the rationale of the task was explained, Chinese subjects said they were not used to talking and thinking about relationships between reified theoretical entities, that is, between things that are not people, situations, or occurrences.

These tasks do not really illuminate the relationship between language and thought. The first task showed that one version of a text was more readily interpretable to Chinese speakers than was another, and the second task further confirmed their difficulties with Western-style texts. The Chinese responses made clear that the whole Western way of talking is alien to them. But in themselves, these results suggest nothing about the cultural or cognitive significance of the language patterns. From a cultural point of view, Bloom did not show that the "theoretical" discourse style is widespread in the West; in fact, it is clearly a specialized speech style (or register) characteristically used by certain well-defined social and professional subgroups (dialect groups) in American culture.[67] From a cognitive point of view, Bloom failed to provide supporting data showing that theoretical thinking by individuals depends on these forms of discourse or that the forms of discourse depend on the structures he has described – even though he implied that their use holds some advantages for English speakers (1981, pp. 46–60).[68]

General proclivity for theoretical, hypothetical thinking in the West

Bloom described a final task that does not seem to serve any specific function relative to the preceding arguments about entification, but that addressed the larger question of accepting premises for the sake of argument and sets the stage for a general discussion of the consequences of engaging so heavily in theoretical, hypothetical thinking. A paragraph describing the relative advantages of two methods of moral training was presented to a sample of Chinese and English speakers. The key idea of the paragraph was that both punishments and rewards could effectively teach moral behavior, but that the former might have adverse consequences (Bloom, 1981, p. 53). Subjects were then asked "what do the two methods have in common?" and were given five answers to choose from.

Virtually all of the English speakers chose the answer indicating that both methods could be effective in getting the child to respect morality. By contrast fewer than two-thirds of the Chinese chose this answer. Most of the remaining subjects chose answers indicating that the second method was better or that none of the alternatives made sense

and then went on to explain, based on their own experience and often at great length and evidently after much reflection, why, for instance, the second method might be better, or why neither method works, or why both methods have to be used in conjunction with each other, or, perhaps, why some other specified means is preferable.   (Bloom, 1981, p. 54)

It is clear that these Chinese subjects understood the paragraph – as compared with the confusions encountered on the three previous paragraphs in this series. Bloom therefore gave an account of these Chinese responses in terms of a different sense of moral responsibility:

they felt that choosing [the] alternative [indicating that both methods were effective] and leaving it at that would be misleading since in their experience that response was untrue. As they saw it, what was expected, desired, must be at a minimum an answer reflecting their personal considered opinion, if not, a more elaborated explanation of their own experiences relevant to the matter at hand. Why else would anyone ask the question?   (Bloom, 1981, p. 54)

In short, Bloom interpreted the responses as an unwillingness to choose an answer that was untrue, an answer that was counterfactual. This interpretation is strengthened by the considerable literature reporting such refusals to take the counterfactual perspective in other groups (see references in Bloom, 1981, p. 54, n26). An equally plausible interpretation, not evaluated by Bloom, is that the Chinese subjects were not answering his specific question at all but were simply reporting the basic message in the paragraph (i.e., although both methods are effective, one method is better overall) or responding to the general issue raised by the paragraph. Failures resulting from understanding but refusing to accept the counterfactual assumptions of the paragraph were indistinguishable from those due to ignoring the specific question.

Bloom contrasted these Chinese patterns with the American subjects' responses:

American subjects, by contrast, readily accepted the question as a purely "theoretical" exercise to be responded to according to the assumptions of the world it creates rather than in terms of their own experiences with the actual world. Not a single American subject made reference to his or her own experience ... no American subject appeared to have any difficulty, either of a cognitive or ethical nature, in leaving the actual world aside to work within the constraints of the theoretical world provided, no matter how simplistic or even inaccurate they might hold the content of that world to be.

(Bloom, 1981, p. 54)

In short, American subjects both accepted the premises of the paragraph and answered the question.

Bloom (1981, pp. 54–59) then proposed broader linkages between abstract, theoretical modeling on the one hand and a detached attitude toward reality and moral consequences in the West on the other. Although Bloom's argument is interesting, as it stands, it is not convincing. Some of the dimensions of "theoretical modeling" that he mentioned (for instance, taking a single perspective or developing single-factor explanations) bear no obvious relationship to the linguistic variables he has discussed. If anything, they have more to do with what is regarded as an acceptable account of events in a culture, which again is more a functional than a structural issue. Further, his argument was based not on a systematic evaluation of substantive evidence but rather on just a quick summarizing of a few historical and literary comparisons of East and West (Hatano, 1982; Jordan, 1982). Nonetheless, the hypothesis should not be rejected out of hand, since others have reached similar conclusions about the advantages and limitations of the dominant mode of theoretical thought in the West (for example, Lukács, 1971 [1923]).

Bloom sought to connect his linguistic analysis with Needham's (1956) well-known analysis of the Chinese failure to develop science because of their reluctance to adopt purely theoretical orientations (Bloom, 1981, p. 55).[69] Inversely, Bloom also argued that such theoretical modeling has its costs for the West, since it

involves the extraction of single patterns of causal explanation from factual data that are in reality characterized by a multiplicity of internal interassociations and interrelationships and hence necessarily gives rise to overly simplistic and constrictive assumptions about the nature of the phenomena it seeks to describe.

(Bloom, 1981, p. 56)

Chinese observers note that this isolation of single patterns of causal explanation is not limited to science:

In choosing to view the world through one theoretical perspective rather than another, to adopt an exclusively political, social, psychological, behavioral, or cognitive view, one easily forgets that one has adopted that perspective for the sake of analysis only and begins to perceive the world and our knowledge of it as inherently compartmentalized in those ways. (Bloom, 1981, pp. 56–57)

Bloom then tied this observation back to the separations of morality from practicality, personal experience from abstract precept:

the kind of thinking that leads one to accept, if only for the sake of argument, that a triangle is a circle, or that two given methods of moral training are effective even when you known [sic] they are not, is a kind of thinking that can often lead not only to an overly simplistic, but also to an alienating [sic], a personally debilitating, and, in fact, an amoral perspective on the world.

(Bloom, 1981, p. 57)[70]

These arguments apparently represented Bloom's attempt to balance his characterizations of Chinese thought with a comparable "deficit" in the West. And Bloom has identified an important, probably distinctive dimension of thinking in the West. However, he never really established that this Western pattern of thinking is hegemonic in the culture (i.e., that the Chinese way of thinking is not also prevalent and valued) or that it stems in any way from the structure of the European languages. Specifically, whereas the Chinese cognitive "deficit" was explained in terms of the absence of a series of essential grammatical devices, the English cognitive pattern was not explained in this way – and it may not be possible to explain it thus if the grammatical opportunities present in Chinese are also present in English. So, despite appearances, Bloom's contrast was still between the presence of certain forms in one language and their absence in another, the presence of a related, valued mode of thinking in the first language and its absence in the other. Bloom simply did not have the sort of comparative framework for his analysis that would permit a neutral characterization of the linguistic and cognitive differences.

Having described these broader implications of his work, however, Bloom then explicitly retreated on the issue of the role of language:

Historically-speaking, it is certainly not the case that structural differences between Chinese and English bear primary responsibility for creating the culturally-specific modes of thinking reflected in . . . this chapter as a whole. From a historical point of view, languages are much more the products of their cultures than determiners of them . . . but if Chinese speakers at some point in the past had felt a sufficient need to venture into the realm of the counterfactual or the theoretical, the Chinese language would have evolved to accommodate that need, as it is doing today. And so, to explain historically why counterfactual and entificational thinking did not develop on a grand scale, one would have to look not only to the characteristics of the language but to the social and intellectual determinants of why a perceived need for such thinking did not arise.

(Bloom, 1981, p. 59)

This amounts to a claim (implicit, really, throughout the discussion) that some of the structures found in a language are developed to serve certain

period, the child will have a variety of unlabeled schemas and will develop other schemas before mastering the linguistic labels appropriate to them, schemas which are free of the influence of language (for example, lawns versus trees, hungry versus thirsty, color versus shape, depressed versus elated, figure out versus confused, succeed versus fail, infer versus explain, and pumpkin versus grapefruit). Although it is reasonable to assume that there are realms of cognition not shaped by language, it is surprising to see Bloom simply accepting without justification the lexemes of his own language as naturally given categories. And he did not give any criteria for identifying how such natural categories may be distinguished from those influenced by language. Bloom's stance here derives from two tacit assumptions underlying his argument: (1) some cognitive schemas are more natural than others and (2) language merely labels ("codes") these natural ones, whereas it actually helps constitute the more complex, artificial ones. It is important to recognize, despite Bloom's assertions, that these were theoretical assumptions, not empirical findings.

Bloom (1981, p. 66) then went on to make his central point, namely that the child builds many cognitive schemas during development "expressly to meet the requirements of linguistic labels" available in the language:[72]

the labels of the language he is learning will guide him to further refine and elaborate many of the schematic perspectives on the world he has already developed so that those perspectives come to include as part of their defining parameters the logico-linguistic links they bear to one another in the adult linguistic world. [For example,] His notion of red will come to include as one of its defining criteria its link to his notion color.[73]   (Bloom, 1981, p. 70)

However, Bloom did not argue that labeled schemas were fundamentally different from unlabeled schemas from an internal structural point of view. Rather, he argued that labeling a schema allows one to do more with it and that a labeled schema "can perform some very special cognitive functions that unnamed schemas cannot perform" (1981, p. 74). Of course this implied that such labeled schemas are only relevant in the contexts requiring those "very special cognitive functions," that is, that the structural effects are contingent on a certain pattern of use. In particular, linguistic labels are especially important in shaping more complex schemas:

the more complex the structured perspective on reality to which a label points, the more extracted that perspective from immediate experience, and the more dependent that perspective, for the definition of its parameters, on the link it bears to other labeled schemas in the linguistic web, the more likely it is that if [the child] is to develop that particular mode of categorizing reality at all, he will have to rely on a linguistic label – lexical, intonational, or grammatical – to point the way and to serve as the locus around which the processes of cognitive construction take place. (Bloom, 1981, p. 70)

(See also Bloom, 1981, p. 33, for more on this issue.) To some degree Bloom's views here were the complement of his earlier acceptance of *some* of our own lexical categories as simple and natural: he expected language to have effect primarily on the development of more complex, decontextual, and interlocked category structures. This contrasts with Whorf's suggestion that even our most elementary, habitually used categories might not be either so simple or so natural. Notice, also, how broad the notion of label has become here: an intonation contour can be a label around which a schema can be constructed. It seems unlikely that such labels will be very subject to explicit manipulation in theoretical thought.

Bloom proposed that such complex schemas develop in a feedback process with language forms (1981, p. 45). Thus the proper use of each linguistic form is acquired by feedback and then the "full meaning" (= a cognitive schema) induced on it.[74] The linkage of the new concepts to linguistic labels creates concepts that are language-specific:

linguistic labels ... lead us to extend our cognitive repertoires in language-specific ways, to develop many schemas through which we come to cognize the world, store information about it and plan our reactions to it that we would be unlikely to develop without their aid. (Bloom, 1981, p. 74)

Bloom ended by arguing that these language-specific schemas help insure the development and continuance of social institutions:

linguistic labels ... [make] it possible for societies to insure not only that their language but also that their institutions, intellectual attainments, and cultural orientations can be passed down from one generation to the next. (Bloom, 1981, p. 73)

This whole line of argument is consistent with the position that language matters only for "higher" cultural achievements. This is radically different from Whorf's position, which encompassed *both* habitual behavior at the most mundane level *and* philosophical and scientific thought.

The particular cognitive schemas associated with the counterfactual, the generic concept, and the entification of properties and actions are "special" in Bloom's view because they do

not merely involve further differentiation of the perceptual world but rather a special kind of abstraction from it – in other words, with the sort of schema that is most likely to be dependent for its development on the directives that language provides. (Bloom, 1981, p. 45)

Unfortunately, Bloom never elaborated the criteria distinguishing linguistic forms which represent a "special kind of abstraction" from the perceptual world from those forms which "merely involve further differentiation" of it. Certainly, the two kinds of forms are not structurally distinctive. Bloom's own judgment of what is more or less abstract or theoretical was apparently the tacit criterion.

In summary, Bloom made three central points in his developmental argument. First, linguistic labels stimulate the development of additional cognitive schemas beyond those which would naturally occur. In itself this claim is relatively uncontroversial. But without any criteria for distinguishing those categories which depend on language from those that do not, the claim lacks theoretical force. Second, labeling processes are essential to developing more complex schemas. Again, in itself this claim is relatively uncontroversial. But without any clear argument about why labeled schemas are so crucial or any standard for what constitutes complexity, the claim once more lacks theoretical force. Third, the labels available in the West promote "a special kind of abstraction." But these forms do not cohere as a structural unity within the Indo-European languages, nor did Bloom provide wide comparative evidence to establish that Indo-European language forms are distinctive from those of the rest of the world's languages. This claim, like the others, lacks real substance. To some extent, Bloom addressed the significance of the presence of labels in the following discussion of cognitive functioning, but overall, his theoretical argument merely made his assumptions clear, and did not present a case for them.

The linguistic shaping of cognitive functioning

Bloom argued that the labeled schemas provided by language are important for adult cognitive functioning in two ways. First, language mediates (serves as the cognitive vehicle for) thought at the social level (Bloom, 1981, pp. 75–76). For thoughts to be communicated, they must be translated into schemas that bear labels, that is, into the set of structured perspectives on the world for which the particular language provides names. Insofar as thought is social, then, the claim is that it necessarily operates through language. But according to Bloom's earlier argument, some dimensions of meaning are not explicitly labeled by language; Bloom claimed that these implicit meanings are always understood through more literal meanings. (It is not clear what this would mean for categories where the label is an intonation contour.) And he did not discuss the communication of thought through nonlinguistic labels at all.

Second, labeled schemas provide accessible anchors of mental perspective for individual thought:

... we seem to call upon this very same subset of schemas that our language labels, not only when we want, through language, to give direction to the behavior and thoughts of others, but also when we want to give direction to our own behavior and thoughts ... and make use of those discrete, structured perspectives on reality as stable points of mental orientation to provide direction to our continuing cognitive activities.   (Bloom, 1981, p. 76)[75]

Thus, the schemas labeled by language are used to direct behavior and thought. (Here again we find echoes of the codability hypothesis.) Bloom never explained why thought or behavior need such direction. His analogy between giving "direction" to others and giving "direction" to our own behavior only makes sense if we accept an implicit separation of a self from its thought and behavior; this raises the question of how the directing self is directed, and so on. Likewise, there is no account of the need for "stable points of mental orientation" and no characterization of the nature of the "continuing cognitive activities."

In support of his claims, Bloom (1981, pp. 77–83) then reviewed research indicating the special contribution of language and labeled schemas in forming abstract concepts or in facilitating performance on complex tasks. He concluded that the more abstract the intellectual task, the more important will be the role of language. Although his claim seems plausible, it is worth mentioning that none of the studies he reviewed establish this point. Bloom generalized as follows:

If ... we are to uncover the more significant effects of language on the way we think, we have to turn our attention away from the cognitive effects of linguistic labels, such as color names, that stake out simple categorizations of the perceptual world, and direct our attention instead to the cognitive effects of linguistic labels that lead us to build those highly complex, abstractly derived perspectives on reality that we [are] unlikely to construct without their aid ... And we have to turn our attention as well, away from tasks such as those of color memory in which perceptual encodings of task relevant information can compete with, or substitute for, linguistic encodings, and direct our attention instead to tasks in which successful performance depends on the use of information that can neither be represented in perceptual terms nor easily disengaged and maintained in mind without the aid of associated linguistic labels. *We have to turn our attention*, in other words, *to tasks* such as those *which require subjects to assume and operate with counterfactual or entified/relational, theoretical perspectives on the world.*   (Bloom, 1981, p. 83, my italics)

Without doubt it would be worthwhile to examine more than color terms and color memory in looking for language effects, but there are no empirical grounds at present to justify Bloom's quite plausible claim that language will have a greater effect in other areas. Moreover, his last sentence, taken literally, implies that the "more significant effects" of linguistic labels at this second level will be found primarily in the West – that is, where "subjects ... assume and operate with counterfactual or

There are many problems with Galda's treatment of Yucatec grammar which are not worth elaborating in detail here. Two examples can stand for many. First, Galda did not mention a third use of *wa* as a general "dubitive" to pose questions (see Blair, 1965, p. 32; McQuown, 1967, p. 244) and, consequently, he misanalyzes many of the Yucatec examples. Second, Yucatec has two ways of expressing simple one-place predicate–argument relationships in the active voice. By contrast there is only one construction type for such relationships in English. The difference between the two Yucatecan forms lies both in the morphological form of the pronouns (known as type A or B) indicating the logical argument and in the relative position of the pronoun before or after the verb: so *pronoun A + verb* contrasts with *verb + pronoun B*. The two constructions both distinguish the logical aspect of the predicate (incompletive and completive respectively) and also suggest either an agentive or patientive role status (respectively) for the argument. Galda described the existence of the two formal options and then collapsed the two together as "subject–theme" relations. This reduction may be warranted from the point of view of *our* logic but completely ignores the point that Yucatec speakers routinely distinguish the two. This is exactly the sort of difference one might seize upon in trying to construct an alternative logic.

What Galda ended up doing, then, was sorting Yucatec forms into three categories: the same as English and our logic (for example, presence of most logical connectives), different from English but readily reducible to our logic (for example, two sorts of one-place predicates can be collapsed into our single logical form), or deficient from the point of view of English and therefore of our logic (for example, no marker of class membership relations).

He then looked for evidence of different logical reasoning among the Maya. First he searched for examples of logical arguments in native texts from the Spanish colonial period. He found that

None of the selected passages are in a form that corresponds exactly to a symbolic argument, although some are fairly close. Consequently, I generally take some liberties with what I take to be the meaning of the text and with what I assume to be hidden premises as well as what seem to me to be unstated but implied conclusions. (1976 [1975], p. 90)

Using this loose approach, he easily found some examples of logical arguments. However, he drew no general conclusions from them.

Second, Galda (1976 [1975], ch. 6) administered some experimental tasks to adult Yucatec speakers in Mexico. He used a modified version of a task originally designed by Hill (1960)[76] to test the logical abilities of American first-, second-, and third-grade schoolchildren. The task consisted of a series of simple logical problems involving two or three statements followed by a yes–no type of question. (The problems were translated from English into Spanish and then into Yucatec.) Answers were scored as "correct" if they were in accordance with a traditional logical solution. Scores were also broken down by type of logical problem.

Yucatec speakers generally performed below the level of the American children. Significantly, the highest scores were obtained by the Yucatec speakers who were most bilingual in Spanish and who were more Westernized. A selected subset of motivated, high-scoring subjects performed the task a second time, receiving additional explanations as to what was desired; this group did as well as the American children. There were also some differences in performance as a function of the logical type of the problem. In particular, and not surprisingly, the largest gap between the groups involved those problems involving logical disjunction signaled by the *wa* particle.

It is difficult to know what to make of these results. As Galda (1976 [1975], p. 117) himself pointed out, there were so many factors that could have affected the results that it is difficult to single out language as the causative factor. It is entirely possible, for example, that cultural familiarity with the task accounts for the lower Yucatec scores. Certainly, there is no indigenous system of formal logic to compare with that of the West, and the linguistic analysis had washed out most of the routine differences between the two languages. But the core of the problem is that Galda's *experiments bore virtually no relationship to his linguistic analysis*, that is, he did not design crucial experiments to test for differences in logical abilities which might hinge on specific linguistic differences. Rather he simply used an existing measure of overall logical ability and, therefore, could only rate subjects as higher or lower. Thus, when he finds a lower score, he cannot then work back to the language analysis as a plausible causal factor. For example, the particle *wa* collapsed some English distinctions into a single form, but since nearly all of the task items used *wa*, it is virtually impossible to sort out any meaningful, reliable pattern. In short, Galda conducted an experiment, but it could not give him any information about the question he was posing about logical systems or language categories.

Galda's study shared a remarkable number of similarities with Bloom's. He looked for structural impediments in language to certain kinds of thinking but, in fact, it is more likely that he was dealing with a difference in the use of language, not a difference in grammar *per se*. By dealing with logical relations rather than referential categories, he was forced to depend completely on translation for his linguistic comparison. He conducted a language-dependent experiment that could only characterize the non-Western group as quantitatively "deficient" rather than as qualitatively different. And finally, the experiment was ultimately unable to address the basic hypothesis because it was not diagnostic of the influence of the language form at issue on some nonlinguistic behavior. Despite the similarities, however, Galda's study was considerably inferior to Bloom's in vision, level of theoretical argument, and general methodology.

Overall conclusions

The work reviewed in this chapter diverges from the research reported in previous chapters in that an effort was made to compare diverse grammatical categories while retaining the focus on experimental assessment of individual behavior. Thus, a partial merger of the concerns of the psychological and anthropological traditions was achieved. The studies dealing with logical relators were especially distinctive in that they were the first studies in either tradition to work with categories without clear denotational value. Despite these innovations, these studies were only marginally successful and continued to exhibit some of the basic problems of the psycholinguistic research on color.

The linguistic analyses were very cursory and unsystematic: the structural roles of the grammatical forms were never characterized, so that, ultimately, elements being compared were isolated from their structural context in almost the same manner as the color terms. The comparisons were not grounded in any broad cross-linguistic framework and were mostly pseudo-comparisons in that they contrasted the presence of a feature or use in one language with its absence in another rather than comparing two different ways of accomplishing a similar referential (or other) end. In other words, despite working with "grammar," these studies never really grappled with anything like a large-scale grammatical pattern or an analogical structuring of meaning.

The cognitive emphasis continued to be on the experimental assessment of individual performance. However, perhaps because of the comparative nature of the research, issues of cultural context repeatedly entered the discussions in a more compelling way. In the studies of form–class differences, diagnostic experiments were developed to help identify nonlinguistic effects, but the connection of these experiments to habitual everyday behavior remained unclear. The ambiguous results of these experiments led, in some cases, to the first serious examination of the cultural context of the research. In short, these studies foregrounded the problem of validity (or representativeness) in comparative experimental research. In Bloom's study, by contrast, the experiments were connected to everyday behavior at the outset but, ironically, because of their language-oriented design, they provided relatively little diagnostic evidence about nonlinguistic behavior. Because of these design problems, the experiments reported here produced little reliable information on the influence of language on habitual nonlinguistic thought and behavior.

Finally, these studies highlighted the importance characterizing the patterns of use of language forms and the relation of those patterns to language structure. This issue was most salient in the work of Bloom, which detailed some of the specialized cultural uses of language that might be relevant to certain specialized forms of thought. A general clarification of the general patterns of interaction between linguistic structure and use will be essential to developing a general theory of language, of the relation of language to culture, and of the relation of language to individual psychological functioning (see the discussions above of the work of Silverstein, Hymes, and Brown respectively).

7. Overview and assessment of previous empirical research

This chapter sets the stage for future empirical work on the linguistic relativity hypothesis. First, the various lines of research reviewed in the first six chapters are briefly characterized as to their overall orientation and most significant problems and contributions. Second, in light of this past research, an evaluation is made of the most promising available approaches and research directions. This evaluation provides the rationale for the design of the specific empirical investigation described in *Grammatical categories and cognition*.

Overview of past empirical research

Whorf's research served as the historical point of departure for our review, since most contemporary empirical research on the linguistic relativity hypothesis has been stimulated by it. His work can also serve as the substantive point of departure, since it still represents the most adequate empirical approach to the issue among the studies reviewed. Subsequent research efforts have characteristically omitted or altered crucial elements of his approach even as they introduced improvements in some areas. Many of these changes stem more from traditional disciplinary preferences than from any substantive necessity.

Boas, Sapir, and Whorf[1]

Boas put forward the basic claim that languages implicitly classify experience in diverse ways for the purposes of speech. Sapir developed these ideas further by suggesting that these language categories, organized as a coherent system, could shape a person's view of reality. Whorf, in turn, clarified the operation and significance of the systematic interrelations among language categories and provided the first empirical evidence of effects on thought.

In terms of actual data in his empirical research papers, Whorf basically compared the semantic structures of two languages and then traced connections between such meaning structures and various cultural beliefs and institutions. He emphasized the importance of grammatical patterns in contributing to the meanings of lexical items and of formal syntactic equivalencies in suggesting meaningful substantive analogies. No subsequent empirical study of this issue has replicated this approach to linguistic analysis.

Individual thought was inferred from the language analysis and empirically verified by reference to related cultural patterns of belief and behavior. This approach allowed Whorf to emphasize the general significance of language patterns for behavior, but, from the point of view of subsequent researchers, it did not provide evidence of the current, direct operation of language influences on individuals or any procedure for sifting through alternative, competing accounts of behavior.

There was an additional element to Whorf's formulation: a reality against which the two linguistic patterns were tacitly compared but which was not seriously analyzed or explicated by him. The practical consequences of this weakness were mitigated somewhat because he did not privilege either of the two languages but rather played them off against each other to establish his comparison. Herein lies the nucleus of a procedure for establishing a neutral basis for the comparison of language–reality relationships, a nucleus that has yet to be exploited in this research area. The key elements in Whorf's approach are displayed in figure 11.

The anthropological linguists

The anthropological linguistic research exemplified by Lee, Mathiot, and Hoijer continued Whorf's emphasis on the relation of the grammatical structure of a language to broad cultural patterns. Although showing some fidelity to Whorf's original concern with the grammatical patterning of meaning, the empirical analyses in this tradition were of uneven quality and showed little useful innovation when contrasted to Whorf's work: little effort was made to relate the categories at issue to other categories in the language or to similar categories in other languages. Later research in this tradition by Hymes, Bernstein, and others made the important point that any claims about structural relativity were dependent on certain commonalities in the cultural uses of language, but

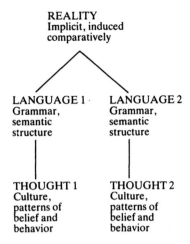

REALITY
Implicit, induced
comparatively

LANGUAGE 1
Grammar,
semantic
structure

LANGUAGE 2
Grammar,
semantic
structure

THOUGHT 1
Culture,
patterns of
belief and
behavior

THOUGHT 2
Culture,
patterns of
belief and
behavior

Figure 11 Whorf's formulation of the linguistic relativity hypothesis

this important theoretical insight remains underdeveloped theoretically and has not yet been explored empirically in cross-linguistic research.

Research in the anthropological tradition typically did not provide clear evidence for a nonlinguistic correlate with grammatical patterns. Cultural analyses were either nonexistent or dominated by the use of linguistic materials such as vocabulary lists or myth texts. So, for example, a purported relation between language and culture would turn out, under scrutiny, to be a relation between the grammatical structure of a language and the lexical structure of the same language. An adequate study of the relation between language and thought should, by contrast, provide clear evidence of a pattern of nonlinguistic belief and behavior. (Ironically, the closest recent approximation to a comparative study of linguistic relativity consistent with the anthropological focus on the relation of the grammar of a language to broad cultural patterns is the work by Bloom – a psycholinguist.) This is not to say that vocabulary items do not reflect nonlinguistic culture or that language texts do not provide important evidence about cultural beliefs, but only that, from a methodological point of view, such materials are not decisive and cannot be persuasive unless supplemented by significant nonlinguistic evidence.

The anthropological linguists initially dealt primarily with case studies of a single exotic language, effectively dropping Whorf's comparative approach. However, early on there was recognition, at least in principle, of the need for systematic, controlled comparisons, and proposals for regionally and typologically controlled comparisons were made by Hoijer and Hymes respectively. The use of some such comparative framework is essential to providing unbiased linguistic comparison and a method for controlling for other cultural effects.

Further, since there was no actual comparison of languages, the issue of a common reality against which they could be assessed was not explicitly raised. It can, of course, be argued that a broader comparative linguistic framework was tacitly present since each of the linguists worked with a descriptive language based on a variety of linguistic types. But, in fact, comparative semantic work was relatively undeveloped during this period and the analyses reviewed were, at best, based on a sensitive interpretation of the particular case or, at worst, based on extrapolating from English glosses. In no case are comparatively based insights brought to bear about the relation of language to the world. Later work by Greenberg, Friedrich, Silverstein, and others pointed the way toward building an effective, typologically based linguistic framework for comparison of referential values, but to date these linguistic advances have not been exploited in actual research on the linguistic relativity issue.

In sum, by contrast with Whorf's formulation, the anthropological case studies represented a truncated approach to the relativity problem. Thought was assessed by reference to linguistic materials, the comparative dimension was eliminated, and the tacit framework guiding the analyses was an English-based view of reality. Only the linguistic analyses had any depth to them as each author explored the interconnected meanings implicit in the structure of an exotic language.

The psycholinguists

Research on color lexicons

By contrast to the anthropologists, the psycholinguists Brown and Lenneberg working in the color tradition shifted completely away from the sort of data central to Whorf's work. They represented language by the denotational value of lexical items, that is, the array of objective stimuli that they could refer to. (Ironically, then, lexical content which had served to represent nonlinguistic "culture" for some anthropological linguists now serves to represent "language" for these psycholinguists.) Eventually this denotational emphasis led to the complete elimination of any concern with structures of meaning or grammatical differences among languages. The only "linguistic" variable remaining in the later studies was "code efficiency." Rather than claiming (with Whorf) that a grammatical equivalence relation can give rise to a characteristic conceptual interpretation of the objects of lexical reference, they claimed that inter-subject agreement in the denotational application of individual lexical items can provide a quantitative index of accuracy in perceptually distinguishing among the pertinent objects of reference. The shift to lexical denotation was undertaken to simplify the research problem. But the simplification crucially altered the terms of Whorf's problematic and, ultimately, underrepresented the structural dimension of language. Inevitably, it led to a conceptualization of language as a mere dependent variable.

Thought was assessed in this tradition by presenting individual subjects with experimentally controlled memory tasks rather than by analyzing naturally occurring patterns of everyday belief and behavior. This use of experiments provided more control over some of the variables affecting performance but was accompanied by a shift of the research emphasis away from Whorf's concern with habitual behavior toward a concern with potential behavior. On the one hand, this approach raised questions about the cultural validity (or representativeness) of the tasks. The considerable gains in control were offset by the ambiguous status of the experiments as representations of *habitual* behavior. On the other hand, the extent to which the experiments adequately represented *potential* behavior also become problematic as research became increasingly concerned with unintended effects due to various design features of the experiments.

The psycholinguists also eliminated, at least initially, Whorf's comparative approach, both in a narrower sense by working only with English and in a broader sense by explicitly using a Western scientific characterization of reality (i.e., the color space). Because the conceptualization of language forms was in terms of an independently known reality (as construed in English), the whole approach undermined *in principle* the possibility of discovering genuinely different linguistic approaches to reality. The approach also invited a "deficit" interpretation since other languages will tend to look deficient from the point of view of a standard based on ours. So, although this work was important in foregrounding the metalanguage problem underlying research on this issue, it did not provide an acceptable solution to it.

Later work in the color tradition by Stefflre and others kept the orientation toward lexical items and experimental assessment of individual behavior but partially restored the comparative approach. But even where two or more languages were compared, serious problems remained on several counts because of the closed, biased metalanguage of description. Further, at most one language ever received serious analysis, and sometimes there was no linguistic analysis at all. For example, by the time the variable "codability" had been transformed into "communication accuracy," no linguistic analysis was really necessary – only stimulus input and behavioral output were actually relevant.

(However, Lucy and Shweder, 1979, eventually did reintroduce attention to linguistic patterns – in the sense of regularities of use – into the communication accuracy formulation.)

Extensions of Lenneberg and Roberts's early color work by anthropologists Berlin and Kay generated the first broad multilanguage comparative framework to be actually applied to the relativity question. Heider later used it to anchor her two-way case study of the relation of language and thought. However, this work retained the lexical orientation and fundamentally Western conception of "color" characteristic of the earlier era. Rather than being a comparatively induced typology of patterns of language–world relationships, it showed instead the distribution of languages relative to a fixed set of parameters drawn from the Western European scientific tradition. So despite its comparative orientation, it actually washed out linguistic differences and suggested that language merely "reflected" reality. The real strength of this work, as in the psychological tradition generally, lay in its methodological rigor and not in its conceptualization of linguistic and cultural differences.

Research on grammar

While retaining the experimental assessment of individual behavior characteristic of the psycholinguistics tradition, Brown, Carroll, Casagrande, Maclay, and Bloom investigated more complex (mostly grammatical) linguistic patterns and thus, in terms of language variables, explored issues closer to those of concern to Whorf and the other anthropological linguists. Unfortunately, the linguistic analyses also showed exactly the same weaknesses as those in the anthropological tradition in that no attempt was made to relate the categories at issue to other categories in the language or to similar categories in other languages. Thus Brown, Carroll, Casagrande, and Maclay each only described a single categorical distinction in a single language even when behavioral data were collected on two or three language groups. In each case, the tacit metalanguage for linguistic characterization was "reality" (a world of objects) as construed in or viewed from English. Typically, a pattern "present" in one language was contrasted with its "absence" in another. (Bloom's work diverged somewhat from this norm in that he did compare two languages and did not deal exclusively with referential categories.) Even though these studies made only token efforts at grammatical analysis and comparison, they did suggest some categories that might be good candidates for further research.

The experimental tasks developed by these researchers typically focused on the relation between a pattern of linguistic responses to a set of stimuli and a pattern of individual nonlinguistic classification and reasoning with respect to the same set of stimuli. Thus, the experimental stimuli consisting of objects in the world or pictures of them served as the bridge by which language and thought were connected. (Bloom followed the general pattern of using common stimuli; however, he did not anchor his experiments referentially, but relied instead on interpretations of texts. This approach led to a number of ambiguities – especially regarding whether he had, in fact, identified any nonlinguistic effects.) Perhaps because of the experimental orientation characteristic of this tradition, broader cultural patterns remained largely outside the purview of most psycholinguistic research. Nonetheless, cultural issues repeatedly intruded into the studies because the researchers encountered differences in the use of language and in the relation of language to other cultural patterns. Despite the ambiguity of Bloom's results, his approach was especially significant in that experimental work and cultural analysis were brought together for the first time.

Towards a new empirical approach

In this section we switch from an historical to a more analytic mode of discussion. Whereas up to this point each study and then each research tradition has been treated as a coherent entity, now the goal will be to extract the crucial features of the linguistic relativity hypothesis and to assemble the most promising available means toward its empirical investigation. The discussion will remain at a general level in this section so as to highlight the logic of the proposed approach and to make clear its continuities and discontinuities with previous approaches. The empirical research reported in *Grammatical categories and cognition* gives specific content to this general framework.

Key dimensions of the hypothesis: language, thought, and reality in comparative perspective

Using Whorf's formulation as the starting point and taking into account the general course of previous research, we can extract the key dimensions of the relativity question. In its most elementary form, the linguistic relativity hypothesis posits that diverse languages influence the thought of those who speak them. Note first that the hypothesis is irreducibly *comparative* – it is a claim about differences and cannot be adequately investigated without comparative data. Second, the hypothesis involves two key notions – *language* and *thought* – and therefore cannot be adequately investigated without data and theory pertinent to both. After a certain point in an individual's development, of course, categories of language may not be readily distinguishable from categories of thought in ordinary behavior. Nonetheless, it is important that there be a clear analytic distinction between linguistic categories and cognitive categories so that the influence of the former on the latter (if any) can be detected and identified. If linguistic and cognitive categories are conflated in the research formulation, then the findings will be ambiguous; if they are directly equated with one another, then what is to be proven will, in effect, have been presupposed.

In addition to language and thought, Whorf's formulation, and most of the others reviewed here, introduced a third crucial notion: *reality*. Reality, in this view, is at least analytically independent of both language and thought. It is invoked to anchor the comparison of diverse language categories, to bridge the analyses of language and of thought, or to do both. Thus, in this American tradition, the research focus has been on the way diverse language categories implicitly classify reality and then on how those implicit classifications, in turn, influence thought about or the view of reality of those who speak them. And a crucial theoretical–methodological problem (whether recognized or not) has been to characterize reality without simply invoking the conception of reality suggested by the investigator's own language.

This tradition has focused, then, on the appropriation for cognitive and cultural ends of structures associated with the referential function of language, that is, the semiotic function of effectively referring to and predicating about the world. Other functions of language (for example, social, expressive, aesthetic, etc.) and their structural correlates have not been emphasized. This formulation makes some sense given that reference-and-predication appears to be the dominant function of language from a semiotic–structural point of view. However, there is no necessary reason why linkages to other functions of language could not also be investigated (for instance, Friedrich's work on the poetic function), and they may be very important.

Need for a multidisciplinary approach

Despite various achievements, the record of past research reveals that one or another of these crucial terms of the problem have been ignored or underdeveloped by each researcher. To a large extent, these weaknesses have followed disciplinary lines. The early anthropological linguists focused on language almost to the exclusion of any other data. Later work in this tradition was consistent with this orientation: increasingly sophisticated views of language were produced, but without correspond-ingly sophisticated psychological or cultural assessment. By contrast, early psycholinguistic work typically had an impoverished view of language, but introduced a variety of specific models of intellectual functioning. These models indicated specific processing regularities which should produce visible behavioral regularities under controlled conditions. Thus both anthropological linguists and psycholinguists showed strength in areas of traditional disciplinary concern. Both language and thought can be treated more adequately by drawing on the best conceptualizations of each tradition.[2]

But some of the weaknesses in past research are more generalized. No research tradition produced a fully explicit yet neutral characterization of reality suitable for research in this area. Anthropological linguists have made some progress on such a characterization for the purposes of linguistic comparison and calibration, while psychologists have made some progress in providing an overt standard against which to assess both language behavior and other behaviors. A new approach will have to integrate these partial solutions. Likewise, neither tradition has fully coped with the intrinsically comparative nature of the hypothesis. There are remarkably few studies which examine both language and thought in two groups. And only Heider (Rosch) has placed such a comparison within an explicitly articulated comparative context.

As should be clear, any new research effort must be multidisciplinary, both in drawing on the existing strengths of the relevant disciplines and in building theory and method where no strength now exists. Such an approach must adopt specific formulations for each of the key terms of the hypothesis – language, thought, reality – and must be explicitly comparative. In some cases, however, the stances taken by the various disciplines on these issues have been contradictory or have reflected fundamental, perhaps irresolvable, differences in their understandings of human action. The following sections analyze the most promising available approaches to dealing adequately with these key components of the hypothesis. Where there are several, sometimes conflicting alternatives, a recommendation is made as to which approach seems most promising or should be undertaken first.

The structure of linguistic reference and its uses

Of the various components of grammar, *referential categories* with clear denotational value have been the main target of research interest. If this traditional focus on the referential function[3] of language is accepted, it is clear that languages exhibit differences in the morphosyntactic structures available for acts of referring. The linguistic relativity hypothesis then asserts that these differences in morphosyntactic structure have detectable effects on thought about reality. This hypothesis may be and has been asserted generally, that is, without reference to conditioning factors such as the different cognitive and cultural uses to which such structures might be put. This form of the hypothesis underlies most of the research that has been reviewed and remains the most promising because the indexical component of such categories, that is, their presuppositional relation to immediate contextual features such as objects and events, provides a crucial anchor (or common reference point) for linguistic comparison and for nonlinguistic assessment of thought.

Whorf's work is still the best available example of a true structural comparison and can serve as the foundation point for further work on the linguistic side of the hypothesis. No other linguistic analysis within the various traditions reviewed is as sophisticated in terms of scope of categories considered within the language and carefulness in comparison across languages. First, Whorf's analysis considered a whole *configuration* of meaning, that is, a semantically integrated, structurally pervasive pattern of categories. Subsequent work has tended to focus on an isolated syntactic (or grammatical) form class (for instance, Navaho verb-stem classes) or on a small lexical set (for instance, color terms) without embedding them in the larger grammar. Whorf's analysis, by contrast, dealt with the complex interrelationship between syntactic and lexical phenomena, showing how they jointly constitute and analogically structure meaning.[4]

Second, Whorf grounded his analysis in *linguistic comparison*: his characterizations of English and Hopi meanings drew on insights gleaned from the way the two languages differentially construe a common dimension of reality. Thus, in a preliminary and informal way, he implemented a comparative method that uses *the reality constituted by both languages as a "neutral" metalanguage for the description of the meaning of each*. Whorf did not assert that languages varied without limit, and the "calibration" of linguistic categories remained the real goal of comparison for him. We can say that linguistic variation is both real and yet constrained – and therefore finite or limited. Whorf's approach contrasts with subsequent work that has tended to avoid language comparison entirely or that has engaged in comparison using descriptive categories for reality derived from only one of the languages being compared. From a contemporary perspective, drawing on work in anthropological linguistics, Whorf's approach can be greatly improved by developing the descriptive metalanguage (or construal of reality) using a larger sample of language types and then situating the particular languages within that larger array of types. This both makes the descriptive language increasingly "neutral" with respect to each particular language and allows the principled extension of the research to new typological cases.

Extending the work of Hymes, we can develop a second level of the relativity hypothesis by positing that the different specific *cognitive and cultural uses of language* (or orientations toward language) influence thought about reality. Silverstein (1979) explicitly takes this approach with regard to the cultural importance of the linguistic function of reference in the West. Other sociolinguistic research such as that on the relation between class-specific speech styles and school achievement can also be conceptualized in this way (see chapter 4).

Of course structure and use do not exist in isolation from one another, and interactions between the two constitute an important area of research. From a synchronic perspective, the usage aspect always takes priority over the structural, since any structural effects are dependent on those structures actually being used in thought. If specific language structures are used differently either qualitatively or quantitatively by various groups, then no safe inferences can be drawn from structural analysis alone. Some of the work in the color tradition showed just such effects of differences in cognitive use. From a diachronic perspective, however, certain structural facts may facilitate the emergence of certain uses of language (for example, the presence of overt marking for a certain concept or modality) or come to shape the uses dependent on them in characteristic ways. Bloom's work can be (re-)conceptualized in this way, although the facts of the case still remain unclear. Alternatively, a certain context of use can give rise, via emphasis on a specific semiotic function, to a specific structural element. For example, perhaps a general cultural trend toward theoretical thinking which is dependent on language forms could give rise to the creation or automatization of specific referential forms to help facilitate such thinking. In the end, an adequate theory will have to deal directly with the interplay between such cognitive and cultural uses and structural–functional configurations in language.

However, given the present state of research, *the concern with use really becomes of interest only once a case has been made that at least one structural difference has some detectable effect on speakers*. Therefore, despite the great potential significance of variation in the cognitive and cultural uses of language, it seems appropriate to bracket this concern for the moment and to continue to remain focused on the structural level. So doing will require assuming a loose isofunctionality across languages of the everyday use of speech to accomplish acts of descriptive reference and to assist cognitive activity.

The structure and uses of thought

Regarding the interpretation of the second variable, thought, there are two overt tensions underlying the alternative research approaches: the individual versus cultural conceptions of thought, and the contrasting standards of control and validity in its assessment. A third, latent issue concerns the difference between habitual thought and various specialized modes of thought, that is, differences in the uses of thought (cf. Fishman, 1960).

Individual and cultural patterns of thought

Although Whorf included the interpreting individual as a central element in his conceptualization, he verified the existence of individual patterns of thought only by reference to cultural patterns of habitual belief and behavior. Most subsequent research has aligned itself with either the individual or the cultural conception of thought. Most anthropologists have seen thought as cultural. They have been concerned to demonstrate the influence of language on *shared beliefs and institutions* without specific reference to individuals. This approach has been criticized by psychologists, for whom thought is essentially an individual phenomenon; their primary concern has been to demonstrate the current vitality of the proposed linguistic effects on the thought and behavior of individuals. These two stances grow quite clearly out of different disciplinary traditions, but reflect different aspects of one and the same problem.

The difference between an individual and a cultural emphasis has sometimes been construed as or confounded with a difference between content and process. In this view, anthropologists focus entirely on content issues, that is, shared cultural categories, whereas psychologists emphasize processes (for example, memory, classification, reasoning). This is fair to the extent that the psychologist uses the term *process* to indicate a conceptualization of thought as a functionally subdifferentiated individual activity. (This is the sense retained in this book.) However, the substantive goal has always been to investigate how these processes are affected by category content rather than how the "pure" process (if such exists) functions. Further, even studies that focus on differences in so-called "modes of thinking" do not concern processes but differences in culturally constituted ways of thinking – that is, differences in cultural goals, strategies, and tools – in short, content at another level. Thus, in both disciplines, the central concern has been the influence of language on socially shared, if individually manifested, interpretations of reality and not on the *mode* of processing as such. A notion of "pure" process remains of dubious value in the area of cultural comparisons.

An emphasis in future research on the assessment of individual behavior offers several advantages. First, since most anthropologists would, all other things being equal, accept regularities in individual behavior as part of culture, individual assessment can be regarded as the more neutral formulation: it speaks to concerns of both groups. (By contrast most psychologists would not accept institutional patterns as evidence of current psychological vitality.) Second, from an analytic point of view, there may be effects on individual thought and behavior that a traditional analysis of cultural beliefs and institutions would not reveal. Languages with remarkable structural parallels can be found in very diverse cultures. (Indeed, a true "linguistic" relativity, insofar as it is an autonomous force, must, by definition, operate somewhat independently of a more general "cultural" relativity.) It may be that such linguistic parallels insure a certain "core" cultural similarity (as suggested by Hoijer) as yet undetected by traditional cultural analysis, or that linguistic influences on individual thought, although present, do not play a significant role in shaping institutional structures. It therefore makes sense to hold general cultural hypotheses in abeyance until it is first established that there is some relation to individual thought. (Although there can be linguistic influences on the individual that have not been recognized as such by cultural analysis, it seems very unlikely that there will be cultural effects unmediated through individual interpretation.) If identified. a relationship of language and individual thought could be used as a basis for re-examining traditional cultural analyses. The initial goal. then. should be to provide data on individual behavior with respect to a linguistic hypothesis formulated in a fashion consistent with Whorf's approach.

Control and validity in assessment

A second, closely related traditional tension is between the emphasis in psychological research on using *experimental controls* to assess individual nonlinguistic behavior and the concern in anthropological research to assure the cultural or *conceptual validity* of any such assessments. The trade-off here is crucial, since experimental control can produce the kind of focused data necessary to decide among competing hypotheses, whereas cultural validity is essential to assure that the findings have meaning beyond the task context.

Evidence gathered in cross-cultural research always remains fundamentally correlational, since the language and culture of a given individual or group cannot be freely manipulated. Such correlational evidence is especially vulnerable to reinterpretation in terms of some unrecognized third variable. The great number of cultural differences between groups make the risk of such erroneous attribution of causal relation very high – particularly in two-way comparisons.

In the present case, the anthropologist may readily demonstrate that a given language pattern is associated with a general cultural pattern, but it is another matter to establish that such patterns actually stem from language. Demonstration of the decisive role of language must come either (1) from an especially persuasive and distinctive configuration of cultural patterns (as Whorf attempted), (2) from exploiting fortuitous contrasts among naturally occurring cases (as Hoijer proposed and as Bright and Bright attempted) including analyses of historical developments and crucial diagnostic cases, or (3) from looking at global patterns of correlation among naturally occurring, typologically classed cases (as Hymes proposed). In short, an ethnographic case-study approach must be supplemented by controlled evidence capable of distinguishing among competing accounts of a given pattern of cultural thought and behavior.

The psychologist introduces experimental controls precisely to help distinguish among various possible influences on behavior and thereby clarify functional interrelations. Controlled assessment typically involves constructing crucial diagnostic situations. Features such as the background of the subjects, the composition of some stimulus set, or the nature of the task itself are varied so as to distinguish among a variety of competing explanations. In the present circumstance, the background status of the subjects (i.e., the language spoken) is the crucial variable, but it cannot be manipulated experimentally, so the most powerful relevant experimental control cannot be employed. (Notice that the language status of a bilingual speaker cannot be manipulated either. Such subjects are irreducibly speakers of two languages and cannot alternately represent two states of monolingualism.) Nonetheless, introducing experimental controls over stimulus and task variables can still be useful, and this approach has been used by some anthropologists (for instance, Casagrande). Typically such controlled test situations simultaneously foreground examples of the hypothesized behavioral differences and provide equivalent opportunities for both groups. The foregrounding is useful because crucial interrelationships may be clearly manifested only infrequently or in certain situations. Providing equal opportunities for each individual within and across groups allows individuals and groups to be directly compared on specific patterns of performance rather than only in terms of global characterizations.

Properly used, these experimental controls can greatly improve the three forms of correlational evidence available to anthropologists in the present case. First, to make alternative interpretations extremely unlikely in the first place, task behaviors can be designed so that the predicted effects of language patterns on behavior can be made very specific and highly characteristic. This both rigorously tests the hypothesis and, at the same time, when the results are positive, reduces the likelihood that any simple alternative explanation will suffice as well, since it will have to predict the same highly characteristic pattern of results. Second, additional examples of crucial naturally occurring behavioral patterns which are culturally contrastive but infrequently manifested can be elicited so as to challenge or bolster an interpretation based on informal observations. Third, to facilitate the further comparative evaluation of alternative explanations of the patterns of data, both the linguistic and cognitive assessment procedures can be developed in such a way that they can be readily extended to additional, typologically selected cases. A direct multilanguage and multicultural comparison provides the surest route to control over additional variables for the present problem. Future research should implement all three of these enhancements to traditional correlational designs.

However, these gains in control do not come without some costs. It is not always clear that behavior exhibited under experimentally controlled conditions adequately represents either speakers' potential behavior or their habitual behavior, that is, that there is a valid link between the experimental task and everyday behavior. The issue has two aspects. The first question is whether the introduction of various controls in and of itself destroys the object of analysis. The problem is especially acute when the object of analysis is known to be inherently context sensitive. The problem can be minimized by selecting materials and designing tasks so as to maximize their representativeness of everyday materials and tasks. This is especially pertinent in cross-cultural situations, where the range of relevant influences on behavior may be especially difficult to discern; but as the history of research in the color tradition with its different stimulus arrays and task designs well illustrates, the problem can emerge in research in familiar contexts as well. The maximization of validity can be accomplished by having a substantial knowledge of the cultures, by indicating the reasons for believing that the task is representative, and by simulating aspects of everyday behavior in the task where possible. Since it is also possible that some incidental feature of the task procedure or stimulus materials could account for the pattern of results, multiple means of assessment are also desirable. And, ideally, the observed patterns of behavior should be consistent with naturalistic evidence.

The second question is whether the introduction of controlled assessment favors one language group over another. In particular, the tasks and/or materials may be more culturally familiar for one group than another. This has been a persistent problem with cross-cultural psychological research for many years and, for this reason, some of the main lines of difficulty with Western research procedures are well understood. Specific procedures (for example, back translation, use of indigenous stimulus materials, local pilot work, etc.) have been developed to handle such difficulties. Again, the problem can be minimized if the design of the tasks is based on a background knowledge of the cultures.

To some extent, this tension between control and validity in assessment is intrinsic, since control, by its very definition, involves a departure from or limitation of everyday situations. Of the work reviewed, only Bloom's seriously tried to combine an analysis of cultural belief with controlled individual assessment. Although his attempt was flawed in crucial respects, this tactic clearly represents the best long-range approach to balancing control and validity. Accordingly, future research should make use of controlled assessment whenever possible to improve the precision of the correlational data. An attempt should be made to maximize the validity of the stimulus materials and tasks and to supplement the assessments with naturalistic observations.

Habitual and specialized thought

Nearly all the research reviewed has focused on the structure of thought, that is, its patterns of organization and operation, as it relates to reality. A second issue, variation in modes of thought across cultures, has almost never been directly examined as part of the linguistic relativity debate. However, the issue has arisen indirectly – most clearly in Whorf's *implicit* distinction between habitual thought and specialized (or formal) thought. Habitual thought consists, in this view, of certain everyday ways of apprehending and dealing with the world of experience characteristic of most normal adult members of a culture. Specialized thought is thought characteristic of some definite subgroup (as with a linguistic dialect) or some definite subset of cultural situations (as with a linguistic register) or both. Specialized thought is typically developed for the performance of very particular, often culture-specific tasks, and often rests on the acquisition of a body of information and strategies not shared by all. In many cases the distinction between habitual and specialized thought may not be easy to draw, especially because habitual thought is not a well-defined mode but a more or less residual category.

Whorf conceived of habitual thought as having priority: categories of everyday thought provide the underlying basis for the categories used by specialists such as scientists or philosophers. However, one can readily imagine the reverse situation, where a specialized mode of thinking spreads to become a habitual mode, widespread in the culture – again Bloom's work points in this direction. Of particular interest in this regard is the relationship between the everyday awareness of and thought about (ideologies of) language and the various specialized uses of language made by specialists in a culture. For example, the development of an overtly reflexive orientation toward language categories in certain social spheres (or "fields") in the West (for example, science, law, philosophy, religion, literature) necessarily grows out of certain everyday habitual uses. But the elaboration of these orientations can become quite extensive and eventually come to influence ideas not only about language but also about ways of thinking in or about everyday domains.

Future research should begin by looking for language effects on habitual thought rather than specialized thought. The assessment of thought should not center on highly trained subjects or specialized bodies of knowledge but rather emphasize simple skills and everyday knowledge. This is advantageous from the point of view of cultural comparison since the various specialized modes of thought are not represented in every culture and cannot, therefore, easily be compared.

The description of reality and the comparative dilemma

As indicated at the outset, most previous research on the linguistic relativity question has introduced nonlinguistic "reality" as a crucial third term. Under this formulation, the linguistic relativity hypothesis devolves into a concern with how the referential categories of language "classify" reality and how these classifications affect thought about or the conception of reality. The key theoretical problem under such a formulation becomes the development of a *neutral description of reality for the purposes of comparison*, that is, a description that does not privilege the categories of any one language or culture at the outset and that cannot be reduced to the categories of a particular language or system of thought. For undertaking studies such as Bloom's which deal with the linguistic encoding of "concepts" or "modes of thinking" rather than "reality," the only difference would be that the universe of possible concepts or modes of thinking must be neutrally described. But providing such a description is unlikely to prove to be substantially easier and may, in fact, prove more difficult.

If, for some reason, the categories of one group *are* privileged in the analysis, then both the linguistic and cognitive analysis will be skewed. On the one hand, the true range of linguistic variation will be obscured as language forms are slotted into the available categories; by comparison with the privileged language, other languages will typically look "deficient." On the other hand, the true range of cognitive variation will be obscured as behavioral tasks are developed favoring dimensions meaningful to the privileged group; other groups will, again, typically look "deficient" by comparison. In short, the description of reality for the purposes of comparison ideally should be neutral with respect to any one cultural or linguistic system. Of course, from a broader perspective, the descriptive enterprise itself cannot be seen as neutral, since it arises historically out of our particular cultural concerns, which may be linguistically shaped (see Lucy, 1985a). This aspect of the problem cannot be adequately explored without a full elaboration of the functional relativity issue, which cannot be undertaken here.

Of the research reviewed, Whorf was the most successful in being neutral in his characterization of reality. But his characterization was *ad hoc* in two senses: it was based largely on the two languages in his study, and no general procedure for constructing such characterizations was developed. Lenneberg, by contrast, developed an explicit general procedure for characterizing certain segments of reality. But his characterization was also faulty in two respects. First, his approach to reality was based on only a single language (or language family) – and hence was not neutral at all in this sense – and, second, it did not provide any principled distinction between reality as such and the representations of language and thought. Thus, in an important respect, he collapsed or conflated all three terms of the hypothesis. Ideally a new approach to the linguistic relativity issue would combine elements of these approaches to produce an explicit, neutral characterization of reality. To achieve this, a clearer formulation of the grounds for the descriptive metalanguage need to be articulated. This must be regarded as *the* crucial theoretical task.

One essential step in building such a descriptive language is to develop it from a *broad comparative sample* of languages and cultures so that it can reflect a maximum range of diversity at the outset and place each specific system relative to the array of possibilities. The parameters of such a typology then provide the terms of description for each individual case. Ironically, however, such a project depends precisely on *already having* available a body of comparative work in anthropology, psychology, and linguistics based on an adequate comparative framework. Because of this dilemma, no full descriptive language can be articulated at the outset but must be built or elaborated in incremental steps (i.e., iteratively) from existing work. A major limitation at present is that meaningful comparative work in psychology, that is, work which takes into account culturally specific categories or understandings of reality within a cross-cultural framework, is essentially nonexistent. Likewise, anthropology at present fails to provide an adequate comparative frame for the description or typology of cultural modes of thought. By contrast, there is a body of work in contrastive linguistics that has attempted to describe the referential categories of languages within an overarching comparative framework.

Because of this situation, the most promising approach at present is to turn to contrastive linguistics for help in developing a provisional, neutral description of reality. In other words, *reality can be described as it appears through the window of language.* The description will be neutral to the extent that it succeeds in not favoring any one language, but it will remain a decidedly linguistic vision of the world and, in this respect, a decidedly partial construal of reality. But since the issue at hand is the effect of variation in the linguistic construal of reality on the cognitive construal of reality, there seems to be little danger in ignoring these effects of language-in-general (speech). (This actually understates the case since, first, normal adult thought always presupposes familiarity with some language – hence a language-informed view of reality is not a procedurally introduced artifact at all – and, second, the sort of comparative work being advocated is absolutely essential for identifying such effects of language-in-general on a generic human view of reality, if such a view exists.) The risks of ignoring coincident nonlinguistic effects on thought cannot be completely eliminated, as mentioned in the previous section, but will be reduced by using the procedures outlined there. And, I hope, as suggested in the introduction, the present work will suggest the outlines of the sort of theory and method needed for comparative psychological research more generally, the sort of research needed to fully situate the current project theoretically.

A description of reality developed in this way is an analytical tool, a theoretical language, constructed for the purposes of comparison, and cannot be seen as a definitive description of reality for everyone or for any specific linguistic or cultural group. No group may recognize all elements of the "reality" constituted by the comparative frame, nor need the frame exhaust the full reality of any specific cultural configuration. Further, to the extent that the theoretical language is concerned with (refers to) language structure and function, it is also a metalanguage. To the extent that the metalanguage is built out of and operates on our own language it is also reflexive, with all that that may entail in terms of theoretical complications (Lucy, 1992).

Summary

The various goals and procedures described here can be summarized as in figure 12 to highlight the contrasts with Whorf's original approach shown in figure 11. I have placed language between thought and reality in

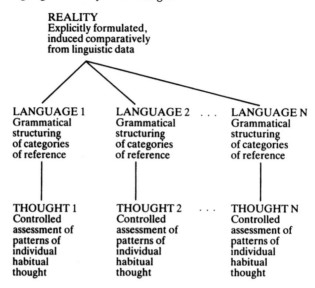

Figure 12 Essential components of research on linguistic relativity

this figure to emphasize that it influences their interrelation. This placement should not be construed as an attribution or endorsement of any specific mechanism (for example, that language is a filter, that reality is known only through language, etc.).

The research described in *Grammatical categories and cognition* completes the analysis presented here by illustrating concretely how the various suggestions for well-grounded empirical research on the linguistic relativity hypothesis can actually be implemented. It departs from the framework just outlined in that THOUGHT is assessed for only two groups. This deficiency can be remedied in future work by employing the same method iteratively.

Notes

1 Development of the linguistic relativity hypothesis in America: Boas and Sapir

1 Whorf (1956a, p. 66) explicitly connected his work with that of Boas and Sapir as well as with that of Leonard Bloomfield. Discussion of his intellectual debt to Boas and Sapir can be found in Carroll (1956, pp. 15–17), Hymes (1961b, pp. 23–27; 1963, pp. 72–73; 1964a, pp. 115–20), Hymes and Fought (1975, pp. 999–1002), and Silverstein (1979, pp. 193–203).

2 I have profited in this subsection from a series of unpublished lectures on Boas given by Michael Silverstein in a 1976 University of Chicago course entitled "Linguistic categories in cognition." (See also Silverstein, 1979.) George Stocking's (1968; 1974) works on Boas have also been of considerable importance in developing this section.

3 In its classificatory aspect, Boas regarded language as continuous with other aspects of human thought which also classify experience in various ways for diverse ends (Boas, 1966a [1911], p. 24).

4 Boas (1916 [1911], pp. 142–43) explicitly equates "phonetic groups" with "word-stems" and then uses "word-stems" in a passage otherwise identical to the one cited here. Most of his examples consist of comparing words in one language with root plus affixes in another. (But see n5 below.)

5 In general Boas argued that the dividing line between stem and affix (lexicon and grammar) is difficult to draw (see his discussion in Boas, 1966a [1911], pp. 23–25 and pp. 33–35). Many of his examples show that what is lexically expressed in one language is grammatically expressed in another. Hence, from a broader point of view, "lexical" categories are part of "grammar" (1966a [1911], pp. 29–30).

6 Boas's (1966a [1911]) examples in his section "Interpretation of grammatical categories" perhaps appear more unusual than necessary because he routinely glosses unmarked forms as specifying a negative value. Such glosses are not always justified. Most obligatory category distinctions include an unmarked form (i.e., neither positive or negative but neutral when used in unmarked sense) which substantially weakens the cognitive force of their "obligatory" status. So, for example, in English, where tense marking is obligatory, the "simple present" is best thought of as a "nonpast" form, since it can signal not only "present" but also "timeless," "future," and "hypothetical."

277

K

7 For a brief discussion of the history of concern with the unconscious nature of linguistic phenomena, see Jakobson (1980); also Lucy (1992).

8 Boas's claim that language categories are distinctive relative to other ethnological phenomena in their unconscious character warrants the inclusion of this issue with his other claims about language, rather than with his claims about the relation of language to thought – where it might also plausibly be placed. See n9 below.

9 Silverstein (1979, pp. 197–98) characterizes "the Boasian question" which Whorf was eventually to take up as "which parts of language emerge in 'secondary rationalization' and thereby historically affect cultural practice." Boas himself certainly never formulated the question in this way – although some of his examples (discussed further below) were suggestive on this point. Whorf, as we shall see, raised the issue only implicitly. For explicit consideration of this issue see Silverstein's own work (1979; 1981a). See also Stocking (1974, pp. 477–78) on this point.

10 Boas defined ethnology at one point as "the science dealing with the mental phenomena of the life of the peoples of the world," and frequently took an explicitly psychological approach to ethnographic problems. (See, for example, Boas, 1966a [1911], p. 59 and all of 1916 [1911]; see also discussions by Hymes, 1961b, p. 24, and Stocking, 1974, pp. 476–78.)

11 For Boas, any apparent advance in the level of thought in more "civilized" men was not in fact an individual phenomenon (or a linguistic one), but rather an historical development in the body of traditions that the individual draws on

> with the advance of civilization, reasoning becomes more and more logical, not because each individual carries out his thought in a more logical manner, but because the traditional material which is handed down to each individual has been thought out and worked out more thoroughly and more carefully.
>
> (Boas, 1916 [1911], p. 206)

The general mechanism for these changes seems to be the rise into consciousness of categories which allow the hypothetical basis of our reasoning to become more clear. Boas did concede that eventually in this development, more individuals will in fact try to free themselves of the fetters of tradition, but on the whole the "civilized" person tends to utilize the beliefs of his scientific tradition in a way that is indistinguishable from that of the "primitive" person (Boas, 1916 [1911], pp. 202–9).

12 Stocking (1974, pp. 476–78) discusses some of the historical reasons for Boas's "ambiguity and even . . . apparent contradiction" on this issue.

13 These arguments emerge most clearly beginning in 1924 and may have been constructed by Sapir on analogy with his work in phonology; see in this regard his classic article "Sound patterns in language" (1949g [1925]).

14 Sapir (1949e [1921]) described at some length the range of formal meaning and substantive content associated with such classifications.

15 Another good example is given in Sapir and Swadesh (1964 [1929–46]).

16 Sapir drew these terms from Carl Jung's work *Psychological types* (1923); see also Sapir's review of this work (Sapir, 1949a [1923], pp. 529–32) and his discussion of it elsewhere (1949c [1924], p. 156). Whorf also made use of Jung's distinctions, as will be discussed below.

17 Boas also comments on the difficulty of recognizing a part within a whole complex, but only in his discussion of sound systems (1966a [1911], pp. 19–20).

18 Those familiar with the Soviet (/Marxist) developmental psychology of Vygotsky (1978 [1930–34]; 1987 [1934]) will recognize strong parallels in the general theory proposed as to the relation of speech and thought. See B. Lee (1985) on Vygotsky's use of Sapir's work. For a general contrast of the American and Soviet approaches see Lucy and Wertsch (1987).

19 Elsewhere, Sapir claims that "Even comparatively simple acts of perception are very much more at the mercy of the social patterns called words than we might suppose" (1949h [1929], p. 162); but his examples turn out to involve the placing of perceptions into "categories," rather than any alteration of immediate sensation.

20 See also Sapir (1949e [1921], p. 218) where he states that the latent thought of all languages is the same, and (1949c [1924], p. 157) where he advocates the study of exotic languages so as not to be misled by the "accidental" forms of our own language in philosophical speculation.

21 Sapir uses "morphological" in a specific sense here:

We may consider the subject matter of morphology as made up of certain logical or psychological categories of thought that receive grammatical treatment and of formal methods of expressing these.

(Sapir, 1949f [1912], p. 97)

22 In this article, Sapir has just reviewed how similar phonological forms (for example, pitch, nasalized vowels, glottal stops, etc.) can be found in widely disparate parts of the world and in societies of very different types. Conversely, languages with quite disparate phonological characteristics can be found in quite similar cultures (for instance, French and English, which have similar geographical and historical backgrounds). Just as phonological form seemed to be in free variation with geographical and social environment, Sapir felt, at this point in his thinking, that much the same degree of freedom also characterized morphological categories.

23 Sapir uses the terms "form" and "content" in a variety of contrasts which can occasionally create confusion. In general, with regard to language he nests the opposition as follows: content: form:: culture: language:: vocabulary: grammar:: grammatical concepts: grammatical processes. He also contrasts latent (universal) content with manifest (variable) form. He sometimes extends the contrast of content versus form (or process) to his discussions of thought and culture. Full explication of his theory would have to work out the details of these usages.

24 See the comments in Sapir (1964 [1931], p. 128; 1949d [1933], pp. 7–11) for similar references to the shaping role of language and to its complete interpenetration with the rest of culture. Berthoff (1988) argues that Sapir did not change his earlier views on the autonomy of language and culture in his later work. She offers an ingenious interpretation of the passage cited, making clear its place in Sapir's discussion of social science methodology. It seems unlikely, however, that Sapir meant his remarks to refer only to social scientists, and Berthoff's own exegesis makes obvious how untenable this view would be.

25 Notice that this statement by Sapir follows soon after his "Sound patterns in language" (1949g [1925]). See also Eggan (1954) and Stocking (1968) on the general development in American anthropology (*c.* 1930) of an image of culture as more structured and less a mere assemblage. It is interesting that the bulk of Sapir's writings on psychiatry and personality post-date this apparent shift in his thinking toward highlighting the importance of shared individual symbolic understandings (cf. Darnell, 1986).

2   Development of the linguistic relativity hypothesis in America: Whorf

1 This volume of Whorf's selected writings, chronologically arranged and with introductory biographical sketch, has become the standard source for his views regarding the relation between language and thought. References in this discussion will be made to this volume rather than to the original sources of publication both for economy of citation and because the pagination of this volume better reflects the sequential development of Whorf's ideas than do the dates of first publication.

2 Berthoff (1988) has disputed the close relation of Whorf's views to those of Sapir. In particular, she criticizes Whorf (in contrast to Sapir) for having a dyadic rather than triadic view of language, by which she seems to mean that he saw language as a simple map of reality and lacked the notion of a dynamic interpretant. I find this reading of Whorf unpersuasive given his emphasis on the constitutive force of linguistic patternment in social life and science. Whorf's studies of the interlocking character of linguistic categories give empirical content to Sapir's programmatic ideas about the formal completeness of language as a heuristic conceptual system – exactly the aspect of Sapir's work that Berthoff praises as distinctive.

3 Whorf's writings on overt and covert categories spanned the years from 1936 through 1939 (1956a, pp. 67–73, 79–83, 87–94, 104–11, 113, 126, 129–32; 1956b [1938], pp. 4–6; 1946a [1939], pp. 162, 173; 1946b [1939], p. 375). Little of this material was published during his lifetime, however, and its significance in his later thinking has perhaps been underestimated (but see Silverstein, 1979; 1981b). Whorf believed that he was "the first to point out the existence of this submerged layer of meaning, which in spite of its submergence functions regularly in the general linguistic whole" (1956a, p. 111). Whorf may be correct insofar as he ascribes general theoretical significance to such a distinction. Compare, however, with Jakobson (1971b [1937]) for contemporaneous concern with categories lacking regular overt morphological marking. It is possible that Whorf was aware of at least some of this work in Eastern Europe; note his passing references (1946a [1939], p. 159; 1956b [1938], p. 4; 1940, p. 15) to the work of Trubetskoy and the Prague School.

4 This distinction between *overt* and *covert* categories cross-cuts several others that he makes. The most important of these is the distinction between *modulus* and *selective* categories, that is, those that may be applied to large segments of the lexicon or to the whole lexicon, as opposed to those that are applicable only to a selected subset in the lexicon. It appears that only selective categories may be covert, as indicated by Whorf's failure to give appropriate examples in his discussion (1956a, pp. 93–99), by the structure of his typology of categories, which also omits the possibility (1956a, pp. 130–32), and by his assertion "Moduli are overt, selective classes either overt or covert" (1956b [1938], p. 6). He does, however, make a few remarks which appear to be at odds with this interpretation: see, for example, his mention of covert derivation (1956a, p. 132). (His discussion, 1956a, p. 97, of the application of verbation and stativation to part of the English lexicon is a borderline example depending on whether verbation and stativation are conceived of as selective or modulus categories in the example.)

Whorf's discussions of category types in languages show the influence of and in some ways extend and improve upon Bloomfield (1933, chs. 10, 12, and 16).

5 Silverstein (1979, p. 197) has noted the "transformational" nature of this approach, which identifies relations among linguistic elements by patterns of formal interaction (see Chomsky, 1957).

6 These grammatical meanings can be understood as equivalent to Bloomfield's (1933, p. 146) *class meaning*, that is, the meaning common to all members of a form class.

7 The relationship among Whorf's terms for various kinds of categories mentioned in n4 can be diagrammed as follows (where dashes indicate empty categories and square brackets indicate redundant terms):

Scope of application

Systematicity of marking	Selective	Modulus
Overt		
Mark	[signature]	signature
Meaning	phenotype	[phenotype]
Covert		
Mark	reactance	—
Meaning	cryptotype	—

8 In the latter piece, one of the last which he wrote, Whorf appears to be moving toward a conception of overt morphological forms as epiphenomenal. The popularized tone of the writing makes it difficult to be certain. See also Whorf (1956a, pp. 197, 240).

9 It is not clear why Whorf did not explicitly use the overt–covert distinction in his last writings on language and thought (from 1939 to 1941). Perhaps he found it superfluous to his argument, too complicated to introduce, or flawed in some way – the first of these seems most likely. For an attempt to bridge the gap and reword Whorf's essential argument with these distinctions (and related ones), see Silverstein (1979).

10 Whorf occasionally criticized those who selected only certain elements in their comparison of languages, elements which he felt tended to minimize the degree of difference between the segmentations of various languages (see, for example, 1956a, pp. 240–42).

11 Hymes (1961a, p. 26) makes a similar evaluation of Whorf's interests.

12 Whorf occasionally made other references to prelinguistic sensation (i.e., aside from Gestalt phenomena: see, for instance, 1956a, p. 267) that also

give evidence of his recognition of this kind of perceptual universal. In an indirect way, his use of pictorial models in his popular writings (1956a, pp. 208, 210, 213, 234, 235, 243) also suggests that he felt he could appeal to nonlinguistic devices to avoid the categorial biases of particular languages.

13 Silverstein sees in Whorf's work "a first attempt to draw out the Boasian implications of how pure referential (semantic) categories and duplex (referential–indexical) ones combine differently from language to language to accomplish ultimately isofunctional referential speech events" (1976b, p. 25). Whorf's understanding of such differences was crucial in his willingness to argue that other languages could be referentially adequate without our familiar categories.

14 For other evidence of Whorf's recognition that at least some linguistic universals might stem from specifically linguistic factors, see the remark (1956a, p. 66, n2) on the "cultural" as opposed to "biological" nature of language and the discussion (1956a, p. 267) of the serial or hierarchical organization of behavior.

15 Whorf recognizes that nonlinguistic communication is possible, but distinguishes the kind of agreement possible in such cases from that obtainable through speech (1956a, pp. 212, 239).

16 "Exotic" in this case would mean languages outside the European languages so frequently contrasted with one another, but which are in many ways very similar. This commonality of European languages is discussed further below. Note that the study of these languages is not the same as acquiring the ability to speak them (1956a, p. 211).

17 Whorf's writings on language and thought may be divided into three groups. The first group (1956a, pp. 51–124), written between 1935 and 1940, concerns itself with the two living languages which Whorf worked on most intensively – Hopi and Nahuatl (Aztec) – and the understandings of grammatical phenomena which emerged from these studies. In these pieces we find many passages which refer to the relation between language and thought, but the argument is not yet mature. Most of these pieces were only published posthumously and Whorf, quite naturally, did not make reference in later published works to some of the terminological distinctions developed in them. They also lack some of the finishing apparent in his other work. The second group (1956a, pp. 134–59) contains but one article, his "The relation of habitual thought and behavior to language," written in 1939 and published in 1941. This piece is central not only temporally but also conceptually; it is his only published presentation of his ideas on this topic to a professional linguistic and anthropological audience during his lifetime, and it takes up the central issues in the most detail. The third group (1956a, pp. 207–70) contains four pieces written for a popular (though educated) audience, in which Whorf tried to bring the understandings and significance of modern linguistic science, including his own ideas, to a wider audience. The latter pieces are consistent on the whole with his professionally articulated position, although his choice of vocabulary and emphasis is somewhat dictated by his readership. The informal tone of these pieces has for some readers obscured the depth of Whorf's understanding of the language and thought issue. The final article in this group is especially

significant, indicating that Whorf was prepared to take his critique of Western scientific and philosophical thought much further than he had in his previous writings.

18 There are other places where Whorf uses lexical examples but, interestingly, most often to show how ephemeral they in fact are, that is, how they depend on a total grammatical (or cultural) configuration to acquire their semantic force (see 1956a, pp. 67–68, 197, 240–41, 258–63; 1956b [1938], p. 8). Where they have an influence on thought, it tends to be due to their highly segmented nature, which allows speakers to reflect upon them, often incorrectly (see, for example, 1956a, pp. 134–37, 258–63). Compare this with the discussion of Boas in chapter 1. See also Silverstein (1981b, 1985b), who develops a similar point with a more sophisticated theoretical foundation.

19 Whorf uses English as a representative of Standard Average European (SAE) and wishes to emphasize by the use of the latter label that all the languages of Europe bear sufficient similarity to one another that they may be taken as one in contrast with Hopi. This rhetorical point aside, however, he deals for the most part with English grammar. The emphasis on patterns in particular languages (versus language in general) is consistent with Whorf's emphasis on the cultural (versus biological) aspect of language. He makes clear that it is indeed the pattern of particular languages which he expects to interact with thought:

> The statement that "thinking is a matter of LANGUAGE" is an incorrect generalization of the more nearly correct idea that "thinking is a matter of different tongues."   (1956a, p. 239; see also p. 252)

20 Only occasionally does Whorf refer to the power of pattern and meaning in language actually to override perceptual reality (see, for instance, 1956a, p. 267, on meaning affecting sound symbolism) rather than merely segment, arrange, or construe it in some way.

21 In general I have not dealt with Bloomfield's considerable influence on Whorf because the former did not address the linguistic relativity issue as such. However, in passing, he too mentioned the impact of language categories on philosophers:

> The categories of a language, especially those which affect morphology (*book: books, he: she*), are so pervasive that anyone who reflects upon his language at all, is sure to notice them. In the ordinary case, this person, knowing only his native language, or perhaps some others closely akin to it, may mistake his categories for universal forms of speech, or of "human thought," or of the universe itself. This is why a good deal of what passes for "logic" or "metaphysics" is merely an incompetent restating of the chief categories of the philosopher's language.   (Bloomfield, 1933, p. 270)

It is important to realize that the two most eminent American linguists of his day, Sapir and Bloomfield, were voicing ideas much like Whorf's.

22 Whorf's discussions of Indian philosophy (1956a, pp. 70, 252–69) reflect his desire to focus on the relations between overall structural patterns. *Manas* (roughly, '[higher] mind') is divided into two great levels, one made up of discrete units (*Rūpa₁*) and the other of patterns among those units (*Arūpa*):

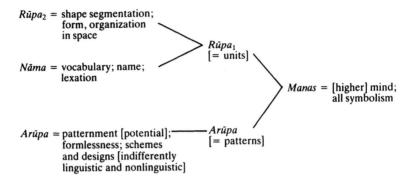

Rūpa₂ = shape segmentation; form, organization in space

Nāma = vocabulary; name; lexation

Rūpa₁ [= units]

Arūpa = patternment [potential]; formlessness; schemes and designs [indifferently linguistic and nonlinguistic]

Arūpa [= patterns]

Manas = [higher] mind; all symbolism

I cannot say to what extent Whorf's glosses are correct, but the merging of linguistic and nonlinguistic patternment under the term *Arūpa* clearly reflects his own view that the two are of the same nature. *Arūpa* is the level he emphasized in his discussions as the focus of the interaction of language and thought; he is interested in the patterning of thought (*Arūpa* + *Rūpa₂*) in relation to the patterning of language (*Arūpa* + *Nāma*) and he is interested in the importance of pattern (*Arūpa*) in the interpretation of units (*Rūpa₁*).

23 The immediate source of Whorf's term *analogy* used in this sense is not clear. The term may come from Bloomfield, who used it in a different, more traditional sense, to refer to formal extensions in grammar:

> A grammatical pattern ... is often called an *analogy*. A regular analogy permits a speaker to utter speech-forms which he has not heard; we say that he utters them *on the analogy* of similar forms which he has heard.
>
> (Bloomfield, 1933, p. 275)

The term analogy is also used in the study of diachronic linguistic change in a different though not unrelated sense (see, for instance, Kuryłowicz, 1973b [1945–49]; see also Sapir, 1949e [1921], ch. 7, on historical "drift").

24 For some remarks on the importance of language in enabling some kinds of thought, or in "socializing" individual thought, see Whorf (1956a, pp. 66–70, 257–63); these remarks fall well short of adequately addressing this issue, however.

25 Whorf does not mean his claims to be "correlational" in the sense that knowing feature X about a language, one can reliably predict (diagnose) feature Y about the culture. Whorf's (1956a, p. 159) view is that there are relations, but only to be discovered by careful analysis of the whole. In this regard his approach is similar to recent approaches in interpretive anthropology. Nonetheless, from a formal methodological point of view, such an approach remains correlational in the sense that no experimental manipulation can be undertaken to prove that causal connections between the features actually exist.

26 In a later essay Whorf gave further lexical examples which involved more explicit reflection on the forms (i.e., folk etymology) (1956a, pp. 261–63).

27 As mentioned in n19 above, Whorf's examples were from English, but recall that he meant them to stand as representative of Standard Average European (SAE), since the European languages are relatively similar as

compared with Hopi. In discussing *cultural* patterns related to the English (SAE) forms, however, he drew on the entire Western tradition.

28 It is possible to read the last line of this quotation as meaning "universal in experience if and only if universal in language." This seems incorrect given the use of the word "unmistakably" (in the sense of "unavoidably"), which indicates that Whorf only meant to refer to the *deterministic* status of the pre-linguistic category, not its existence. Even if this interpretation is discounted, Whorf still seems to have been guilty of a logical error. He essentially deduced from the following plausible proposition:

> If a classification exists in all languages, then it is based on something that is given in experience to all people in similar form (i.e., if *x* then *y*),

the following invalid conclusion:

> If a classification is based on something that is given in experience to all people in similar form, then it exists in all languages (i.e., if *y* then *x*).

The latter proposition runs up against a number of alternative possibilities, namely that certain universal concepts or experiences might never be taken up as language categories, might be taken up only by some languages, might be taken up only under certain conditions by languages, etc. Compare here the earlier discussion of Whorf's tendency to consider universals of experience only when confronted with similarity between languages.

29 It may be significant that Whorf chose as his example *men* instead of, for example, *boys*, where the plural marker (suffixed *-s*) would show more clearly the formal parallel with *days*. He apparently wanted to emphasize the grammatical or structural nature of the linkage and to avoid implying that formal analogies were limited to overlapping overt morphological markings. (Cf. Bloomfield, 1933, pp. 214–15.)

30 Whorf refers to this as "counting itself," a somewhat misleading label which draws attention to the absence of any perceptible objects.

31 Silverstein (1979), in linking Whorf's work to that of Boas, interprets Whorf's use of the term *objectification* somewhat more broadly as a general process characteristic of speakers of various languages which has to do with the equation of a language category with something objectively perceptible in the world. This contrasts with the claim made here that Whorf intended "objectification" to be a specific phenomenon pertaining to English and that refers specifically to giving imaginary entities the properties of objects (for example, spatial extent, substance, etc.). Silverstein remains unconvinced by my reading (and by my gloss of his). Given the ambiguity in Whorf's text, Silverstein's alternative term *referential projection* might be a more suitable way of labeling the more general process. More recently, Silverstein has used the term *objectualization* to specify the general process of construing the meanings of linguistic categories in terms of corresponding objects in the world. See the related remark on Silverstein's reading of Whorf in chapter 1, n9 above. See also Whorf (1956a, p. 261 – and the surrounding discussion) on the projection of language forms and Boas (1966b [1917], p. 207) on "the objectivating tendency of our mind."

32 Tensors, in Whorf's analysis, are a distinct "part of speech" in Hopi (1956a, pp. 143, 146). They are similar to our adverbs of time and degree and are used to express intensities. More discussion of tensors and of this particular example is given in Whorf's Hopi grammar (1946a [1939], pp. 170, 178–80).

33 For clarity I confine the discussion to the particular English patterns mentioned by Whorf. In chapter 2 of *Grammatical categories and cognition* we will examine this grammatical category more thoroughly.

34 The bridge here is, therefore, "filling a nominal slot in the grammar." The direction of influence is from the more complex forms (where a one-to-one match of form with meaning has been developed) to unitary forms (where such a match is not possible). The more complex form is then felt to be implicit in the unitary form, with all the attendant meaning implications thus entailed (cf. Kuryłowicz, 1964; Silverstein, 1979).

35 Whorf's well-known claim that the Hopi language has no forms that refer directly to what we call "time" (in, for instance, 1956a, pp. 57–58) must be read in this context. He consistently uses quotation marks to distinguish reference to our Western, objectified view of "time" from a more linguistically neutral view of time. The various attempts to discredit Whorf's Hopi data typically ignore this subtlety (see, for example, Malotki, 1983).

36 An argument can be made that the lines of influence must run in the reverse direction for lexical categories.

37 Even the difference between phase nouns (i.e., those referring to cycles) and physical object nouns can also be construed as a covert distinction in English, whose reactances include certain constraints on locative and locative-plus-article combinations (see Whorf, 1956a, p. 142, n5), but this fact has no especially interesting consequences in Whorf's illustrations.

38 Michael Silverstein (personal communication) suggests, I think correctly, that if Whorf had begun with Hopi selective categories, the English covert categories would have played a more prominent role in the argument. For obvious rhetorical reasons, he grounded the discussion in English.

39 At times Whorf appears to distinguish between culture and behavior, but there is not enough material to develop a good picture of what he might have intended. In this discussion, culture and behavioral norms are used interchangeably – the latter being the observable aspect of the patterns relevant to the former. Use of "culture" in opposition to "language" should be taken to imply not that language is not a part of culture, but rather that we are referring to the influence of a part on a broader whole, especially to other parts of the whole which are not specifically linguistic.

40 Whorf's emphasis on the mediating significance of the individual microcosm was somewhat unusual for this era. Although his interest in individual psychology pre-dated his contact with Sapir (e.g., Whorf, 1956a, pp. 35–42), his approach was consistent with the approach to culture taken by Sapir in his later work (see Darnell, 1986; and the papers collected in part 3 of Mandelbaum, 1949). It is important to be clear also that Whorf's focus is on the operation of the socially shared or collective aspect of individual functioning and not on individual personal experiences or associations (see 1956a, p. 36).

3 Approaches in anthropological linguistics: typical ethnographic case studies

1 Characteristically, Lee did not cite references in this article. The wording in this passage, however, is reminiscent of some of Sapir and Whorf's terminology and is the closest Lee ever came to a direct reference to their ideas. Given the date of publication and her academic affiliations in California, it is most likely she was familiar with the ideas of Sapir. The wording is also reminiscent of the approaches of Humboldt and Cassirer.

2 I do not mean to suggest here that there is no difference between grammar and lexicon (as traditionally conceived) in their relations to the broader cultural world. Substantively, grammatical categories may be more general than lexical ones. Formally, the lexicon may exhibit a higher degree of susceptibility to speaker awareness as contrasted with grammatical phenomena of other types (Brown and Lenneberg, 1954; Silverstein, 1981a). The argument here is only against the equation of lexemes with culture (in opposition to the rest of grammar) and with the underlying premise that structure and meaning are separable in this way.

3 Mathiot (1967a; 1968; 1969) introduces an elaborate abstract analytic framework for semantic analysis which cannot be further described here without serious digression from our topic. Suffice it to say that while she generates many important insights regarding the semantics of grammatical number, they do not appear to stem from or depend on the formalism in any significant way.

4 Although Hoijer was obviously familiar with Whorf's work (see Hoijer, 1946), there is no mention of him in his 1964b [1948] piece written prior to the reprinting of Whorf's key articles in 1949 (Trager, 1950 [1949]).

5 The research conducted by Osgood, Suci, and their associates is not reviewed here because, for the most part, it is concerned with purely linguistic responses, what might be called experimental studies of lexical semantics, and because its methodological approach systematically obscures just the sort of differences we are concerned with. The basic approach and findings of this tradition are presented in Osgood, Suci, and Tannenbaum (1957). For an account of an attempt to incorporate a nonlinguistic element into such studies, see Osgood (1960). The study by Kaplan (1954) is concerned with interpreting personality variables on the basis of Rorschach responses (not too successfully).

6 This would be called an ergative pattern in current terminology. See Silverstein (1976a) for a discussion.

7 Hoijer also may have intended this analysis to extend Whorf's arguments about the tendency of English speakers to read into nature "fictional acting entities [i.e., underlying agents], simply because our verbs must have substantives in front of them [i.e., surface subjects]" (Whorf, 1956a, p. 242).

8 Clearly this is a problem with all semantic interpretation not grounded in wide comparative perspective. Specifically, compare this view with the discussion by Kuryłowicz (1973a [1946]) of the cognitive logic of ergative patterning. For some contemporary remarks on the possible cultural significance of Navaho case-marking patterns, see Witherspoon (1980). Most of the criticisms raised in this section continue to apply to the latter.

9 Hoijer (1954, p. 100) also makes passing mention (without references) to work on Navaho religion by Washington Mathews and Father Berard Haile.

10 In a recent study which is similar in approach to Hoijer's, Fusi (1985) analyzes the semantics of certain Māori "possessives" and suggests a relation to Māori cultural conceptions of ownership and possession. The linguistic analysis is perceptive and the "nonlinguistic" cultural correlate more plausible than Hoijer's. However, Fusi remains fully within the tradition described here in that he does not spell out the language–culture linkage precisely (it remains a "thematic association") and does not show that the linguistic and cultural patterns are distinctively associated (it remains a case study). No argument is offered as to why the linguistic forms should be considered causal.

11 The interdisciplinary conference on the Whorfian problem organized by Hoijer in 1954 foundered on just this problem of the place and relevance of meaning in the study of language (Hoijer, 1954).

12 See Mathiot (1969, p. 251) on form–meaning variation in language, but not necessarily in cognition.

4   Approaches in anthropological linguistics: theoretical and methodological advances

1 Carroll (1967) lists publications stemming from this project.

2 We will not be concerned with those who simply presuppose without adequate empirical data the universality of fundamental language forms.

3 Hymes (1963) presents some historical perspective on the concern for typological approaches. He discusses the cycles of interest in typology in the history of linguistics, the different emphases of typological concern, and the leading contemporary exponents of this approach.

4 Hymes (1974b) also uses the term "style" in a somewhat different sense, as will be discussed further below.

5 In general Jakobson and other members of the Prague School of linguistics were consistently concerned with typological issues, even when this perspective was out of favor in American linguistics (Hymes, 1963, p. 95).

6 The specific study Hymes gives as an illustration is too idiosyncratic (and unconvincing) to warrant detailed description here. Parts of it are described further below in another context.

7 Friedrich, in the piece considered here, is concerned with making methodological issues explicit. A similar orientation – but somewhat less developed – informs his article on "Shape in grammar" (1970).

8 Friedrich's first component corresponds to the types of basic verbal categories derived by Jakobson and called "specific content" by Hymes. Friedrich, then, is typologizing within one of these basic categories, exploring variation at one level of generality lower than Jakobson.

9 Formal is meant quite broadly here as the particular arrangement of basic features of the substantive dimension. Since these basic features are themselves substantive, the pattern is not "purely formal" in the sense of without content. Friedrich discusses this problem in terms of context-free and context-dependent descriptions of the same phenomenon (1974, p. 35).

10 Since this entire argument is summarized from Silverstein (especially 1976a and 1981a), specific citation will be made only for quoted passages.

11 For this simplified account, all examples will be confined to the level of the individual proposition. It should be noted, however, that a major goal of Silverstein's approach was to show that case-marking phenomena cannot, in fact, be adequately understood at the level of individual propositions and that attempts to do so are ultimately misleading.

12 Silverstein distinguished between discourse-reference ("pragmatic" reference) and propositional-reference ("semantic" reference), corresponding, respectively, to the extensional and intensional reference-values of language signs. The two kinds of referential features correspond to these two kinds of referential value. As should be clear, these sorts of features are distinct from the "basic features" introduced earlier in the discussion of Friedrich's work.

13 Silverstein (1976a) showed that the ordering of features can be established independently of any considerations of case marking. This may be so from a formal point of view, but, as a matter of practice, specific features are of interest precisely because they in fact appear to be the ones relevant to describing a specific grammatical pattern – in this instance, case marking. Further, while the feature space can be ordered independently of any *one* grammatical dimension, it cannot be adequately ordered independently of *any* grammatical dimensions whatsoever. In this sense the ordering is independent of any single grammatical dimension, but is dependent, ultimately, on evidence derived from the whole array of such dimensions available for analysis. This issue is explored further in chapter 2 of *Grammatical categories and cognition*.

14 The argument developed in this section immediately followed the discussion of case marking in Silverstein (1973). I present here Silverstein's (1980; 1981a) more recent development of these points, which differs in certain respects from the preliminary formulation.

15 Silverstein (1981a) gave a more formal characterization of the principle of ordering in the following terms:

> It would appear that, insofar as the markedness of noun phrase categorizations is concerned, languages follow an ordering principle based on what we can term THE UNAVOIDABILITY AND TRANSPARENCY OF METAPRAGMATIC REFERENCE.   (1981a, p. 241)

The precise meaning of this characterization can only be grasped by studying the original argument in some detail, but it essentially attempts to characterize how the ordering of noun-phrase types is "natural" from the point of view of events of speaking. Again, more detail is given in chapter 2 of the companion case study to the present volume.

16 The experiments alluded to were conducted under hypotheses other than Silverstein's. He has reinterpreted their findings as consistent with his own analysis.

17 In fact, he explicitly avoids doing so (Silverstein, 1973, p. 20).

18 Only once, that is, unless one takes Whorf's prevailing concern for the errors of modern positive science and positivist philosophy as an *implicit* suggestion that this problem of the linguistic influences upon thought is of greater significance in our modern societies.

19   This should not be confused with Whorf's distinction between identifying a morphological form and understanding its *use*, by which he meant syntactic and semantic constraints on use of the form within the framework of the grammar. The focus here is on the overall utilization of language categories in cognitive and cultural activities – as the subsequent discussion will make clear.

20   Silverstein would call Wasco–Wishram a single dialect. For a fuller account of historical changes in Chinookan tense–aspect systems see Silverstein (1974). For more on Chinookan case-marking see Silverstein (1976a).

21   For more on this diminutive–augmentative contrast, see Silverstein (1981b; 1986b).

22   Hymes uses the shift in Sapir's views (from language as autonomous to language as functionally integrated) to show how step one and step two are conceptually independent. It may be, rather, that the shift in Sapir's views (if there is one) stems not from a shift within step two, but rather from a recognition of the inseparability of the two steps. Either way, Sapir's later theoretical work rejected the notion of an autonomous language.

23   The allusion to work on communicative functions is probably a reference to Jakobson (1960); cf. Hymes (1974a, p. 10).

24   Whorf's approach is characterized as joint determination ([3] in the schema) on the cultural dimension and either joint determination ([3] in the schema) or language primacy ([1] in the schema) on the individual level. Hymes underrated the significance of Whorf's remarks about the relatively conservative nature of language as opposed to the rest of culture, with the result that his joint determination is asymmetric in important ways, i.e., joint determination with language as dominant.

25   Silverstein is building here on a substantial body of research within anthropological linguistics on the context-dependent nature of some forms of reference and on the importance of the nonreferential functions of language. Regarding the latter, see Hymes (1974b, esp. pp. 435ff.) for a contrasting approach in terms of a dichotomy between the *referential* and *stylistic* functions of language.

26   The eventual introduction of a sixth factor can be foreseen given the structure of his argument, and a reformulation is currently being developed (Silverstein, 1985b; 1992): two factors concern the form and function of the described signal relative to reference, two factors will deal with the form and function of the metalinguistic signal relative to reference, and two factors will deal with the relationship of form and function between the described signal and the metalinguistic signal. Clarification of these points owes much to remarks by Silverstein, Richard Parmentier, and others at a workshop and conference on metapragmatics held at the Center for Psychosocial Studies, Chicago, in June and July 1985 (see Lucy, 1992).

27   In Silverstein (1985b) this becomes *unavoidable dual segmentability* to emphasize that "in segmenting a form . . . you also segment the form that counts in reference." A similar notion of duality is used to define *unavoidable referentiality* in Silverstein (1981b) and (1985b).

28   A more complete critique of this tradition is given in Silverstein (1979, pp. 208–16).

29   Since neither aspect nor status is indexical, Silverstein probably meant here to refer to Whorf's (1956a, pp. 144–45; pp. 113–15) discussion of the use in

Hopi of aspect in combination with an indexical category he called assertion or validity-form to achieve some of the meanings of English tense.

30 Notice that such a claim would have to extend to other accounts of intralinguistic shifts in form and meaning, such as the "laws of analogy" proposed by Kuryłowicz (1973b [1945–49]) for historical changes in languages. Some of these "laws" of historical change match quite closely the sort of interpretive shifts Whorf claims speakers are making. Silverstein (1979, p. 233) attempts just such an integration, that is, to account for Kurłowicz's laws by reference to a dialectical tension between ideology and structure.

31 See the clarification of these terms developed in chapter 2.

32 This is not to deny certain strong similarities between the phenomena discovered by Whorf and those discovered later by the transformational grammarians, but only to assert that the two sets of specific theoretical terms had different meanings.

33 To some extent an argument can be made concerning the doubly misleading nature of overt categories (see discussion in chapter 2), but not by *opposing* them to covert categories in the way Silverstein develops the argument.

34 The argument can also be made that the analysis of the nature of experienced reality is precisely an analysis of the language's categories (covert as well as overt). This is, perhaps, the force of the immediately following remark by Silverstein:

> Whorf is thus constrasting native awareness of the suggestive referential patterns of surface lexical forms, with the linguist's awareness of the cryptotypic semantic structure behind those surface forms, achieved by excruciating analysis in a comparative framework.   (1981b, p. 19)

But the statement is difficult to assess given the placement of overt and covert categories in opposition and the various possible interpretations here for term "awareness."

35 This whole line of argument, the generalization of Whorf's approach to nonreferential functions of speech, is more fully developed in Silverstein (1979).

5 Approaches in comparative psycholinguistics: experimental studies on the lexical coding of color

1 The importance of Whorf's work for the development of psycholinguistics is discussed in Casagrande (1956, p. 42; 1960, pp. 777–78), Sebeok (1965, pp. v–vi), Newman (1967, p. 6), and Brown (1976, pp. 127–29).

2 There is a long history of research on color terminology which will not be taken up here as it has played only a minor role in this tradition. For reviews of this material see Segall, Campbell, and Herskovits (1966, pp. 137–48), Berlin and Kay (1969, pp. 134–51), and Bornstein (1973).

3 Lenneberg, perhaps stimulated by his own German background (see E. R. Brown, 1975, p. v), first became interested in these problems through his work on the philosophy of E. Cassirer (Lenneberg, 1955).

4 Though jointly authored, the theoretical approach in this study is explicitly credited to Lenneberg (Lenneberg and Roberts, 1956, p. iii).

5   The brevity of Whorf's discussion can be accounted for in part by the role these examples play as an introduction to his overall argument. Lenneberg's discussion does not take account of this factor or of the logic of the other empirical examples presented by Whorf.

6   Lenneberg (1962) later somewhat altered his view that language was fundamentally denotational, recognizing a difference between meaning and reference and the irreducibility of the former to the latter. But in the absence of an understanding of the social nature of language, he was forced to conclude that meaning must reflect the operation of innate, biologically governed concepts.

7   Later, in Lenneberg and Roberts (1956), this dismissal of the need for comparative work was modified, and the circumstances under which inter-cultural comparison is necessary were characterized.

8   At this point in his remarks Lenneberg added the following footnote: "These conditions, aspects, and relationships are primarily but not exclus-ively expressed by grammatical categories." So, by his own analysis, the aspects of meaning involved in codification tend to lie in grammatical, not lexical forms.

9   Note that the use here of the term "objectification" differs from Whorf's. "Objectification" here involves intentional equation of the meaning of a linguis-tic form with an object or an objective property (a property of an object).

10   At times it even appears that Lenneberg would have liked to have dealt with codability quite independently of any consideration of meaning (or content) whatsoever by examining, for example, "the efficiency of the code within stated contexts" (1953, p. 467). Recall also the remark just cited in the text regarding the theoretical possibility of excluding considerations of meaning entirely. (Notice, however, that use of "intuited" meaning is in fact crucial to his procedure.) Whereas Whorf placed the analysis of meaning at the center of his concerns, Lenneberg saw it as peripheral.

11   Many years later Brown recalled several more practical motives for choosing to work with color and to take an intra-cultural approach:

Eric and I picked a lexical contrast rather than a grammatical one to work with because it looked simpler and because we had neither the means nor the impulse to travel to one of the Indian reservations in the Southwest. We planned to test Whorf's hypothesis *within one language[:] English.*
(Brown, 1976, p. 128)

We allowed ourselves to imagine a universal law relating referent codability to recognition ... On this grand scale it seemed a matter of indifference whether the first test were intra-cultural or inter-cultural and, of course, convenience favored the former.   (Brown, 1976, p. 129)

12   Lenneberg and Roberts even made explicit that they intended to restrict the informants' range of response:

before each informant names individual colors, it is suggested that he be shown the extent of the entire sample of colors to be named. This is essential because in many languages differing degrees of precision in naming are possible.   (1956, p. 21)

See also Brown and Lenneberg (1954, p. 459).

13 Lenneberg later formalized his argument (Lenneberg and Roberts, 1956, pp. 3–4) in a way which makes the underlying emphasis on generic language–thought relations clear. He described the goal as being to establish experimentally the relationship between a series of language conditions C_i and a series of corresponding nonlinguistic behaviors K_i in a given language. The degree of overall correspondence can be labeled F. This process can be repeated with a second language, and the degree of correspondence can be labeled V. A comparison of the two groups is between the degrees of correspondences F and V and not between the two language conditions (i.e., C_i and C_j), because the latter are incommensurable. This makes explicit that the focus of the intra-cultural approach is on mechanisms (or relations) of Language and Thought interaction for which each individual language becomes then merely another token of the type Language, albeit with stronger or weaker correspondence to the nonlinguistic conditions. Thus, Lenneberg wrote:

> The reason for doing cross-cultural work in this instance is to prevent us from over-generalizing our theory rather than to validate our hypothesis.
> (Lenneberg and Roberts, 1956, p. 4)

Clearly, this is not a methodology for investigating the significance of language differences.

14 Lenneberg himself later came to realize that this set of lexical items cannot possibly stand for all of language (Lenneberg, 1962, p. 103). His reformulation is discussed further below.

15 Claims for the universal similarity of the perception of color (Rivers, 1901; Bornstein, 1973; 1975) and for the universal presence of equivalent color stimuli in the environment (Segall, Campbell, and Herskovits, 1966, p. 40; McNeill, 1972) remain somewhat controversial. For reviews and analyses of the relative importance of perceptual apparatus and social environment in the development of color term systems, see Ember (1978), Zollinger (1984), and Zimmer (1984).

16 These arguments about essential meaning difference apply equally well to both figures 1 and 2 in Lenneberg and Roberts (1956).

17 Reviewing this research on color, Hickerson concluded:

> The approach is, in effect, ethnocentric, since the standard was the ability of the native language to match the imposed categories set by the selection of color samples. (1975, p. 319)

18 Lenneberg later acknowledged that the criterion for selecting language categories was their utility for testing:

> The language of experience is particularly well-suited for research because its *referents* have ... advantages over the *referents* of most other types of words ... (1967, p. 337, my italics)

The advantages he subsequently cites make no reference to language as such.

19 The core of Lenneberg's later stance can be captured by quoting a few lines summarizing his position. Notice that his conceptualization of language alternates between biologically given universals and individually created

variation. There is no recognition of the possibility of a social or cultural level of organization which is neither universal nor individual.

The words that constitute the dictionary of a natural language are a sample of labels of categories natural to our species . . .

The abstractness underlying meanings in general . . . may best be understood by considering concept-formation the primary cognitive process, and naming . . . the secondary cognitive process . . . Cognition must be the psychological manifestation of a physiological process . . . *Words tag the processes by which the species deals cognitively with its environment.*

This theoretical position also elucidates the problem of translation or the equation of meanings across natural languages. If words label modes of cognizing, we would expect that all semantic systems would have certain formal commonalities . . . Man's cognition functions within biologically given limits. On the other hand, there is also freedom within these limits. Thus every individual may have highly idiosyncratic thoughts or conceptualize in a peculiar way or, in fact, may choose somewhat different modes of cognitive organization at different times faced with identical sensory stimuli . . . Given this degree of freedom, it becomes reasonable to assume that natural languages always have universally understandable types of semantics, but may easily have different extensions of meanings, and that, therefore, specific semantic categories are not coterminous across languages.

It does not follow from this that differences in semantics are signs of obligatory differences in thought processes, as assumed by Whorf (1956[a]) and many others. The modes of conceptualization that happen to be tagged by a given language need not, and apparently do not, exert restrictions upon an individual's freedom of conceptualizing.   (1967, pp. 332–34)

There is some evidence of a possible shift in Lenneberg's view in his last writings (for example, 1975, pp. 24–25).

20   Martin (1986) provides a history of the use and misuse of the "snow" example which rightly criticizes the lack of careful attention to linguistic analysis of "Eskimo" languages. Here, inattention to linguistic detail represents only part of the problem.

21   Although Whorf was making the characteristically Boasian point that what is treated by lexical alternation in one language may be handled grammatically in another, it should be emphasized that the "snow" example is plucked from one of his popular articles, where he made no pretense of developing a formal argument.

22   In a retrospective article Brown indicated two pragmatic motives for choosing the domain of color:

1. The -etic level of description for color by which we meant a culture-free, finely-differentiated description already existed. More than a century of psycho-physical study of absolute thresholds and difference limens in terms of the dimensions of hue, brightness, and saturation had given us the basic description we needed. Furthermore, a large sample of precision-manufactured color chips intended to be psychologically evenly spaced was already in existence and could be purchased from the Munsell Color Company.   (1976, p. 129)

2. The cross-cultural files contained very many instances of differences between languages in color lexicon.   (1976, p. 130)

These remarks confirm that Brown and Lenneberg believed that they had a culture-free description of color. That the category color itself might be problematic or that the scientific description was a refinement of our cultural conception of color was not seriously considered. The "cross-cultural files" referred to here are presumably the Human Relations Area Files – mentioned in Brown and Lenneberg (1954, p. 458) as the Yale Cross-Cultural Index. The variety of color lexica across languages played no substantive role in Brown and Lenneberg's discussion, however.

23 Brown and Lenneberg's study was not, strictly speaking, comparative, but comparative data gathered by the same methods are mentioned in the discussion (1954, p. 461).

24 The emphasis on elementary (irreducible) building blocks of experience is drawn from the logical empiricists/positivists (discussion and references in Lenneberg and Roberts, 1956, pp. 30–31). Wittgenstein's (1958 [1953]) criticisms of this tradition are pertinent here.

25 Brown and Lenneberg hedge on whether Whorf really made the claim for a causal relation of language to thought, for reasons that should be clear from the discussion in chapter 2. Their own contribution in this regard (1954, p. 457) is quite preliminary.

26 For comparison with the work of Berlin and Kay (1969), which will be described later, note that the 240 Munsell colors were all at maximum saturation for a given hue and brightness. No justification for the use of maximum saturation colors is given. Brown comments:

As one leafs through the [Munsell] Book of Color it is apparent that most of the highly codable colors are on the perimeter where one finds the maximally saturated version of each hue. We thought it important to include in our array some colors of very high codability and, therefore, some of high saturation. There were, however, 240 chips at maximum saturation and we could hardly use them all. So we asked five judges to examine a systematic array of 240 colors and pick out the best red, orange, yellow, green, blue, purple, pink, and brown. These terms are the most frequent color terms in English.   (1976, pp. 130–31)

The set of twenty-four probes included these 8 color chips as well as 16 others drawn so as to sample the "color space" evenly (i.e., apparently, to sample the 240 maximum saturation colors evenly).

27 This array was a pared-down version of the 240-sample array of colors at maximum saturation, now arranged with hue and brightness displayed in two dimensions in sequential order. However, the array was split in two with one part above the other for presentational convenience.

28 An additional problem with this approach is that the encoders (subjects giving names) were naming relative to a framework of 24 test colors. The recognition task operated within a framework of 120 colors in an array. Thus the contextual conditions differ substantially between the naming and recognition conditions. Brown (1976, p. 133) discusses the problem and says had it been corrected, the correlation might have been much higher. Lantz and Stefflre (1964, p. 480) controlled for this difference by exposing the full

120-sample array before naming. If Brown and Lenneberg's scoring technique is used on essentially the same conditions (Brown and Lenneberg's condition C is the same as Lantz and Steffire's condition III), the relationship is in fact somewhat weaker and still not significant ($r = .32$ rather than .415).

29 The contextual determination of reference may be taken as a general principle of speech. Speakers select specific terms depending on the degree of precision necessary to extend (pick out a referent) adequately in a given context. The term *flower* may serve to distinguish a given plant adequately when the only alternatives are trees and rocks. A term such as *rose* may be necessary if other flowering plants are present. The effectiveness of the term *flower* as an encoding, then, depends on the referential context. Elsewhere, Brown (1958a) himself discusses just this point.

30 Lenneberg and Roberts (1956) provide an extended discussion (1956, Step II, pp. 15–17) of the "Theoretically Possible Properties of Stimulus Groups, Given the Nature of the Continuum" which includes, significantly, from the point of view of future research, such features as the existence, size, and centrality of a category focus. This is followed (1956, Step IV, pp. 17–21) by a description of the procedure used for eliciting color terms (without stimuli present) and then mapping them and their foci relative to a referential grid of 320 Munsell colors at maximum saturation. (Mapping is not part of the Brown and Lenneberg, 1954, procedure despite the allusion to it by Lenneberg and Roberts, 1956, p. 31.) The results, in the form of a composite mapping (1956, Step VI, pp. 21–30), are presented for each of three groups: English speakers, Zuni monolingual speakers, and English–Zuni bilinguals. These composite mappings show the location of the most commonly used verbal encodings and their foci. In this study English color terms were apparently elicited from English speakers rather than being drawn from word-frequency lists as in Brown and Lenneberg (1954); thus English has two foci each for "blue" (named *blue* and *light blue*) and for "green" (named *green* and *light green*). The compound terms would not have been encountered by those working from word-frequency lists. Lenneberg and Roberts say: "It does not matter in scoring that some of these names appear to be composed of two words" (1956, p. 27). This effectively discards the original idea behind using Zipf's law. It is not clear what effect including these foci in the target sample would have had on the codability findings of Brown and Lenneberg (1954). See also Lenneberg (1957, 1961) in regard to the form of color categories and categories in general. Brown (1976) points out, aptly, that much of subsequent research on focal colors is really presaged in these discussions. Berlin and Kay mention the Lenneberg and Roberts study only briefly (1969, pp. 5, 103, 149).

31 The age of those in the Zuni sample is supposedly a problem because they are unrepresentative of the population at large. But certainly they are representative of monolingual Zuni – especially when compared with speakers of other languages. Note in this regard that the Harvard and Radcliffe students used as the English sample are hardly "representative" of all English speakers.

32 This information on the Zuni study was presented within the context of a discussion of the implications of the color codability findings for research in philosophy, communication, psychology, and anthropology. It was not a focus of the empirical portion of the report.

33 Lenneberg and Roberts (1956, p. 24) use a solidus (/) to indicate a glottal stop in Zuni.

34 An examination of Lenneberg and Roberts's Zuni data reveals that the term covering our "yellow" and "orange," *ihupz/inna*, is tied as one of the two most frequently mentioned terms and that a term for "orange" is also very common: */olenchi(nanne)* ('like the orange' – where */olenchi*, 'orange,' is presumably a loan word derived from English *orange*). (Compare also in this regard Hickerson's, 1975, suggestion that Zuni has two different kinds, or levels, of color terms.) However, since repetitions (using the same expression for more than one color) are not indicated, no conclusion can be drawn about codability as measured by interpersonal agreement.

35 Because of the ambiguous use of the gloss 'becoming,' it is not clear how Newman's and Hickerson's data interrelate. It would appear that *lhupz/i-nna*, 'be or become yellow [verbal],' is Newman's A and that */oneya-nne*, 'pale, yellowed (like corn pollen) [nominal],' is Newman's B. The nominal form would then refer to an 'intrinsic' color.

36 Brown later observed: "[Brown and Lenneberg (1954)] caused no great stir . . . A few friends took notice, and it became fairly common to hear that the Whorf thesis had been confirmed in its weak form but not in its strong form" (1976, p. 134).

37 Virtually all of the work in this latter category was done by persons associated with Brown or Lenneberg at Harvard. Other reviews of research in this tradition during this period can be found in Brown (1965, pp. 332–48; 1976); see also Lucy and Shweder (1979).

38 This approach was first developed by Lantz (1963, cited by Lantz and Stefflre, 1964). A summary of this work is given in Brown (1965, pp. 332–40).

39 Lantz and Stefflre's argument bears some similarity to Vygotsky's (1987 [1934]) proposals for studying the development of inner speech by observing children's external egocentric speech.

40 Most comparative work on color (by, for instance, Ray, 1953; Lenneberg and Roberts, 1956; and Landar, Ervin and Horowitz, 1960) lacked a cognitive dimension. Some unpublished material apparently exists; for example, Lenneberg (1967, p. 348) reported a comparison of hue discrimination by English, Zuni, and Navaho speakers. Brown (1956, pp. 291–94) described a study using color stimuli with Navaho and English speakers, but the focus of the study was not on color or color terms.

41 This was the core of Lenneberg's (1967, pp. 344, 354) criticism of the communication accuracy measure. Brown (1965, pp. 333, 335, 340) was apparently more willing to argue that the measure still bore a relation to a specific language.

42 Lucy and Shweder (1979) attempted to provide a more language-characteristic measure of communication accuracy by developing a measure of "group communication accuracy" which depended on aggregating a sample of judgments as to what were good descriptors.

43 Lenneberg (1960; 1962) elsewhere raised functional questions, but quasi-evolutionary ones rather than socially constituted ones.

44 Lucy (1981) takes up the problem of relativity of use in a comparative study, but without reference to Lantz and Lenneberg's findings.

M

45 By disciplinary affiliation, Berlin and Kay's work belongs in the tradition of anthropological linguistics. However, their work is grouped here with the comparative psycholinguistics tradition because of the strong historical continuity in substantive concerns (color), methodological techniques (experimental), and even theoretical assumptions (primacy of denotation). The subsequent development of a psychophysiological explanation for their findings is also consistent with this placement.

46 The "universal" here is an *implicational universal* (i.e., *if* X is the case in language$_i$, *then* Y will also be the case). See the discussion in chapter 4 above and in Berlin and Kay (1969, ch. 4).

47 There were minor modifications of the Lenneberg and Roberts procedure: a neutral hue series (white–grey–black) was added to the array, thereby increasing the number of chips from 320 to 329; only "basic color terms" were sought during elicitation (and used during mapping) rather than all commonly used color expressions; informants were instructed to indicate the colors which "under any conditions" could be called by the name rather than "all of the color chips subsumed under one name"; informants were allowed to indicate more than one focal chip; typically, only one bilingual informant was used for each language rather than several monolinguals; and informants were retested on three occasions (Lenneberg and Roberts, 1956, pp. 19–20; Berlin and Kay, 1969, pp. 5, 7, 103–104).

48 Berlin and Kay's (1969) methods, findings, and theories have been the subject of a number of critiques (for instance, Wescott, 1970; Hickerson, 1971; Caskey-Sirmons and Hickerson, 1977; Durbin, 1972; Collier, 1973; see also the references in the discussion earlier of Zuni and other cases where noncolorimetric values are joined with what we would call "color"). The critiques, however valid, have in no way affected the general acceptance of the research. In addition to Kay and McDaniel (1978) there have been some other extensions (e.g., Hays, Margolis, Naroll, and Perkins, 1972; Heider, 1971; 1972a,b; Collier *et al.*, 1976; Burgess Kempton, and MacLaury, 1983; Kay and Kempton, 1984) and revisions (e.g., Kay, 1975). See also Hardin (1988) and the references in n15 above. Work using this paradigm continues to the present.

49 For example, one problem with the original Berlin and Kay formulation was that most people of whatever language group had never seen colors equivalent to the focal colors in the array (colors of this degree of purity occur either rarely or not at all in nature); so the proposal of successive encoding of such colors by various languages was very problematic. This problem is alleviated somewhat by the reworking in Kay and McDaniel (1978, p. 617).

50 Some of the required work in this area was done by Heider (1971; 1972a, b). See also Collier *et al.* (1976), Garro (1986), and Lucy and Shweder (1979; 1988).

51 For the 20 languages directly investigated, the criteria involved what would count as a basic color term and what aspects of meaning (here, denotational value in the color array) will count in the comparison. For the additional 78 languages coded from written sources, the criteria involved what would count as a basic color term and, given the number of terms and some translation values, what the denotational value of those terms must be.

52 E. Rosch published under the name E. Heider before 1973.

53 Heider's rationale for not taking up Lantz and Stefflre's findings is not entirely clear. She seemed (see Heider, 1972b, p. 11) to draw on Lenneberg's (1967, ch. 8) argument that the structure of a language was bypassed by the communication accuracy measure of codability. This need not be the case with communication accuracy. (See the following note; also Lucy and Shweder, 1979, Experiment V.)

54 Heider (1972b, p. 19) dismisses Stefflre *et al.*'s results because they employ the Farnsworth–Munsell array and thus involve no focal colors. Ironically, she does not see the implications of this for the general validity of her own results using the Berlin and Kay array.

55 Heider (1972b, p. 17) did conduct a numerical correction for discriminability differences, but it was apparently unreliable.

56 Witkowski and Brown (1982) have criticized Lucy and Shweder's (1979) efforts to produce a perceptually unbiased array. Their criticisms founder, however, on an ambiguous use of the notion of "salience." See discussion in Lucy and Shweder (1988, n2).

57 The category boundary is defined in a separate psychophysical task as "that wavelength at which an equal mixture of green and blue is perceived" by American English-speaking subjects (Kay and Kempton, 1984, p. 68). In subsequent tasks both groups show noticeable departures from the psychophysical patterns predicted from this scaling.

6   Approaches in comparative psycholinguistics: experimental studies on grammatical categories

1 Brown's initial comparison centered on the status of words not shared between the child and adult lists. It is not clear whether the general characterizations of vocabulary differences were made on the same basis.

2 Brown (1958b, p. 253) separated "form-class" patterns such as noun and verb from what he called "cases of forced observation" in grammar such as the application of verb tense. As will become clear in chapter 2 of *Grammatical categories and cognition*, the subdivision of nouns into mass and particular nouns (equivalent to mass and individual nouns in Whorf's terminology and to mass and count nouns in contemporary terminology) which Brown introduced in this third study (1958b, p. 250) as "form classes" can reasonably be regarded as "forced observations." In fact, parts of Brown's (1957, p. 3; 1958b, p. 250) own discussions are consistent with this interpretation.

3 For mass nouns the experimenter began "Have you ever seen any sib?" For particular nouns the experimenter began "Do you know what a sib is?" Brown did not give the full protocols for these noun cases.

4 Brown (1958b, pp. 252–53) reports that children do better than adults on this particular task, apparently because adults do not believe that it is actually a naming task and respond in unexpected ways. Brown argued, however, that in a more appropriate adult task (for instance, learning some technical subvocabulary) the expected effects would be found.

5 Of course, an argument could be made that adult speech directed to children will be tailored in these ways. Brown (1965, p. 339) seemed to suggest this at one point, but he did not elaborate.

6 Brown (1958b, pp. 255–58) pointed toward such a functional relativity at another point when discussing the possible influence of degree of societal complexity or differentiation on the tendency to create specialized superordinate and subordinate terms. Also relevant here is his argument for the importance of "function" or "usual utility" in the development and deployment of vocabulary items (Brown, 1958a; 1965, pp. 317–21, 328).

7 Building on the work of Bruner, Goodnow, and Austin (1956), Brown (1956, 1958b) attempted to use a single formal definition of "category," whether linguistic or nonlinguistic. From a contemporary perspective, his definition seems too broad, but his effort points up the continuing need for a systematic, unified theory of what constitutes a category.

8 Although Maclay's (1958) orientation was primarily methodological and he did not discuss or take an explicit stand on key theoretical issues, his implicit framework was much the same as that of Carroll and Casagrande. Another study, encountered too late to be incorporated into the discussion but which is similar in spirit to the work of these three researchers, is that of Hooton and Hooton (1977), which compared shape and color classification preference as a function of adjectival word order. It seems to have had no impact on subsequent discussions.

9 Carroll and Casagrande argued that "there are no boundaries between the parts of experience except those which are created by our perceptions" (1958, p. 19). Language categories are then applied and "are 'arbitrary' in the sense that they could be replaced by other, equally acceptable ways of categorizing experience" (1958, p. 19). But they did not suggest that these categories were completely without constraint. In general they believed that the discovery of commonalities across languages is an empirical problem.

10 Rather than defining what was a grammatical category, Carroll and Casagrande provided examples from English:

Not all categories of experience are symbolized by discrete words; some are represented by grammatical phenomena such as are indicated in the following contrasts: *horse* v. *horse's* [± possessive]; *petunia* v. *petunias*; [± plural]; *he* v. *him* [± possessive]; *ecstacy* v. *ecstatic* [noun v. adjective]; *reprimand* v. *reprimanded* [± past]; *green* v. *greener* [± comparative]; *the very old man* v. *the very idea* [adverb v. adjective]; and the classic *dog bites man* v. *man bites dog* [± patient].   (1958, p. 19, my insertions in brackets)

11 Carroll and Casagrande emphasized the important point that the success of translation depends partly on the purpose of translation. The notion of a single "best" translation that is independent of any context or use is problematic. See also Casagrande (1954) on this.

12 Carroll and Casagrande also mentioned some of the inherent trade-offs involved in using an experimental approach in a cross-cultural situation:·

Use of [an interlinguistic design] entails an advantage and a danger: it may become possible to select linguistic features in two languages which are strikingly and fundamentally different, but it becomes difficult to assure oneself that any observed behavioral correlates are *not* due to irrelevant factors such as dissimilar cultural backgrounds and experiences.

> (Carroll and Casagrande, 1958, p. 22)

Casagrande's empirical results particularly highlighted this problem.

13 Maclay (1958, p. 221) preferred the term linguistic *response* here.

14 All Hopi speakers were fluent in Hopi but spoke English as well, with varying degrees of competence.

15 Carroll did not present a statistical analysis. Since the results were not reported by individual subject, no *post hoc* analysis is possible.

16 Carroll analyzed the data as if the subject responses were independent and finds a significant correlation ($p < .01$) between language and nonlinguistic response pattern. As Carroll admitted, this statistical treatment cannot be justified.

17 Carroll and Casagrande (1958, pp. 19, 26) consistently distinguished lexical and syntactic phenomena rather than seeing them as interrelated.

18 These are the same Navaho classifier forms that were discussed by Hoijer and that were reviewed in chapter 3 above. They were a popular example of an "exotic" grammatical category in the 1950s (see, for instance, Brown, 1956; 1958b).

19 This task yielded the clearest results of the several tasks administered by Casagrande (1960 [1956], pp. 779–82). It was interposed between the other procedures "well after the child had become accustomed to the experimental situation" (Carroll and Casagrande, 1958, p. 27). To my knowledge, results from the other tasks have never been reported.

20 Although Casagrande sometimes treated the verb forms as encouraging attention to "shape or form" (Carroll and Casagrande, 1958, p. 30), he also made clear that verb-form classes can also refer to material (Carroll and Casagrande, 1958, pp. 28, 31). In this example, rope and stick can be seen as different either in shape or in material. In some of the other items, shape alone varies, but material never serves as a basis for classification by itself.

21 Apparently each child's dominant language was used to administer the task and a Navaho interpreter was used for the Navaho-speaking children (Carroll and Casagrande, 1958, p. 28).

22 Casagrande analyzed the data by item. However, since each subject did each item, the results across items were not independent for statistical purposes. Nor did he test against the possibility of random selections – which might have been a problem in the case of the English-dominant group. However, given the regular pattern of the data and the sample size, the results are probably reliable.

23 These data were not analyzed statistically. Without a breakdown by subjects, *post hoc* analysis is not possible.

24 Despite the obvious logic of including such white English-speaking children in the study (i.e., so as to have one set of subjects with the same language and different cultures and another set with the same culture but different languages), it appears that the comparison group was not part of the original design: it is not mentioned in Casagrande (1960 [1956]), and its inclusion was not strongly motivated in Carroll and Casagrande (1958, pp. 28, 30).

25 To my knowledge, precise results of this study of Harlem schoolchildren have never been published.

26 Casagrande grouped three- and four-year-olds for the Navaho, but not for the English. If the English scores are also grouped for these two ages, then the Navaho score is slightly higher.

27 Although Casagrande (in contrast to Maclay – see below) tried to be careful about the semantics of these verb-stem classes – referring to matches predicted by them simply as "verb stem" choices – the overall nonlinguistic hypothesis about the relative ordering of "form" to the other dimensions of classification must tacitly accept the characterization of these classes having to do with "form." If the stems distinguish more than (or something other than) "form," then the linkage to the "form" of referents in the classification task actually has more to do with a happenstance of our provisional label for the classes than with any fact about meaning patterns in Navaho.

28 Fishman went on to cite Hockett's (1954) suggestion that language patterns will be more influential in some verbally dependent activities such as story-telling, religion, and philosophy than in more practical ones. This whole line of thought points toward a functional relativity of the sort mentioned elsewhere in this chapter and discussed in detail in chapter 4.

29 Maclay (1958, p. 222) did not give the actual forms, but his initial glosses corresponded to Casagrande's: 'rope-like,' 'long,' and 'fabric-like.'

30 Maclay's formal methodology was relatively rigorous. Some items were included to test the validity of the design, and there were also three pre-test items to insure that subjects understood the instructions. Presentation order and the arrangement of objects before the subjects were randomized. Maclay apparently gave instructions in English to all subjects except Navaho monolinguals (half of that group), for whom an interpreter was used.

31 Although Maclay says "Function" in the text, his table of test items says "Function or Material." Inspection of individual items reveals that a material-based match is possible in each of the items theoretically pitting function against form. All language groups prefer "Function or Material" as a basis for grouping when it is available.

32 Ironically, the crucial "Color" oppositions are between "blue" and "green," which are not distinguished grammatically or lexically in Navaho (Landar, Ervin, and Horowitz, 1960; Ervin, 1961).

33 Recall, however, that some linguists, notably Hoijer, had in fact stressed the frequency question and that others such as Hymes and Newman were well aware of it (see Hymes, 1961a, pp. 327–28, on Maclay's study).

34 Neither study made mention of the other, even though they were both part of the Southwest Project in Comparative Psycholinguistics.

35 Maclay's wording here is a bit odd – he seems to be suggesting that similar categories might exist but not be obligatory. Alternatively, he may just mean that if a category does not exist, it cannot be obligatory.

36 Using Maclay's own formulation, this can be stated more precisely. His general hypothesis was as follows:

> If Language A unites referents x and y and Language B separates them, then speakers of Language A should be more likely than speakers of Language B to exhibit the same non-linguistic response to them. (1958, p. 221)

Maclay never showed that Language B (i.e., English, "Pueblo") separated the referents that Language A (i.e., Navaho) grouped.

37 Maclay's ignorance of other work may account for his lack of excitement

about one interesting pattern in his data: when available, "Function or Material" was the preferred dimension of sorting for all groups. Considering both his and Casagrande's studies together, the most plausible ordering of preferences for the groups would be as follows:

English: material/function > form > size   > color
Navaho: material/function > form > color > size
Pueblo: material/function > form > color > [size].

There may also be some tendency for monolinguals to show greater preference for form-based classifications. It is against such a cross-cultural baseline that one could look for a linguistic influence.

38   Bloom (1981, pp. 80–84; 1984, pp. 285–86) did briefly contrast his work with the research on color terms and color memory, where he felt subjects' performance was dominated by perceptual factors.

39   Chatterjee (1985) has claimed that linguistic relativity is an *inevitable* concomitant of a structuralist approach to language and has characterized both Whorf and Chomsky as structuralists trying to break free of their structuralist–relativist inheritance. Although Chatterjee cited some historical connections in favor of his views, he did not develop a detailed substantive argument. With respect to Whorf, Chatterjee's second claim seems to be inconsistent with the body of his work.

40   Bloom restricted his discussion to true counterfactuals as opposed to all hypotheticals. Even so, his analysis of English was sketchy: it ignored the modal nature of counterfactuals, the significance of tense–aspect shifts, and certain alternative indicators of conditionality such as *could*. (Cf. the comments in Liu, 1985, pp. 266–67.) As will become clear below, his analysis of Chinese is also controversial. The discussion here follows Bloom's analysis.

41   Chinese does not mark tense, but time can be indicated somewhere in the clause by forms meaning 'yesterday,' 'in the future,' 'now,' etc.

42   In many ways Bloom's approach was the polar opposite of Lenneberg's. Whereas Lenneberg called two linguistic labels equivalent when they picked out the same sensory experiences, Bloom called them equivalent when they described the same conceptual schema. Lenneberg ignored the conceptual/semantic value of the label; Bloom ignored the perceptual/pragmatic concomitants of the label. Lenneberg's codability involved a coding of outer reality; Bloom's codability involved a coding of inner thought.

43   At least in principle comparison can be grounded in a function other than reference, although it is not clear at present what other linguistic functions might serve.

44   Note that 'was' in the Chinese should be 'is + past time marker.'

45   Bloom (1984, p. 279) reported similar results for Japanese, which also does not have English-type marking of the counterfactual.

46   Bloom (1981, p. 31) presented a second version of the task using a less abstract version of the question: "If all chairs were red and this table were a chair, would it be red?" However, he did not report the results except to say "equivalent cross-linguistic differences arise."

47   Bloom (1984, p. 278) reported similar results for Japanese, which also does not have English-type marking of the counterfactual.

48   Ironically, nonpsychological reviewers (for instance, Elman, 1983; Jordan,

1982) have found Bloom's study interesting and significant in part precisely because of its methodological rigor.

49   The number of cues was manipulated by taking advantage of the grammatical option available in English to truncate predicates in cases of structural parallelism (for example, If I were you, I would finish my dinner; [I would] turn off the TV; and [I would] start studying].

50   Au implied that this second study would also address the problem of difference between subjects, but it did not.

51   Au found no difference between her story and Bloom's when using a "more idiomatic" version of his story which she constructed. This version kept the original logic of the story but marked counterfactuals more clearly. As will be noted below, Bloom (1984, p. 283) criticized her revised version for being "less counterfactual" in content.

52   In work with English-, Afrikaans-, and Sepedi-speaking subjects, Vorster and Schuring (1989) also found a steady developmental/educational increase in comprehension of counterfactual materials. Although it is very cursory, the discussion of Sepedi counterfactual marking included in this study is interesting.

53   Au was aware of this – having reported that Bloom's story "was written by a Chinese speaker, under Bloom's guidance as to content, and Bloom translated it into English" (personal communication from Bloom in Au, 1983, p. 158 n3). One reviewer (Jordan, 1982, p. 747) also remarked on Bloom's extensive contact with knowledgeable Chinese professors.

54   Note that Bloom did not question the grammaticality of her revised version. Au reported that both her own story and her revision of Bloom's story had been checked by a native speaker of Chinese.

55   Both Takano (1989, pp. 144–45) and Vorster and Schuring (1989, p. 35) criticize Bloom and Au for neglecting to systematically provide "control" stories to show that the behaviors observed in their tasks are due to the linguistic variable at issue (for example, counterfactual markers) rather than some other cultural or situational variable. This argument is valid insofar as one is making a claim about subjects' response to existing stories. Such controls do not, however, help evaluate Bloom's claim that one language group characteristically introduces the crucial linguistic forms whereas another does not, that is, that language guides the very construal of events. Since differences at this level inevitably affect the salience of the linguistic variable at issue when it is introduced, mechanical adherence to the control paradigm may actually conceal real differences arising from the routine presence or absence of the linguistic variable.

56   Au (1984) calls these subjects "nearly monolingual" even though they have been studying English for ten years. It is not clear why she did not just use a group of monolinguals and meet Bloom's challenge directly.

57   Au, Cheng, and Liu do not really dispute Bloom's observations about the rarity of decontextualized counterfactual arguments in Chinese or about the difficulty Chinese speakers have in mastering the English counterfactual mode. Nor have other reviewers (for instance, Elman, 1983; Jordan, 1982; and Hatano, 1982) disagreed with the cultural analysis, though some have expressed skepticism about its origin and significance.

58 For example, regarding the use of such terms as *success* or *thought* without an article, he said that the English speaker

> shifts from discussion of a particular instance or particular instances to discussion of a generic concept conceptually extracted from those instances. (With abstract rather than concrete nouns – the shift is signaled by the dropping of the article altogether, rather than by its use in circumstances that do not readily yield a referential interpretation.)   (Bloom, 1981, p. 35)

This pattern is actually characteristic of *all* mass nouns, whether concrete or abstract.

59 Under this analysis, Bloom's argument would have to be recast as a claim that the availability of certain structural or semantic potentials can facilitate certain functional (pragmatic) shifts to metalevel reference. For example, one could argue that an overt morphological marking of [+ definite] facilitates creating the necessary shift. Generic reference would then be a straightforward extension of the usual interpretation of such a [+ definite] form with successive broadening of the scope of presupposition: definite in immediate (nonspeech) context → definite in ongoing speech context → definite in cultural universe (actual speech contexts) → definite in cultural universe (possible speech contexts, code potential). A more plausible syntactic candidate for facilitating a functional shift would be an interaction between a syntactic category overtly marking [definite] with one marking [plural] (or count/mass, with rules for deriving one from the other).

60 The definite/indefinite distinction in Chinese is signaled by word order (before or after the verb), and number is usually left unstated to be inferred if needed from context or made clear by the use of one of the available demonstratives or quantifiers. (Equivalents exist for English *this*, *that*, *these*, *one*, *single*, *the average*, *several*, and *all*.)

61 The sentence was *Taishu shih ch'ih lopo ti tungwu*, which Bloom glossed as '(The) kangaroo/s is/are eat turnip/s of animal/s,' where the solidi are designed to show all possible meanings since there is some syntactic ambiguity in Chinese from the perspective of English.

62 Bloom himself did not immediately illustrate this point. I have drawn this example from later in his discussion and created this layout of it (Bloom, 1981, p. 41).

63 Despite an apparent similarity, Bloom's argument actually bore little relationship to Whorf's argument about analogical structures. For example, he did not establish (or attempt to establish) that "theoretical" is an aspect of noun meaning.

64 No other reason for entification was subsequently proposed in the text. As suggested here and becomes clear below, Bloom treated linguistic structure as arising historically from the functional demands of theory construction.

65 Since it makes little sense for Takano to have used Bloom's original materials once he knew they were flawed, it seems likely that he only discovered the interpretive alternative *after* conducting the replication. Perhaps this is why Takano never took the obvious step of showing that, contra Bloom, an Asian sample would respond like an American sample once they had corrected materials. This would provide exactly the proper "control" that Takano is so concerned to advocate in his discussion (see n55 above).

66   This was a crucial claim because it was the closest Bloom came to implying that the availability of certain English syntactic options was essential to solving the task. Ironically, the paragraph did not utilize the relevant syntactic forms (i.e., contain entifications), with the possible exception of the word *humidity*. Also, the task was so complex that many factors could account for the results.

67   Bloom was ambiguous about the relationship between this specialized register and everyday discourse patterns. At one point he asserted that this specialized mode of theoretical discourse becomes "part of the speaker's everyday linguistic and cognitive activity" (1981, p. 53). But then later he asserted conversely that the theoretical mode of discourse present in science and philosophy must arise ultimately from proclivities already present in the cognitive activities of individuals (1981, pp. 54–55). Also, in this regard, Bloom's (1981, pp. 52–53) discussion of the differences between the meaning of the term "theoretical" to English and Chinese speakers is quite relevant.

68   There is no reason in principle to rule out the possibility that a specific structural pattern might give rise to or encourage the development of a distinctive mode of discourse. This was, of course, Bloom's basic hypothesis at the level of the individual, although he rejected it at the level of culture or language (1981, p. 59).

69   Bloom made an important clarification:

A disinclination towards the theoretical in this context should not be understood as implying a disinclination towards framing explanations of reality in terms of highly abstract notions ... but rather as involving a disinclination towards entertaining such abstract notions as truth commitment-free [sic] hypotheses that retain purely theoreticals [sic] status until confirmed by empirical evidence.   (1981, p. 55)

70   Bloom (1981, p. 57 n29) then went on to use this argument to attack Kohlberg's theory of moral development.

71   Contrast this with the structure of Whorf's argument (see figure 5 above): Language → Individual → Culture. See also Parmentier (1985, pp. 360ff.).

72   Notice that Liu's (1985) study raises questions about the extent to which the development of counterfactual reasoning skills during childhood in fact depends on the existence of such language forms.

73   Both *red* and *color* are natural schemas in Bloom's account; language merely labels them and then links them together. What the schemas look like before this linkage remains completely obscure: what is color conceived of without reference to red or red conceived of without reference to color?

74   Bloom's formulation is similar in some respects to that of Vygotsky (1987 [1934] – especially chs. 5, 6). Bloom (1981, pp. 64, 77) discusses Vygotsky's work, but not this aspect of it. See also Sapir (1949e [1921], pp. 14–15) for a similar argument.

75   Compare with Vygotsky's (1978, ch. 4) general argument that interpsychological functions (activities) become intrapsychological functions and with

Lantz and Stefflre's (1964) account of memory as communication with oneself over time.

76 Galda only used a subset of Hill's items. He then added to the list a few problems of his own design. Additionally, for a few subjects, he administered a task involving the construction of simple truth tables.

7 Overview and assessment of previous empirical research

1 A much condensed summary of the account developed in chapters 1 and 2 appeared in Lucy (1985b).

2 Interestingly, there do not appear to be any important differences among disciplines or individual researchers in the proposed *strength* of the language and thought relationship within this body of empirical research. In general, contrary to widespread belief and assertion (see, for instance, Rosch, 1987), the work of serious investigators cannot be readily divided into those proposing strong ("language determines") and weak ("language influences") versions of the hypothesis.

3 To avoid confusion in this section, the term *function* will be employed to refer to the semiotic ends of speech such as reference. The term *use* will be employed to refer to the implementation of a semiotic function or its structural precipitates for cognitive or cultural ends.

4 Fishman's (1960) influential "systematization of the Whorfian hypothesis" inaugurated a long tradition of separating lexical and grammatical approaches to the linguistic relativity problem. The study developed in *Grammatical categories and cognition* follows Whorf's conceptualization on this point.

References

Aarsleff, H. (1982). *From Locke to Saussure: essays on the study of language and intellectual history*. Minneapolis: University of Minnesota Press.

Alisjahbana, S. T. (1986). The relation of language, thought and culture as reflected in the development of the Indonesian language. *International Journal of the Sociology of Language, 62*, 25–49.

Astrov, M. (1950). The concept of motion as the psychological leitmotif of Navaho life and literature. *Journal of American Folklore, 63*, 45–56.

Au, T. K. (1983). Chinese and English counterfactuals: the Sapir–Whorf hypothesis revisited. *Cognition, 15*, 155–87.

(1984). Counterfactuals: in reply to Alfred Bloom. *Cognition, 17*, 289–302.

Bauman, R. and J. Sherzer (eds.). (1974). *Explorations in the ethnography of speaking*. Cambridge: Cambridge University Press.

Berlin, B. and P. Kay (1969). *Basic color terms: their universality and evolution*. Berkeley: University of California Press.

Bernstein, B. (1971). *Class, codes, and control*. Vol. I: *Theoretical studies toward a sociology of language*. London: Routledge & Kegan Paul.

Berthoff, A. E. (1988). Sapir and the two tasks of language. *Semiotica, 71*, 1–47.

Blair, R. W. (1965). Yucatec Maya noun and verb morpho-syntax (doctoral dissertation, Indiana University, 1964). *Dissertation Abstracts, 25*, 6606.

Bloom, A. H. (1981). *The linguistic shaping of thought: a study in the impact of language on thinking in China and the West*. Hillsdale, NJ: Lawrence Erlbaum.

(1984). Caution – the words you use may affect what you say: a response to Au. *Cognition, 17*, 275–87.

Bloomfield, L. (1933). *Language*. New York: Holt.

Boas, F. (1916). *The mind of primitive man*. New York: Macmillan. (Original work published in 1911.)

(1942). Language and culture. In *Studies in the history of culture: the disciplines of the humanities* (pp. 178–84). Menasha, WI: Banta. (Published for the Conference of Secretaries of the American Council of Learned Societies.)

(1965). *The mind of primitive man* (rev. edn.). New York: The Free Press. (Revised edition first published in 1938.)

(1966a). Introduction. In F. Boas (ed.), *Handbook of American Indian languages* (reprint edited by P. Holder) (pp. 1–79). Lincoln, NE: University of Nebraska Press. (Reprinted from *Bureau of American Ethnology Bulletin*, 1911, *40*(1), 1–83. Washington, DC: Smithsonian Institution.)

(1966b). Introduction [to the] International Journal of American Linguistics. In F. Boas (ed.), *Race, language, and culture* (pp. 199–210). New York: The Free Press (Macmillan). (Reprinted from Introductory, *International Journal of American Linguistics*, 1917, *1*, 1–8.)

(1966c). The methods of ethnology. In F. Boas (ed.), *Race, language, and culture* (pp. 281–89). New York: The Free Press (Macmillan). (Reprinted from *American Anthropologist*, 1920, *22*, 311–21.)

Bolton, R. (1978). Black, white, and red all over: the riddle of color term salience. *Ethnology*, *17*, 287–311.

Bornstein, M. H. (1973). Color vision and color naming: a psychophysiological hypothesis of cultural difference. *Psychological Bulletin*, *80*, 257–85.

(1975). The influence of visual perception on culture. *American Anthropologist*, *77*, 774–98.

Bourdieu, P. (1984). *Distinction: a social critique of the judgement of taste* (trans. R. Nice). Cambridge, MA: Harvard University Press. (Original work published in 1979.)

Bourdieu, P., and J.-C. Passeron (1977). *Reproduction in education, society, and culture* (trans. R. Nice). London: Sage. (Original work published in 1970.)

Bright, J. O., and W. Bright (1965). Semantic structures in northwestern California and the Sapir–Whorf hypothesis. *American Anthropologist*, *67*, 249–58.

Brown, E. R. (1975). Eric Lenneberg [dedication]. In E. H. Lenneberg and E. Lenneberg (eds.), *Foundations of language development: a multidisciplinary approach*, Vol. I (pp. v–vi). New York: Academic. (Also appears in Vol. II with same pagination.)

Brown, R. L. (1967). Wilhelm von Humboldt's conception of linguistic relativity. *Janua Linguarum, series minor*, *65*. The Hague: Mouton.

Brown, R. W. (1956). Language and categories [appendix]. In J. S. Bruner, J. J. Goodnow, and G. A. Austin, *A study of thinking* (pp. 247–321). New York: Wiley.

(1957). Linguistic determinism and the part of speech. *Journal of Abnormal and Social Psychology*, *55*, 1–5.

(1958a). How shall a thing be called? *Psychological Review*, *65*, 14–21.

(1958b). *Words and things*. New York: The Free Press (Macmillan).

(1965). *Social psychology*. New York: The Free Press (Macmillan).

(1976). Reference: in memorial tribute to Eric Lenneberg. *Cognition*, *4*, 125–53.

Brown, R. W., and D. Fish (1983). The psychological causality implicit in language. *Cognition*, *14*, 237–73.

Brown, R. W., and E. H. Lenneberg (1954). A study in language and cognition. *Journal of Abnormal and Social Psychology*, *49*, 454–62.

Bruner, J. S., J. J. Goodnow, and G. A. Austin (1956). *A study of thinking*. New York: Wiley.

Burgess, D., W. Kempton, and R. MacLaury (1983). Tarahumara color modifiers: category structure presaging evolutionary change. *American Ethnologist*, *10*, 133–49.

Burnham, R. W., and J. R. Clark (1955). A test of hue memory. *The Journal of Applied Psychology*, *39*, 164–72.

Carroll, J. B. (1956). Introduction. In J. B. Carroll (ed.), *Language, thought, and reality: selected writings of Benjamin Lee Whorf* (pp. 1–34). Cambridge, MA: The Massachusetts Institute of Technology Press.

(1967). Bibliography of the Southwest Project in Comparative Psycholinguistics (appendix). In D. H. Hymes and W. Bittle (eds.), *Studies in southwestern ethnolinguistics* (vol. 3 of Studies in General Anthropology) (pp. 452–54). The Hague: Mouton.

Carroll, J. B., and J. B. Casagrande (1958). The function of language classifications in behavior. In E. E. Maccoby, T. M. Newcomb, and E. L. Hartley (eds.), *Readings in social psychology* (pp. 18–31). New York: Henry Holt.

Casagrande, J. B. (1954). The ends of translation. *International Journal of American Linguistics, 20*, 335–40.

(1956). The Southwest Project in Comparative Psycholinguistics: a progress report. *ITEMS, 10*, 41–45. (Newsletter of the Social Science Research Council, New York.)

(1960). The Southwest Project in Comparative Psycholinguistics: a preliminary report. In A. Wallace (ed.), *Men and cultures* (Selected papers of the Fifth International Congress of Anthropological and Ethnological Sciences, Philadelphia, September 1–9, 1956) (pp. 777–82). Philadelphia: University of Pennsylvania Press.

Caskey-Sirmons, L. A. and N. P. Hickerson (1977). Semantic shift and bilingualism: variation in the color terms of five languages. *Anthropological Linguistics, 19*, 358–66.

Casson, R. W. (ed.). (1981). *Language, culture, and cognition: anthropological perspectives*. New York: Macmillan.

Chatterjee, R. (1985). Reading Whorf through Wittgenstein: a solution to the linguistic relativity problem. *Lingua, 67*, 37–63.

Cheng, P. W. (1985). Pictures of ghosts: a critique of Alfred Bloom's *The linguistic shaping of thought. American Anthropologist, 87*, 917–22.

Chomsky, N. (1957). Syntactic structures. *Janua Linguarum, series minor, 4.* The Hague: Mouton.

(1965). *Aspects of the theory of syntax*. Cambridge, MA: The Massachusetts Institute of Technology Press.

Cole, M., and S. Scribner (1981). *The psychology of literacy*. Cambridge, MA: Harvard University Press.

Collier, G. A. (1973). Review of Berlin and Kay 1969. *Language, 49*, 245–48.

Collier, G. A. *et al.* (1976). Further evidence for universal color categories. *Language, 52*, 884–90.

Comrie, B. (1981). *Language universals and linguistic typology: syntax and morphology*. Chicago: University of Chicago Press.

Conklin, H. (1955). Hanunóo color categories. *Southwest Journal of Anthropology, 11*, 339–44.

Darnell, R. (1986). Personality and culture: the fate of the Sapirian alternative. In G. Stocking (ed.), *Malinowski, Rivers, Benedict and others: essays on culture and personality* (pp. 156–83). Madison, WI: University of Wisconsin Press.

Dougherty, J. W. D. (ed.). (1985). *Directions in cognitive anthropology*. Urbana, IL: University of Illinois Press.

Durbin, M. (1972). Basic terms – off color? [Review of B. Berlin and P. Kay, *Basic color terms: their universality and evolution*]. *Semiotica, 6*, 257–78.

Eggan, F. (1954). Social anthropology and the method of controlled comparison. *American Anthropologist*, *56*, 743–63.

Elman, B. A. (1983). [Review of A. Bloom, *The linguistic shaping of thought: a study in the impact of language on thinking in China and the West*]. *Journal of Asian Studies*, *42*, 611–14.

Ember, M. (1978). Size of color lexicon: interaction of cultural and biological factors. *American Anthropologist*, *80*, 364–67.

Ervin, S. M. (1961). Semantic shift in bilingualism. *American Journal of Psychology*, *74*, 233–41.

Fearing, F. (1954). An examination of the conceptions of Benjamin Whorf in the light of theories of perception and cognition. In H. Hoijer (ed.), *Language in culture* (Comparative Studies of Cultures and Civilizations, no. 3; Memoirs of the American Anthropological Association, no. 79) (pp. 47–81). Chicago: University of Chicago Press.

Fishman, J. A. (1960). A systematization of the Whorfian hypothesis. *Behavioral Science*, *5*, 323–39.

Friedrich, P. (1970). Shape in grammar. *Language*, *46*, 379–407.

(1974). On aspect theory and Homeric aspect. *International Journal of American Linguistics*, *40* (2, part 2, memoir 28).

(1986). *The language parallax: linguistic relativism and poetic indeterminacy*. Austin, TX: University of Texas.

(1990). Language, ideology, and political economy. *American Anthropologist*, *91*, 295–312.

Frijda, N. H., and J. P. Van de Geer (1961). Codability and recognition: an experiment with facial expressions. *Acta Psychologica*, *18*, 360–67.

Fusi, V. (1985). Action and possession in Maori language and culture: a Whorfian approach. *L'Homme*, *94*, 117–45.

Galda, K. (1976). Logical reasoning and the Yucatec Maya language (doctoral dissertation, Stanford University, 1975). *Dissertation Abstracts International*, *36*, 8109A.

Garro, L. C. (1986). Language, memory, and focality: a reexamination. *American Anthropologist*, *88*, 128–36.

Glanzer, M., and W. H. Clark (1962). Accuracy of perceptual recall: an analysis of organization. *Journal of Verbal Learning and Verbal Behavior*, *1*, 225–42.

(1963). The verbal loop hypothesis: binary numbers. *Journal of Verbal Learning and Verbal Behavior*, *3*, 301–309.

Goodenough, W. (1964 [1957]). Cultural anthropology and linguistics. In D. H. Hymes (ed.), *Language in culture and society: a reader in linguistics and anthropology* (pp. 36–39). New York: Harper & Row.

Goody, J., and I. Watt (1968). The consequences of literacy. In J. Goody (ed.), *Literacy in traditional societies* (pp. 27–68). Cambridge: Cambridge University Press.

Gordon, P. (1985). Evaluating the semantic categories hypothesis: the case of the count/mass distinction. *Cognition*, *20*, 209–42.

Greenberg, J. H. (1966a). Language universals. In T. A. Sebeok (ed.), *Current trends in linguistics*. Vol. III: *Theoretical foundations* (pp. 61–112). The Hague: Mouton.

(ed.). (1966b). *Universals of language* (2nd edn.). Cambridge, MA: The Massachusetts Institute of Technology Press. (First edition, 1963.)

(ed.). (1978). *Universals of human language* (Vols. 1–4). Stanford, CA: Stanford University Press.

Gumperz, J. H., and D. H. Hymes (eds.). (1964). The ethnography of communication. *American Anthropologist*, *66* (6, part 2).

(1972). *Directions in sociolinguistics*. New York: Holt, Rinehart, & Winston.

Hardin, C. L. (1988). *Color for philosophers: unweaving the rainbow*. Indianapolis, IN: Hackett.

Hatano, G. (1982). Cognitive barriers in intercultural understanding [review of A. H. Bloom, *The linguistic shaping of thought: a study in the impact of language on thinking in China and the West* and S. Bochner (ed.), *The mediating person: bridges between cultures*]. *Contemporary Psychology*, *27*, 819–20.

Haugen, E. (1977). Linguistic relativity: myths and methods. In W. McCormack and S. Wurm (eds.), *Language and thought: anthropological issues* (pp. 11–28). The Hague: Mouton.

Havránek, B. (1964). The functional differentiation of the standard language. In P. Garvin (ed. and trans.), *A Prague school reader on esthetics, literary structure, and style* (pp. 3–16). Washington, DC: Georgetown University. (Original work written in 1932.)

Hays, D. G., E. Margolis, R. Naroll, and D. R. Perkins (1972). Color term salience. *American Anthropologist*, *74*, 1107–21.

Heider, E. R. (1971). Focal color areas and the development of color names. *Developmental Psychology*, *4*, 447–55.

(1972a). Probabilities, sampling, and ethnographic method: the case of Dani colour names. *Man*, *7* (n.s.), 448–66.

(1972b). Universals in color naming and memory. *Journal of Experimental Psychology*, *93*, 10–20.

Hickerson, N. P. (1971). [Review of B. Berlin and P. Kay, *Basic color terms: their universality and evolution*]. *International Journal of American Linguistics*, *37*, 257–70.

(1975). Two studies of color: implications for cross-cultural comparability of semantic categories. In M. D. Kinkade, K. L. Hale, and O. Werner (eds.), *Linguistics and anthropology: in honor of C. F. Voegelin* (pp. 317–30). Lisse: The Peter de Ridder Press.

Hill, S. (1960). A study of the logical abilities of children (unpublished doctoral dissertation, Stanford University, Stanford, CA; citation drawn from Galda, 1976 [1975]).

Hockett, C. G. (1954). Chinese versus English: an exploration of the Whorfian thesis. In H. Hoijer (ed.), *Language in culture* (Comparative Studies of Cultures and Civilizations, no. 3; Memoirs of the American Anthropological Association, no. 79) (pp. 106–23). Chicago: University of Chicago Press.

Hoijer, H. (ed.). (1946). *Linguistic structures of native America*. New York: Viking Fund.

(1953). The relation of language to culture. In A. L. Kroeber (ed.), *Anthropology today* (pp. 554–73). Chicago: University of Chicago Press.

(1954). The Sapir–Whorf hypothesis. In H. Hoijer (ed.), *Language in culture* (Comparative Studies of Cultures and Civilizations, no. 3; Memoirs of the American Anthropological Association, no. 79) (pp. 92–105). Chicago: University of Chicago Press.

(1964a). Cultural implications of some Navaho linguistic categories. In D. H. Hymes (ed.), *Language in culture and society: a reader in linguistics and anthropology* (pp. 142–48). New York: Harper & Row. (Reprinted from *Language*, 1951, *27*, 111–20.)

(1964b). Linguistic and cultural change. In D. H. Hymes (ed.), *Language in culture and society: a reader in linguistics and anthropology* (pp. 455–62). New York: Harper & Row. (Reprinted from *Language*, 1948, *24*, 335–45.)

Holland, D., and N. Quinn (eds.). (1987). *Cultural models in language and thought.* Cambridge: Cambridge University Press.

Hooton, A. B. and C. Hooton (1977). The influence of syntax on visual perception. *Anthropological Linguistics*, *19*, 355–57.

Hymes, D. H. (1961a). Linguistic aspects of cross-cultural personality study. In B. Kaplan (ed.), *Studying personality cross-culturally* (pp. 313–59). New York: Harper & Row.

(1961b). On typology of cognitive styles in language (with examples from Chinookan). *Anthropological Linguistics*, *3*(1), 22–54.

(1962). The ethnography of speaking. In T. Gladwin and W. C. Sturtevant (eds.), *Anthropology and human behavior* (pp. 13–54). Washington, DC: Anthropological Society of Washington.

(1963). Notes toward a history of linguistic anthropology. *Anthropological Linguistics*, *5*, 59–103.

(1964a). Introduction [to part III: World view and grammatical categories]. In D. H. Hymes (ed.), *Language in culture and society: a reader in linguistics and anthropology* (pp. 115–20). New York: Harper & Row.

(ed.). (1964b). *Language in culture and society: a reader in linguistics and anthropology.* New York: Harper & Row.

(1966). Two types of linguistic relativity (with examples from Amerindian ethnography). In W. Bright (ed.), *Sociolinguistics, proceedings of the UCLA sociolinguistics conference, 1964 (=Janua Linguarum, series maior, 20)* (pp. 114–67). The Hague: Mouton.

(1974a). *Foundations in sociolinguistics: an ethnographic approach.* Philadelphia: University of Pennsylvania Press.

(1974b). Ways of speaking. In R. Bauman and J. Sherzer (eds.), *Explorations in the ethnography of speaking* (pp. 433–51). Cambridge: Cambridge University Press.

(1980). Speech and language: on the origins and foundations of inequality among speakers. In D. H. Hymes, *Language and education: essays in educational ethnolinguistics* (pp. 19–61). Washington, DC: Center for Applied Linguistics.

Hymes, D. H., and J. Fought (1975). American structuralism. In T. A. Sebeok (ed.), H. Aarsleff, R. Austerlitz, D. Hymes, and E. Stankiewicz (assoc. eds.), *Current trends in linguistics.* Vol. XIII: *Historiography of linguistics* (pp. 903–1176). The Hague: Mouton.

Jakobson, R. O. (1959). Boas' view of grammatical meaning. In W. Goldschmidt (ed.), *The anthropology of Franz Boas: essays on the centennial of his birth* (pp. 139–45). San Francisco: Chandler.

(1960). Concluding statement: linguistics and poetics. In T. A. Sebeok (ed.), *Style in language* (pp. 350–77). Cambridge, MA: The Massachusetts Institute of Technology Press.

(1971a). Shifters, verbal categories, and the Russian verb. In R. O. Jakobson, *Selected writings*. Vol. II: *Word and language* (pp. 130–47). The Hague: Mouton. (Reprint of mimeo, Russian Language Project, Harvard University, Cambridge, MA, 1957.)

(1971b). Signe zéro. In R. O. Jakobson, *Selected writings*. Vol. II: *Word and language* (pp. 211–19). The Hague: Mouton. (Originally published in 1937.)

(1980). On the linguistic approach to the problem of consciousness and the unconscious. In *The framework of language* (Michigan Studies in the Humanities) (pp. 113–32). Ann Arbor: Horace H. Rackham School of Graduate Studies.

Jordan, D. K. (1982). [Review of A. Bloom, *The linguistic shaping of thought: a study in the impact of language on thinking in China and the West*]. *American Anthropologist*, *84*, 747–48.

Jung, C. (1923). *Psychological types; or The psychology of individuation* (trans. H. Baynes). New York: Harcourt, Brace, & Co.

Kaplan, B. (1954). A study of Rorschach responses in four cultures. *Papers of the Peabody Museum of American Archaeology and Ethnology, Harvard University*, *42*, 1–44.

Kay, P. (1975). Synchronic variability and diachronic change in Basic Color Terms. *Language in Society*, *4*, 257–70.

Kay, P., and W. Kempton (1984). What is the Sapir–Whorf hypothesis? *American Anthropologist*, *86*, 65–79.

Kay, P., and C. K. McDaniel (1978). The linguistic significance of the meanings of Basic Color Terms. *Language*, *54*, 610–46.

Kluckhohn, C. (1960). Navaho categories. In S. Diamond (ed.), *Culture in history* (pp. 65–98). New York: Columbia University Press.

Kluckhohn, C., and D. Leighton (1946). *The Navaho*. Cambridge, MA: Harvard University Press.

Koerner, E. (1977). The Humboldtian trend in linguistics. *Cahiers Linguistiques d'Ottawa*, *5*, 22–40.

Kuryłowicz, J. (1964). *The inflectional categories of Indo-European*. Heidelberg: Carl Winter Universitätsverlag.

(1973a). La Construction ergative et le développement "stadial" du langage. *Esquisses Linguistiques* I (pp. 95–103). Munich: Wilhelm Fink Verlag. (Originally written in 1946.)

(1973b). La Nature des procès dits "analogiques." *Esquisses Linguistiques* I (pp. 66–86). Munich: Wilhelm Fink Verlag. (Reprinted from *Acta Linguistica*, 1945–49, *5*, 15–37.)

Kuschel, R., and T. Monberg (1974). 'We don't talk much about colour here': a study of colour semantics on Bellona Island. *Man*, *9* (n.s.), 213–42.

Labov, W. (1975). Academic ignorance and black intelligence. In M. Maehr and W. Stallings (eds.), *Culture, child, and school: sociocultural influences on learning* (pp. 63–81). Monterey, CA: Brooks/Cole. (Reprinted from *The Atlantic*, 1972, *229*[6], 59–67.)

Laitin, D. D. (1977). *Politics, language, and thought: the Somali experience*. Chicago: University of Chicago Press.

Landar, H. J. (1959). Four Navaho summer tales, part III. *Journal of American Folklore*, *72*, 298–309.

Landar, H. J., S. M. Ervin, and A. E. Horowitz (1960). Navaho color categories. *Language*, *36*, 368–82.

Lantz, D., and E. Lenneberg (1966). Verbal communication and color memory in the deaf and hearing. *Child Development, 37*, 765–79.

Lantz, D., and V. Stefflre (1964). Language and cognition revisited. *Journal of Abnormal and Social Psychology, 69*, 472–81.

Lee, B. (1985). The intellectual origins of Vygotsky's semiotic analysis. In J. V. Wertsch (ed.), *Culture, communication, and cognition: Vygotskian perspectives* (pp. 66–93). Cambridge: Cambridge University Press.

Lee, D. (1938). Conceptual implications of an Indian language. *Philosophy of Science, 5*, 89–102.

(1940a). Noun categories in Wintu. *Zeitschrift für Vergleichende Sprachforschung, 67*, 197–210.

(1940b). The place of kinship terms in Wintu·' speech. *American Anthropologist, 42*, 604–16.

(1944). Categories of the generic and the particular in Wintu·'. *American Anthropologist, 46*, 362–69.

(1959a). The conception of the self among the Wintu indians. In D. Lee (ed.), *Freedom and culture* (pp. 131–40) Englewood Cliffs, NJ: Prentice-Hall. (Reprint of Notes on the conception of the self among the Wintu Indians, *Journal of Abnormal and Social Psychology*, 1950, *45*, 538–43.)

(1959b). Linguistic reflection of Wintu thought. In D. Lee (ed.), *Freedom and culture* (pp. 21–30) Englewood Cliffs, NJ: Prentice-Hall. (Revised from original in *International Journal of American Linguistics*, 1944, *10*, 181–87.)

Lenneberg, E. H. (1953). Cognition in ethnolinguistics. *Language, 29*: 463–71.

(1955). A note on Cassirer's philosophy of language. *Philosophy and Phenomenological Research, 15*, 512–22.

(1957). A probabilistic approach to language learning. *Behavioral Science, 11*, 1–12.

(1960). Language, evolution, and purposive behavior. In S. Diamond (ed.), *Culture in history: essays in honor of Paul Radin* (pp. 869–93). New York: Columbia University Press for Brandeis University.

(1961). Color naming, color recognition, color discrimination: a reappraisal. *Perceptual and Motor Skills, 12*, 375–82.

(1962). The relationship of language to the formation of concepts. *Synthese, 14*, 103–9.

(1967). *Biological foundations of language.* New York: Wiley.

(1975). The concept of language differentiation. In E. H. Lenneberg and E. Lenneberg (eds.), *Foundations of language development: a multidisciplinary approach* (Vol. I, pp. 17–33). New York: Academic.

Lenneberg, E. H., and J. M. Roberts (1956). The language of experience: a study in methodology. *International Journal of American Linguistics, 22* (2, part 2, Memoir 13).

Liu, L. (1985). Reasoning counterfactually in Chinese: are there any obstacles? *Cognition, 21*, 239–70.

Lucy, J. A. (1981, December). *Cultural factors in memory for color: the problem of language usage.* Paper presented to Annual Meeting of the American Anthropological Association, Los Angeles, CA.

(1985a). The historical relativity of the linguistic relativity hypothesis. *The Quarterly Newsletter of the Laboratory of Comparative Human Cognition, 7*, 103–8.

(1985b). Whorf's view of the linguistic mediation of thought. In E. Mertz and

R. Parmentier (eds.), *Semiotic mediation: sociocultural and psychological perspectives* (pp. 73–97). Orlando, FL: Academic.

(1988, November). *Consciousness as a methodological problem.* Paper presented at the 87th Annual Meeting of the American Anthropological Association, Phoenix, AZ.

(1989, April). *Vygotsky and the culture of language.* Paper read at the Biennial Meeting of the Society for Research in Child Development, Kansas City, MO.

(1992). Reflexive language and the human disciplines. In J. A. Lucy (ed.), *Reflexive language: reported speech and metapragmatics.* Cambridge: Cambridge University Press.

Lucy, J. A., S. Gaskins, and V. Castillo Vales (1990). [Linguistic and nonlinguistic influences on color memory: a comparison of English, Spanish, and Yucatec]. Unpublished data.

Lucy, J. A., and R. A. Shweder (1979). Whorf and his critics: linguistic and nonlinguistic influences on color memory. *American Anthropologist, 81,* 581–615.

(1988). The effect of incidental conversation on memory for focal colors. *American Anthropologist, 90,* 923–31.

Lucy, J. A., and J. V. Wertsch (1987). Vygotsky and Whorf: a comparative analysis. In M. Hickmann (ed.), *Social and functional approaches to language and thought* (pp. 67–86). Cambridge: Cambridge University Press.

Lukács, G. (1971). *History and class consciousness: studies in Marxist dialectics* (trans. R. Livingstone). Cambridge, MA: The Massachusetts Institute of Technology Press. (Original work appeared in 1923.)

Lyons, J. (1968). *Introduction to theoretical linguistics.* Cambridge: Cambridge University Press.

Maclay, H. (1958). An experimental study of language and non-linguistic behavior. *Southwestern Journal of Anthropology, 14,* 220–29.

McNeill, N. B. (1972). Colour and colour terminology. *Journal of Linguistics, 8,* 21–33.

McQuown, N. A. (1967). Classical Yucatec (Maya). In R. Wauchope and N. A. McQuown (eds.), *Handbook of Middle American Indians.* Vol. V: *Linguistics* (pp. 201–47). Austin, TX: University of Texas Press.

Malotki, E. (1983). *Hopi time: a linguistic analysis of the temporal categories in the Hopi language.* Berlin: Mouton.

Mandelbaum, D. G. (ed.). (1949). *The selected writings of Edward Sapir in language, culture, and personality.* Berkeley: University of California Press.

Martin, L. (1986). "Eskimo words for snow": a case study in the genesis and decay of an anthropological example. *American Anthropologist, 88,* 418–23.

Mathiot, M. (1964). Noun classes and folk taxonomy in Papago. In D. H. Hymes (ed.), *Language in culture and society: a reader in linguistics and anthropology* (pp. 154–61). New York: Harper & Row. (Reprinted from *American Anthropologist,* 1962, *64,* 340–50.)

(1967a). The cognitive significance of the category of nominal number in Papago. In D. H. Hymes and W. Bittle (eds.), *Studies in southwestern ethnolinguistics* (pp. 197–237). The Hague: Mouton.

(1967b). The place of the dictionary in linguistic description. *Language, 43,* 703–24.

(1968). An approach to the cognitive study of language. *International Journal of American Linguistics*, *34* (1, part 2). (Publication 45 of the Indiana University Publications in Anthropology and Linguistics.)

(1969). The semantic and cognitive domains of language. In P. L. Garvin (ed.), *Cognition: a multiple view* (pp. 249–76). New York: Spartan Books.

Needham, J. (1956). *Science and civilization in China.* Vol. II: *History of scientific thought.* Cambridge: Cambridge University Press.

Newman, S. (1954). Semantic problems in grammatical systems and lexemes: a search for method. In H. Hoijer (ed.), *Language in culture* (Comparative Studies of Cultures and Civilizations, no. 3; Memoirs of the American Anthropological Association, no. 79) (pp. 82–91). Chicago: University of Chicago Press.

(1967). Introduction. In D. H. Hymes and W. Bittle (eds.), *Studies in south-western ethnolinguistics* (pp. 1–12). The Hague: Mouton.

Osgood, C. (1960). The cross-cultural generality of visual–verbal synesthetic tendencies. *Behavioral Science*, *5*, 146–69.

Osgood, C., G. Suci, and P. Tannenbaum (1957). *The measurement of meaning.* Urbana: University of Illinois Press.

Owen, M. G., III. (1969). The semantic structures of Yucatec verb roots (doctoral dissertation, Yale University, 1968). *Dissertation Abstracts International*, *30*, 476B.

Parmentier, R. J. (1985). Semiotic mediation: ancestral genealogy and final interpretant. In E. Mertz and R. J. Parmentier (eds.), *Semiotic mediation: sociocultural and psychological perspectives* (pp. 359–85). Orlando, FL: Academic.

Penn, J. (1972). Linguistic relativity versus innate ideas: the origins of the Sapir–Whorf hypothesis in German thought. *Janua Linguarum, series minor, 120.* The Hague: Mouton.

Ray, V. F. (1953). Human color perception and behavioral response. *Transactions of the New York Academy of Sciences, 16*, 98–104.

Reichard, G. A. (1949). The character of the Navaho verb stem. *Word, 5*, 55–76.

Rivers, W. H. R. (1901). Primitive colour vision. *Popular Science Monthly, 59*, 44–58.

Rollins, P. C. (1972). Benjamin Lee Whorf: transcendental linguist (unpublished doctoral dissertation, Harvard University, Cambridge, MA).

(1980). *Benjamin Lee Whorf: lost generation theories of mind, language, and religion.* Ann Arbor, MI: University Microfilms International for the Popular Culture Association.

Rosch, E. (1987). Linguistic relativity. *ETC.: A Review of General Semantics* [*et cetera*], *44*, 254–79.

Rumsey, A. (1990). Wording, meaning, and linguistic ideology. *American Anthropologist, 92*, 346–61.

Sapir, E. (1947). The relation of American Indian linguistics to general linguistics. *Southwestern Journal of Anthropology, 3*, 1–4.

(1949a). From a review of C. G. Jung, "Psychological types." In D. G. Mandelbaum (ed.), *The selected writings of Edward Sapir in language, culture, and personality* (pp. 529–32). Berkeley: University of California Press. (Excerpts from original which appeared in *The Freeman*, 1923, *8*, 211–12.)

(1949b). Grading: a study in semantics. In D. G. Mandelbaum (ed.), *The selected writings of Edward Sapir in language, culture, and personality* (pp. 122–49). Berkeley: University of California Press. (Reprinted from *Philosophy of Science*, 1944, *11*, 93–116.)

(1949c). The grammarian and his language. In D. G. Mandelbaum (ed.), *The selected writings of Edward Sapir in language, culture and personality* (pp. 150–59). Berkeley: University of California Press. (Reprinted from *American Mercury*, 1924, *1*, 149–55.)

(1949d). Language. In D. G. Mandelbaum (ed.), *The selected writings of Edward Sapir in language, culture, and personality* (pp. 7–32). Berkeley: University of California Press. (Reprinted from *Encyclopaedia of the social sciences*, 1933, *9*, 155–69.)

(1949e). *Language: an introduction to the study of speech.* New York: Harcourt, Brace, and Company. (Original work published in 1921.)

(1949f). Language and environment. In D. G. Mandelbaum (ed.), *The selected writings of Edward Sapir in language, culture, and personality* (pp. 89–103). Berkeley: University of California Press. (Reprinted from *American Anthropologist*, 1912, *14*, 226–42.)

(1949g). Sound patterns in language. In D. G. Mandelbaum (ed.), *The selected writings of Edward Sapir in language, culture, and personality* (pp. 33–45). Berkeley: University of California Press. (Reprinted from *Language*, 1925, *1*, 37–51.)

(1949h). The status of linguistics as a science. In D. G. Mandelbaum (ed.), *The selected writings of Edward Sapir in language, culture, and personality* (pp. 160–66). Berkeley: University of California Press. (Reprinted from *Language*, 1929, *5*, 207–14.)

(1949i). Time perspective in aboriginal American culture: a study in method. In D. G. Mandelbaum (ed.), *The selected writings of Edward Sapir in language, culture, and personality* (pp. 389–462). Berkeley: University of California Press. (Originally published as *Geological Survey Memoir 90; Anthropological Series, no. 13.* Ottawa: Canada Department of Mines, Government Printing Bureau, 1916.)

(1949j). The unconscious patterning of behavior in society. In D. G. Mandelbaum (ed.), *The selected writings of Edward Sapir in language, culture, and personality* (pp. 544–59). Berkeley: University of California Press. (Reprinted from E. S. Dummer [ed.], *The unconscious: a symposium* [pp. 114–42]. New York: Knopf, 1927.)

(1964). Conceptual categories in primitive languages. In D. H. Hymes (ed.), *Language in culture and society: a reader in linguistics and anthropology* (p. 128). New York: Harper & Row. (Title provided by Hymes; reprinted from *Science*, 1931, *74*, 578.)

Sapir, E., and M. Swadesh (1964). American Indian grammatical categories. In D. H. Hymes (ed.), *Language in culture and society: a reader in linguistics and anthropology* (pp. 101–7). New York: Harper & Row. (Reprinted from *Word*, 1946, *2*, 103–12. First half written by Sapir c. 1929. Completed by Swadesh in 1946.)

Sebeok, T. A. (1965). Preface. In C. E. Osgood and T. A. Sebeok (eds.), *Psycholinguistics: a survey of theory and research problems* (bound with A. R. Diebold, *A survey of psycholinguistic research, 1954–1964,* and G. A.

Miller, *The psycholinguists: on the new scientists of language*) (pp. v–vi). Bloomington, IN: Indiana University Press.

Segall, M. H., D. T. Campbell, and M. J. Herskovits (1966). *The influence of culture on visual perception*. Chicago: Bobbs-Merrill.

Shweder, R. (1984). Anthropology's romantic rebellion against the enlightenment, or there's more to thinking than reason and evidence. In R. A. Shweder and R. A. LeVine (eds.), *Culture theory* (pp. 27–66). Cambridge: Cambridge University Press.

Silverstein, M. (1973, January). *Hierarchy of features and ergativity*. Paper presented to the Chicago Linguistic Society, Chicago, IL.

　(1974). Dialectal developments in Chinookan tense–aspect systems: an areal-historical analysis. *International Journal of American Linguistics*, *40* (4, part 2, memoir 28).

　(1976a). Hierarchy of features and ergativity. In R. M. W. Dixon (ed.), *Grammatical categories in Australian languages* (Australian Institute of Aboriginal Studies, Linguistic Series, no. 22.) (pp. 112–71). Canberra: Australian Institute of Aboriginal Studies.

　(1976b). Shifters, linguistic categories, and cultural description. In K. Basso and H. Selby (eds.), *Meaning in anthropology* (pp. 11–55). Albuquerque: University of New Mexico Press.

　(1977, February). *Cognitive implications of a referential hierarchy*. Paper presented to the Committee on Cognition and Communication, University of Chicago.

　(1979). Language structure and linguistic ideology. In P. Clyne, W. Hanks, and C. Hofbauer (eds.), *The elements: a parasession on linguistic units and levels* (pp. 193–247). Chicago: Chicago Linguistic Society.

　(1980, November). *Cognitive implications of a referential hierarchy*. Paper presented at the Max-Planck-Institut für Psycholinguistik, Nijmegen, The Netherlands.

　(1981a). Case-marking and the nature of language. *Australian Journal of Linguistics*, *1*, 227–44.

　(1981b). The limits of awareness. *Working Papers in Sociolinguistics*, no. 84. Austin: Southwestern Educational Laboratory.

　(1985a). Language and the culture of gender: at the intersection of structure, usage, and ideology. In E. Mertz and R. J. Parmentier (eds.), *Semiotic mediation: sociocultural and psychological perspectives* (pp. 219–59). Orlando, FL: Academic.

　(1985b, June). *Metapragmatics and metapragmatic function*. Paper presented at a Conference on Reported Speech and Metapragmatics, Center for Psychosocial Studies, Chicago, IL.

　(1986a). *Noun phrase categorial markedness and syntactic parametricization*. Paper presented at Eastern States Conference on Linguistics, State University of New York, Buffalo, NY.

　(1986b, January). *"Relative motivation" in denotational and indexical sound symbolism of Wasco–Wishram Chinookan*. Paper presented at Conference on Sound Symbolism, University of California, Berkeley, CA.

　(1987). Cognitive implications of a referential hierarchy. In M. Hickmann (ed.), *Social and functional approaches to language and thought* (pp. 125–64). Cambridge: Cambridge University Press.

(1992). Metapragmatic discourse and metapragmatic function. In J. A. Lucy (ed.), *Reflexive language: reported speech and metapragmatics.* Cambridge: Cambridge University Press.

Spradley, J. P. (ed.). (1972). *Culture and cognition: rules, maps and plans.* San Francisco: Chandler.

Stam, J. H. (1980). An historical perspective on "Linguistic relativity." In R. W. Rieber (ed.), *Psychology of language and thought: essays on the theory and history of psycholinguistics* (pp. 239–62). New York: Plenum.

Stefflre, V., V. Castillo Vales, and L. Morley (1966). Language and cognition in Yucatan: a cross-cultural replication. *Journal of Personality and Social Psychology, 4*, 112–15.

Stocking, G. (1968). *Race, culture, and evolution: essays in the history of anthropology.* New York: The Free Press.

(1974). The Boas plan for the study of American Indian languages. In D. H. Hymes (ed.), *Studies in the history of linguistics* (pp. 239–62). New York: Plenum.

Takano, Y. (1989). Methodological problems in cross-cultural studies of linguistic relativity. *Cognition, 31*, 141–62.

Trager, G. (1950). *Benjamin Lee Whorf: four articles on metalinguistics.* Washington, DC: Foreign Service Institute, Department of State. (Reprinting of four articles by B. L. Whorf. First reprinting appeared in summer 1949. Second reprinting with corrected cover and title page, table of contents, and pagination appeared in April 1950. A later, 1952, version was apparently entitled *Collected Papers on Metalinguistics.*)

Turton, D. (1980). There's no such beast: cattle and colour naming among the Mursi. *Man, 15* (n.s.), 320–38.

Tyler, S. A. (ed.). (1969). *Cognitive anthropology.* New York: Holt, Rinehart, & Winston.

Van de Geer, J. P. (1972). Codability in perception. In S. Moscovici (ed.), *The psychosociology of language* (pp. 3–10). Chicago: Markham.

Voegelin, C. F. (1949). Linguistics without meaning and culture without words. *Word, 5*, 36–42.

Vorster, J., and G. Schuring (1989). Language and thought: developmental perspectives on counterfactual conditionals. *South African Journal of Psychology, 19*, 34–38.

Vygotsky, L. S. (1978). *Mind in society: the development of higher psychological processes* (ed. and trans. M. Cole, V. John-Steiner, S. Scribner, and E. Souberman). Cambridge, MA: Harvard University Press. (Essays translated, rearranged, and abridged from the Russian originals written 1930–34.)

(1987). Thinking and speech. In R. W. Rieber and A. S. Carton (eds.), *The collected works of L. S. Vygotsky.* Vol. I: *Problems of General Psychology* (trans. N. Minnick) (pp. 39–285). New York: Plenum. (Original work published 1934.)

Weinreich, U. (1968). *Languages in contact.* The Hague: Mouton.

Wescott, R. W. (1970). Bini color terms. *Anthropological Linguistics, 12*, 349–60.

Whorf, B. L. (1940). [Concerning descriptive linguistics at Yale]. *Main Currents in Modern Thought, 1* (1), 15.

(1941). A brotherhood of thought. *Main Currents in Modern Thought, 1* (4), 13–14.

(1946a). The Hopi language, Toreva dialect. In H. Hoijer (ed.), *Linguistic structures of native America* (pp. 158–83). New York: Viking Fund. (Written in 1939.)

(1946b). The Milpa Alta dialect of Aztec, with notes on the Classical and the Tepoztlán dialects. In H. Hoijer (ed.), *Linguistic structures of native America* (pp. 367–97). New York: Viking Fund. (Written in 1939.)

(1956a). *Language, thought, and reality: selected writings of Benjamin Lee Whorf* (ed. J. B. Carroll). Cambridge, MA: The Massachusetts Institute of Technology Press. (Original works written 1927–41.)

(1956b). Report on linguistic research in the department of anthropology of Yale University for the term September 1937–June 1938 (incomplete) [Written in part with G. Trager]. In *Microfilm collection of manuscripts on Middle American cultural anthropology*, no. 51: <Miscellanea>, pp. 1–9. Chicago: University of Chicago Library. (Original work written 1938.)

Witherspoon, G. (1980). Language in culture and culture in language. *International Journal of Anthropological Linguistics*, *46*, 1–13.

Witkowski, S. R., and C. H. Brown (1982). Whorf and universals of color nomenclature. *Journal of Anthropological Research*, *38*, 411–20.

Wittgenstein, L. (1958). *Philosophical investigations* (trans. G. E. M. Anscombe) (3rd edn.). New York: Macmillan. (Original work published in 1953.)

Woolard, K. A. (1989). *Double talk: bilingualism and the politics of ethnicity in Catalonia*. Stanford, CA: Stanford University Press.

Zimmer, A. C. (1984). There is more than one level in color naming – a reply to Zollinger 1984. *Psychological Research*, *46*, 411–16.

Zipf, G. K. (1935). *The psycho-biology of language: an introduction to dynamic philology*. Boston, MA: Houghton Mifflin.

Zollinger, H. (1984). Why just turquoise? Remarks on the evolution of color terms. *Psychological Research*, *46*, 403–9.

Index

Printed in the United States
85655LV00004B/61-78/A